Case Studies in Sustainability Management and Strategy
The oikos collection

About the editor

Jost Hamschmidt is a Lecturer at the University of St Gallen and Managing Director of oikos Foundation, St Gallen, Switzerland. He received a master in Business Administration from the University of Kassel (Germany), a BA in Technology Management from the University of St Etienne (France) and holds a PhD in Environmental Management from the University of St Gallen. In April 2002 he became Managing Director of the oikos Foundation, an international reference point for sustainability research and teaching in Business Education. His areas of interest include NGO–management, sustainability, entrepreneurship and strategy. In 2001/2002 he was a post-doc visiting fellow at the Haas School of Business, University of California, Berkeley and for the fall term 2007/08 he has been invited as a visiting scholar at Harvard Business School (USA). He is married to Dr Monika Kurath and a father of two children.

CASE STUDIES IN
SUSTAINABILITY MANAGEMENT AND STRATEGY

The oikos collection

Edited by Jost Hamschmidt

Greenleaf
PUBLISHING

2 0 0 7

© 2007 Greenleaf Publishing Ltd, except, where otherwise stated, reprinted with permission

Published by Greenleaf Publishing Limited
Aizlewood's Mill
Nursery Street
Sheffield S3 8GG
UK
www.greenleaf-publishing.com

Printed in Great Britain on acid-free paper by CPI Antony Rowe, Chippenham, Wiltshire.

FSC
Mixed Sources
Product group from well-managed
forests and other controlled sources

Cert no. SGS-COC-2953
www.fsc.org
© 1996 Forest Stewardship Council

Cover by LaliAbril.com.

British Library Cataloguing in Publication Data:
    A catalogue record for this book is available from the British Library.

    ISBN-13: 9781906093013

Contents

List of Contributors

- Wolfgang Amann, Henley College, UK
- Steve Bowden, Waikato School of Management, New Zealand
- Oana Branzei, Ivey School of Business, Canada
- John Buffington, Kenan-Flagler Business School, USA
- Eva Collins, Waikato School of Management, New Zealand
- Daniel Corsten, London Business School, UK
- Magali Delmas, University of California at Santa Barbara, USA
- Rajiv Fernando, ICFAI Center for Management Research, Hyderabad, India
- Dan Goldstein, University of Oregon, USA
- Jens Hamprecht, ETH Zurich, Switzerland
- Kai Hockerts, Copenhagen Business School, Denmark
- Aileen Ionescu-Somers, IMD Lausanne, Switzerland
- Kate Kearins, Auckland University of Technology, New Zealand
- Robert Letovsky, St Michael's College, USA
- Ted London, University of Michigan, USA
- Kevin McKague, York University, Canada
- Alexander Nick, IMD Lausanne, Switzerland
- Erica Plambeck, Stanford University, USA
- Monifa Porter, Stanford University, USA
- Debapratim Purkayastha, ICFAI Center for Management Research, Hyderabad, India
- Mike Russo, University of Oregon, USA
- Murray Silverman, San Francisco State University, USA
- Ulrich Steger, IMD Lausanne, Switzerland
- Tom Thomas, US EPA, San Francisco, USA

Acknowledgments

This book would not have been possible without the generous support of the founders of the oikos Foundation: BAER, BP Switzerland, Ernst Schweizer AG, Gasser Baumaterialien, Fondation Looser, Helvetia, Knecht & Müller AG, Rhomberg Bau and Stiftung Drittes Millennium. Their support for oikos in general and the oikos Case Writing Competition in particular have provided the platform on which to build the collection of cases for this book. In that context, a special thank you goes to Stephan Baer, Josias Gasser, Randolph Koller, Hubert Looser, Peter Müller, Hansruedi Schweizer, Gabriela Seiler, Peter Schwer and Hansruedi Zulliger, whose long commitment to oikos has always been and continues to be a strong encouragement and driver for our work. Thank you! At the same time, I am indebted to all the members of the oikos Case Writing Competition's award committee—their ongoing support provided a strong academic base for this publication: Tima Bansal, Frank M. Belz, Magali Delmas, Thomas Dyllick, Minna Halme, Kai Hockerts, Steven Kobrin, Andy Hoffman, P.D. Jose, Michael Lenox, Mette Morsing, Stefano Pogutz, Forest Reinhardt, Carlos Romero-Uscanga, David Vogel, Michael Yaziji and Friedrich M. Zimmermann. Helpful comments on the final draft were given by Alexander Barkawi, Michael Pirson, Claude Siegenthaler and Lars Stein. Many thanks!

Part 1
Introduction

1.1
Preface

This book has been produced to provide teaching cases for management education in the field of sustainability, management and strategy. The collection is based on the winning cases of the oikos Case Writing Competition[1]—an annual competition organized by oikos: the International Student Organization for Sustainable Economics and Management. oikos aims to support the integration of sustainability issues into teaching and research at the world's faculties for economics and management. The oikos Case Collection reflects this objective and aims to add relevant content to corporate sustainability education at management schools worldwide. We see the case method as one important teaching concept that is able to intertwine theoretical concepts with hands-on experiences, based on real-life organizations. We believe that this is a method that prepares the business students of today to deal with contemporary challenges.

In view of the growing importance of various sustainability trends, management schools are increasingly integrating long-term economic, environmental and social issues into their teaching and research. Climate change, water scarcity, labor standards and human rights issues are among the many examples of issues that future decision-makers will will need to face in their careers. Business education needs to reflect this and provide a broadened understanding of value creation. Sustainability is a concept that demands that organizations consider the legitimate expectations of different stakeholders in their value creation processes. At the same time, it underlines the fact that many sustainability trends offer interesting new business opportunities that entrepreneurs will seize. As a result, value creation processes need to be reorganized in order to create economic capital while developing social capital and preserving natural capital.

Indeed, organizations are increasingly dealing with these challenges. The 12 case studies in this book explore both the opportunities and pitfalls companies and NGOs face in targeting sustainability issues and how their values and core assumptions impact their business strategies.

---

1 For more information on this competition please consult Chapter 6.4 or http://www.oikos-foundation.unisg.ch/homepage/case.htm.

Surprisingly, there are only a few cases on multinational companies represented here. Although there is a growing need, the production of excellent teaching cases in the field of sustainable economics and management lags far behind. Despite the tide of publications on corporate social responsibility and sustainability management, few suitable cases on multinationals seem to be available. Therefore, we hope to stimulate the production of new cases with this volume. As an incentive, the reader will find in Chapter 1.2 an introduction to the characteristics of excellent cases. And in Chapter 6 we provide additional information on external sources dealing with the case writing process, international case competitions and case collections. We also present specific information on the oikos Case Writing Competition and provide short CVs of the oikos Award Committee, an international board of 20 selected scholars from Europe, the Americas and Asia. Finally, we provide background information on oikos, the International Student Organization for Sustainable Economics and Management.

Jost Hamschmidt
St Gallen, June 2007

1.2
Cases in Corporate Sustainability
What Makes an Excellent Case?

The case method of teaching was developed by Faculty of the Harvard Business School[1] and the Ivey School of Business in the 1920s. The basic idea was to simulate real business challenges in the classroom in order to breathe life and instill greater meaning into the lessons of management education. Case studies can be important tools for creating learning processes on different levels—students are forced to struggle with exactly the kinds of decisions and dilemmas managers confront every day. In this reflection of reality, the values and goals of the student are systematically challenged. Uncertainty is key: students are asked what *they* think, how *they* would act, and what challenges *they* feel are important. The use of a case study should create a classroom in which students succeed by exercising the skills of leadership and teamwork in the face of real problems. Facts, figures and theories play an important role; but contexts, emotions and value judgments have a large influence, too. Guided by a faculty member, students cooperate, analyze and synthesize conflicting data and points of view. The objective is to define and prioritize goals, to persuade and inspire others who think differently, to make tough decisions with uncertain information, and to seize opportunities in the face of doubt.

These attributes are especially valuable in the context of sustainability and strategy; organizations are now continually forced to value the different aspects of sustainability and their interrelations: How do social issues impact the economic bottom line? How can an environmentally sound strategy create a positive impact on employee motivation and thus have measurable impact on economic performance? What comes first and why? These are just some of the many questions that may arise.

---

1   This introductory paragraph is based on information available at http://www.hbs.edu/case and McNair and Hersum 1954.

What makes an excellent case in sustainability management? There are multiple case "recipes" available, e.g. via the Internet, and a vast literature about case writing and teaching.[2] Many of these tips and hints can be applied to sustainability cases. In this section we propose ten features of an excellent case, which are derived from experience with the oikos Case Writing Competition. They also echo the lessons of a classic article by Clyde Freeman Herreid.[3]

1. **An excellent case provides a learning opportunity on a relevant topic.** The case should tackle a decision situation with impact on the future of an organization and implications for corporate strategy. It should be a real case, not just a story. And it should identify clear-cut management decisions (i.e. merge or not; compete or cooperate).

2. **An excellent case tells an engaging story.** It should have an interesting plot that relates to the experiences of the target audience. It needs a hero, a dilemma and a solution. The solution may not exist yet; it will be what the students need to supply once the case is discussed.

3. **An excellent case is accompanied by teaching goals and a teaching note.** It should be explicit which audience is being addressed with the case. Undergraduates have a different background compared to MBA students. What does the case do for the course and the student? What theories are employed? How should the students be involved (e.g. group works, student preparation, class interaction). Cases can be choreographed with role-plays and/or voting. Students need to be systematically challenged to argue. Excellent cases provide suggestions for frameworks and literature for faculty *and* students.

4. **An excellent case is based on a recent situation.** To appear real the story should have the trappings of a current challenge. If a student has just seen the problem mentioned in the media, so much the better. Thus, a case on corporate strategies to deal with climate change will arouse the students' interest more than one on Shell's Brent Spar Platform disposal challenge.

5. **An excellent case includes quotations.** Digital technology has made the life of case writers easier; nowadays it has become simple to produce a short film on the "hero" of a case. A face and a voice is the best way to gain empathy for the leading characters: let them speak in their own voices. If this is not possible, use quotations and add life and drama to the case. Quotations from other sources, e.g. leading newspapers, advertisements or internal documents, should be used as well. They make your case more authentic.

6. **An excellent case is relevant to the audience.** Cases should be chosen that involve situations that the students know or are likely to face. This improves the empathy factor and makes the case clearly something worth studying. Thus, for a graduate student in finance, a case involving George Soros's opinion on Tobin taxes might be of greater interest than barter trade in Papua New Guinea.

---

2   See e.g. Heath 2006; Leenders *et al.* 2001.
3   Herreid 1997.

7. **An excellent case is conflict-provoking.** It should provide food for thought and should leave room for different interpretations. It should fuel the debate on an issue. Take, for example, the Hindustan Lever case in this book (pp. 146-163): Is it really sustainable?

8. **An excellent case is decision-forcing.** Not all cases have to be dilemmas that need to be solved, but there must be an urgency and a seriousness in such cases. Best-practice cases are often boring for the reader whereas, in dilemma or decision cases, students are forced to face challenges head-on. Provide a time-line and sufficient data in order to enable well-reasoned options.

9. **An excellent case has generality.** Cases should be of more use than addressing a minor or local problem; they should have general applicability. The case writer should make sure that the case provides useful generalizations and clear take-aways. Patterns should be recognizable and key insights should be aimed for—for on-the-job application or for confidence in mastering similar challenges in the future. (Take, for example, the Body Shop case in this book [pp. 228-253]: what are the implications for other takeovers?)

9. **An excellent case is as short as possible.** This is basically a matter of attention span. Cases should be long enough to introduce the facts of the case but they should be carefully designed in order to keep interest high. Complexity can be introduced in stages. Case series can help in structuring the information. Data can be provided accompanied by some questions and a first decision point before additional information is introduced. Remember that the average person is not able to digest more than three pieces of information at a time. (Take, for example, the Mobility case in this book [pp. 254-278]: why is it structured as it is?)

10. **Finally: an excellent case is one that is revised after a first try in class.** Very often case writers take implicit knowledge for granted and the perception of the case presented in class is different from what was expected. Different mental models and understandings of the foundations of management might also hinder the applicability of cases in different geographical and cultural contexts. This is a growing challenge in a world economy, where regional contexts are often key to understanding markets and society in order to guarantee long-term business success.[4] At the same time, this represents a great opportunity, since an explicit description of business models and dilemmas in a specific context does contribute to a better understanding of cultural foundations and underlying values of the environments in which businesses are operating.

---

4   See e.g. Friedman 2001.

1.3
Teaching Notes
Combining Contents with Concepts

Excellent cases are always linked to learning objectives, which include concepts, theories and methodologies. However, the underlying conceptual ideas are sometimes not wholly explicit in the case; therefore, teaching notes provide the means for an educator to explore the full learning potential of a case in class. Within the oikos Competition we have observed a surprisingly widespread lack of knowledge concerning concepts, goals and contents of case teaching notes. In this section we therefore provide a brief description of what useful teaching notes should look like.[1]

Teaching notes should provide useful background information in order to better understand a case. According to the European Case Clearing House,[2] which holds the world's biggest case collection, only about 50% of their registered cases are accompanied by teaching notes. However, 80% of the 50 most popular cases do provide teaching notes. This leads us to the assumption that teaching notes confer important benefits to case instructors.

All of the cases included in this book have excellent teaching notes, which are available for faculty, free of charge, by request from Greenleaf Publishing at the following link:

http://www.greenleaf-publishing.com/oikos_notes

Basically, teaching notes are guidance documents which enable potential case instructors to teach a case, providing a case summary, teaching goals, key issues, con-

---

1 See also Lapierre/Cardinal (2003): *Guidelines for Writing Teaching Notes*. HEC Montreal. Online resource available at: http://www.hec.ca/en/casecentre/case/guide_redaction_np_a.pdf.
2 See http://www.ecch.com/about/writing-teaching-notes.cfm; see also the information in Chapter 6.3.

cepts, open questions and potential approaches to the case. While the style, length and design of a teaching note may vary widely, we consider here the following elements:[3]

- **Case summary.** The case summary is a short version of the case and high-lights the major points. What is the context and storyline? Who are the main players? What is issue framed by the case? The aim is to provide the case instructor with the key elements of the story as concisely as possible.

- **Case teaching objectives, target audience, targeted courses.** A teaching note explicitly clarifies the teaching objectives (e.g. concerning content and theoretical concepts), target audiences (e.g. undergraduates, MBA or execu-tive MBA students). It should also mention the courses in which the case can be applied. Is the case suitable for a mainstream marketing, strategy or man-agement course or should it be taught in an environmental management or CSR course? What knowledge base is needed in order to successfully deal with the case?

- **Sources of the case material.** The case author should explain how the case was developed, including the steps involved in information gathering and data collection (e.g. interviews with company representatives and/or stake-holders, annual reports, media reports, Internet searches, press coverage, internal documents, scientific articles, etc.).

- **Teaching approach and didactic elements.** The teaching note should enable the transfer of knowledge. Cases are question-oriented and the teaching note should systematically help the instructor to raise relevant questions in order to promote a learning experience. It should also provide possible answers to questions that are likely to arise during in-class discussion. Questions can be developed to prepare students for in-class discussion, in order to open or to advance the discussion. It might be helpful to develop an ideal structure for this, where each issue is allocated a certain amount of time. These guidelines serve as a starting point for the instructor and will have to be adapted to suit particular circumstances. Other didactic elements can be the introduction of additional information during the course, the use of the blackboard, online research during class, suggestions for group work, role-plays, or student assignments in order to consolidate the learning process.

- **Analysis and methods.** Of course, the questions posed in a case require answers. Therefore, the teaching note should include the necessary links to concepts and theories and provide comprehensive response options to the questions. The frameworks provided should also help the students to develop their personal synthesis and should encourage further reflection. It should be noted that an excellent case will have multiple "solutions" to business chal-lenges. Teaching notes should therefore reflect possible trade-offs among competing alternatives (e.g. how to evaluate a short-term cost reduction against a long-term reputational risk). The identification of trade-offs and the

---

3   The proposed elements include the standard elements of ECCH requirements for a teaching note; see http://www.ecch.com/uploads/teachingnote.pdf.

understanding of the logic of these trade-offs will improve the students' strategic perspective on business challenges in a sustainability context.

- **Further reading, references, media support.** A further reading and reference list, useful in mastering the concepts and theories addressed by the case, should be provided. Suggestions for reading assignments for students are helpful; and references to relevant websites and other sources of information are becoming increasingly important. The use of additional multimedia support, if available, should be briefly outlined.

- **Feedback and perspectives.** Teaching notes should also communicate any tips or hints the author has gained from their personal teaching experience with the case. What has worked well and what has not and for what reasons? If there is information available on the real outcome of a case, it should be included in the teaching notes. Also helpful are suggestions for other possible avenues of exploration, which could provide the basis for a more detailed study or some form of knowledge transfer in other contexts.

These are some basic suggestions for constructing teaching notes. We also acknowledge that there are a variety of other valid approaches. In essence, however, the user of teaching notes will be well served if they are: brief (a maximum of ten pages), well structured and comprehensive.

1.4

Introduction to the Cases[1]

According to management luminary Sumantra Ghoshal,[2] management schools need to reconsider the basic foundations of their management approaches and curricula. Ghoshal asks that business education be much more in tune with societal trends and not just seek narrow goals at the expense of the well-being of the world community. This calls for a broadened understanding of value creation. The following 12 cases deal with this challenge. They describe new patterns of value creation, new alliances and the challenges of dealing with existing paradigms. In this chapter we briefly introduce the cases and their core characteristics.

Managing Multiple Value Creation Processes

The cases open with four cases that examine value creation processes in the context of sustainability. The first is "Seventh Generation: Balancing Customer Expectations with Supply Chain Realities," written by Mike Russo and Dan Goldstein (University of Oregon). Seventh Generation is a US-based maker of environmentally sensitive household non-durables such as soaps, detergents, paper products, and diapers. Faced with the prospect of being without a product when a contract manufacturer could no longer make its natural baby wipes, the company substituted conventional wipes. But some of the ingredients in these conventional baby wipes proved unacceptable to its customers. The case provides a broad background on the industry in which Seventh Generation competes, and the developing green niche within it. A history of the company's cir-

---

1 This chapter draws on the case summaries provided by the case authors and reflects the comments of the oikos Case Writing Competition's Award Committee. Since the reviews are double-blind, no reviewer is cited. The editor is extremely grateful for the extensive reviews provided by the oikos Award Committee (see also Chapter 6.4).
2 Ghoshal 2005; see also Mintzberg 2005, Hoffman 2004 and Zell 2005.

cuitous journey to become the leader in its field is then presented, with special reference to the importance of its corporate values to strategy and staffing. The case closes with a meeting to decide what to do about the baby wipes problem. It is an excellent example of the dilemma when companies are caught between consumer expectations and supply chain deliveries. Thus, the Seventh Generation case deals with a problem that is relevant for many producers with "responsible brands." It is written in a captivating fashion and easy to understand for students, because the products are close to everyone's daily life.[3] It can be used to illustrate and discuss a number of important issues for socially responsible businesses, including building a values-driven organization, questions of environmental differentiation and strategy, communication with customers, and managing sustainability-oriented trade-offs.[4]

Our second case comes from New Zealand and is about a start-up trying to differentiate itself from competitors through sustainability. The case "Phoenix Organic: Valuing Sustainability while Desiring Growth" brings out the multiple tensions of a fast-growing organic beverage company. By May 2004, Phoenix Organic had grown from its bathtub beginnings with its ginger fizz product 17 years earlier to become New Zealand's leading manufacturer of premium certified organic and natural beverages. It had done so while living up to its founders' vision of creating "a business that was good for the planet and good for the health of its people." Yet, despite a growth rate of 25% over the last three years, sales were still only NZ$6.5 million. Having carved out a strong niche in the New Zealand non-alcoholic beverage industry, the question was how to produce future growth—through new products such as the chai Phoenix had launched, through new channels such as supermarkets, through developing overseas markets such as Australia or Malaysia, or through some combination of all of these strategies? The challenge focuses on how to combine economic growth with the Phoenix philosophy: being good for the planet and also good for people's health. The Phoenix case explores the challenges of operating a sustainable business.[5] It highlights aspects of a business with a distinctive niche (organics) strategy and explores the tensions between growth and sustainability. The case was originally written for an undergraduate strategy case competition and has also been used in a postgraduate course on strategy and sustainability. It is suitable for undergraduate and MBA courses in strategy, entrepreneurship, business, government and society, or environmental management. Although the focal business has a sustainability focus, the case provides sufficient information for a regular strategy case analysis to be performed by students who may not otherwise be exposed to sustainability issues in the curriculum in an explicit way.

The third case in this section is written by Murray Silverman (California State University) and Tom Thomas (US EPA): "Kimpton Hotels: Balancing Strategy and Environmental Sustainability." It captures the strategic repositioning of a hotel chain, founded by Bill Kimpton, an investment banker-turned-hotelier who became a pioneer in the hospitality industry.[6] By 2005, Kimpton Hotels was comprised of 39 hotels

---

3   The case is accompanied by an excellent set of video sequences featuring key players of Seventh Generation, available from Mike Russo at mrusso@lcbmail.uoregon.edu.

4   For additional readings on these issues, please refer to Reinhardt 1998 and Tapscott and Ticoll 2003, especially ch. 1, pp. 3-36.

5   See also the Phoenix website at http://phoenixorganics.co.nz.

6   See the company website at http://www.kimptonhotels.com.

throughout North America and Canada, each one designed to create a unique and exceptional guest experience. While Kimpton was known for designing hotels that reflected the energy and personality of their distinct locations, by 2004 the company's top executives realized that uniting its hotel portfolio under a single recognizable brand could add considerable value. One aspect of the branding effort was to add the Kimpton name to each property, as in "Hotel Monaco San Francisco: A Kimpton Hotel." Another aspect of their efforts to establish the Kimpton brand was the development and rollout to all of their hotels of a major environmental initiative they named EarthCare. EarthCare was built on an already-established commitment to environmental and social responsibility. Their Hotel Triton was a model for the program, as it already included initiatives such as: energy-efficient lighting solutions, low-flow/high-pressure showerheads and sink aerators, and toilets that reduce water use, a linen and towel re-use program, non-toxic, non-allergenic, all-natural cleaning products, low-VOC paints used to paint walls and ceilings, and more. Planned future initiatives went well beyond those in the Triton.

There were two basic ground rules for the rollout: new initiatives couldn't cost more than what was already budgeted for operations and capital improvements, and they couldn't adversely affect customer perceptions or satisfaction.

The case allows students to explore whether there is a "business case" for the Earth-Care program as well as posing a number of implementation issues, including: (1) potential resistance by general managers to centralized initiatives; (2) potential resistance by hotel staff to new products and procedures; (3) the possibility that investments might have slower payback period, lower rate of return, and result in intangible benefits; (4) the problem that, for some products, required investments might exceed existing budgets.

The case was developed to be cross-disciplinary and can be included in courses in environmental management, business and society, or strategic management. Because of its focus on a hotel chain's efforts to integrate environmental initiatives into its business, it is tailor-made for environmental management courses exploring the development of an environmental strategy. In terms of business and society courses, the case can be tied into environmental stakeholders and proactive voluntary initiatives at the firm level. In the context of strategic management courses, it offers students a chance to examine the strategic benefits of environmental responsibility initiatives. Cutting across all these courses, the case provides an opportunity to explore the oft-mentioned question as to whether an environmental strategy or initiative has a business case for implementation.

Kimpton Hotels is a well-written case that does an excellent job of integrating business strategy and environmental priorities on an important industry. It works well because it poses a clear business challenge and addresses both the costs and benefits of sustainability and social responsibility. The Kimpton Hotel case frames these issues as part of an overall corporate strategy and also scrutinizes the potential risks associated with environmental programs. It is also a flexible case, since it integrates aspects of strategy, organizational behavior, marketing, and operations management.

A final case on multiple value creation processes is contributed by Magali Delmas (UC Santa Barbara), Monifa Porter, and Erica Plambeck (Stanford University). Their case, "Environmental Product Differentiation by the Hayward Lumber Company," traces the greening of Hayward Lumber Company, a family-owned company based in

California.[7] As an initial step toward serving an environmentally focused market niche, the firm began selling Forest Stewardship Council (FSC)-certified lumber to meet a growing demand for green building materials in California's central coast market. The company found that, while supplying FSC wood afforded entry into the green build market, horizontal expansion into higher-margin green building materials created a great opportunity for revenue enhancement. The case details the problems of competing certification standards, and the components of Hayward's environmental strategy. It closes with descriptions of several propositions for strategic growth of the firm, to reach stated environmental and sales goals. A three-part video complements the case.[8] This case can be used to analyze the elements of a competitive environmental differentiation strategy and to examine the value of eco-labels as a competitive differentiator. Similar to the Kimpton Hotel case, it can be also used to investigate synergies between environmental strategy and business strategy. It is intended for use in courses on corporate environmental strategy, business and society, or environmental entrepreneurship.

The case describes a small-business perspective and has sophisticated linkages with strategy and marketing. It is well written and an engaging story, and is also supported by excellent background information.

Innovative Partnership Models

Partnerships between non-governmental organizations (NGOs) and large corporations are on the increase and offer tremendous learning potential for the partners involved. It is interesting to observe that, today, NGOs such as Greenpeace cooperate with multinational corporations such as Coca-Cola.[9] The two cases in this section focus on partnership models.

The first, "Transforming the Global Fishing Industry: The Marine Stewardship Council at Full Sail?" produced by the Swiss Institute for Management Development (IMD Lausanne), illustrates a partnership between a large NGO with a multinational company in order to develop new institutions for managing global fish stocks. The case states that about three-quarters of the world's commercial marine stocks are fully exploited, overexploited, depleted, or recovering. Over the last few decades, government initiatives to manage this natural resource more sustainably have been rather ineffective. The Marine Stewardship Council (MSC)[10] is a small NGO set up by Unilever and the WWF in 1997 to contribute to reversing the decline in global fish stocks by setting up an eco-labeling scheme. The case study briefly highlights the MSC's history to provide the necessary background on key events and challenges in the past, including the current crisis in the global fishing industry—largely associated with the so-called "Tragedy of the Commons" (catch as much as you can). It offers insights into the launch

7   See http://www.haywardlumber.com.
8   Available from https://www.gsb.stanford.edu/multimedia/Hayward/index.html.
9   In January 2007, Greenpeace International Executive Director Gerd Leipold and E. Neville Isdell, Chairman of the Coca-Cola Company, presented a joint project on climate-friendly cooling systems at the World Economic Forum 2007. For a deeper analysis of similar phenomena, see Yaziji 2004.
10   For more information please check the MSC website at http://www.msc.org.

of the MSC and its early efforts at introducing a functioning market mechanism for sustainable fishing products (no market, no supply, and vice versa).

The key management challenge of this case study is the challenge associated with operating a certification and eco-labeling system acceptable to many different stakeholders: the fishing industry, food processors, retailers, national governments, supranational institutions, the conservation community, and consumers. As a result of these often conflicting demands and the MSC's failure to recognize the need for reforms, the organization encountered a crisis of credibility.

Since then, through changes, in particular in governance, certification criteria, and communication, the MSC has become more effective. Overall, it can be seen as a "best-practice example" of business–NGO cooperation. At the beginning of 2006, about 5–6% of the total wild edible capture groups were certified according the MSC standard. More than 300 seafood products in 24 countries bear the MSC eco-label. The case critically examines several remaining key challenges: for example, some NGOs (including Greenpeace) still question the usefulness of sustainability standard and are calling for a stricter interpretation to more effectively ensure the long-term productivity of the marine environment. On the other hand, certification is still too costly and time-intensive for many actors in the industry. There is also still a clear lack of consumer awareness and demand, although retailers have pushed labeled products into supermarkets. Weaker—and therefore cheaper—labels (for example, from the French Carrefour Group) are emerging. The case concludes that, to date, it is uncertain how the MSC can successfully build scale and a global brand when still facing these barriers.

This case sheds light on the growing importance of certifiable standards and the challenges they face. Standards such as MSC are becoming increasingly important as tools for the self-regulation of environmental and social issues. This case lends itself to a debate in which student groups are assigned different stakeholder interests to think through. Furthermore, the emergence of competing standards provides an opportunity to talk about different company strategies with respect to standards (proactive, defensive, accommodating, etc.).

This case provides valuable lessons that can be transferred beyond the MSC to other environmental or social standards and to other situations in which stakeholder engagement is required. Lessons from this case are relevant to students working in NGO, governmental, and industry settings.

Another perspective on standards development and the cooperation between companies and NGOs is provided by Jens Hamprecht (ETH Zurich) and Daniel Corsten (London Business School) with their case "Purchasing Strategies and Sustainability: The Migros Palm Oil Case." The case describes the launch of a strategy in the field of corporate sustainability which actually went far beyond market demands. It also deals with the firm's capabilities to form and transform rules, norms, and standard models of customers as well as other actors in the market. The case is based on an issue that began to emerge in the Swiss media in 1999: the role of the palm oil industry in the destruction of the rainforest. Given this development in the public debate, the Swiss retailer Migros began to investigate purchasing sustainable palm oil for its products. To increase the legitimacy of Migros's efforts and to gain support by experts, Migros began to collaborate with WWF Switzerland. Jointly, the two parties developed their own standard on sustainable palm oil production. When Migros purchased the first palm oil supplies complying with this standard, the company added fuel to the public debate. It communicated to the public that the palm oil industry was a problem and that Migros was not contributing to it. Once Migros had gained a reputational advantage for its project, it initiated talks on an industry standard for sustainable palm oil production. Today, this standard gains increasing acceptance in the global consumer goods industry.[11]

The case has multifaceted aspects and learning opportunities. It explores the difficulties of judging scientific data in the management of corporate sustainability. It illustrates how opinion makers use numbers and statistics to let one and the same issue in the management of the natural environment appear as either dramatically important or irrelevant. And it identifies how a business can respond to the attempts of a competitor to transform institutions. It provides relevant information for students on an important issue and it is highlights entrepreneurial strategies for creating institutional change, balancing trade-offs and the challenges of corporate–NGO partnerships.

Sustainability Strategies in the South

Three cases focus on sustainability strategies in the South. While Wolfgang Amann, Ulrich Steger, and Aileen Ionescu-Somers (IMD Lausanne) present "Hindustan Lever: Leaping a Millennium," a classic base-of-the-pyramid case from a corporate perspective, the second case of John Buffington (UNC Kenan-Flagler)and Ted London (University of Michigan) takes a social entrepreneurship perspective. Finally, Kevin McKague and Oana Branzei (York University), with their case series on City Water Tanzania, highlight the failure of a World Bank Project in Dar es Salaam, Tanzania.

The Hindustan Lever case series centers on a new business model developed by Hindustan Lever (HLL)[12] in order to tap the business and sustainability potentials hidden in rural India and focuses on a win–win partnership with rural, female self-help groups (SHGs). HLL assists these SHGs to access micro-credit, which is usually restricted, Self-help groups buy HLL products and sell them in their villages in a decentralized way, thus creating various opportunities for rural communities: training and income opportunities for women that are otherwise hardly available as well as better living conditions, e.g. through the hygiene products on offer. Section A of the case describes the cornerstones and key decisions in the inception phase of the project. It details the value chain and expected deliverables for the stakeholder groups. Section A stops at the point in time when the entire system has been set up and launched and reveals no insights regarding the actual results. Section B illustrates that performance clearly lagged behind the expectations. Women dropped out of the scheme, sales decreased during the harvest season, and the system risked losing momentum. HLL needed to make a decision whether to patiently wait for the system to eventually take off, or to implement changes to the complex system of interdependent variables and players. Section B points out that innovation alone, as presented in Section A, does not in itself create a

---

11   See the dynamic development of the membership base of the Roundtable on Sustainable Palmoil (RSPO) at http://www.rspo.org.

12   Website: http://www.hll.com.

sustainable model. Learning, not reality avoidance, and a careful evolution of the system over time are key success factors. Section C presents the actual changes that were implemented, the quite impressive successes over time, and the vision forward. Within less than a decade, HLL envisages building up a pool of 100,000 self-employed women covering 500,000 villages, and reaching 500 million people. HLL would thus undoubtedly create opportunities for rural women to live in improved conditions, while changing their families' overall standard of living for the better.

The case is a vehicle for discussion and insight on how multinational corporations (MNCs) can radically change their perception of the poor rural sector as a potential customer base and their role in developing economies in general. Instead of seeing themselves as serving only the richer sectors of society with sufficient purchasing power, leaving the poor to governments and NGOs, MNCs can also play a role within this sector. Through innovative thinking and creation of partnerships, new dynamics can be established to boost wealth in these communities, breaking the traditional moulds and boosting growth and development. While many cases have been written outlining great ideas for marketing (with strong local characteristics) and sustainability, this case series moves beyond the presentation of a real-life innovation with only potential and unmeasured enormous effects. The case series emphasizes a key aspect hitherto neglected: the crucial role of learning and adaptation over time in order to make the model last and evolve. It is also very useful as a means for students to better understand India. Along with China, India is currently frequently to be found at the top of managers', educators' and academics' radar screens. This case series sensitizes them in respect to local characteristics and crucial factors for success in this future market. However, one controversial question remains: to what extent is HLL's initiative truly sustainable?

John Buffington and Ted London choose a very different perspective. Their case study, "Building a Sustainable Venture from the Ground Up: TMI's Earth Brick Machine," discusses a number of unique and complex challenges that will be facing the business and non-profit leaders of tomorrow, particularly with regards to the increasing overlap between the business and non-profit sectors. Specific challenges addressed involve operating and marketing in remote areas with scarce resources, venture formation, managing from a distant location, and technology transfer and piracy.

In 2002, The Mountain Institute (TMI),[13] a non-profit organization, received a patent for a machine that makes environmentally friendly bricks from dirt, allowing for low-cost construction of housing and other structures. TMI saw this technology not only as an environmental win but also as a tool for economic development in the developing countries where it operated, making the machine a true vehicle for sustainable development. Two years before receiving the patent, the organization began initial pilot-testing in Tibet, a market as rugged as its terrain.

This effort resulted in the construction of a number of small cottages and a medical clinic. Encouraged by this initial success, in mid-2002 TMI was poised to launch the technology on a wider scale. To do so, however, the organization saw the need for a deeper understanding of the new "business" challenges it faced. In fact, based on the assumed value proposition of the machine, an idea had been gaining momentum

13   See http://www.mountain.org.

within TMI that would take it into new territory: the launch of an independent for-profit venture.

Finally, the City Water Tanzania case series, provided by Kevin McKague (York University) and Oana Branzei (Ivey School of Business), explores the development of a public–private partnership in Tanzania. The first part of the case examines how the Tanzanian government intends to address a pressing deterioration in the infrastructure and services of Dar es Salaam's Water and Sewerage Authority (DAWASA). The decision process unfolds in the spring of 2002, on the heels of the Cochabamba uprising and increasing dispute over the involvement of the World Bank and the International Finance Corporation (IFC) in other water development projects in Ghana, Mauritania and South Africa. At that time, the World Bank was already sponsoring similar projects in Angola, Benin, Guinea-Bissau, Niger, Rwanda, São Tomé and Senegal, despite some vocal local opposition. Section A's decision point concerns: (a) the privatization of the utility in line with the ongoing economic reforms; (b) the choice between partnering with an international operator (as required by the World Bank) and local models (government-led or entrepreneurial ventures); and (c) the implications of these choices for Dar es Salaam's residents, donors, investors, and politicians. Section B describes the Tanzanian government's privatization of DAWASA. It details the terms of the lease contract with an international operator, City Water, discussing the alternatives that were considered and discarded, the bidding process, and the roles and motivations of the parties. The key questions revolve around: (a) the adequacy of the decision; (b) the responsibility for the next steps; and (c) milestones and metrics to gauge the success of the privatization. Section C provides a dual role-play, casting students in the position of Edward Lowassa, Tanzania's Minister of Water, and Cliff Stone, a former director of sales for Africa for Biwater and now part of City Water's management. The two role-plays ask each party to review the progress by May 1st, 2005. Each party reviews their accomplishments and shortcomings, two years after the signing of the lease in February 2003. Section C triggers a negotiation between representatives of the two sides (Lowassa and Stone) and an analysis of their competing expectations and only partial fulfillment of their assumed roles. Section D summarizes the decision of the negotiation: the break-up of City Water Tanzania, and its aftermath, including litigation and forgone opportunities to meet the needs of the local residents. The case series addresses the critical issue of water in a developing country with its economic, social, and environmental implications. It can be used for a critical discussion of privatization and foreign aid (World Bank and IFC).

Responsible Business Models and Stakeholder Tension

The case "Body Shop: Social Responsibility or Sustained Greenwashing," written by Rajiv Fernando and Debapratim Purkayastha (ICFAI Hyderabad, India), deals with a contemporary strategy pattern: the acquisition of small, innovative but strong brands by multinational companies.[14] It is also about the issue of sustainability rhetoric and

---

14 E.g. the acquisitions of Odwalla by the Coca-Cola Company or Ben & Jerry's by Unilever.

greenwashing. In March 2006, The Body Shop International Plc (Body Shop), a retailer of natural-based and ethically sourced beauty products and a long-time darling of sustainable business proponents, announced that it had agreed to an acquisition by the beauty care giant L'Oréal in a cash deal worth £652 million (US$1.14 billion). The announcement brought in its wake a spate of criticism against Body Shop and its founder, Dame Anita Roddick. The company was strongly associated with Roddick's social activism. Since its inception, it had endorsed and championed various social issues such as opposition to animal testing, developing community trade, building self-esteem, campaigning for human rights, and protection of the planet. Through these initiatives, the company had cultivated a loyal base of customers who shared these values.

L'Oréal, on the other hand, had been severely criticized by activists for allegedly testing its cosmetics on animals and selling its products by making women feel insecure. Moreover, Nestlé owned a 26% stake in L'Oréal and Nestlé was one of the most boycotted companies in the world for its alleged unethical business practices and aggressive promotion of baby milk in developing countries.

Some of Body Shop's critics and customers said that they felt betrayed by the deal as Roddick had previously been vocal in her criticism of companies such as L'Oréal. Some groups called for a boycott of Body Shop's products. However, Body Shop and Roddick defended the deal by saying that the acquisition by L'Oréal would not compromise its ethics; the merger would, in fact, give Body Shop a chance to spread its values to L'Oréal. L'Oréal also announced that Body Shop's values would not be compromised and that it would continue to operate as an independent unit.

This case discusses the reactions of consumers, activists, and CSR experts to the acquisition of Body Shop by L'Oréal. The acquisition throws up some questions such as: Is Body Shop guilty of greenwashing? Does it have the influence to extend its values to L'Oréal? The case also looks into the issue of whether L'Oréal was trying to improve its own image and to buy CSR through this deal.

This case provides a rare opportunity to discuss in the classroom the complexity of hypocrisy in the light of a presumably authentic wish to contribute to the integration of sustainability into business thinking globally. It provides a great opportunity to have a structured intellectual and nuanced debate about Body Shop's ethical challenges—a case and a challenge that often evokes emotional either-you-are-for-or-you-are-against arguments that hinder critical reflection and stop the debate. It is a well-structured case with excellent details about the progress of the company, which serves to provide sufficient insights to avoid a simple pro or anti argumentation.

The case series "Mobility Car Sharing: From Ecopreneurial Start-up to Commercial Venture," contributed by Kai Hockerts (CBS Copenhagen), describes the development of a social entrepreneurial venture from its cooperative self-help roots in 1987 until 2002. This case aims to help students explore the different challenges the car-sharing entrepreneurs faced while turning their organization from a self-help start-up into a viable commercial venture. Consisting of five separate parts, the case series highlights different managerial issues in each. Although the first four follow a chronological order, teachers may focus only on selected parts. The case can be used in different settings—electives on environmental management, strategy, or social entrepreneurship—but it also has interesting links on aspects of free-riding, collective action, and entrepreneurship. The case can be used to highlight the difficulties environmental niche players face when moving into the mass market. The last section of the case is also very helpful in illustrating the measurement of environmental impacts. The case introduces critical concepts such as the rebound effect and sufficiency. It is superbly written and has an interesting story on voluntarism versus professionalism. It also portrays in a very good way how business success can contradict with the original principles of an activity.

Wind power has become a major industry but the social acceptance of wind turbines is becoming a major obstacle for its development.[15] Local protests against wind power have added fuel to the debate about the so-called NIMBY (not in my back yard) effect. Robert Letovsky's case "Catamount Energy and the Glebe Mountain Windfarm: Clean Energy vs NIMBY" illustrates this development. It focuses on the environmental and economic consequences of a proposed wind farm in the state of Vermont in the northeastern United States. The project, once fully operational, would supply only a relatively small percentage of the state's overall electricity needs. However, it represents to some an important opportunity in light of concerns regarding global climate change and the emissions associated with fossil fuels. For others, however, the proposed project along the top of Glebe Mountain represents a brutal violation of Vermont's scenic beauty, a threat to the state's crucial tourist industry, and a threat to hikers' and hunters' access to the outdoors. The case gives an overview of the worldwide wind-generated electricity (WGE) industry, reviewing the pros and cons of WGE and focusing on how the industry has evolved in certain countries and US states. The case then reviews the tourist industry in the state of Vermont, and describes both the proposed Glebe Mountain project and the firm proposing the project, Catamount Energy Corporation (CEC). It ends with a description of the consultative process that CEC initiated as it sought regulatory approval of the project and how opposition to the Glebe Mountain project began to mobilize.

Ideally, this case should be assigned after students have had a chance to discuss global energy trends and climate change. The case allows students to explore the ongoing debate over WGE, and the issue of NIMBY, which has impacted several proposed wind farm projects, as well as major projects for other energy sources. Alternatively, the case would work well in a strategic management/business policy course, as it deals with the issue of stakeholder management. Finally, the case could be used in an advanced marketing management/public relations course, as it allows students to evaluate one firm's attempt to build public support for a controversial project.

The case outlines the various groups that have aligned themselves—both for and against—the proposed Glebe Mountain project. These groups include a group of local residents determined to block the project (the Glebe Mountain Group); another group of local environmentalists equally committed to the project (Fairwinds Vermont); the firm promoting the project (Catamount Energy Corporation); local and state governments and regulatory authorities; and media observers from across the state. Other stakeholders who have expressed an interest or who may be affected by the Glebe Mountain project include electricity ratepayers in the state, taxpayers at both the state and local levels, and outdoorsmen's groups. Students can be asked to come up with measures that address each of the stakeholder groups, using an established framework for classifying responses to stakeholder demands.

---

15 For a comprehensive discussion of the social acceptance of renewable energy innovation, especially wind power, please refer to Wüstenhagen 2007.

Part 2
Managing Multiple
Value Creation Processes

CASE 1
Seventh Generation
Balancing Customer Expectations with Supply Chain Realities

Daniel R. Goldstein and Michael V. Russo[1]

University of Oregon

Martin Wolf put down the telephone and thought about how depressing these calls were getting. As Director of Product Quality and Technology at Seventh Generation, a seller of natural household products, it was his responsibility to field phone calls from customers about the ingredients in company products. It was one thing to answer questions about the effects of Seventh Generation's environmentally sensitive soaps, detergents and other goods on adults. But responding to inquiries about how company products might influence the health of infants was another matter. The emotional character of these customer interactions only heightened Wolf's anxiety. One mother, practically in tears, stated that after years of "trusting the green leaf" (Seventh Generation's logo, from a Littleleaf Linden tree), she felt betrayed by the company's decision to change the ingredients of the wipes without informing customers. Wolf was left wondering if this type of customer contact was in his job description.

His mind wandered to the situation at the company sixth months ago, prior to his arrival. Seventh Generation's contract manufacturer of baby wipes informed the company that it could no longer manufacture the baby wipes as it had. The previous formula, designed to be environmentally sensitive in manufacture and healthy in use, avoided the harsh synthetically derived ingredients typically found in most infant personal care products (see Exhibit 1.1 for a comparison of ingredients in wipes currently

1   The authors gratefully acknowledge the financial support of the Dreyfus Foundation and the American Chemical Society, which underwrote the preparation of this case, accompanying video (available from Mike Russo at mrusso@lcbmail.uoregon.edu), and teaching note. © Michael V. Russo 2006.

EXHIBIT 1.1 Ingredients in Seventh Generation Tushies
and Conventional Baby Wipes[2]

The following substances are found in Seventh Generation and conventional baby
wipes:

Seventh Generation	Conventional Wipes
Water	Water
Aloe vera	Aloe vera
Glycerin	Propylene glycol
Citric acid	Citric acid
Vitamin E	Vitamin E
Alkyl polyglycoside	Polysorbate 20
Sodium hydroxymethylglycinate	Disodium cocoamphodiacetate
	Methylchloroisothiazolinone
	Methylisothiazolinone
	Quaternium 15
	Potassium sorbate
	Disodium EDTA
	Fragrance

Alkyl polyglycoside
A surfactant derived from cornstarch and palm oil.

Aloe vera
A plant extract with the demonstrated ability to help skin heal.

Citric acid
A naturally occurring substance used as a chelating agent and acidifier. Citric acid
can be an irritant.

Disodium cocoamphodiacetate
A surfactant derived from coconut oil.

Disodium EDTA
Used to chelate (bind) metals.

Glycerin
A naturally occurring substance found in virtually every living organism. Glycerin is
a desiccant (keeps the wipe from drying-out) and solvent (has both water-soluble
and oil-soluble properties) to help remove soil from baby's skin.

Methylchloroisothiazolinone
A synthetic antimicrobial.

Methylisothiazolinone
A synthetic antimicrobial.

(continued over)

2   Personal Communication, Martin Wolf.

(from previous page)

Polysorbate 20
A surfactant derived from sugar.

Potassium sorbate
Potassium sorbate is a potassium salt version of sorbic acid, a naturally occurring, polyunsaturated fat used to inhibit mold growth. It is widely used in the food and cosmetics industries. Most potassium sorbate is prepared synthetically. Potassium sorbate may be irritating.

Propylene glycol
A synthetic (petroleum-derived) dessicant (keeps the wipe from drying out) and solvent (has both water-soluble and oil-soluble properties) to help remove soil from baby's skin.

Quaternium 15
A synthetic antimicrobial.

Sodium hydroxymethylglycinate
A synthetic antimicrobial based on the naturally occurring amino acid glycine.

Vitamin E (Tocopheryl acetate)
A form of Vitamin E. Helps soothe and heal skin.

---

sold by Seventh Generation and conventional counterparts). After its initial introduction, sales of the wipes had steadily grown. Seventh Generation had secured substantial shelf space for the product in natural goods stores and, increasingly, in more mainstream outlets like Albertsons, Kroger, and Safeway.

The problem was that the manufacturer of the wipes could no longer justify the expense of the frequent changeovers of its manufacturing line from conventional wipes to natural wipes, and proposed to simply make conventional wipes for Seventh Generation. With no other alternative, the company decided that since this product was no worse than others in the marketplace, it would substitute the conventional wipes and sell those under its own label.

This decision was complicated and illustrated that Seventh Generation was not a monolith. While all employees viewed protection and enhancement of the natural environment as a core value of the company, there were other considerations as well. Gregor Barnum, Director of Corporate Consciousness at Seventh Generation, put it this way: "There are voices that give primary weight to human health, others that give primary weight to the environment, and others that give primary weight to profitable operation."[3] One reason to ship the conventional product was the declaration by Martin Wolf's predecessor that although the conventional wipes contained some ingredients Seventh Generation generally avoided, the formula was safe. Contributing to the decision was the sense that the company would be without a product otherwise, and that customers would purchase wipes from competitors that used conventional formulas.

---

3   Personal communication, October 6, 2006.

Not much happened at first. It may have been that shoppers, especially mothers with young children, were simply too busy to notice the changes to the ingredients. But starting about three months after the newly formulated wipes hit the shelves, it became increasingly clear that customers had not accepted the new formula. From that point on, the frequency of calls to Wolf's office had escalated—a disturbing trend. The issue had attracted no media interest. But as he noted, "If one person is calling, it means 200 more people have the same complaint and aren't letting us know."[4]

Wolf wondered whether or not the issue was ripe for discussion. Was there something Seventh Generation could do to stem the increase in complaints about this product choice? Did it bear some responsibility to change the product or stop selling it, based on its operating principles and ongoing relationship with customers? Trust was a powerful driver of consumer choice, one that could take years to earn. Wolf didn't want to throw that away now. The segment of the household nondurable goods industry the company served was growing rapidly, and Seventh Generation was well positioned to thrive in the new environment.

Industry Background

The global household nondurable products industry was valued at $156 billion annually (at the wholesale level), with US sales representing approximately 50% of that figure.[5] The industry was very mature and highly competitive, as population growth (and therefore market growth) in the primary markets of the US and industrialized Europe had stagnated.[6] Because of the market's maturity, gains in market share were captured in three ways: competing fiercely on price, struggling for shelf space in static distribution channels, and introducing new and innovative products.[7] All of these methods were costly.

The industry's consumers wielded significant purchasing power, as they frequently viewed most household nondurable products as undifferentiated.[8] Brand loyalty had steadily declined for many products since the 1960s, and in times of economic duress price was frequently the only discriminating purchase criterion.[9]

These facts, coupled with cyclical fluctuations in the commodity prices of raw materials, resulted in somewhat low profit margins for many products. To boost overall margins, companies grew earnings by attempting to develop a set of loyal customers and weaning them off lower-margin standard products and onto higher-margin innovative products.[10] Another strategy was to enter emerging markets, where more and more

4   Casewriter interview, September 6, 2005.
5   Bossong-Martines, Eileen M. 2004. *Standard & Poor's Industry Survey*, 172(51): Section 1. "Household Non-Durables Industry Survey." McGraw-Hill.
6   Ibid.
7   Ibid.
8   Ibid.
9   Pierce, Lynn M. 2005. *Encyclopedia of American Industries. Vol. 1: Manufacturing Industries*. 4th ed. Farmington Hills, MI: Thompson/Gale.
10 Bossong-Martines, Eileen M. 2004. *Standard & Poor's Industry Survey*, 172(51): Section 1. "Household Non-Durables Industry Survey." McGraw-Hill.

EXHIBIT 1.2 Industry Leader Financial Statistics (1995–2004) (continued opposite)

(Dollar Figures in Millions)

	1995	1996	1997	1998	1999	2000	2001	2002	2003	2004
Procter & Gamble[11]										
Sales	$33,434	$35,284	$35,784	$37,154	$38,125	$39,951	$39,244	$40,238	$43,377	$51,407
Operating Margin	16.2%	17.5%	19.5%	20.6%	23.2%	22.3%	22.6%	22.5%	23.3%	22.5%
Net Profit Margin	7.9%	8.6%	9.5%	10.2%	10.9%	10.6%	11.2%	12.6%	13.2%	12.6%
ROE	25.0%	26.0%	28.3%	30.9%	34.4%	34.4%	36.6%	36.9%	35.4%	37.5%
Unilever[12]										
Sales	$49,505	$57,323	$49,114	$44,895	$43,650	$45,259	$45,590	$45,839	$48,353	$50,246
Operating Margin	11.2%	11.1%	10.5%	13.2%	13.1%	16.5%	19.4%	21.9%	20.9%	13.9%
Net Profit Margin	4.7%	4.8%	5.9%	6.6%	6.7%	6.3%	6.3%	8.3%	11.6%	9.8%
ROE	13.7%	15.2%	14.3%	13.1%	19.3%	37.3%	24.1%	42.4%	71.6%	65.0%

11 Noh, Charles W. 2005. "Proctor & Gamble," *Value Line*, July 8.
12 Smith, Jason A. 2005. "Unilever N.V/Unilever PLC," *Value Line*, August 5.

EXHIBIT 1.2 (from previous page)

	1995	1996	1997	1998	1999	2000	2001	2002	2003	2004
Kimberly-Clark[13]										
Sales	$13,789	$13,149	$12,547	$12,298	$13,007	$13,982	$14,524	$13,566	$14,348	$15,083
Operating Margin	16.2%	19.9%	18.1%	18.7%	21.5%	22.9%	21.8%	18.7%	22.8%	22.3%
Net Profit Margin	8.0%	10.7%	11.2%	11.0%	12.4%	12.9%	12.0%	12.9%	12.0%	11.9%
ROE	30.2%	31.3%	34.0%	34.8%	31.6%	31.2%	30.9%	30.9%	25.4%	27.2%
Colgate-Palmolive[14]										
Sales	$8,358	$8,749	$9,057	$8,972	$9,118	$9,358	$9,428	$9,294	$9,903	$10,584
Operating Margin	17.1%	17.9%	18.5%	20.2%	21.7%	22.8%	24.0%	23.0%	24.9%	24.6%
Net Profit Margin	6.5%	7.3%	8.2%	9.5%	10.3%	11.4%	12.5%	13.9%	14.4%	13.0%
ROE	32.2%	31.2%	34.0%	40.7%	51.1%	72.5%				
Clorox[15]										
Sales	$1,984	$2,218	$2,533	$2,741	$4,003	$4,083	$3,903	$4,061	$4,144	$4,324
Operating Margin	23.3%	24.0%	23.4%	23.6%	23.5%	24.0%	22.9%	23.2%	25.2%	24.7%
Net Profit Margin	10.1%	10.0%	9.8%	10.9%	9.8%	10.3%	9.8%	7.9%	12.4%	12.6%
ROE	21.3%	23.8%	24.1%	27.5%	24.9%	23.4%	20.2%	23.8%	42.3%	35.5%

13   Noh, Charles W. 2005. "Kimberly-Clark," *Value Line*, July 8.
14   Kaplan, Jerome H. 2005. "Colgate-Palmolive," *Value Line*, July 8.
15   Kaplan, Jerome, H. 2005. "Clorox Co.," *Value Line*, July 8.

households could afford their products. These strategies yielded industry average operating margins of 21% in 2004.[16]

Competing in the industry required going up against such giants as Procter & Gamble and Unilever, which together accounted for around half of global market share. Other major players included familiar names like Kimberly-Clark, Colgate-Palmolive, and Clorox (See Exhibit 1.2). Recent years had also seen superstores like Wal-Mart introduce private label products into the market, further intensifying competition.

Producers were formidable rivals, paying large fees to retailers to display their goods prominently. This practice was controversial and critics noted that competitors with less capital were often relegated to the bottom shelf or were forced out of the market entirely. Tom Chappell, CEO of Tom's of Maine, a purveyor of environmentally sensitive personal care products, commented about his experience with these tactics. He stated, "It's common practice for a sales executive from a major company to go into a chain store account with a new product and say 'We want you to take this new toothpaste, and we recommend that you discontinue three or four Tom's items to find room on the shelves.' "[17]

Green Household Products

As relatively new members of the natural products portfolio, green household products suffered from a reputation for ineffectiveness and questionable environmental performance. For example, early green detergents lacked the cleaning power of conventional detergents. Worse, some product claims were exposed as highly inflated.[18] Despite this handicap, green products were making a spirited comeback: sales were estimated to be growing at over 20% annually in natural food stores and 17.6% of American households reported using at least one natural household product. This resurgence had created a healthy niche industry estimated to be worth over $450 million in annual sales.[19]

This growth trend was expected to continue due to the increased patronage of baby boomers looking to green household products as one way to live healthier as they grew older.[20] In addition, in mature markets such as household nondurables, there was a general trend towards premium products during periods of economic prosperity, which supported periodic faster growth among natural household products versus the industry as a whole.[21]

The industry's primary channels of distribution were natural foods stores, such as Whole Foods Market, as well as smaller local outlets, direct mail, and online catalogs.

16   Noh, Charles W. 2005. "Household Products Industry." *Value Line*, April 8.

17   Estabrook, Barry. 2004. "Clean 'n' Green." *On Earth*, 26(4).

18   Crane, Andrew. 2000. "Facing the Backlash: Green marketing and strategic reorientation in the 1990's." *Journal of Strategic Marketing*, 8: 277-296.

19   Duber-Smith, Darrin C. 2004. "The Market for Natural Household Products." http://www. NPICenter.com

20   Ginsberg, Jill M. and Bloom, Paul N., 2004. "Choosing the Right Green Marketing Strategy." *MIT Sloan Management Review*, 46(1): 79-84.

21   Bossong-Martines, Eileen M. 2004. *Standard & Poor's Industry Survey*, 172 (51): Section 1. "Household Non-Durables Industry Survey." McGraw-Hill.

Mainstream supermarket chains, such as Albertsons and Safeway, also had begun to stock an increasing inventory of these products. In large measure, this was an attempt to replace sales of price-driven conventional products that had been lost to large discounters, such as Wal-Mart and Costco. Over time, this effect had been powerful. Between 1988 and 2003, mainstream grocery chains saw their market share of all grocery and consumable sales shrink to 56% from a high of 90%. This was forecast to drop to a 49% share by 2008[22] (see Exhibit 1.3). By carrying higher-margin goods unlikely to be available at these discounters, supermarkets were hoping to regain customers.

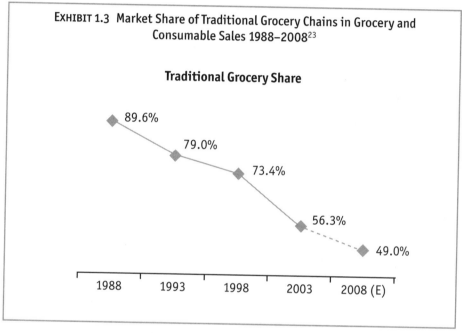

EXHIBIT 1.3 Market Share of Traditional Grocery Chains in Grocery and Consumable Sales 1988–2008[23]

Traditional Grocery Share

89.6%

79.0%

73.4%

56.3%

49.0%

1988   1993   1998   2003   2008 (E)

Seventh Generation was the only company competing in the natural household products market that had built a strong brand, sold a wide range of products, and was widely available in catalogs, natural food stores, and mainstream grocery stores. Most of the industry was fragmented, as many companies were young and had yet to build strong brand images. In addition, many companies sold only one product line so consumers had few choices when looking for one-stop companies from which to purchase all of their green household products.[24]

Some mainstream household products companies responded to this new industry niche by introducing green product lines of their own, as evidenced by Kimberly-Clark's line of recycled-fiber bathroom tissue. These companies, which might lack the green

---

22   Jacobson, Amy. 2005. "New Formats Edging out Traditional Supermarket." *Spins Industry Partner Newsletter*, 9: 3.

23   Ibid.

24   An example of this is the company BonaKemi, which solely produces environmentally sound hardwood finishing products.

credentials that many consumers sought, often looked to third-party green certification institutions (such as Green Seal) to provide verification of their claims.[25] In order for mainstream companies to boost credibility and enter this side of the industry, they were pursuing strategic acquisitions of green start-ups, much as they did in the natural foods industry.[26] Two notable examples of this trend were Unilever's acquisition of Ben & Jerry's and Groupe Danone's acquisition of Stonyfield Farms.

As the green household products industry continued to move out of niche channels, its companies were seeking to overcome a collective image as products for "tree huggers" and become fully accepted in the mainstream market place. Wider consumer acceptance would require an increased understanding of environmental and health issues within the general public, a challenging proposition considering the complexity of these topics and the small amount of time a company had to deliver information to a customer in a supermarket.[27] Seventh Generation was a company betting that it could meet this challenge. If so, the green consumer movement seemed ready to deliver the company increased sales.

Green Consumers

What is a green consumer? The term was notoriously hard to understand and the market segment equally difficult to define. Early attempts to use socio-demographic factors to segment these customers produced contradictory results while further studies attempting to use attitudes, environmental knowledge, education, social consciousness, and related behaviors were also frequently inconclusive.[28] Making things more confusing for market researchers, environmental concern reported in marketing surveys appeared vastly over-reported in comparison to consumers' actual buying habits.[29] One early explanation for over-reporting of environmental concern was the survey questions posed to consumers. Who wouldn't say yes when asked "do you feel we should protect the natural environment?" The problem was that the values linked to purchases and other behaviors were quite different from the general values observed in surveys with these types of questions.[30]

25   http://www.greenseal.org.
26   Estabrook, Barry. 2004. "Clean 'n' Green." On Earth, 26(4).
27   Ottman, Jacquelyn A. 2003. "Green Marketing: Empower the People." In Business, 25(6): 32.
28   See Straughan, Robert D. and Roberts, James A. 1999. "Environmental segmentation alternatives: A look at green consumer behavior in the new millennium." Journal of Consumer Marketing. 16(6): 558-575; Peattie, Ken. 1999. "Trappings versus Substance in the Greening of Marketing Planning." Journal of Strategic Marketing, 7(2): 131-148; Kilbourne, William E. and Beckmann, Suzanne, C. 1998. "Review and Critical Assessment of Research on Marketing and the Environment." Journal of Marketing Management, 14: 513-532.
29   Crane, Andrew. 2000. "Facing the Backlash: Green marketing and strategic reorientation in the 1990's." Journal of Strategic Marketing, 8: 277-296.
30   Dembkowski, S. and Hanmer-Lloyd, S., 1994. "The Environmental Value-Attitude-System Model: A Framework to Guide the Understanding of Environmentally-Conscious Consumer Behavior." Journal of Marketing Management, 10(7): 593-603.

But some of these contradictions could be explained if the trade-offs required to purchase different types of green products were examined. Although a consumer may wish to purchase a green product, the perceived trade-offs in terms of ease of purchase, quality versus conventional products, and price might still be too high. A 2002 survey reporting that 49% of Americans viewed environmentally safe alternative products as too expensive to purchase validated this perception.[31] Simply put, most consumers would not buy a green product if it was inconvenient to use or purchase, or didn't meet their performance expectations.

Recent years, however, had produced an increased understanding of these contradictions and as a result there had been some success in segmenting green consumers. A 2002 Roper Organization survey segmented all consumers into five "shades" of greenness:[32]

- **True Blue Greens (9%).** These consumers act and speak out on their environmental beliefs. Typically, they are financially stable and well-educated families. True Blues are four times more likely to avoid products made with no environmental claims.

- **Greenback Greens (6%).** Not politically active in environmental or activist causes, these consumers still consistently buy green products. Greenbacks weigh any trade-off they may face when purchasing green products, unlike True Blues, who typically disregard them.

- **Sprouts (31%).** Sprouts are the environmental fence sitters and will buy green products when the economy is doing well or when they are appealed to properly. Sprouts often have a "pet" environmental issue, such as animal rights, which they will support in their purchasing habits, while disregarding most other issues.

- **Grousers (19%).** Grousers feel guilty about the environment, but wash their hands of its problems. Grousers feel that environmental problems are the concern of the government and large corporations, not individuals. They are usually uneducated about the environment and feel that they cannot affect change, two factors regularly linked to green purchasing behavior.

- **Basic Browns (33%).** Browns have no concern for the environment and feel that they display mainstream behavior. Generally coming from low income and low education levels, Basic Browns feel they have more pressing problems to worry about than protecting the environment.

These segments showed that between 15 and 46% of the population were receptive to green products, depending on the economy and on the confidence and trade-offs necessary to make purchases. Moreover, the aforementioned growth in the baby boomer segment could be expected to fuel further growth in green spending as these individuals continued to grow older and become more concerned with their health and a healthy environment.

---

31   RoperASW, 2002. "Green Gauge Report 2002: Americans Perspective on Green Business, Yes . . . But." November.
32   Ibid.

Seventh Generation: A Circuitous Route to Success

Seventh Generation sold a line of over 50 natural household products including paper products made from recycled fibers and chemical-free household cleaners and detergents. Seventh Generation's prices, although somewhat variable, are typically 40–60% higher than competing natural products and could be more than twice as expensive as conventional products. There was no doubt that the company was a force in niche channels. In natural food stores, Seventh Generation accounted for 69% of all toilet paper sales, 74% of all paper towel sales, 42% of all laundry liquid sales, and 35% of all laundry powder sales.[33]

Seventh Generation essentially was a product design, marketing, and distribution company, having no manufacturing facilities at its Burlington, Vermont headquarters. In 2005, its entire staff numbered only 42. To manufacture, it relied on close relationships with suppliers that manufactured to its specifications. At company headquarters, two staff scientists worked on product development and testing to ensure that products met Seventh Generation's strict environmental standards.

Seventh Generation had gone through several transformations since beginning as a wholesale natural products catalog in the late 1980's. Originally named Renew America, it was run by a Washington DC non-profit that developed and sold energy-saving household devices. In 1988, Renew America decided to sell its catalog business and made an offer to Vermont entrepreneur Alan Newman. At the time, Newman was running a company called Niche Marketing, a provider of marketing services to progressive and non-profit companies, including Renew America. Newman initially refused the offer, but when Renew America was unable to find a suitable buyer, it simply gave him its catalog business. Newman didn't like the name and at the suggestion of a Native American employee, changed it to Seventh Generation, a name based on the Iroquois philosophy that all decisions should be considered in light of their impact on the next seven generations.[34]

Using direct mailings, the company generated some consumer response and by 1989 sales were meeting Newman's expectations. Although not yet profitable, Newman felt that the company had a real shot at sustained growth and success. However, he had no previous experience growing a company on this scale and needed to raise additional capital to help his new company reach its potential. It was about then that Newman met someone looking for a new way of doing business, Jeffrey Hollender.[35]

Hollender had just quit his job as the president of the audio books division at Warner Communications. He had landed the job after selling Warner his first successful business: a series of taped courses offering such educational fare as *How to Lose Your Brooklyn Accent* and *How to Marry Money*. Although financially successful at a very young age, Hollender found his work unfulfilling. He had long harbored lofty goals of making a positive impact on society and felt that the work he was doing at Warner was taking him in another direction. He quit to conduct research for his first book, *How to Make the World a Better Place,* which led him to Vermont and Seventh Generation. The book offered a number of ideas on how to live life in a more sustainable and environmentally

33   Estabrook, Barry. 2004. "Clean 'n' Green." *On Earth*, 26(4).
34   McCuan, Jess. 2004. "It's Not Easy Being Green." *Inc. Magazine*, 26(11): 110-118.
35   Ibid.

friendly way, laying out specific directions on how to conserve more paper, support environmental organizations, and produce less waste.

After they met to discuss the topics surrounding Hollender's book, it was clear that the two men had similar business interests. Moreover, Hollender's acumen for raising money as well as his business connections and reputation were just the things that Newman needed to continue to grow Seventh Generation. The two co-wrote Seventh Generation's first business plan, billing it as a green household products wholesale company using direct mailings as its marketing channel. It would be a niche player, buying products from small-scale green entrepreneurs who could not get their products into other channels. The product line would be limited to green household non-durable products.

Pitching this plan to investors, the pair was able to raise $850,000 in capital by selling 54% of the company to 40 different investors. The two partners contributed the remainder evenly. Hollender became CEO and took over product development and long-term planning while Newman became President and oversaw day-to-day operations.[36]

The additional capital proved essential. Shortly after the deal, monthly orders climbed 1000% following increases in the catalog's circulation and some key Earth Day publicity. The new funds enabled Newman and Hollender to buy a new facility, hire 80 new employees, and begin rapidly increasing the breadth of their product line. By 1990 sales had reached $7 million, increasing from just $1 million the year before. Hollender raised another $5 million from investors and forecast sales to increase up to $20 million within another year.[37]

Economic conditions would put a damper on these estimates, however, as the first Persian Gulf War and ensuing recession of the early 90s would test Seventh Generation's consumer appeal and management savvy.

Uncertain Ground

The world had changed, but Seventh Generation hadn't.

—Alan Newman

It was like falling through the air and not knowing where the ground is.

—Jeffrey Hollender

1991 saw sales plummet. At a point when the company was organized to sell $20 million of goods, it sold only $6 million.[38] It appeared that many of Seventh Generation's green products were discretionary to its customers and when hit with economic hard

36   Ibid.
37   Ibid.
38   Hollender, J. 2004. *What Matters Most: How a Small Group of Pioneers is Teaching Social Responsibility to Big Business, and Why Big Business is Listening.* New York: Basic Books: 255.

times, most switched back to cheaper standard products. The company struggled to maintain sales levels and was forced to lay off over 50 employees. This was not enough to keep the company afloat, however, and another difficult round of layoffs ensued, forcing management to dismiss many employees that had been with the company since its founding.

At the executive level, a rift developed between Hollender and Newman as they envisioned disparate strategies for getting the company back on track.[39] Newman still believed Seventh Generation should stay in the catalog business in order to provide a channel of distribution for small, green entrepreneurs who had no other means of reaching potential customers. Hollender, on the other hand, believed the best way to both grow the business and stay true to the company's mission of spreading sustainable business practices was to become a player in the mainstream marketplace. He wanted to build Seventh Generation as a solid brand and position it in natural foods stores as well as in mainstream grocery channels.

The stress of keeping the company afloat proved too much for Newman, who left to take a six-month sabbatical in the midst of the company's turmoil. The move incensed Hollender and the board of directors, who felt betrayed by Newman's departure; Newman was not allowed to return to Seventh Generation, even after repeated requests.[40] In the words of Seventh Generation's board chairman at the time, "Alan Newman was never interested in making money. He was one of those people who believe it doesn't matter. I saw Alan as an impediment."[41]

Seventh Generation was facing potential bankruptcy and Hollender now had the additional problem of managing numerous employees who were loyal to Newman and who viewed Hollender with suspicion. The company needed money badly and management decided that taking the company public was the best way to obtain it. Although to Hollender, going public did not seem like the most socially responsible course of action, nothing would be accomplished by letting the company go bankrupt. After buying out Newman's stock, Seventh Generation raised $7 million dollars with an IPO starting at $5 a share in 1994.[42]

The Recovery

Our number one goal and priority is to build our brand—to build Seventh Generation as the brand name of leading environmental products.[43]

—Jeffrey Hollender

39   McCuan, Jess. 2004. "It's Not Easy Being Green." *Inc. Magazine*, 26(11): 110-118.
40   Ibid.
41   Ibid.
42   Newman used the proceeds from selling his shares in Seventh Generation to build the now-famous Vermont microbrewery, Magic Hat. See McCuan, Jess. 2004. "It's Not Easy Being Green." *Inc. Magazine*, 26(11): 110-118.
43   D.R., 1996. "Adjusting to a Changing Market." *In Business*, 18(4): 18-21.

Hollender then moved forward, acting on his vision of turning Seventh Generation into a strong household products brand that would positively influence society by becoming a fixture in the homes of mainstream America. He did not see the direct mail business model as a means to this end and also had problems with the nature of the business, once commenting: "If one, two, or three percent of the people we mail to respond, where do all those other catalogs go?"[44] More importantly, the catalog business was losing money, even though it accounted for 80% of Seventh Generation's revenues at the time.[45] As of December 31, 1994, the catalog reported an operating loss of $1 million on net revenues of $6.3 million.[46]

Seventh Generation decided to sell the catalog in 1995 to Gaiam, Inc., a Colorado company formed specifically for the purchase. Gaiam agreed to buy the catalog for $1.3 million along with the assumption of $500,000 in liabilities. The transaction also included agreements for Seventh Generation to sell their branded products to the catalog as well as a $200,000 licensing agreement for Gaiam to continue to use the Seventh Generation name.[47] After the sale, Hollender noted, "The sale of the catalog operations will help reduce the company's overall operating losses. We expect that revenue from the sales of branded products to the new catalog company will improve the financial performance of our wholesale business."[48] Most employees went to go work for Gaiam, and Seventh Generation's staff, once 140 strong, shrank to only seven.[49]

The spin-off of the catalog proved a shrewd decision. Sales from Seventh Generation's core wholesale business increased from $1.7 million in 1995 to $4 million in 1996.[50] On solid ground once again, Seventh Generation was able to focus on developing new products and building tight relationships with natural foods stores like Whole Foods Market as well as mainstream grocery chains like Albertsons and Kroger. Its product line began to firm up, and featured strong sellers such as recycled paper products, hypo-allergenic soaps and detergents, and biodegradable disposable diapers.

But although Seventh Generation had posted sales of $11 million in 1999 (an increase of 40% per year since the sale of the catalog[51]) its stock price was still in the doldrums, trading at around $0.70.[52] Company officials worried that the stock, which they viewed as undervalued, would attract a hostile takeover. Hollender, noted, "If we don't come along to make an offer to buy the company, somebody else will."[53] Seeing the future start to clear up and fed up with the expenses and hassles of running a public company, Seventh Generation became privately held once again, purchasing back the outstanding shares at a premium of $1.30 per share.[54] It obtained funding from another round of private equity fundraising, which secured $4.6 million in capital. The private acquisition only required about $3 million. This left $1.6 million to cover transaction costs

44   Ibid.
45   McCuan, Jess. 2004. "It's Not Easy Being Green." *Inc. Magazine*, 26(11): 110-118.
46   *In Business*. 1995. "Seventh Generation Sells Catalog Business." May/June vol. 17(3): 6.
47   Ibid.
48   Ibid.
49   D.R., 1996. "Adjusting to a Changing Market." *In Business*, 18(4): 18-21.
50   Ibid.
51   Johnson, Jim. 2000. "Seventh Generation Goes Private." *Waste News*, 5(39): 4.
52   McCuan, Jess. 2004. "It's Not Easy Being Green." *Inc. Magazine*, 26(11): 110-118.
53   Johnson, Jim. 2000. "Seventh Generation Goes Private." *Waste News*, 5(39): 4.
54   Ibid.

and pay off outstanding debt.[55] The move would save Seventh Generation $200,000 per year in public reporting costs as well as $100,000 annually in interest payments.[56]

A New Approach

At about this same time, Hollender had a revelation about the natural products industry as a whole. Seeing the success of natural foods in mainstream retail chains, he observed, "People don't buy organic apples because they are worried about the pollution of a stream, for the most part they are worrying about consuming pesticides."[57] He repositioned Seventh Generation as a purveyor of healthy, safe, and effective products, switching the tagline from "Products for a Healthy Planet," to "Healthier for You and the Environment."[58] Academic research supported this repositioning.[59] Product attributes were promoted by spotlighting their health benefits, especially in regard to asthma, allergies, and chemical sensitivities. These ailments were known to be aggravated by the presence of chlorine, petroleum products, and volatile organic compounds that were found in traditional chemical-based household products. Seventh Generation's products contained no chlorine or solvents, and instead used vegetable-based oils. In the cases where the company violated these guidelines there were detailed ingredient labels prominently displayed. This practice was not employed by its mainstream competitors.

With its new marketing campaign, Seventh Generation made a major nationwide move into mainstream retail chains in 2001, expanding beyond its home turf in the grocery chains of the northeastern United States. This positioned it to capitalize on two key trends in the industry. First, the large baby boomer generation had been steadily aging (see Exhibit 1.4), and this segment had become increasingly willing to pay a premium for products that were healthy and safe.[60] Second, traditional supermarkets continued to look for a way to differentiate themselves from mega-discount stores and warehouse chains such as Wal-Mart and Costco as well as gain access to the typically wealthier green consumer.[61] Seventh Generation provided supermarkets with the opportunity to meet both of these goals and as a result the company received major discounts on shelving fees. Its products were displayed prominently and supermarkets resisted pressure from competitors to reduce these concessions.[62]

55   Ibid
56   Ibid.
57   Estabrook, Barry. 2004. "Clean 'n' Green." *On Earth*, 26(4).
58   Janoff, Barry. 1999. "Supermarkets go Au Naturel." *Progressive Grocer*, 78(3): 75-79.
59   Dembkowski, S. and Hanmer-Lloyd, S. 1994. "The Environmental Value-Attitude-System Model: A Framework to Guide the Understanding of Environmentally-Conscious Consumer Behavior." *Journal of Marketing Management*, 10(7): 593-603.
60   Ginsberg, Jill M. and Bloom, Paul N. 2004. "Choosing the Right Green Marketing Strategy." *MIT Sloan Management Review*, 46(1): 79-84.
61   Estabrook, Barry. 2004. "Clean 'n' Green." *On Earth*, 26(4).
62   McCuan, Jess. 2004. "It's Not Easy Being Green." *Inc. Magazine*, 26(11): 110-118.

EXHIBIT 1.4 Growth Estimates for US Population by Age Group[63]

(Numbers are in Thousands)

	2000–2050	2000–2010	2010–2020	2020–2030	2030–2040	2040–2050
Numerical Change						
TOTAL	**137,729**	**26,811**	**26,869**	**27,780**	**28,361**	**27,908**
Ages 0–4	8,862	2,208	1,506	1,340	2,027	1,781
Ages 5–19	19,736	479	4,146	4,877	4,494	5,740
Ages 20–44	26,822	369	4,189	6,115	6,912	9,237
Ages 45–64	30,665	18,573	2,641	-1,373	6,331	4,493
Ages 65–84	35,050	3,326	13,243	14,487	2,790	1,204
Ages 85+	16,594	1,856	1,145	2,334	5,806	5,452
Percent Change						
TOTAL	**48.8**	**9.5**	**8.7**	**8.3**	**7.8**	**7.1**
Ages 0–4	46.1	11.5	7.0	5.8	8.4	6.8
Ages 5–19	32.2	0.8	6.7	7.4	6.3	7.6
Ages 20–44	25.8	0.4	4.0	5.6	6.0	7.6
Ages 45–64	49.1	29.7	3.3	-1.6	7.7	5.1
Ages 65–84	113.8	10.8	38.8	30.6	4.5	1.9
Ages 85+	388.9	43.5	18.7	32.1	60.5	35.4

Seventh Generation's new strategy was effective and survived through the tough economic times of the early 2000s. By 2004, its annual sales were estimated to top $25 million.[64] As of 2004, sales from mainstream grocery chains accounted for 30% of Seventh Generation's revenues and Hollender expected them to account for 50% by 2006.[65] Though it was "not even a fly on the back of a Procter & Gamble," the company wasn't a microorganism either.[66]

Hollender saw such growth as synonymous with positive change, noting, "Why should we [society] manufacture products that damage the environment and make people sick when we have the technology to do it in a way that's far safer?"[67] But in order to continue growth at their rapid rate and take toxic chemicals off the shelves,

63   US Census Bureau, 2004, "US Interim Projections by Age, Sex, Race, and Hispanic Origin," http://www.census.gov/ipc/www/usinterimproj.
64   Ibid.
65   Estabrook, Barry. 2004. "Clean 'n' Green." *On Earth*, 26(4).
66   Kanter, Larry. 2006. "The Eco-Advantage: The Green 50." *Inc Magazine*, 28(11): 90.
67   Estabrook, Barry. 2004. "Clean 'n' Green." *On Earth*, 26(4).

Seventh Generation had to continue building a company with a distinctly values-driven character.

Corporate Counter-Culture?

> We have an expectation that people will be as committed to their personal growth here as they are to their professional growth. And as a company, we explicitly support the personal growth of our people. But that is not a challenge that everyone wants to take on. So we have to be very particular about hiring. The most important thing is that the people we hire get our mission and values so they can become part of the community we've built.[68]
>
> —Judith Joyce, Director of Community Development and Human Resources

Hiring at Seventh Generation reflected the belief that skills could be taught to a capable person, but values could not. At Seventh Generation, prospective employees had to clear both a competency and a values hurdle. Consequently, staff members thought of themselves as a community of people with diverse backgrounds and personalities, working towards the same common goals and ideals (see Exhibit 1.5 for the company's mission and values statement). This type of fit was viewed as crucial to success within the company, and was illustrated by the layoff of a highly qualified Harvard MBA. Although a very capable and skilled employee, this person did not make decisions in line with Seventh Generation's priorities, which at times placed stakeholder interests ahead of immediate financial benefit.

To better codify and communicate the company's mission and vision, Seventh Generation created a Values and Operating Principles Committee (VOPS) that consisted of employees and a senior management representative. The group knew that Seventh Generation faced some risk with a values-driven strategy, and wanted to maintain consistency and set precedent for future actions by the company. When formed, the group was tasked with creating an updated business plan that could be justified in terms of the company's mission statement. This proved a formidable challenge. Gregor Barnum, Director of Corporate Consciousness, described the result as a learning process: "they made a business plan and tried to make it fit the mission and that is not how you do business in a socially responsible company."[69]

More recently, the group has enjoyed some success developing protocols for situations that could misalign the company with its stated goals. For example, in 2003 there was a strike at the Albertsons grocery chain in southern California. Seventh Generation had no policy for selling products into a strike zone, but the situation made the VOPS group uneasy. Senior management, after a lengthy dialogue with the VOPS group,

68   Seventh Generation Corporate Responsibility Report, 2004. "Widening the Lens."
69   Casewriter interview, September 6, 2005.

EXHIBIT 1.5 Vision, Mission, and Values and Operating Principles[70]

Our Vision

Leadership, Inspiration, and Positive Change
A company with the authority to lead, the creativity to inspire, and the will to foster positive social and environmental change.

Make The World a Better Place
A community in which individuals possess the resources, knowledge, courage, and commitment to make the world a better place.

Sustainability, Justice, and Compassion
A society whose guiding principles include: environmental sustainability, social justice, and compassion for all living creatures.

An Earth Restored
An earth that is restored, protected, and cherished for this generation and those to come.

Our Mission

Trust & Authenticity
We are committed to becoming the world's most trusted brand of authentic, safe, and environmentally responsible products for a healthy home.

Service & Inspiration
We are dedicated to setting the standard for superior service and to providing our customers with the resources and inspiration they need to make informed, responsible decisions.

Balance
We strive to achieve balance between the fiscal, social, and environmental responsibilities of our company.

An Exceptional Workplace Community
We are committed to creating an exceptional workplace community, one that inspires honesty and trust, respect and compassion, and a spirited sense of play. A community that provides opportunities for growth and the freedom to realize our full potential.

Community Participation
We will fully participate in and provide leadership to each community of which we are a part.

(continued over)

(from previous page)

Our Values & Operating Principles

Trust
To provide authentic, high-quality, and competitively priced products that build trust in our brand and our mission.

Service
To provide service that exceeds the expectations of our customers.

Responsibility
To understand that our social and environmental responsibility can best be fulfilled through the financial success of our Company.

Empowerment
To empower employees by creating a work environment in which each person is entrusted with responsibility and held accountable; personal and professional development are strongly encouraged; mistakes are understood as opportunities for growth; and everyone is provided with the tools, information, and resources to do their best.

Community
To create a workplace community in which respect and dignity are promoted, honest communication is fostered, open minds and hearts are valued, trust is cultivated, fun and playfulness are encouraged, and a "can do" attitude is expected.

Leadership
To be leaders and role models in the communities and markets we serve.

decided to continue to sell products into the strike zone while making a donation to the striker's hardship fund equivalent to the profits earned on those sales.

Despite considerable growth, the Seventh Generation work atmosphere remained casual and open, with many employees dressed as if they could slip out for a quick hike at a moment's notice. Gregor Barnum often was accompanied at work by his dog Puck. Yet, like others at Seventh Generation, he was serious about his work. When probed, he elaborated on why he enjoyed working at Seventh Generation: "it's great working for a place where meetings can range in topic from product positioning to corporate responsibility to 19th century philosophy and everybody is on board."[71]

Seventh Generation invested considerable effort toward maintaining its values-driven mission. Staff retreats reinvigorated its commitment to values, and what those values meant in practice. Joint outings like snow-shoeing or rafting helped to create a sense of community within the company.[72] And the company insisted that all employees serve on committees like the community service group or "green team," to connect

71   Ibid.
72   Hollender, J. 2004. "What matters most: Corporate values and social responsibility." *California Management Review*, 46: 111-119.

them with broader needs of the community and planet. Seventh Generation was also a pioneer in the use of "360-degree" reviews, and all employees had the opportunity to critique the performance of Hollender and other corporate officers.[73] Hollender considered such reviews to be consistent with his commitment to transparency.

One of the many challenges facing Seventh Generation, with its hope for rapid growth to $100 million in annual revenues, was maintaining this culture and sense of community while doubling its workforce in less than five years. Penny Tudor, Director of Quality Assurance, summed up why she thought the company would be successful in the midst of its expansion, "It all comes back to making sure you hire like-minded people who understand the company's mission around corporate responsibility. People have to know why they're here."[74]

Seventh Generation's Communication Strategy

By entering into mainstream distribution channels, Seventh Generation had created a convenient point of sale that helped to eliminate some of the trade-offs necessary when purchasing green products. By changing the focus of its products' benefits from environmental to personal, the company also was widening its potential customer base beyond the "True Blue" and "Greenback Green" consumer. In order to build green credibility with consumers it employed a third-party company to publish a thorough corporate social responsibility report each year that documented the sustainability of its operations from suppliers to the post-consumer recycling bins and trash dumps.[75]

These actions bolstered sales and improved the future outlook for Seventh Generation. However, its products still had not attained mainstream status. Company executives worried that a majority of consumers still did not understand—even in personal terms—the advantage of using chemical-free products in the home. In fact, fifty-one percent of consumers surveyed by the Roper Organization reported that they knew little or nothing about environmental issues and problems.[76]

Seventh Generation tried to do its part to educate consumers by putting general information on its products' packaging. It also used some edgy advertising to attract attention. Rather than advertise, the company conducts educational promotions such as a self-declared "Made Without Chlorine Month." For this promotion, Seventh Generation distributed toilet paper with a list of facts on it entitled "Learn Facts about Chlorine That Will Scare the Crap Out Of You," in order to educate its consumers about chlorine's link to cancer.[77] Although unorthodox, the promotion proved popular.

The Internet was believed to be a real advantage for Seventh Generation, because it allowed the company to meet the needs of its most inquiring customers. For these individuals, its website, seventhgeneration.com, provided a wealth of information on com-

73   Ibid.
74   Seventh Generation Corporate Responsibility Report, 2004. "Widening the Lens."
75   www.seventhgeneration.com
76   RoperASW, 2002. "Green Gauge Report 2002: Americans Perspective on Green Business, Yes . . . But." November.
77   Ivinsky, Pamela A. 2000. "Double Duty." *Print,* 54(2): 8.

pany products. In November, 2006, across the top and down the side of its home page were these tabs:

- Household Hazards
- Making a Difference
- About Us
- Get Coupons

- Living Green
- Our Products
- Find a Store
- Visit our Blog

Several of these tabs replicated those that would appear on any commercial site, but others provided useful information on sustainability and health issues and engaged customers. For example, visitors could sign up to receive email copies of "The Non-Toxic Times," a newsletter that contained "ideas, news, and resources for a clean home, a healthy family, and a safer world." The site also served to strengthen the Seventh Generation brand image.

In mid-2006, the company launched its blog, inspiredprotagonist.com. The home page of the site proclaimed this mission for the blog:

> In an age when despairing doom and global gloom rule the wires and extinguish those inspired fires that could ignite the needed change, the Inspired Protagonist seeks to cut the cords of negativity that bind us and replace them with hopeful strands of thought and deed that weave new worlds of possibility. This is the home of the voice of Seventh Generation and of all our friends and kindred spirits. It's the place for different thinking, dynamic action, deeper traction, and daring dialogue that move people to move our culture forward. Let us together reboot the present and reinvent the future through alternative patterns of being and sharing, doing and caring.

The site provided a place for Jeffrey Hollender, others in the company, and a host of interested parties to exchange ideas about subjects much wider than green household products. From events in Vermont to global politics, the blog represented a stream of thoughts and ideas about the state of human enterprise, consumption, and coexistence with the natural environment.

The Baby Wipes Problem

Martin Wolf had been working on a new natural formula for Seventh Generation's baby wipes when a meeting of top management was called. Seventh Generation was running out of stock on the conventional baby wipes and needed to decide if it was going to continue selling them or stop ordering and shipping the conventional product until a new natural formula was completed. Management personnel from all of Seventh Generation's divisions were present at the meeting (see Exhibit 1.6 for a list of attendees).

Jeff Phillips, head of finance and operations, argued that the company should continue to sell the conventional product while the natural formula was being developed. His position was supported by sales chief John Murphy, who added that the loss of revenues and shelf space was unacceptable and that, after all, the conventional formula had been deemed "safe." Opposition to this viewpoint was strongest from Sue Holden,

EXHIBIT 1.6 Baby Wipes Meeting Attendees

- Jeffrey Hollender, President & CEO
- Jeff Phillips, Executive Vice President of Finance & Operations
- Karen Fleming, Vice President of Marketing
- John Murphy, Vice President of Sales
- Jay Leduc, Vice President of Operations
- Sue Holden, Manager, Consumer Relations
- Martin Wolf, Director, Product Quality & Technology

Manager of Consumer Relations, who wanted to stop shipping conventional formula baby wipes until a new natural formula could be developed. She felt strongly that Seventh Generation had betrayed their customers and needed to act to win their trust back. Martin Wolf and Karen Fleming, VP of Marketing, both supported this point of view as well. For them, this approach was more consistent with Seventh Generation's brand, and felt the company's actions needed to resonate with its image.

Financially, all agreed that the implications of the decision were not trivial. One measure of the impact of Seventh Generation's decision would be seen on store shelves. Selling through existing supplies would take 30–60 days, and after that it would take another 60–90 days for the newly-formulate wipes to arrive. Even a week's loss of sales would register an impact on Seventh Generation's bottom line. Added to this was the significant cost of clearing store shelves of conventionally formulated wipes, if that option was selected.

One of three courses of action were available:

- Clear the shelves immediately and wait until the newly formulated wipes were available for sale (90–150 days of empty shelves).

- Sell-through existing wipes, order no additional conventional wipes, and then wait until the newly formulated wipes were available (60–90 days of empty shelves).

- Sell-through existing products, order enough conventional wipes to fill the gap until the newly formulated wipes were available, and switch over to the new wipes without having to leave shelves empty.

Jeffrey Hollender, who had moderated the meeting, remained silent on the subject until his management team had fully voiced its range of opinions. The group waited anxiously for Hollender to decide on a course of action.

Teaching notes for this case are available from Greenleaf Publishing. These are free of charge and are available only to teaching staff. They can be requested by going to:
http://www.greenleaf-publishing.com/oikos_notes

CASE 2
Phoenix Organic
Valuing Sustainability While Desiring Growth[1]

Eva Collins and Steve Bowden

Waikato School of Management, New Zealand

Kate Kearins

Auckland University of Technology, New Zealand

> I believe that there are some significant issues related to sustainability for businesses that get beyond a certain point.
>
> —Chris Morrison, Managing Director

For business school students wanting to do business differently, Phoenix Organic should be an inspiration. Start by collecting empty beer bottles after a night at the pub(s), wash off the labels and cigarette butts, and refill them with potent home brew. Sell them at a profit to a cult market and, 17 years later in 2004, lean back and enjoy the fruits of a $NZ6.5 million business. You don't even have to finish your degree.

All of the above is correct but it wasn't that simple. The reality was that the founders of Auckland-based Phoenix Organic made a series of strategic decisions that, coupled with some good luck and more hard work, allowed them to claim a niche in New Zealand's beverage industry. And they did it while maintaining their vision to create a business that was good for the planet and good for the health of its people.

How It All Started

"It was all very subsistence. We literally just were hanging in there and I worked nights doing dishes in a restaurant, and we were definitely hand-to-mouth," remembered Roger Harris, Director of Sales and Marketing and also one of Phoenix's founders. Phoenix relied on government business development money and personal scrimping to get the company going in those early days.

Harris met Managing Director, Chris Morrison, and partner Deborah Cairns in 1987—all part of a circle of people involved in organic urban gardening. Morrison and Cairns had started a small business making naturally fermented ginger fizz in their Auckland flat. "We used to go around the pubs and pick up the old Steinlager bottles and take them home and soak them in our bath to get the cigarette butts out and all that filthy stuff," Morrison remembered. A friendly restaurant owner let them sterilise the bottles, which they then took back and refilled with ginger fizz using a jug and funnel. "All very primitive," Morrison admitted, but a product whose natural properties they all felt attuned to.

Morrison and Cairns made ginger fizz for about a year. The business started to grow, taking over more of the couple's time. Cairns dropped out of the course she was taking and the couple had the first of four children. All was well, if hectic and slightly chaotic, when Morrison met Harris. "He had a similar vision to us—to make a healthy alternative to the drinks out there, one with a premium edge," Morrison said. Harris tells it slightly differently. "I think they saw me as the big mouth that wouldn't shut up . . . that could be quite useful out there in the trade, selling," he said.

Harris had his work cut out for him. Ginger fizz was developing a strong following, but was a challenge to market and sell to cafés. "I was out there growing distribution, but the product was not ideal. One of the problems was that it really needed to be treated as a very volatile, fresh product, but the perception was that it was just another soft drink." He had to explain to puzzled café owners that the ginger fizz had to be handled gently and refrigerated—or it would blow up! The ginger fizz had a kick that could be downright dangerous. In hot weather it could explode and ricochet around the old van that Harris used for deliveries. Once a crate took off like a rocket and smashed against the roof of the van. Harris decided the business needed to upgrade. "I thought, there's got to be a better way, we can't keep doing this, it's going to kill me," Harris said.

From a Flat to a Firm

Phoenix began as a part-time partnership—almost a hobby for the three founders. "We had lived it quite fluid and loose and I think that was a good idea because you just don't know what is going to happen," Harris said. But moving to a professional business required the trio to make some very strategic decisions about what they wanted to achieve.

Harris believed there was one key decision that saw Phoenix grow from a little-known bathtub brew to an internationally recognised brand: pasteurisation. "That was a significant quantum leap for us, the day we learnt finally how to pasteurise," he said. With that technological leap, a whole range of new opportunities opened up, including the chance to modify its only product, its flagship ginger fizz. The three realised that there were a number of negatives with the brand—not the least of which was its tendency to explode.

"I could see at that point that we needed to re-brand and we needed to exit from ginger fizz for a number of reasons. It was a real enthusiast product and it had a lot of cult around it, but it needed to change, it needed to reflect what we now knew about the market and where we wanted to head. So we made that change," Harris said.

Morrison agreed that the technological advance of pasteurisation changed the company dramatically. "It expanded our range," he said, which meant moving into new premises and hiring more staff. Since its bathtub beginnings, the company had moved three times, most recently to a two-acre property with custom-built premises and plenty of room for expansion.

Making a Range of Drinks

The process for making drinks was pretty simple. First, ingredients were inspected and tested to ensure they were of the required standard before being blended each evening for the following day's production. Usually two drinks in the same bottle format were prepared—two organic juices, or two sparkling waters, for example. More quality assurance tests were carried out prior to bottling. Phoenix had two fillers—one for juice products and one for carbonated products, each operating at around 100 bottles per minute. Once filled, bottles were sealed with aluminium caps applied in a three-head roll-on capper, and passed through a spray tunnel pasteuriser to ensure the drinks were free of micro-organisms. Bottles were then labeled and boxed before being sent to the onsite warehouse awaiting delivery to point of sale. With a shelf-life of twelve months, drinks were produced to order and distributed within three weeks. Waste and recalls were minimal.

The product range had expanded from the early ginger fizz. First to be added was lemonade and cola in 1990, both with honey as the sweetener. Then came a range of sparkling fruit-flavoured waters, including the unusual feijoa—seldom found outside New Zealand. Later came sparkling mineral water, vegetable juice and Chai tea (see Exhibit 2.1 for a complete list of Phoenix products). In 2004, the company was considering adding a liquid chocolate that cafés could use to make hot chocolate. Phoenix produced five to six million bottles of drinks each year. Ginger beer (without the explosive fizz) was still one of its leading products, at around 7% of sales. Very close behind were orange mango, apple and feijoa juice. Organic juices were increasing in popularity, 30–50% annually. Sparkling feijoa water was also popular.

EXHIBIT 2.1 Phoenix Organic Products

Range	Products	Container	Ingredients (varies per product)	Claims
Honey-Sweetened Drinks	Lemonade Natural cola Ginger beer	330 ml resealable green glass bottle	Carbonated water, honey, juice, concentrate, natural flavour, yeast, root ginger	GE···FREE
Sparkling Fruit-Flavoured Waters	Lime Blackcurrant Melon Feijoa	330 ml resealable clear glass bottle	Carbonated water, honey, juice or juice concentrate, natural fruit flavour, vitamin C (ascorbic acid)	GE···FREE
Sparkling Mineral Water	Sparkling mineral water	330 ml resealable clear glass bottle	Carbonated mineral water	Sourced from a deep aquifier naturally filtered through 220 metres of solid rock for over 50 years. Bottled straight from New Zealand source
Vegetable Juices	Vegetable juice	250 ml & 1 l resealable clear glass bottles	Organic vegetable juices, tomato 62%, carrot 27%, celery 9.9%, spinach 0.9%, beetroot 0.5%, sea salt	Can cleanse and repair the body / CERTIFIED ORGANIC 484 / IFOAM ACCREDITED / GE···FREE
Organic Juices	Orange mango & apple juice* Pear & apple juice* Apple juice* Feijoa & apple juice* Guava & apple juice Boysenberry & apple juice	275 ml resealable clear glass bottles * Also available in 1 l resealable clear glass bottles	Organic juice/juice concentrate, organic puree, natural fruit flavour, natural fruit aroma, vitamin C (ascorbic acid)	CERTIFIED ORGANIC 484 / IFOAM ACCREDITED / GE···FREE
Organic Drinks	Organic lemonade Organic cola Organic ginger beer	330 ml resealable green glass bottles Also cluster packs of 4	Carbonated water, organic sugar, organic fruit concentrate, natural flavouring, yeast, root ginger	CERTIFIED ORGANIC 484 / IFOAM ACCREDITED / GE···FREE
Natural Herbal Drinks	Wildberry herbal, Orange Mango herbal, Guava Apple herbal	250 ml clear glass bottles	Filtered water, fruit juice concentrate, fruit puree, natural flavour, vitamin C, herbal extracts	Revitalise, energise, relax / GE···FREE
Chai	Phoenix chai (Chai latte)	Concentrate	Filtered water, spices, tea, organic sugar, natural flavours, emulsifier (lecithin), sea salt, citric acid. Contains caffeine	GE···FREE

Filling the Niche

The company's founders wanted Phoenix to be something new, something different. "We knew at the beginning that we wanted to break the monotony, the sameness and the oligopoly of the brand in those days. Seventeen years ago it was Coke and Frucor and if you wanted anything else, you were looking at the wrong country," Harris said.

Phoenix intentionally targeted the developing café culture. Coca-Cola had dominated for years. But Harris argued that while Coca-Cola made plenty of money, it also left a gap in the market. "There was a whole trade that was emerging called the café trade and it needed products that were packaged, that had the point of difference, that reflected the premium, that could command those margins, that could carry the retail value," he said. Phoenix tried to tap into that new market by developing what cafés needed and wanted.

Early on, Phoenix spotted that cafés needed to distinguish themselves in ways that would justify charging $NZ3–$NZ4 for a drink. Harris said that Coca-Cola's approach had been to go in and offer café owners the standard "big red box" (the fridge that distributors supply with their products) and the usual beverage suspects. But the Coca-Cola brand, which was so powerful in many ways, was a handicap here. "Coke was going to, just by the presence of their branding alone, to say something to the audience about what the product was. It says, 'lunchbar, lunchbar, lunchbar'. And that turns off big chunks of their audience."

According to Harris, café owners knew that they did not have many realistic choices. Phoenix, small and smart enough to be flexible and innovative, attempted to fill that niche. Its success was demonstrated by its presence in some 2,000 cafés in New Zealand, a market penetration of close to 70%.

Harris would go to cafés and say, "I know you have needs over and above what I can meet. So what I'll get you is a fridge where we'll design the product layout, and we'll put Coke in there. We'll put water in there; we'll put fresh orange juice in there. All we want is an agreement with you that gives us enough of the fridge to get the volume we need to pay for the fridge and make this a profitable business." In return, Phoenix got to occupy prime fridge real estate. "We own eye level, we own down to your navel, and they can have the rest," Harris commented.

The Ties That Bind

Ask Chris Morrison why he thinks Phoenix has been so successful and he will cite the relationships Phoenix had built up with suppliers and customers. "We've built up respect and trust with our market and those things don't happen overnight. We're not a flash in the pan, we've done the hard yards, and we've built it up with no money. I think that's why we've been successful and why we're in quite a strong position now— because we've paid our dues, and really been fairly modest about it. And made sure that we have good relationships with people, not only customers, but our suppliers, and the whole spectrum of people we deal with in the company."

Even though it had grown into a multi-million-dollar company, Phoenix still had a strong "family business" flavour to it. Morrison preferred to deal with small companies that could buy into "the Phoenix way of doing things." And, in return, he said, "We really cement the relationship, people feel like they are being looked after by us, it's very much a personal approach."

The emphasis on strong relationships extended to the company's 25 staff (See Exhibit 2.2 for Phoenix's organisation chart). The company prides itself on upskilling staff, listening to their needs and being responsive. Having staff that were relatively happy at their work meant that productivity went up and turnover went down. "That's a huge benefit to the company, and so I think it's very important to put a lot of energy in that area", Morrison said. "We are very fortunate to have great staff at Phoenix and we try very hard to look after everyone."

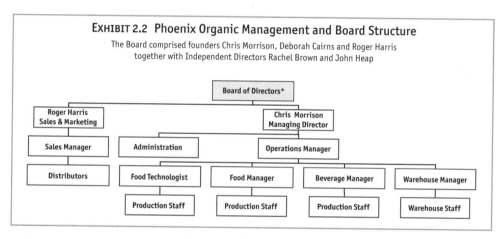

EXHIBIT 2.2 Phoenix Organic Management and Board Structure

The Board comprised founders Chris Morrison, Deborah Cairns and Roger Harris together with Independent Directors Rachel Brown and John Heap

Morrison also realised that some jobs were repetitive and of limited scope by their very nature. "It's damn hard for people to come to work every day and work on a production line and load bottles eight hours a day . . . that can be pretty tough," he said. So, social activities outside work were seen as important too. At the end of each summer (the company's busy period) staff went away for an all-expenses-paid long weekend within New Zealand. In 2003 they went to Great Barrier Island. In the winter they went skiing in Queenstown for four days, with the company paying 50% of the costs. Morrison said these events had been a great success.

Riding the Organic Wave

Harris saw Phoenix benefiting from a growing global public awareness of food safety issues such as mad cow disease. "The owners of the supermarkets in New Zealand suddenly lit up one day and said, 'hey, what are organics?'" Harris said. Suddenly, supermarket buyers were being told to start taking organics seriously. "It was just unprecedented," Harris recalled.

Phoenix decided to take advantage of the significant market shift represented by the new interest in organics. The company had been tracking world media for a long time and believed that organics was a global trend that would eventually hit New Zealand. When Morrison and Harris started to get early intelligence that suggested the wave was coming soon, they moved. "We had a strategy session about three years ago that decided we wanted to create an umbrella organic brand," Harris said. "Chris and I thought, 'We've been in organics forever, we're not going to be left on the sideline. This is our opportunity.'"

The plan was designed to work with the café trade, but also be the vehicle to help Phoenix make it big in supermarkets. The plan was to develop an organic food brand, starting with jams and salsas, complementary to its beverage products, ultimately making Phoenix a household name for all organics. It seemed like a great idea at the time. It wasn't.

Harris was upfront about what he thinks went wrong. "It's a mistake for organisations which are fast growing and relatively light in terms of size to try and pick off too many different diverse areas. It becomes a distraction. It's incredibly tempting. You're really growth-addicted."

Phoenix encountered a number of difficulties with the organic food concept. The big supermarkets did take more organic products, but they often segregated them into small organic sections instead of mainstreaming them with similar products. In Harris's words, they were 'ghetto-ised.' For Phoenix, it was the kiss of death. "I could see this problem of having too diverse an offer and not having the resources to really do the thing properly," Harris said. "We were going to run the risk of basically stretching ourselves too thin, exhausting our resources trying to keep too many different balls up in the air."

Phoenix did not abandon the supermarket channel for its beverages; however, Harris found specialists to help Phoenix tailor beverage products to that trade. In 2004, Phoenix's beverages were in all the national supermarket chains and accounted for about 20% of its business. But selling to supermarkets demanded new strategic thinking. "As we start to develop product for supermarkets, we're looking at what the need is there and we're starting to see that the single-serve beverage isn't actually the main answer. We need cluster packs, we need one-litre bottles, we need bulk," Harris said. However, Phoenix could approach both the two main supermarket chains in New Zealand and others as "the largest organic beverage company in the country."

Getting Enough

Phoenix was totally committed to organics and in the future hoped to have all of its beverages fully certified as organic by BioGro, New Zealand's leading internationally accredited organic certification body. Some products were "natural" rather than "organic" (see box insert below for a definition of organic food). Going organic raised some significant issues for the company. "Our ingredients are often up to 100% more expensive, plus we often have to carry ingredients from season to season," Morrison said. And, organics aside, Operations Manager John Evans pointed out that the natural flavours used by Phoenix could cost two to three times more than did artificial substitutes.

> ### Organic Food is . . .
>
> - Grown naturally without the routine use of synthetic agricultural chemicals such as fungicides, herbicides, insecticides, growth regulators, and soluble fertilisers
>
> - Processed with nil or minimal use of synthetic additives like stabilisers, emulsifiers, antioxidants, preservatives, colours, and flavour enhancers
>
> - Much more than spray-free or residue-free because it is produced under positive agri-ecological management systems which work in harmony with nature
>
> Source: BioGro

With the market overall, and supermarkets in particular, wanting to give only a 20% premium for organic products there was little margin. "This has meant we have had to work more efficiently and smarter than our competitors. Sourcing a range and quantity of ingredients is also difficult and requires good long-term planning and strong relationships with suppliers," Morrison said. "Strategically it's tough. But we're market leaders in this area, and it gives us an edge. And it also keeps our competitors at bay. They'll have a look at it and think the margins aren't there, it's too hard, it's too difficult. There's only a certain amount of suppliers and Phoenix already has good relationships with them."

In addition to the challenge of tight profit margins, the demand for organic ingredients far outstripped supply. "We can't just go out in the middle of the down season and say I'd like some more strawberries, because there aren't that many organic strawberry growers," Morrison noted. About 60% of the company's production was organic. Some of Phoenix's natural products were being converted to organic, but it remained a challenge merely to source enough certified organic ingredients.

Saving the World and Making Money

Phoenix was a privately held company. Morrison estimated total sales at about $NZ6.5 million in 2004, up from $NZ4 million in 2002 and $NZ5 million in 2003. Phoenix had been growing at 25–30% per annum with similar predictions for the immediate future. Morrison acknowledged that it was not easy for a business to grow at that rate without outside capital. "Cash flow is extremely tight," he said, although inventory turnover was relatively efficient at under three weeks. The land Phoenix bought in 2001 and its new buildings and planned extensions for 2004, were mainly financed through borrowing. Profits were continually ploughed back into the business.

Exports made up 10% of sales and were, Morrison predicted, the most likely source for future growth. Sales in Australia had increased from less than $NZ10,000 a month to \$NZ60–70,000 a month with the deployment of personnel into Sydney on a one-week-a-month basis. When considering further expansion into Australia, Morrison suggested that the next step might be to use a contract manufacturer. He felt that investing in plant and equipment in Australia would be too expensive given current debt levels. Morrison was reluctant to accept the compromises and loss of control that would likely come with outside capital. "We built this company. We don't necessarily want somebody else telling us to do it a different way. We're quite happy with the results we've achieved; we think we're doing it quite well."

Social and environmental sustainability was one aspect of the business that Morrison, also Chair of New Zealand's Sustainable Business Network, was unwilling to compromise on. Even in the bathtub days, the three founders always tried to make their products in an ethical manner, providing a healthy, natural premium product with the least impact on the environment. They believed that the market had caught up to their early thinking. "In the last 10 years we've seen more interest from the market in things that are important to us—safety, accountability, values, integrity and sustainability," Morrison said.

Gradually, Phoenix had evolved from an instinctive, ad hoc approach to sustainability to adopting internationally recognised sustainability protocols. In 1996, the local council's Cleaner Production Programme got Phoenix management thinking more about its water, waste and energy reduction systems. Three years later the founders were introduced to The Natural Step, a Swedish framework for sustainability that they implemented at Phoenix. The company even had a Sustainability Director, employed part-time, Rachel Brown. "My role is to ensure that everything the company does operates in a way that is environmentally and socially responsible," Brown said. From her earlier cleaner production role involving Phoenix, Brown had gone on to the Auckland Environmental Business Network which Morrison eventually chaired before it went nationwide as the Sustainable Business Network in 2002.

Creating (and Implementing) a Strategic Sustainability Plan

Meanwhile, back at Phoenix, Brown, Morrison and others spent time coming up with a long-term sustainability plan that covered five key areas. The plan considered staffing issues, reduction of fossil fuel use, avoiding persistent chemicals, protecting the environment and using resources efficiently. Sticking to this plan meant some hard choices. To offset the environmental impacts of the fossil fuels used in transportation, Phoenix ran a Greenfleet programme and encouraged Auckland distributors to use low-sulphur diesel.

The choice between glass and plastic illustrated the dilemmas associated with having a sustainability philosophy. It would have been a lot cheaper for the company to stop using glass bottles and put everything into plastic. Plus, plastic was lighter than glass was and required less fuel per shipment. But plastic was a non-renewable resource and Brown believed that plastic contamination of the beverages could potentially cause long-term health effects for people. Glass also fitted better with the company's upmarket image. "What are the social implications? What are the economic implications? So we have to go through those for all the major decisions," Brown said.

Phoenix was also constrained in how far it could unilaterally take its sustainability programme. The company would prefer glass bottles that were returnable and refillable, but the only provider of glass bottles in New Zealand—ACI—did not make refillable glass. On its own, Phoenix was not big enough to influence that market dynamic, but it was an active participant in the local organic cluster of many small enterprises.

The company's sustainability ethic also limited its product options. Bottled water would seem to have been a natural for Phoenix, but most water was sold in plastic. Brown also pointed out that there should have been no reason for people in New Zealand to be drinking bottled water. "The fact that our rivers have become polluted or that people are not feeling confident about drinking water out of the tap is really a worry," she said. Instead of joining the rush to make a profit from bottled water, the Phoenix philosophy suggested New Zealand should look seriously at how to restore people's confidence in drinking tap water.

Another critical issue for the company was genetic engineering. The company had a clear stand promoting a 'GE-free' New Zealand. "Not only is there a question over the damage to our natural ecosystems, but there seems to me a strong economic case for remaining GE-free," Morrison said.

Morrison also suggested that Phoenix was targeted more by competitors eager to tarnish its environmental good-guy image. "The whole sustainability thing is interesting because you go down that track and you start talking about what good business is about etc. from a sustainable perspective, and then you're opening yourself up to criticism. People are just desperate to knock you down." He didn't really mind the extra scrutiny, however. "I think it's really important for organic businesses to make sure that they're squeaky-clean."

Despite the challenges, Phoenix's directors clearly saw its social and environmental sustainability image as a winning combination and the company had collected a number of awards for its sustainable business practices. "The fact that they're doing all this sustainability stuff keeps this loyal customer base going. It makes it very difficult for other companies to copy because the company brand is so interlinked with the owners, and their beliefs systems, and their value base," Brown said.

Mapping the Beverage Landscape

Phoenix was pretty much out on its own in the organics beverage market, the only player of any real size. But it was selling in a market where not everyone was concerned whether their drinks were organic or not. So, the wider non-alcoholic beverage industry whose players were arguably less environmentally and socially concerned made for a very competitive landscape. Per capita consumption of soft drinks (carbonated beverages) in New Zealand was high by world standards at 360 bottles per year (although lower than the US at 450). However, the market was considered mature and had been growing at 4–5% annually.[2] Coca-Cola New Zealand had dominated soft drinks since coming to New Zealand in 1939 and in 2004 continued to sell the majority of soft drinks in New Zealand, including the top six brands. Private label soft drinks had eaten into the virtual monopoly of Coca-Cola in recent years, while Pepsi had remained a minor player in New Zealand with less than 10% market share.

Coca-Cola was also active in other non-alcoholic beverage segments beyond soft drinks. The 2002 acquisition of Rio Beverages had gained Coca-Cola access to New Zealand's second largest juice company. Key brands from the acquisition—Keri and Robinsons—accounted for 20% of Coca-Cola's New Zealand production in 2004. The largest juice company in New Zealand was Frucor—itself acquired by the French multi-national Groupe Danone in January 2002. Frucor's origins dated back to the 1961 launch of Fresh-Up under the old Apple & Pear Marketing Board. In 1988, Frucor had been spun off from the Marketing Board and in 1999 Frucor had acquired the Pepsi bottling business in New Zealand from Lion Nathan.

Both Frucor and Coca-Cola had brands in other segments such as bottled water and energy drinks. Bottled water was the fastest-growing beverage segment in New Zealand—as it was throughout the Asia-Pacific region. Energy drinks had also shown strong growth, with Frucor's V brand being number 1 in Australasia. Coca-Cola's new regional managing director, George Adams, saw real growth potential in both water and juice: "New Zealand is a very small bottled-water consumer because no one has taken the market and built it, no one has told consumers it tastes better than tap water, that it is treated and convenient. The juice business is low due to a reasonably under-developed market, which needs a big player with serious distribution money to grow it. We want to lift juice—it is a market which responds to innovation in packaging and flavours. Over the next two years we will bring more innovation to the business."[3] Frucor had a stronger reputation for innovation stemming from its introduction of V and Mizone.

EXHIBIT 2.3 Grocery Sales By Category[4]

Source: Grocers' Review, October 2003; AC Neilson

	2003 (NZ$)	2002 (NZ$)
Carbonated Beverages	199,864,802	180,314,022
New Age Beverages	27,219,073	25,789,626
Fruit Juice & Drinks	124,039,971	115,803,445
Non-Carbonated Beverages	44,123,295	44,589,664
Non-Carbonated Mineral Water	20,448,717	13,490,378

2   Kennedy, G. (2004, February 5) "Kiwi's thirsty enough?" *National Business Review*, p. 28.
3   Ibid.
4   Without being exact, a Frucor spokesperson kindly estimated that sales through non-grocery channels were generally similar in scale to grocery sales for the industry overall.

EXHIBIT 2.4 Phoenix versus the Big Dogs in New Zealand, 2003

Sources: Phoenix, Coca-Cola, Frucor, Groupe Danone, Neilson Media research

Company	Staff	Advertising ($000)	Key Brands	Corporate Global Sales (NZ$m)
Phoenix	25	40	Phoenix	6.5
Frucor	500	13,619	V, Fresh-Up, Just Juice, G Force, Mizone, Evian, Pepsi	25,265
Coca-Cola	1000	28,298	Coca-Cola, Fanta, Sprite, L&P, Pump, Keri, Powerade	33,500

Coca-Cola planned growth in soft drinks from a strategy of 'expandable consumption'—based on research that showed it didn't seem to matter how many bottles were bought, it all got drunk. "If soft drinks are in the home they will be used, so we are constantly widening our distribution to have the product within an arm's length of desire," argued George Adams. "Seventy per cent of product is bought on impulse. It's all about . . . understanding placement and making it easy for people to buy."[5]

Aside from Coca-Cola and Frucor, other competitors with Phoenix included Arano, Juice Express and Charlies in juices. The overlap with Phoenix was not that large and Phoenix had co-operated with Arano in the past, with Phoenix supplying carbonated drinks and Arano juices to specific events. The closest competitor to Phoenix in terms of products and style was probably San Pellegrino. Having already established a high-end position in Australia, San Pellegrino had made inroads into the café and restaurant market in New Zealand. Manufactured in Italy, San Pellegrino offered a collection of lightly carbonated flavoured mineral waters. Exhibit 2.5 shows the range of drinks in a typical Auckland café, along with the relative selling price of the different drink options.

The Australian non-alcoholic beverages market was similar to New Zealand in both preferences and trends. Key differences were in terms of size—where the Australian market was approximately five times as large—and in terms of a larger number of competitors.

5   Ibid.

EXHIBIT 2.5 Drinks Available at an Auckland CBD Café in March 2004 (continued opposite)

Main Refrigerator	Producer	Product Description	Selling Price $NZ	Container	Size	Claims
Top Shelf	Arano juice	Spirulina fruit cocktail	4.00	Plastic bottle	375 ml	No preservatives, no animal protein
		Berri-licious fruit smoothie with Echinacea and acerola	4.00	Plastic bottle	375 ml	Medicinal herbs
		Orange juice	3.00	Plastic bottle	250, ml	No preservatives
	Takaneti Agri (Iran)	Pomegranate juice	2.50	Tetrapak	200 cc	
	Fresh n' Fruity Yoghurt to go	Wildberry • Peach & Passionfruit • Strawberry Sensation	2.50	Plastic bottle	300ml	National Heart Foundation approved 99.5% fat-free
2nd Shelf	Phoenix organic	Guava & Apple Juice • Pear & Apple Juice • Orange Mango & Apple Juice • Feijoa & Apple Juice	3.00	Glass bottle	275 ml	Organic
3rd Shelf	Sanpellegrino (Italy)	Pompelmo—sparkling grapefruit beverage Aranciata Rossa—red sparkling orange beverage Limonata—sparkling lemon beverage	3.00	Glass bottle	200 ml	
	Valfrutta Co-operative Agricole (Italy)	Pera—Suco & Polpe (thick pear juice) Pesca gialla—Suco & Polpe (thick peach juice)	2.00	Glass bottle	125 ml	
4th Shelf	Coca-Cola Amatil (Australia)	Diet Coke Coca-Cola	2.50	Glass bottle	330 ml	
	Red Bull Gmbtt (Austria)	Red Bull Energy Drink	4.00	Aluminium can	250 ml	Vitalises body and mind
	Frucor Beverages	V Guarana Energy Drink	2.50	Aluminium can	250 ml	Invigorates, replenishes energy
5th Shelf	San Pellegrino (Italy)	Sparkling Natural Water Sparkling Natural Water	5.00 3.00	Glass bottle	500 ml	Natural, with natural CO_2
	Bundaberg (Australia)	Ginger Beer—brewed soft drink	3.50	Glass bottle	375 ml	Naturally brewed to be better
	Rutaruru Water	Pump Mini Spring Water	1.50	Plastic bottle	400 ml	
Separate Refrigerator		Primo Flavoured Milk • Chocolate, Banana & Strawberry	2.00	Plastic bottle	350 ml	Reduced fat, a big dose of calcium, and zero preservatives. Natural

(from previous page)

Other Options	$NZ
Water (Self help)	Free

Coffee

Short black	3.00
Cappucino • Long black • Flat white	3.50
Latte • Mochaccino • Hot Chocolate	4.00
Soy Milk	.50

Tea

English Breakfast • Earl Grey • Lemon and Ginger • Green Peppermint • Chamomile	3.50

Milkshakes

Kafien Krazy • Chocoholic • Strawberry Fields • Bananarama • Vanilla Ice • Sublime • Creaming Soda	4.50

Future Challenges . . .

Ironically, Phoenix's successes had started to work against it in some segments of the market. There were some very top-end cafés that would not take the Phoenix brand because it was getting more commonplace. The company was also attracting more attention from the big players in the New Zealand beverage industry, which was one of the reasons Phoenix was looking so closely at its Australian options. To continue operating only in New Zealand *and* maintain historical growth levels, Harris said Phoenix would have to find ways to take the brand bigger, which would mean selling cheaper or launching other products. Either option would likely draw fire from bigger competitors like Coca-Cola and Frucor.

The company was leery about going head to head with the really big players. "Going directly against Coke or Frucor is inherently stupid in my opinion," Harris said. He found the Phoenix niche a safer scene. "There are certain rules for survival in this game and a lot of them are around understanding your market, understanding your niche. Once you get that down, you know your niche, then you can see what your tolerance is for other decisions."

The recent growth trends augured well for Phoenix's immediate future; however, Morrison was aware of the risks. "We've still got to be realistic. We're not a huge company and we're still vulnerable. There could be something that happened that pulled us down." One risk he saw was the danger of growing too big and losing the focus on sustainability. "I believe that there are some significant issues related to sustainability for businesses that get beyond a certain point. Issues that the Stephen Tindalls of this world face every single day." Tindall was owner of New Zealand's largest discount retailer and chairman of the New Zealand Business Council for Sustainable Development, a complementary but somewhat rival organisation to the one Morrison chaired. Going out on the hustings for sustainability didn't worry Morrison. He was committed to the idea and believed there was much work to be done in convincing others to take up what he saw as a necessary but ongoing challenge, even for businesses like his own.

. . . and Opportunities

To maintain growth, Phoenix was hoping to get its products into more service stations and more distant overseas markets such as Japan and Malaysia. But the biggest growth was coming from supermarkets and Australia. "With our brand and our type of product, after the service stations, my view has been that we need more export business, we need Australia," Harris said.

In terms of new products, the Phoenix team accepted that Phoenix was going to remain a beverage company. But within that frame there was plenty of room for innovation. Hot drinks were one possibility, Harris pointed out. "The trade we work with deals in hot and cold beverage, and we want to be meaningful and useful to our trade, *and* give our salespeople a year-round opportunity." The company was already marketing "the Chai experience." Chai is a creamy, milky, spicy tea—and Harris was enthusiastic about its potential. "We're talking about students . . . we're talking about people who haven't become coffee fanatics yet. They're looking for something that maybe isn't the mainstream, that isn't like everyone else." Phoenix wanted to increase its focus on organics, but knew that could prove difficult in a number of ways.

Not surprisingly, the founders had considered the what-if scenario of a buyout by a larger corporation. Morrison was unenthusiastic, acknowledging the hard work done by Phoenix in establishing the organic beverage niche. What if organics became much more popular? Would one of the big players suddenly become very interested? Morrison did not dismiss the possibility entirely but saw a danger that public companies and shareholders would be completely focused on the financial bottom line. Plus, Morrison still maintained his enthusiasm for the job: "I don't think we're halfway through the journey and I'm very keen to see us grow. I find it very stimulating and exciting and get a huge amount of my personal needs met out of business."

So growth remained very much part of Phoenix's agenda in May 2004. The relevant questions were how would growth impinge on the business's core sustainability values? And which growth options would be most sustainable all round?

Teaching notes for this case are available from Greenleaf Publishing. These are free of charge and are available only to teaching staff. They can be requested by going to:
http://www.greenleaf-publishing.com/oikos_notes

CASE 3
Kimpton Hotels
Balancing Strategy and Environmental Sustainability[1]

Murray Silverman
San Francisco State University, USA

Tom Thomas
US EPA, San Francisco

Michael Pace faced a dilemma. He was Kimpton Hotels' West Coast Director of Operations and Environmental Programs, General Manager of its Villa Florence Hotel in San Francisco, and the main catalyst for implementing its "EarthCare" program nationally. He was determined to help the boutique hotel chain "walk the talk" regarding its commitment to environmental responsibility, but he also had agreed not to introduce any new products or processes that would be more expensive than those they replaced. Now that the first phase of the program had been implemented nationwide, he and the company's team of "eco-champions" were facing some difficult challenges with the rollout of the second, more ambitious, phase.

For example, the team had to decide whether to recommend the purchase of linens (towels, sheets, pillow cases, etc.) made of organic cotton, which vendors insisted would cost at least 50% more than standard linens. It would cost an average of $100–150k to switch out all the linens in each hotel. If they couldn't negotiate the price down, was there some way they could introduce organic cotton in a limited but meaningful way? All linens are commingled in the laundry, so they can't be introduced one floor at a time. Maybe they could start with pillowcases—though the sheets wouldn't be organic, guests would be resting their heads on organic cotton. Would it even be worth spending so much on linens? From a PR perspective, would it make that much of a difference? Should they wait and see, phase it in over time, or drop the idea altogether?

They would face similar issues when deciding whether to recommend environmentally friendly carpeting or furniture.

And then there was recycling. The program had been field tested at Kimpton hotels in San Francisco, a singular city in one of the most environmentally progressive states in the US. Now the eco-champions team had to figure out how to make it work in cities like Chicago, which didn't even have a municipal recycling program in place. In Denver, recycling actually cost more than waste disposal to a landfill, due to the low cost of land in eastern Colorado. Pace knew that the environmental initiatives most likely to succeed would be those that could be seamlessly implemented by the General Managers and employees of the 39 unique Kimpton hotels around the country. The last thing he wanted to do was to make their jobs more difficult by imposing cookie-cutter standards.

Kimpton had recently embarked on a national campaign to build brand awareness by associating its name with each unique property. Pace knew that the success of Kimpton's strategy would rest heavily on its ability to maintain the care, integrity, and uniqueness that customers had come to associate with its chain of boutique hotels. Other hotel companies had begun investing heavily in the niche that Kimpton had pioneered. To differentiate itself, the company had to continue to find innovative ways to offer services that addressed the needs and values of its customers, and EarthCare was a crucial part of its plans. But could Pace find a way to make it happen within Kimpton's budget, and without adversely affecting the customer experience? Would Kimpton be able to keep the promises made by its new corporate brand?

The US Hotel Industry

By the summer of 2005, the absence of any major terror attacks since September 11, 2001 had encouraged Americans to begin traveling again. Buoyed by a rebound in business travel and continued growth in leisure related spending, the lodging industry had shown steady growth since mid-2003. In 2004, the industry posted impressive gains in room occupancy levels, REVPAR (revenue per available room) and average room rates (see Exhibit 3.1). In the previous year, demand had been dampened by the outbreak of the war with Iraq and the soft US economy. Industry pre-tax profit increased

EXHIBIT 3.1 Hotel and Lodging Industry Trends

Source: Smith Travel Research

Year	2000	2001	2002	2003	2004
Room Rates	$85.43	$85.35	$83.48	$83.41	$86.70
Revenue per Available Room	$55.78	$52.83	$50.84	$50.71	$54.70
Occupancy	65.3%	61.9%	60.9%	60.8%	63.1%
Income (pre-tax)	$22.5m	$16.2	$14.2	$12.8	$14.5

in 2004 to $14.5B over $12.8B in 2003, but was still far below the recent peak of $22.5B in 2000.

The US hotel industry was comprised of 55,000 properties and 4.5 million rooms. Its 2004, $112B revenues included room sales (75%), food and beverages (18%) and miscellaneous such as phone charges, movies, etc. (7%). Revenues in 2003 were $105B. There were many large hotel chains (see Exhibit 3.2), however, no single lodging company accounted for more than 15% of all US hotel rooms. Hotels can be segmented into luxury (Four Seasons, Fairmont, Carlton), upscale (Embassy, Sheraton, Radisson, Courtyard), mid-market (Holiday Inn, Ramada, Comfort Inn) and economy (Motel 6, Days Inn, Red Roof). Within the upscale segment there are two strategic niches: boutique hotels in urban areas which differentiated themselves through unique décor, amenities and service and bed & breakfasts (B&Bs) which were typically small, independent properties featuring unique settings and décor.

Exhibit 3.2 Large Hotel Companies

(Based on number of affiliated rooms worldwide)

Source: Standard & Poors Industry Surveys, Lodging & Gaming, McGraw-Hill, December 2004

Company	Major Chains	No. of Properties	No. of Rooms
Cendant Corp.	Days Inn, Ramada (US), Super 8, Howard Johnson, Travel Lodge	6,399	518,435
InterContinental Hotels Group	Holiday Inn, InterContinental	3,500	538,000
Marriott International	Marriott, Courtyard Residence Inn, Fairfield Inn,Renaissance, Ramada (outside US)	2,753	496,920
Arcor SA	Motel 6, Mercure, Ibis, Novotel, Red Roof Inns, Hotel Sofitel, Formule 1	3,950	455,000
Choice Hotels International	Comfort Inn, Quality Inn, Econo Lodge	4,678	375,859
Hilton Hotels	Hilton (US), Hampton Inns, Doubletree, Embassy Suites, Homewood Suites	2,157	345,141
Best Western Int'l	Best Western	4,105	312,329
Starwood Hotels & Resorts	Sheraton, Westin	736	227,815
Carlson Hospitality Group	Radisson, Country Inns & Suites by Carlson, Regent International Hotels	885	147,000
Hyatt Corp.	Hyatt Regency	121	59,000
TOTAL		29,494	3,498,423

Kimpton Hotels built a portfolio of unique properties in the upscale segment of the industry, and they are credited with inventing the "boutique" hotel segment in 1981.[2] By 1999, boutique hotels accounted for about 15% of San Francisco's estimated 31,000 rooms, according to PKF Consulting. Boutique hotels constituted about 1% of the industry nationwide and the segment was growing. The Starwood Hotel chain entered the segment with its 'W' hotels and Continental Hotels PLC with Hotel Indigo. In San Francisco, Kimpton was the recognized market leader with 67% of the city's boutique hotels. Joie de Vivre Hotels had 20% of the local market, and Personality Hotels on Union Square had 12%. With 2004 sales of $400 million, up from $350 million in 2003, Kimpton planned to add at least three to five properties per year in major markets such as New York, Boston, Washington, DC and Miami.

Approximately 55% of hotel customers were individuals attending a business meeting, conference or group meeting. Foreign travelers contributed significantly to room demand, especially in major cities. Competition for these customers was based on many factors including price, location, brand loyalty, customer service and value-added services. It appeared that the industry's earning recovery had been limited by consumer price-shopping on the Internet, and by cost pressures driven by rising healthcare costs, energy costs and property taxes. Companies were intensifying efforts to win customer loyalty. Efforts included reward programs for frequent visitors and targeting a hotel's best customers for direct marketing programs.

The longer-term outlook for the industry seemed very positive. US demographic trends were highly favorable. Baby boomers, then in their peak earning years, would be seeking elaborate or expensive vacations. In addition, more and more Americans would be retiring and traveling in their leisure time.

The Greening of the US Hotel Industry

The US hotel industry with its 4.5 million rooms, common areas and lobbies, conventions, restaurants, laundry facilities and back offices have a significant environmental impact. According to the American Hotel and Lodging Association, the average hotel toilet is flushed 7 times per day per guest, an average shower is 7.5 minutes long, and 40% of bathroom lights are left on as nightlights. A typical hotel uses 218 gallons of water per day per occupied room. Energy use is pervasive, including lighting in guest rooms and common areas, heating and air-conditioning and washing and drying towels and linens. The hotel industry spends $3.7 billion per year on electricity.[3]

Guestrooms generate surprisingly large amounts of waste, ranging from one-half pound to 28 pounds per day, and averaging 2 pounds per day per guest. In California, 2% of all food waste comes from the hotel and lodging industry. A shortlist of other environmental impacts of the hotel industry includes: non-refillable amenity bottles (shampoos, etc.) generate large amounts of plastic waste; products used to clean bathrooms and furniture contain synthetic additives; paints contain high levels of volatile

2   Sloan, Gene, "Let the Pillowfights Begin", *USA Today*, 8/27/2004.
3   California Green Lodging Program, http://www. Ciwmb.ca.gov/epp.

organic compounds; back-office and front-desk activities generate large amounts of waste paper; and furniture, office equipment, kitchen and laundry appliances are usually not selected for their environmental advantages.

Opportunities for reducing a hotel's environmental footprint are plentiful, and many can yield bottom-line savings. Reduced laundering of linens, at customer discretion, has already been adopted enthusiastically across the spectrum of budget to luxury hotels, to the point that 38% of hotels currently have linen reuse programs. Low-flow shower heads can deliver the same quality shower experience using half the water of a conventional shower head. Faucet aerators also can cut the water requirements by 50%. A 13 watt compact fluorescent bulb gives the same light as a 60 watt incandescent, lasts about 10 times longer and uses about 70% less energy. Waste costs also can be significantly reduced. For many hotels, 50–80% of their solid waste stream is compostable, and a significant part of the remaining waste is recyclables, such as paper, aluminum and glass.

Fairmont Hotels & Resorts, a Canadian-based hotel chain, generated considerable savings since implementing its environmental programs in the early 1990s. While concern for the environment drove Fairmont's program, many of its initiatives resulted in bottom-line benefits. Examples of the types of environmental initiatives and their associated savings at the Fairmont Hotels & Resorts are listed in Exhibit 3.3. Fairmont Hotels also pursued initiatives and made investments that did not produce readily apparent bottom-line benefits. For example, one of their hotels purchased 20% of their energy as renewable energy (solar, wind and hydro) even though the cost was higher. They supported the expense of a Corporate Office of Environmental Affairs and a Manager of Environmental Affairs. They also financially supported efforts related to habitat restoration and preservation of endangered species.[4]

In addition to bottom-line savings, environmental programs held the potential to generate new business. Governmental bodies and NGOs, corporations and convention/meeting planners were showing increased interest in selecting hotels using environmental criteria. California had recently launched its Green Lodging Program. State employees were encouraged to select from the GLP's list of certified hotels. The state's $70 million annual travel budget was an incentive for hotels to be certified by the program. The criteria for certification include recycling, composting, energy- and water-efficient fixtures and lighting, and non-toxic or less toxic alternatives for cleaning supplies. State governments in Pennsylvania, Florida, Vermont, and Virginia also had developed green lodging programs.

CERES, a well-respected environmental non-profit, had developed the Green Hotel Initiative, designed to increase and demonstrate demand for environmentally responsible hotel services. Some major corporations endorsed the initiative, including Ford Motor Company, General Motors, Nike, American Airlines, and Coca-Cola. CERC, the Coalition for Environmentally Responsible Conventions, and the Green Meetings Industry Council were encouraging meeting planners to "green" their events by, among other things, choosing environmentally friendly hotels for lodging and meeting sites. This trend toward booking lodging and meeting sites based on green criteria was in its very early stages. Industry insiders believed that environmentally driven demand was

---

4   Fairmont Hotels & Resorts, *The Green Partnership Guide*, 2nd ed., 2001.

EXHIBIT 3.3 Fairmont Hotels & Resorts: Sampling of Environmental Cost-Saving Initiatives

- The Fairmont Royal York Hotel in Toronto recycles over 212,000 pounds of cardboard and paper annually, saving 2,025 trees and $79,000 in landfill fees.
- Prior to establishing a recycling program for kitchen grease, the Fairmont Winnipeg spent over $1 million to have its sewer system cleared of kitchen grease build-up. Kitchen grease is now picked up and recycled free of charge.
- The breakfast buffet at Fairmont Tremblant eliminated individual servings of jams in 22 ml glass jars. Instead, the kitchen prepares seven varieties of homemade jams and serves them in large attractive jars with serving spoons. With over 49,500 breakfasts served a year, the restaurant saved over $19,000 per year.
- The Fairmont Royal York has over 34,000 light fixtures. The hotel switched 1,920 bulbs in the guest bathrooms and 5,500 bulbs in the guestrooms from incandescent to compact fluorescent bulbs, saving $57,135 annually. In public areas and staircases, over 773 bulbs have been switched with additional savings of $23,095 per year.
- The staff at the Fairmont Hotel Vancouver separates organic waste (from room service, meetings, and conference meals) from its regular waste stream. The organic waste is picked up from the hotel (free of charge) and used to make a rich organic fertilizer. This produced a 50% reduction in landfill wastes and an annuals savings of $11,000.

Source: Fairmont Hotels & Resorts, *The Green Partnership Guide*, 2nd ed., 2001.

extremely limited at this point and the ultimate impact of this movement was uncertain.

Environmental progress in the US hotel industry has been very limited. With a few exceptions, most hotels were doing very little beyond pursuing the low-hanging fruit, in the form of easy-to-implement cost-saving initiatives. Those hotels have been reducing their environmental footprint as a welcome consequence of their cost-cutting efforts, but they were not necessarily committed to a comprehensive environmental program. During a 1998 effort by Cornell University's School of Hotel Administration to identify hotels employing environmental best practices, researchers were "surprised by the dearth of nominations." The four US hotels selected as champions—The Colony Hotel, Hotel Bel Air, Hyatt Regency Chicago, and Hyatt Regency Scottsdale—were primarily focused on cost savings in energy and waste streams.[5] In contrast to the US, hotels in Canada and Europe seemed to be embracing the hotel greening process, as exemplified by the Fairmont Hotel & Resorts effort to institutionalize innovative approaches to reducing their environmental footprint throughout their operations.

5   Enz, Cathy A. and Siguaw, Judy A., "Best Hotel Environmental Practices", *Cornell Hotel and Restaurant Administration Quarterly*, October 1999.

Kimpton's Business Philosophy and Strategy

Kimpton Hotels was founded in 1981 by the late Bill Kimpton, who once said, "No matter how much money people have to spend on big, fancy hotels, they're still intimidated and unsettled when they arrive. So the psychology of how you build hotels and restaurants is very important. You put a fireplace in the lobby and create a warm, friendly restaurant, and the guest will feel at home." By 2005, Kimpton had grown to include 39 hotels throughout North America and Canada, each one designed to create a unique and exceptional guest experience (see Exhibit 3.4). Every hotel lobby had a cozy fireplace and plush sitting area, where complimentary coffee was served every morning, and wine every evening. Guest rooms were stylishly decorated and comfortably furnished, offering amenities such as specialty suites that included Tall Rooms and Yoga Rooms. Every room offered high-speed wireless Internet access, and desks with ample lighting. Rather than rewarding customer loyalty with a point program, Kimpton offered customization and personalization. "We record the preferences of our loyal guests," said Mike Depatie, Kimpton's CEO of real estate, "Someone may want a jogging magazine and a Diet Coke when they arrive. We can get that done."

Business travel (group and individual) accounted for approximately 65% of Kimpton's revenues, and leisure travel (tour group and individual) the other 35%. The selection of hotels for business meetings and conferences was through meeting and conference organizers. Around 35% of all rooms were booked through their call center, 25% through travel agents, 25% through their web site, and the remainder "came in off the street." The Internet portion of their business continued to grow, but they didn't cater to buyers looking for the "steal of the century." Rather, they were increasingly being discovered by the 25% of the customer pool that market researchers called "unchained seekers," many of whom used the Internet to search for unique accommodations that matched their particular needs or values.

Steve Pinetti, Senior Vice President for Sales and Marketing noted, "If I were to drive a customer to the airport after their stay and ask them what their experience was like, the right answer would be, "It felt great." They don't have to know why; it could be the bed, the room, the wine, or the friendly employees. The next time they want to book a room, though, they'll come to us." Kimpton's REVPAR tends to meet or exceed norms within its upscale segment, due primarily to its relatively high occupancy rates. Occupancy rates rose to 68% in the fourth quarter of 2004, up from 63% during the same quarter in 2003. REVPAR during the same period rose from $87 to $102.[6]

Historically, Kimpton prospered by purchasing and renovating buildings at a discount in strategic nationwide locations that were appropriate for their niche segment. The hotel industry in general had been slow to enter the boutique niche, and Kimpton enjoyed a substantial edge in experience in developing value-added services for guests. "All hotels are starting to look alike and act alike, and we are the counterpoint, the contrarians," according to Tom LaTour, Kimpton president and CEO. "We don't look like the brands, we don't act like the brands, and as the baby boomers move through the age wave, they will seek differentiated, experience-oriented products."

Kimpton's top executives took pride in their ability to recognize and develop both undervalued properties and undervalued people. Kimpton's hotel general managers

6   Parets, Robyn, National Real Estate Investor, http://www.nreionline.com, March 2005.

Exhibit 3.4 List of Kimpton Hotels

City, State	Style/Theme	Room	Year
Aspen, Colorado			
Sky Hotel	Play & Action	90	2001
Boston, Massachusetts			
Onyx Hotel	Emerging Art	112	2004
Cambridge, Massachusetts			
Hotel Marlowe	Discovery	236	2003
Chicago, Illinois			
Hotel Allegro Chicago	Be a Star	483	1998
Hotel Monaco Chicago	Indulge Your Senses via Body, Mind & Soul	192	1998
Burnham Hotel	Architecture	122	1999
Cupertino, California			
Cypress Hotel	Good Life: Body, Mind & Soul	224	2002
Denver, Colorado			
Hotel Monaco Denver	Adventure	189	1998
Miami			
Mayfair Hotel & Spa	Tranquility and Sensuality	179	2005
New Orleans, Louisiana			
Hotel Monaco New Orleans	Indulge Your Senses via Exotic Pleasures	250	2001
New York, New York			
70 Park Avenue Hotel	Private Residence	205	2004
Portland, Oregon			
Hotel Vintage Plaza	Italian Romance	107	1992
Fifth Avenue Suites Hotel	Patron of the Arts	221	1996
Salt Lake City			
Hotel Monaco Salt Lake City	Indulge Your Senses via Guilty Pleasures	225	1999
San Diego, California			
Solamar	Art Lies Within	235	2005

(continued over)

(from previous page)

City, State	Style/Theme	Room	Year
San Francisco, California			
● Villa Florence Hotel	Celebration of Italy	183	1986
● Monticello Inn	Literary	91	1987
● Prescott Hotel	Private Residence	164	1989
● Tuscan Inn	Family	221	1990
● Harbor Court Hotel	Energy & Well-being	131	1991
● Hotel Triton	Art, Music and Eco	140	1991
● Sir Francis Drake Hotel	Classic San Francisco	417	1994
● Hotel Monaco San Francisco	Sophisticated World Travel	201	1995
● Serrano Hotel	Fun & Games	236	1999
● Palomar Hotel	Art in Motion	198	1999
● Argonaut Hotel	Adventure	252	2003
Seattle, Washington			
● Alexis Hotel	Art of Living	109	1992
● Hotel Vintage Park	Washington Wine	126	1992
● Hotel Monaco Seattle	Animals	189	1997
Tacoma, Washington			
● Sheraton Tacoma Hotel	Business, conference center	319	1984
Vancouver, BC			
● Pacific Palisades	Fun, Fresh and in the Now	233	2000
Washington, DC			
● Hotel Rouge	Playful Interactions	137	2001
● Topaz Hotel	Wellness	99	2001
● Hotel Monaco DC	Indulge Your Senses	184	2002
● Hotel Madera	Home Away From Home	86	2002
● Hotel Helix	Your 15 minutes	178	2002
● Hotel George	George Washington w/contemporary flair	139	2003
Whistler, BC			
● Summit Lodge	Romance, premier ski resort	81	2000

were often refugees from large branded companies who did not thrive under hierarchical, standardized corporate structures. At Kimpton, they were afforded a great deal of autonomy, subject only to the constraints of customer service standards and capital and operating budgets.

This sense of autonomy and personal responsibility was conveyed down through the ranks to all 5,000 Kimpton employees. Kimpton's flexible corporate structure avoided hierarchy, preferring a circular structure where executives and employees were in constant communication.[7] Steve Pinetti liked to tell the story of a new parking attendant who had to figure out how to deal with a guest who felt that he had not been adequately informed of extra charges for parking his car at the hotel. The attendant decided on the spot to reduce the charges, and asked the front desk to make the necessary adjustments. He had heard his general manager tell everyone that they should feel empowered to take responsibility for making guests happy, but he fully expected to be grilled by his GM, at the very least, about his actions. A sense of dread took hold as he was called to the front of the room at a staff meeting the very next day, but it dissipated quickly when his general manager handed him a special award for his initiative.

Establishing the Kimpton Brand

While Kimpton was known for designing hotels that reflected the energy and personality of their distinct locations, by 2004 the company's top executives realized that uniting its hotel portfolio under a single recognizable brand could add considerable value. Cross-selling of hotel rooms in different cities, for instance, would be easier for salespeople handling corporate accounts if the properties all shared the Kimpton name. So the company launched what it called the first Lifestyle Hotel Collection, with the theme "Every Hotel Tells a Story." One aspect of the branding effort was to add the Kimpton name to each property, as in "Hotel Monaco San Francisco, a Kimpton Hotel." According to CEO LaTour, "We think of our hotels as a family, all having their own first names and sharing the last name Kimpton. We are ready to tell the world the Kimpton story."[8]

The distinctive value proposition associated with the Kimpton brand guaranteed the customer a unique and satisfying experience along five different dimensions, what the company referred to as Care, Comfort, Style, Flavor, and Fun.

- **Care.** Just as Kimpton treated its guests with a strong dose of friendly personal attention and TLC, its culture also emphasized concern and responsibility for the communities in which it did business, and the people it employed. Each hotel's GM and staff expressed this sense of care by engaging in their own forms of community outreach, employee diversity, and environmental quality initiatives.

---

7   French, Liz, americanexecutive.com, December 2004.
8   Kimpton Hotels press release, "Boutique Meets Lifestyle as Kimpton Hotels Let the Secret Out with Launch of National Brand Campaign."

- **Comfort.** Kimpton focused intently on making its guests feel comfortable, their plush rooms and intimate public spaces providing a home away from home. They kept overhead costs in check by limiting the range of services they provided, forgoing the gyms, spas, swimming pools, and other space-hungry amenities that larger chains regularly offered.

- **Style.** No two Kimpton hotels were alike. Each attempted to draw upon the distinctive character of the city and neighborhood in which it was located. Interiors tended to be upscale and stylish rather than opulent or ornate.

- **Flavor.** The restaurants located in each hotel were designed to stand on their own, catering to local clientele rather than rely on hotel guests for the bulk of their business.

- **Fun.** Employees were encouraged to bring their personalities to work, and to make sure that guests enjoyed their stay. According to Mike Depatie, "We don't try to make people Kimpton people. We want them to express the best of what they are."

An important part of Kimpton's story was its longstanding commitment to social responsibility. Staff at each hotel had always been encouraged to engage with local community non-profits that benefited the arts, education, the underprivileged and other charitable causes. Kimpton maintained these local programs even in periods of falling occupancy rates and industry downturns. These local efforts evolved into the company-wide "Kimpton Cares" program in 2004, as part of the company's corporate branding effort, expanding their social and environmental commitments to the national and global arenas. At the national level, Kimpton supported the National AIDS Fund (in support of its Red Ribbon Campaign) and Dress for Success (which assisted economically disadvantaged women struggling to enter the workforce) by allotting a share of a guest's room fee to the charity. At the global level, Kimpton embarked in a partnership with Trust for Public Land (TPL), a non-profit dedicated to the preservation of land for public use. In July 2005, Kimpton committed to raising $15,000 from its total room revenues to introduce the TPL Parks for People program, and created eco-related fund raising events in each of its cities to further support the campaign. Kimpton's EarthCare program was designed to be instituted through a comprehensive environmental program rolled out to all of Kimpton's hotels. "As business leaders, we believe we have a responsibility to positively impact the communities we live in, to be conscious about our environment and to make a difference where we can," says Niki Leondakis, Kimpton's Chief Operating Officer.

Kimpton's top executives consider the "Kimpton Cares" program, and its Earthcare component, essential parts of the company's branding effort. Steve Pinetti noted, "What drove it was our belief that our brand needs to stand for something. What do we want to stand for in the community? We want to draw a line in the sand. We also want our impact to be felt as far and wide as it can. Hopefully, through our good deeds, we'll be able to influence other companies."

The early evidence suggested that the branding effort also had financial payoffs. Kimpton was receiving significant PR coverage of its Earthcare program in local newspapers and travel publications. According to Pinetti, "The number of people who visit our Kimpton web site has tripled in the year since we began the branding effort. Membership in the company's 'InTouch' guest loyalty program, which markets to previous guests via email, rose from 86,000 in the 1st quarter of 2004 to 112,000 in the 4th quarter.[9] Consumer surveys showed big gains in awareness that each hotel is part of a bigger organization, with properties in other cities." As for the firm's "Kimpton Cares" program and its new EarthCare initiative, anecdotal evidence pointed to top-line benefits. "We've booked almost half a million dollars in meetings from a couple of corporations in Chicago because of our ecological reputation," said Pinetti. "Their reps basically told us, 'Your values align with our values, and we want to spend money on hotels that think the way we do.'" Kimpton believed that companies that identified with being socially responsible would look for partners like Kimpton that shared those values; and that certifications like the California Green Lodging program would attract both individuals and corporate clientele.

However, Pinetti noted, "The cost-effectiveness wasn't clear when we started. I thought we might get some business out of this, but that's not why we did it. We think it's the right thing to do, and it generates a lot of enthusiasm among our employees." Kimpton's Real Estate CEO Mike Depatie believed that incorporating care for communities and the environment into the company's brand has been a boon to hiring. "We attract and keep employees because they feel that from a values standpoint, we have a corporate culture and value system that's consistent with theirs. They feel passionate about working here." While the hotel industry was plagued with high turnover, Kimpton's turnover rates were lower than the national averages.

The Hotel Triton

Kimpton's environmental consciousness reaches back to 1985 when they introduced the Galleria Park Hotel in San Francisco as an urban retreat with an open space "park" within the hotel. In 1995, Kimpton's commitment picked up steam as they converted an entire floor of the 140-room Triton hotel in San Francisco into an 'eco-floor'. With assistance from Green Suites International, a supplier of environmental solutions for the lodging industry, the Triton introduced the following initiatives in the 24 rooms on its eco-floor:

- Energy-efficient lighting solutions including compact fluorescent bulbs and sensor nightlights (cutting energy costs by 75%).

- Bathroom amenity dispensers using biodegradable hypoallergenic soaps, lotions, and shampoos.

- Programmable digital thermostats to control guestroom energy consumption.

- Low-flow/high-pressure showerheads and sink aerators, and toilets that reduce water use.

- Linen and towel reuse program.

9   Tate, Ryan, "Kimpton Hotels Remakes its Beds", *San Francisco Business Times*, January 28, 2005.

- Non-toxic, non-allergenic, all natural cleaning products.

- Facial and bathroom tissues made from 100% recycled materials with at least 30% post-consumer waste paper.

- Recycling receptacles.

- Bedding and bath towels made from organically grown cotton (1.5 pounds of agricultural chemicals are used on average to produce the conventionally grown cotton in a single set of queen-size sheets).

- Water filters to improve water quality and air filters to improve air quality.

- Low-VOC paints used to paint walls and ceilings.

For Michael Pace, the sustainability light bulb came on when he was general manager of the Monticello Hotel, prior to taking over as GM of the Triton. At first, his interest was piqued by recycling efforts at the Monticello. But one day, he says, "I had a personal epiphany, where I realized how lucky I am. I'm living the American Dream, and I pass by a dozen homeless people on my way to work every day. I just realized that I wanted to do more than focus on myself and my job. The more I got involved, the more I saw the positive impact these efforts could have."

When Pace became GM of the Triton in 2003, he felt that the eco-floor concept should be expanded throughout the Triton hotel's rooms and common areas. He immediately began to institute most of the eco-floor initiatives in the hotel's other guestrooms. He worked closely with the hotel staff to sort the hotel's entire waste stream, and was able to reduce waste hauling expenses from $2,200 to $600 per month.

As a result of Pace's conversion efforts, in 1994, the Triton was recognized as one of four properties in Northern California to qualify at the Leadership Level for the State's new Green Lodging program. More importantly, the Triton was ready to serve as the template for the EarthCare program and the rest of Kimpton's hotels.

Planning the EarthCare Program Rollout Campaign

Pinetti and Pace realized that they were too busy to handle all the planning and operational details of the national rollout, so they turned to Jeff Slye, of Business Evolution Consulting, for help. Slye was a process management consultant who wanted to help small and medium-sized business owners figure out how to "ecofy" their companies. He knew that entrepreneurs were typically far too busy to do much about the resources they don't like to overuse, and the waste they don't like to generate. He had heard that Kimpton was trying to figure out how to make its operations greener and integrate this effort into their branding effort. When they first met in October 2004, Pinetti and Pace handed him a 10-page document detailing their objectives and a plan for rolling out the initiative in phases. Kimpton's program was to have the following eco-mission statement:

Lead the hospitality industry in supporting a sustainable world by continuing to deliver a premium guest experience through non-intrusive, high quality, eco-friendly products and services.

Our mission is built upon a company wide commitment towards water conservation; reduction of energy usage; elimination of harmful toxins and pollutants; recycling of all reusable waste; building and furnishing hotels with sustainable materials; and purchasing goods and services that directly support these principles.

Slye worked with Pinetti and Pace to fill various gaps in their plan and develop an "ecostandards program," a concise report outlining a strategy for greening the products and operational processes that Kimpton used to deliver a superior experience to its guests. In December 2004, Pinetti asked Slye to present the report to Kimpton's COO, Niki Leondakis. Leondakis greeted the proposal enthusiastically, but noted that it needed an additional component: A strategy for communicating the program both internally (to management and staff) and externally (to guests, investors, and the press). As important as these external audiences were, Slye knew that the internal communications strategy would be particularly crucial, given the autonomy afforded each Kimpton hotel, each with its own set of local initiatives. Getting everyone on board would require a strategy that respected that aspect of Kimpton's culture. Slye kept that in mind as he worked with Pace to draft a communications strategy.

They decided to create an ad hoc "eco-champions" network throughout the company. The national "lead" (Pace) and "co-lead" (Pinetti) would head up the communications effort, and would be accountable for its success. Each of five geographic regions (Pacific Northwest, San Francisco Bay Area, Central US, Washington DC, and Northeast/Southeast), covering six or seven hotel properties, would also have a lead and co-lead who would help communicate the program to employees, and be the local point-person in the chain of command. One of their key roles would be to solicit employee suggestions regarding ways to make products and processes greener.

In addition, a team of national eco-product specialists (EPS) would be key components of the network. These specialists would be responsible for soliciting staff input, and identifying and evaluating greener products as potential substitutes for existing ones. Products would be tested for effectiveness and evaluated on the basis of their environmental benefits, effect on guest perceptions, potential marketing value, and cost. Pinetti and Pace determined that specialists would be needed initially for six product categories: beverages, cleaning agents, office supplies, engineering, information technology, and room supplies.

Pinetti and Pace knew that the various regional leads and national product specialists would have to be selected carefully. The program's success would depend largely on the enthusiasm and capability that team members would bring to the task. They faced a dilemma: ask for volunteers, or handpick preferred candidates? They decided to identify likely candidates and invite them to participate, an approach made possible by Kimpton's tractable size and intimate culture. As they anticipated, everyone they approached responded enthusiastically and volunteered on the spot.

Meanwhile, Pace and Pinetti asked all general managers to report on their existing environmental initiatives, to get baseline feedback on what individual hotels were doing already. They turned the results into a matrix they could use to identify gaps and monitor progress for each hotel.

They also sent out to all Kimpton Directors of Operations (regional managers) a briefing that laid out the communications strategy, including the mission statement, a description of the new eco-champions network, an overview of the phased rollout of products and processes (See Exhibit 2.5), and a "talking points" document that explained to employees the benefits of the new program (See Exhibit 2.6).

National Rollout of the EarthCare program

By February 2005, the new network of eco-champions was in place, and everyone had agreed on the two basic ground rules for the transition: new initiatives couldn't cost more than what was already budgeted for operations and capital improvements, and they couldn't adversely affect customer perceptions or satisfaction. This ground rule mandated that any new product or service could not cost more than the product or service it replaced. All leads, co-leads, and product specialists began meeting via conference call every Friday morning to discuss the greening initiative, and share accounts of employee suggestions, progress achieved and barriers encountered. One revelation that emerged early in the process was that, due to the uniqueness of each hotel and autonomous nature of the organization, all plans and proposals would have to be presented in a clear, concise package in order to ensure effective implementation.

To help communicate the program's goals and achievements, and help motivate employees seeking recognition, the team began to post regular updates and success stories in Kimpton's internal weekly newsletter, *The Word*, which was distributed throughout the organization and read by all GMs. They also ran an EarthCare contest to further galvanize interest, which generated over 70 entries for categories such as "Best Eco-Practice Suggestion," "Most EarthCare Best Practices Adopted," and "Best Art and Humor Depicting EarthCare."

Potential benefits of the program became clear when the team of eco-product specialists began researching the availability of non-toxic cleaning agents. Common cleaning products such as furniture polish, carpet cleaner, spot remover, air fresheners, disinfectants, and bleach can contain hazardous compounds such as toluene, naphthalene, trichloroethylene, benzene and nitrobenzene, phenol, chlorine, and xylene. These and other hazardous ingredients found in many cleaning products are associated with human health concerns including cancer, reproductive disorders, respiratory ailments, and eye or skin irritation. An EPA-funded study by the Western Regional Pollution Prevention Network found that 41% of all standard cleaning products they tested were potentially hazardous to the health of individuals using them. Cleaning chemicals may also include ozone-depleting substances, and toxic materials that can accumulate in the environment and harm plant and animal life. The health and environmental consequences for Kimpton were substantial, as one of its suppliers (Sierra Environmental) estimated that every housekeeping worker handles 60 pounds of cleaning agents per year. With an average of 15 room cleaners, times 39 hotels, it adds up.

The eco-specialists learned that one of Kimpton's incumbent vendors did have a Green Seal-certified non-toxic line, but the products were selling at a 10–15% premium over standard products. They discovered that virtually every product they were inter-

Exhibit 3.5 Rollout of Kimpton's EarthCare Program

Phase I

Phase I initiatives are designed to make hotel staff comfortable with the concept of greener management by introducing non-disruptive and cost-reducing operational practices.

- Recycling program ("Back-of-house"). Bottles, cans, paper, cardboard.
- Cleaning chemicals. Tub & tile cleaners, glass cleaners, deodorizers, and disinfectants all have to be switched to non-toxic, natural products.
- Promotional materials printed on recycled paper, using soy-based inks.
- Complimentary coffee served in lobbies every morning must be organically grown.
- Towel/linen reuse. Sheets and towels are replaced only at guest's request.

Phase II

Hotels that successfully complete their implementation of Phase I initiatives will then move to Phase II, which focuses on investments in water and energy conservation, organically grown cottons, and extending Phase I initiatives.

- Water conservation. Install 2.0 GPM sink aerators, 2.5 GPM showerheads, and phase in 1.6 GPF toilets.
- Energy conservation. Install motion sensors in rooms, fluorescent bulbs in corridors and back-of-house.
- Use recycled content paper for copying and notepads back-of-house, toilet paper and tissues in-room.
- Serve organic coffee in rooms and meeting rooms, organic tea in lobby.
- Switch to organic linens and towels, if feasible.

Phase III

The most fundamental changes are anticipated when hotels are renovated and new hotels are acquired and converted. In addition to implementing Phases I and II, this will require extensive investment in building materials, labor, and appliances. The good news is that rooms can be designed, rather than retrofitted, to be more energy-efficient, and green building materials can be ordered in larger quantities, thus lowering costs.

- Install only Energy Star-rated appliances, computers, and electronic.
- Use only low-VOC paints.
- Install energy-efficient lighting, heating, and air-conditioning.

EXHIBIT 3.6 Internal Talking Points Document

QUICK FACTS ON THE DIFFERENCE YOU WILL MAKE . . .

Printing on 35% post consumer recycled paper: Kimpton will save:

- 24,000 pounds (12 Tons) of wood
- 3,720 pounds (1.75 Tons) of solid waste
- 7,260 pounds (3.6 Tons) of CO_2 emissions
- 58,230,000 BTUs of total energy

** Assumes 30 Hotels participate using 1 case/5,000 sheets per month

Using Green/Eco friendly cleaning products: Kimpton will:

- Improve worker productivity by between 0.5 percent and 5 percent by reducing cleaning supply toxins (US institutions spend more than $75 million a year on medical expenses and lost time wages due to chemical-related injuries).
- Reduce environmental pollution as traditional cleaning products are responsible for approximately 8% of total non-vehicular emissions of volatile organic compounds (VOCs).

Recycling waste: Recycling 50% of hotel waste Kimpton properties will:

- Save over $250,000 per year in waste disposal costs.
- Reduce unnecessary landfill waste by over 100,000 gallons per year.

** Assumes 30 Hotel participate

Recycling glass: Recycling 100 glass bottles/month, Kimpton will:

- Save the equivalent of powering one hundred 100-watt light bulbs for 1,440 hours (60 days).

Recycling aluminum: Recycling 20 Aluminum cans/day, Kimpton will:

- Save the equivalent of nearly 1,500 gallons of gas—enough to run a car for nearly three years.

ested in was more expensive than those currently used. At the extreme, eco-friendly paper products were priced 50% above standard products.

They knew that this would not satisfy the imperative that the greening initiative should not increase operating costs. Determined, they just kept going back to the vendors and asking them to keep working on it until they could supply a greener product of the same quality at the same, or lower, price. Eventually, existing or new vendors were able to meet these criteria, and now the typical hotel uses eco-friendly products such as organic coffee and tea, air fresheners, and cleaning agents at no extra cost, and saves thousands of dollars a month by recycling waste materials that were previously shipped to landfills.

By 2005, the Internet had become a popular supply channel, with BuyEfficent.com emerging as the major online catalog from which hotels purchase their products. Assisting the eco-product specialists, consultant Jeff Slye discovered that it could be a nightmare getting the web site to add new eco-vendors, and more than once had to personally obtain and supply vendor and product codes in order to purchase greener products through the site. While efforts such as these are time consuming, part of the long-term payoff for the company and its eco-champions is knowing that they've made it easier for the entire industry to follow in their footsteps.

The team of eco-champions also quickly learned that the national rollout effort would have its share of potential operational risks and challenges, which would need to be addressed. Among them:

- **Potential resistance by GMs to centralized imperatives.** Kimpton's culture of uniqueness and autonomy might be threatened by a green management program mandated by corporate headquarters. GMs might chafe at what they see as corporate intrusion upon their autonomy. They may see it as just the first step in a trend that will ultimately lead to centralization of the firm as a result of its rebranding effort. Local vendors and distributors may not offer green products. Search and acquisition costs may increase if GMs have to work with a broader range of vendors.

- **Potential resistance by hotel staff to new products and procedures.** Kimpton's relatively low turnover meant that some employees had been working there for many years, and had become accustomed to familiar ways of doing things (Informal queries by management, for example, revealed that many cleaning staff equate strong chemical odors with cleanliness.) Also, many of the service staff do not speak English fluently, and may have difficulty understanding and accepting management's rationales for switching to new procedures or greener cleaning products.

- **Investments might have slower payback period, lower rate of return, intangible benefits.** Unless informed, guests will not be aware that their rooms have been painted with low-VOC paints. Likewise, organic cottons are not likely to feel or look superior to traditional materials. The gains in operating costs achieved by installing longer-life and more energy-efficient fluorescent lighting can take years to pay off, while higher acquisition costs can inflate short-term expenses. The same logic applies to water conservation investments. Will GMs be around to enjoy the benefits? Will corporate executives and investors be patient? What if consumer tastes or Kimpton's branding strategies change before investments have paid off?

- **For some products being considered in Phase II, required investments might exceed existing budgets or fail to meet the cost parity criterion.** Linens and towels made from organic cotton could cost at least 50% more than the cost of conventional products and, the initial cost of converting an average Kimpton hotel to organic cotton linens would run between $100–150, 000. Other environmentally friendly products such as environmentally friendly carpeting and draperies and sustainable flooring would have a price premium. Will additional budget be provided? Will savings in other areas be allowed to pay for it?

- **Marketing the program can be challenging.** How should the EarthCare program be promoted, given customer concerns regarding the impact of some environmental initiatives on the quality of their guest experience? Guests might be concerned, for example, whether low-flow shower heads or fluorescent lighting will meet their expectations. Environmental awareness and concern varies considerably by geographic region, from very high on the West Coast and in the Northeast, to considerably lower in the South and Midwest. Will this affect customer perceptions and demand? Will the program affect the quality rating of Kimpton's hotels? According to the American Automobile Association's Diamond Rating Guidelines, some water saving shower heads and energy-saving light bulbs could lower a hotel's diamond rating.[10] Eventually, information about the Earthcare program was to be disseminated through their web site, guest directory and sales brochures that would go to travel agents, corporate travel planners and meeting planners. Should the program be marketed more aggressively?

- **Regional differences in recycling infrastructure and regulatory environment.** California had a mandated recycling program requiring 70% recycling of solid waste by 2007, so San Francisco's disposal service provided free recycling containers. Other localities may not be so generous.

Even in the face of these challenges, Kimpton executives believed that the EarthCare program was the smart, as well as the "right," thing to do. According to Tom LaTour, Chairman and CEO:

> It's good business. It's not just because we're altruistic, it's good for business. Otherwise the investors would say, what are you guys doing? A lot of people think it's going to cost more. It's actually advantageous to be eco-friendly than not.

Niki Leondakis, COO, saw the program's impact on marketing and employee retention:

> Many people say we're heading toward a tipping point: If you're not environmentally conscious, your company will be blackballed from people's choices. Also, employees today want to come to work every day not just for the pay-

---

10   *AAA Lodging Requirements & Diamond Rating Guidelines*, AAA Publishing, Heathrow, FL, June 2001.

check but to feel good about what they're doing . . . It's very important to them to be aligned with the values of the people they work for, so from the employee retention standpoint, this helps us retain and attract them so we can select from the best and the brightest.[11]

Investors appear to be happy with Kimpton's efforts to manage their properties in a more sustainable manner, as the firm announced a new round of financing in June of 2005. Private investors poured $157 million into the company for a new wave of expansion and renovation. Yale University put up most of the funds, making an investment valued at close to 1% of its $12.7 billion endowment.

By July 2005, Phase I of the EarthCare initiative had been successfully implemented at all Kimpton hotels. The percentage of waste materials recycled at its hotels in San Francisco had gone from 10–20% to over 50% (by volume) since the program's inception. Chemical cleaning agents were no longer used in any of Kimpton's hotel rooms. Every hotel served organic coffee in its lobby, and printed promotional materials on recycled paper with soy-based ink. The challenges of Phase II lay ahead.

Questions for discussion

1. Explore whether there is a "business case" for Kimpton's environmental sustainability initiative, its EarthCare program:
   a. What are the costs and benefits associated with the EarthCare program?
   b. Based on these costs and benefits, how might you justify the program to investors?
   c. Is it necessary for there to be a "business case" to justify implementation of the EarthCare program?

2. In your opinion, does Kimpton's EarthCare program involve any potential risks to their business model? For example, could the eco-initiative adversely affect customer perceptions, general manager autonomy, or costs?

3. To what extent does the EarthCare program have marketing value? Would you actively promote the program? If so, how? If EarthCare lost its marketing value would you continue it?

4. How would you measure the success of the EarthCare program?

5. Would you require each potential product to stand on its own, meeting the criteria that it cost no more than existing products? Or should the greening program be treated as a whole, with some products allowed to exceed existing costs as long as the entire program is "cost-neutral." What are some advantages or disadvantages of each approach?

---

11 From "Environmental Evangelism: Kimpton walks the eco-walk", Carlo Wolff, *Lodging Hospitality*, March 1, 2005.

6. How would you "institutionalize" Kimpton's environmental sustainability initiative? If Michael Pace or other key personnel leave Kimpton's or are unable to devote their time and enthusiasm, would the program continue? How could the company keep it from eventually losing steam?

7. What do you see as the primary challenges in implementing Phase II and III? How would you address those challenges?

Teaching notes for this case are available from Greenleaf Publishing. These are free of charge and are available only to teaching staff. They can be requested by going to:
http://www.greenleaf-publishing.com/oikos_notes

CASE 4

Environmental Product Differentiation by the Hayward Lumber Company

Magali Delmas, Erica Plambeck and Monifa Porter[1]

Stanford Graduate School of Business, USA

For 82 years, the Hayward team has derived its wealth from the forests. Many of the forest practices that have fed our families and the company over that period were not very environmentally responsible. We have both a unique opportunity and a moral obligation to give something back to the forests from which our economic prosperity is derived, to promote wood as a responsible renewable resource, and to improve our profitability. Our pioneering work in greening the construction process will be our legacy—as a company and as individuals. It is the right thing

---

1 Monifa Porter prepared this case under the supervision of Magali Delmas and Erica Plambeck as the basis for class discussion rather than to illustrate either effective or ineffective handling of an administrative situation. Numbers in the case have been modified and disguised to protect proprietary information.

A three-part video complements this case; available from https://www.gsb.stanford.edu/multimedia/Hayward/index.html.

to do for our forests and our environment. It strongly promotes our people strategy, and it is economically feasible.

—Bill Hayward, President, CEO, and Chief Sustainability Officer, Hayward Lumber Company[2]

Bill Hayward looked up to the photo of his great-grandfather hanging on his office wall. The man who started the company almost a century ago would have been intrigued by the new markets into which young Hayward was taking the family business. He glanced back to the blueprints spread across his desk and again concluded that the project was ambitious, but by no means foolhardy. Bill Hayward needed to create a real-world example of the cost case for building green and in so doing, as he had written on his office wall: "be the change he hoped to see in the world."[3] He hoped to capture new information on how to both build and sell green and to fortify his company's environmental leadership position.

In 2000, Hayward had announced his intention to make Hayward Lumber the leading supplier of environmentally friendly building materials on the California central coast and a model for sustainable business. By April 2003, he had already begun to capture the market niche by selling the most credible and trusted high-performance green building materials on the market. In addition, his company had begun to take steps to shift to procuring only green products for use within the company and to mitigate waste through recycling and efficiency auditing. It was time to take an even bigger step in greening his company. He looked back to the construction cost estimates for what could be the world's first environmentally designed truss plant.

Company Overview

Homer T. Hayward founded the Hayward Lumber Company (HLC), a privately held family business, in 1919. Headquartered in Monterey, California, the company operated six lumberyards serving the central coast region, located in Pacific Grove, Salinas, Santa Barbara, Paso Robles, San Luis Obispo, and Santa Maria, California. Bill Hayward, the founder's great-grandson, began managing the company in 1992. Hayward Lumber Company, a professional builder supply business, earned net sales of approximately $115 million in 2002, in an industry with national annual revenues of about $130 billion. The company was the 44th largest building supply company in the United States, the 5th largest in California, and the dominant player in the California central coast market. Hayward's team of 450 employees supplied builders of single-family homes with sawn lumber, oriented strand board (OSB),[4] windows, doors, kitchen cabinets, and other building materials. See Exhibit 4.1. Competitors in the central coast

---

2   "Our Restorative Business," Bill Hayward. Memo to Hayward Lumber Company Management. April 27, 2000.

3   Mahatma Gandhi (1869–1948), "We must become the change we want to see," Cole's Quotables, quotation #3410, http://www.quotationspage.com/collections.html (March 23, 2006).

4   Oriented strand board is a composite wood product similar to plywood.

EXHIBIT 4.1 Hayward Lumber Company Sales by Product Type ($000s)

Source: Hayward Lumber Company

	1998 Actual	1999 Actual	2000 Actual	2001 Actual	2002 Estimate	2003 Budget	2003 % of Total
Lumber/Plywood	42,263	50,241	53,418	64,468	61,047	60,995	50.6%
Roof Truss		2,257	2,855	3,707	4,129	4,965	4.1%
Wall Panels					100	1,500	1.2%
FSC Lumber			300	1,070	1,012	1,800	1.5%
Sheetrock					1,220	2,100	1.7%
Moldings	1,117	1,110	1,213	3,018	3,304	3,678	3.1%
Doors	3,440	3,700	3,233	6,773	6,565	7,730	6.4%
Windows	2,347	2,727	4,500	8,135	9,170	9,288	7.7%
Cabinets	3,144	3,518	4,617	4,831	4,366	4,558	3.8%
Building Materials	4,854	5,794	7,125	10,769	12,425	12,211	10.1%
Other	7,617	7,810	7,015	8,402	9,949	11,607	9.6%
Total Sales	64,782	77,157	84,276	111,173	113,287	120,432	100.0%

market included Big Creek Lumber, Birk and Pace, Weirick Lumber, Terry Company, and San Rafael. With three lumberyards, San Rafael was the largest competitor.

The customers of Hayward Lumber Company were single-family residential home-builders. About half of HLC's revenues were from custom builders that built between two and six homes annually. The other half of HLC's customers built tract housing and up to 200 homes annually in the California central coast region. Traditionally, the construction industry was highly fragmented, specialized and very much relationship-based. Builders contracted and subcontracted with architects, construction crews, plumbers, mechanical and electrical engineers, and interior designers who worked separately to complete a single building. Because of tight construction timelines and having to manage a complex set of relationships, most builders preferred tried and true building methods rather than innovative techniques. Using traditional methods and maintaining long-term relationships with subcontractors assured them of the quality and timeframe of each aspect of the project.

HLC added value for builders by cutting lumber to meet the specific requirements of each construction project and stacking it onto delivery trucks such that it could be removed in exactly the order it was needed at the construction site. HLC would deliver at the specific day and time requested by the builder. Early delivery would clutter the construction site and risk shrinkage and rain damage. Late delivery would cause workers to stand idle and disrupt the construction schedule. In either case, HLC would lose future business. HLC prided itself on being "on time, as promised (OTAP)," as their logo declared. See Exhibit 4.2. Reliability commanded a premium in the construction busi-

EXHIBIT 4.2 Hayward Lumber Company Logo in 1990s

Hayward Lumber Company Logo in 2003

(introduced to support "whole systems" strategy)

Source: Hayward Lumber Company

ness and the company used OTAP measures to gauge their success in meeting customer demand reliably.

HLC's volume of business was physically limited by the size of its lumberyards and the acreage available to stack inventory for pick-and-pack delivery. On average, a full service lumberyard typically required four to seven acres of land, 6,000 to 10,000 square feet of materials storage space, access to a rail spur and $450,000 of inventory on the ground. The capital investment required to start a full-service lumberyard in the central coast region of California was about $12 million in 2003.

The forests that supplied HLC and most lumberyards in the Western United States were located primarily in Washington and Oregon. The supply chain for traditional wood products, heading southbound from forest to final product, was mature and well established. Whole logs were cut from commercial forests and shipped by truck to nearby mills where they were milled into various lengths and sizes. The lumber was then shipped by rail from the mills to the lumberyards and stored there until it was sold and trucked to a construction site. Lumberyards were regionally focused to serve area builders, usually within a one-day trucking range of the yard.

Historically HLC generated most of its revenue from selling and delivering sawn lumber and OSB to job sites. Twenty-five percent of Hayward's wood products was too specialized to be carried in stock. The company had long-standing expertise in procuring rare products and hard-to-find materials.

Bill Hayward

In the early 1990s, the builder supply industry in California was devastated by restriction in the supply of lumber and economic recession. In 1990, strict environmental regulation was imposed to protect the habitat of the spotted owl, restricting clear-cuts to at most 40 acres. The timber harvest in California dropped by 33 percent from 1989 to 1992. From 1990–1992, the number of building permits issued in California fell by 40 percent. Profit margins in the builder supply industry fell from 38 percent to 23 percent and 22 lumber and building materials stores in the central coast market went out of business. See Exhibits 4.3–4.4. During this time period, the Hayward Lumber Company was struggling with internal control—wildly inaccurate inventory assessments—as well as the crisis in its business environment. HLC, which had remained profitable during both the Great Depression and the massive recession of the early 1970s, was headed for a $1.8M loss in 1992, the first loss in company history.

In October of 1992, 29-year-old Bill Hayward was appointed president and CEO of the company. Both a maverick and a hard-nosed fiscal manager, Hayward immediately cut labor costs and increased revenue. He replaced the entire corporate staff and all branch managers as well as cutting HLC's labor force by 25 percent. Hayward aggressively lowered prices on lumber to obtain new market share.

Hayward billed his first four-year plan as the "Arounga Strategy," named after a small staff wielded by Masai cattle herders in the East African savannah. The Masai used the staff to protect their herds from lions and other predators. Hayward hoped to use his Arounga Strategy of *product diversification* and *inventory cost control* to protect his

Exhibit 4.3 HLC Gross Margin and Return on Sales

Source: Hayward Lumber Corporation

	1996	1997	1998	1999	2000	2001	2002	2003
Gross Margin (%)	19.58	˙19.00	20.70	21.60	23.80	25.90	24.80	24.90
Return on Sales (%)	.02	0.20	0.70	1.50	3.30	1.80	0.60	1.60

Exhibit 4.4 Building Permits Issued, by County

Source: "Building Permits," US Census Bureau, http://censtats.census.gov/bldg/bldgprmt.shtml

Single-Family Permits

County	1992	1993	1994	1995	1996	1997	1998	1999	2000	2001
Monterey	736	869	1,466	1,323	1,496	1,713	1,178	1,506	1,492	894
San Benito	365	404	491	422	443	630	745	579	533	300
San Luis Obispo	666	855	1,047	985	1,176	1,329	1,730	1,579	1,547	1,687
Santa Barbara	719	549	700	792	775	903	1,026	601	731	933

small company from the lions of a shifting market and rapidly consolidating competitors. The strategy included selling higher-margin products such as cabinets, doors, and windows in addition to basic lumber. (Even when economic conditions resulted in drastically fewer housing starts, remodeling tended to remain a steady source of revenues from door, window, and cabinet sales.) Hayward implemented just-in-time inventory management. Because the lead-time for HLC to obtain lumber from the Northern mills was two weeks, HLC requested that builder-customers order two weeks in advance of construction. Hayward installed computer information systems for tracking orders, changes in builders' construction schedules, and inventory. HLC would order lumber on the basis of actual orders and inventory levels. HLC aimed to take receipt of the lumber "just-in-time" to load it onto a truck and deliver it to the job site "on time as promised." The projected losses the company faced when Hayward took the helm were due in large part to weak inventory management. By tightly controlling inventory, Hayward reduced shrinkage and financial inventory costs and improved its on-time delivery performance. Space in the yard was used primarily to pick-and-pack lumber for delivery to builders rather than for storage. Hence, HLC could drive a larger volume of business through its lumberyards without acquiring more land.

By 2003, there were far fewer lumber supply firms in the market than there had been in the late 1980s. HLC had survived the rapid concentration and consolidation by implementing the Arounga Strategy. Increased volume and product diversification at HLC proved key to its survival. Revenue shifted from almost entirely lumber in 1992 to about half lumber and half higher-margin building materials in 2003, and sales per lumberyard grew from $6 million to $12 million.

Taking an Environmental Leadership Position

With a lifetime in the builder supply business, Bill Hayward was well attuned to changes in the market and trends among builders. However, he was surprised to learn that a small number of renegade "dark green" builders were building to environmentally stringent building specifications and in the process, were doing business very differently than traditional builders. They were buying Forest Stewardship Council (FSC)-certified lumber, holding it for months at a time, and seeking out and using non-traditional building materials to meet high standards of energy efficiency, health and safety, and environmental sustainability. Hayward hired a director of sustainability to investigate this trend. She discovered a growing market opportunity to supply nontraditional environmentally friendly materials to builders in a very traditional manner: pick-and-pack delivery from the lumberyard.

Bill Hayward was committed to transforming his company into the central coast's supplier for environmentally sustainable building materials, not only to serve this new market, but also to protect the resource that his family had depended on for generations. Hayward also believed that the employees of the company would be invigorated by an environmental strategy. He delivered a mandate to his executive management team to expand the existing product line to include environmentally friendly products, eliminate environmentally undesirable products from the company's offerings, capture existing demand for green building supplies, and create new demand by educating key customers on the value of building green. The first step toward environmental product differentiation was to sell FSC-certified lumber.

Forest Stewardship Council-Certified Wood

In 1993, 130 representatives of environmental organizations, lumber companies, forest product retailers, indigenous peoples' groups, forestry certification groups, and scientists from around the world gathered to create the Forest Stewardship Council (FSC).[5] See Exhibit 4.5. This wide-ranging group of timber industry stakeholders from World Wildlife Fund to Home Depot came together in response to activists protesting in retail outlets and the increased consumer awareness of harmful lumber harvesting practices. They formed FSC to promote "sustainable" forest management—to protect fragile ecosystems, ensure long-term viability of forest resources, empower indigenous people to reap the benefits of their forestlands, and maximize the economic value of the forests within the contexts of these environmental and social goals. The scope of the founding assembly, which uniquely included indigenous people and expressly sought to balance social benefits with environmental and economic concerns, set FSC apart from other certifying bodies.

FSC certification gave consumers the opportunity to choose wood products generated from a "sustainable" forest. The Forest Stewardship Council codified a standard-

---

5 "The History of FSC-US," Forest Stewardship Council, http://www.fscus.org/about_us (March 23, 2006).

EXHIBIT 4.5 Forest Stewardship Council Principles

Principle 1: Compliance With Laws and FSC Principles

Forest management shall respect all applicable laws of the country in which they occur, and international treaties and agreements to which the country is a signatory, and comply with all FSC Principles and Criteria.

Principle 2: Tenure and Use Rights and Responsibilities

Long-term tenure and use rights to the land and forest resources shall be clearly defined, documented and legally established.

Principle 3: Indigenous Peoples' Rights

The legal and customary rights of indigenous peoples to own, use and manage their lands, territories, and resources shall be recognized and respected.

Principle 4: Community Relations and Workers' Rights

Forest management operations shall maintain or enhance the long-term social and economic well-being of forest workers and local communities.

Principle 5: Benefits From The Forest

Forest management operations shall encourage the efficient use of the forest's multiple products and services to ensure economic viability and a wide range of environmental and social benefits.

Principle 6: Environmental Impact

Forest management shall conserve biological diversity and its associated values, water resources, soils, and unique and fragile ecosystems and landscapes, and by so doing, maintain the ecological functions and the integrity of the forest.

Principle 7: Management Plan

A management plan—appropriate to the scale and intensity of the operations—shall be written, implemented, and kept up to date. The long-term objectives of management, and the means of achieving them, shall be clearly stated.

Principle 8: Monitoring and Assessment

Monitoring shall be conducted—appropriate to the scale and intensity of forest management—to assess the condition of the forest, yields of forest products, chain of custody, management activities and their social and environmental impacts.

Principle 9: Maintenance of High Conservation Value Forests

Management activities in high conservation value forests shall maintain or enhance the attributes which define such forests. Decisions regarding high conservation value forests shall always be considered in the context of a precautionary approach.

Principle 10: Plantations

Plantations shall be planned and managed in accordance with Principles and Criteria 1–9, and Principle 10 and its Criteria. While plantations can provide an array of social and economic benefits and can contribute to satisfying the world's needs for forest products, they should complement the management of natural forests while reducing pressures on them, and promoting their conservation and restoration.

Source: "Principles and Criteria," The Forest Stewardship Council, http://www.fscus.org (March 21, 2006)

ization and accreditation process to certify third-party independent certifiers rather than actually certifying forests and forest products directly. Environmental, social, and economic standards of forest management were defined through a complex consensus-building process that incorporated the positions of all of the assembled stakeholders. These broad standards were adapted to local realities and operationalized for implementation by national working groups. The accreditation process provided assurance that third-party certifying bodies would competently and independently verify that forests adhere to the FSC standards. See Exhibit 4.6.

Certifying bodies were also accredited by the FSC to monitor the entire supply chain. They would provide "chain-of-custody certification" to authenticate the wood as it moved from forest to mill to manufacturer to the end consumer. Chain-of-custody certification was complex, costly, and inefficient—less than 10 percent of the wood harvested from FSC-certified forests reached consumers under an FSC label.

In 1995, in response to the FSC certification, the American Forest and Paper Association created the Sustainable Forestry Initiative (SFI) certification process. This was greatly criticized by environmentalists for weak environmental standards and lack of credible and objective third-party evaluation. Following its inception, SFI underwent a number of improvements, including the participation of outside auditors such as PricewaterhouseCoopers. However, environmental NGOs continued to criticize them for lack of chain-of-custody certification and the exclusion of indigenous people and the public at large in development of the standard.

While environmentalists criticized the SFI standard, retailers largely accepted it because FSC-certified products were more expensive and difficult to source. SFI products were offered at no additional cost and were easily available for purchase from mills. In 2003, 42.5 million hectares of land in Canada and the United States were SFI-certified. These woodlands, managed by only 200 different companies, accounted for 85 percent of all wood produced in North America. In contrast, FSC-certified woodlands were fragmented and dispersed: 25.5 million hectares in 66 different countries, including 4 million hectares in the United States under 500 different landowners. Similarly, only a small fraction of saw mills were FSC-certified. These mills would process both FSC and non-FSC-certified wood, but not simultaneously. Before cutting FSC-certified wood, a mill operator was required to shut down and clear the premises of non-FSC-certified wood, in order to meet stringent FSC chain-of-custody requirements. Because the set-up time was costly in lost output, a mill operator would typically only produce a batch of FSC-certified wood three or four times per year. FSC-certified woodlands, FSC-certified saw mills, and manufacturers of FSC-certified products were geographically dispersed, suffering from high transportation costs and delays. Hence, retailers might have the opportunity to order a particular FSC-certified product only once in three months.

The demand for FSC-certified wood was stimulated by the Leadership in Energy and Environmental Design (LEED) Green Building Rating System, a voluntary standard developed by the US Green Building Council[6] to promote high-performance sustainable buildings. The LEED system awarded points for making various environmentally preferable choices, including choosing FSC-certified lumber. By achieving various

6   "LEED: Leadership in Energy and Environmental Design," US Green Building Council, http://www.usgbc.org/DisplayPage.aspx?CategoryID=19 (March 23, 2006).

EXHIBIT 4.6 Comparison of Forest Certification Systems Operating in North America (continued opposite)

Source: Metafore/Certification Resource Center & "Forest Certification Comparison Matrix," Forest Certification Resource Center, http://www.certifiedwoodsearch.org/matrix/matrix.asp (March 23, 2006). Reprinted with permission of Metafore (http://www.certifiedwood.org).

	American Tree Farm System	Canadian Standards Association	Forest Stewardship Council	Sustainable Forestry Initiative
Basis for Company Participation	Voluntary	Voluntary	Voluntary	Required for American Forest & Paper Association (AF&PA) membership. Voluntary for third-party certification and non-member licensees.
Scope	Private, non-industrial forests in the United States.	Primarily focused on forests in Canada.	Used by all types of forest ownership around the world.	Primarily focused on industrial forests in the United States and Canada.
Governance	A program of the American Forest Foundation, an independent, non-profit and non-governmental organization. Each state's program is self-governing.	CSA is an independent non-profit organization accredited by the Standards Council of Canada. CSA operates within Canada's National Standards System and according to nationally and internationally accepted standardization procedures and processes.	An independent, non-profit and non-governmental organization. Governed by a Board of Directors and membership formed in three chambers, social, environmental, and economic. Board is elected by members.	Program of AF&PA, the national trade association for US forest products industry. The Sustainable Forestry Board (SFB), an independent non-governmental organization ($\frac{2}{3}$ from non-industry interests), manages the SFI standard, certification process, dispute resolution & quality control. AF&PA manages the application of the SFI product label.
Chain of Custody tracking	None	Chain of Custody tracks products from forest through each stage of manufacturing and distribution.	Chain of Custody tracks products from forest through each stage of manufacturing and distribution.	Participants required to have auditable monitoring system to account for all wood flow and use of Best Management Practices.
Issues Covered by Standards	Standards address environmental and silvicultural[7] issuess. Many indicators are discretionary.	Standards address environmental, silvicultural, social, and economic issues.	Standards address environmental, silvicultural, social, and economic issues. Most indicators are mandatory.	Standards address environmental, silvicultural, and social issues. Additional indicators are discretionary.

This matrix compares the forest certification systems currently operating in North America. Environmental management systems, such as ISO 14001, are not included because they do not specifically address on-the-ground aspects of forest management.

7   Silviculture is the art and science of controlling the establishment, growth, composition, and quality of forest vegetation for the full range of forest resource objectives: "The Meaning of 'Silvicultural,'" BC Ministry of Forests, http://www.for.gov.bc.ca/hfp/training/00014/meansilv.htm (March 21, 2006).

(from previous page)

	American Tree Farm System	Canadian Standards Association	Forest Stewardship Council	Sustainable Forestry Initiative
Assessment: performance-based (monitor performance directly) vs systems-based (ensure management systems in place to measure & monitor performance)	Performance-based monitoring and an assessment of the forest management plan.	Primarily systems-based assessment incorporating elements of ISO 14001.	Performance-based monitoring and an assessment of the forest management plan.	Primarily systems-based assessment incorporating elements of ISO 14001.
Third-party, independent certification	Third-party certification is required. Volunteer foresters provide initial certification and repeat audits every five years.	Third-party certification is required. Accredited registrars and independently certified auditors provide initial certification, surveillance audits every year, and full re-registration every three years.	Third-party certification is required. Accredited certifiers provide initial certification and annual surveillance audits.	Third-party certification is optional. Accredited registrars and independently certified auditors provide initial certification, an audit after three years and repeat audits every five years. Annual surveillance audits for label users.
On-product label	None	Yes. Minimum threshold is 70%. Product labels required to conform to ISO 14020, ISO 14021.	Yes. Minimum threshold varies with product. 70% for solid wood.	Yes, for third-party certifications only. Minimum threshold is 66%. (ATFS-recognized)
Number of participants	51,000 Certified Tree Farmers in 46 states.	There are 17 companies in Canada with 53 forest management certificates. There are 24 companies with 56 Chain of Custody certificates.	There are 761 Forest Management certificates and 4458 Chain of Custody certificates in 81 countries.	In the United States and Canada, there are 81 organizations with 116 certified operations and 24 label users.
Total acreage	33,000,000 acres in the US.	167,008,935 acres in Canada.	171,136,997 acres globally, 64,229,656 acres in North America.	146,244,242 third-party-certified acres in Canada and the US.

The American Tree Farm System® (ATFS), is a registered service mark of the American Forest Foundation.

The Forest Stewardship Council, and FSC, are registered trademarks of the Forest Stewardship Council A.C.

The Sustainable Forestry Initiative® (SFI), and the Sustainable Forestry Initiative®, SFI, are registered service marks of the American Forest & Paper Association.

point thresholds, a building was designated LEED-Certified: Silver, Gold, or Platinum. To achieve points for certified wood, builders were required to use at least 50 percent FSC-certified lumber in the project, with the wood costs representing at least two percent of the total project cost. See Exhibit 4.7. The US federal government was committed to building to the LEED standard, as were many corporations, universities and individuals. Many new schools and post offices in California were LEED-certified.

EXHIBIT 4.7 LEED Green Building Rating System®, MRc7

Source: US Green Building Council, http://www.usgbc.org/Docs/LEEDdocs/LEED_RS_v2-1.pdf, p. 54 (March 21, 2006); Reprinted by permission of US Green Building Council. Please see http://www.usgbc.org for updates.

1 Point   **Certified Wood**

Intent

Encourage environmentally responsible forest management.

Requirements

Use a minimum of 50% of wood-based materials and products, certified in accordance with the Forest Stewardship Council's Principles and Criteria, for wood building components including, but not limited to, structural framing and general dimensional framing, flooring, finishes, furnishings, and non-rented temporary construction applications such as bracing, concrete form work and pedestrian barriers.

Submittals

❑ Provide the LEED Letter Template, signed by the architect, owner or responsible party, declaring that the credit requirements have been met and listing the FSC-certified materials and products used. Include calculations demonstrating that the project incorporates the required percentage of FSC-certified materials/products and their cost together with the total cost of all materials for the project. For each material/product used to meet these requirements, provide the vendor's or manufacturer's Forest Stewardship Council chain-of-custody certificate number.

Potential Technologies & Strategies

Establish a project goal for FSC-certified wood products and identify suppliers that can achieve this goal. During construction, ensure that the FSC-certified wood products are installed and quantify the total percentage of FSC-certified wood products installed.

HLC: Selling FSC-Certified Wood

Initially, HLC's demand for FSC-certified wood came primarily from custom home-builders. Luxury home buyers tended to be less sensitive to price and many were will-ing to pay a premium for a home that was "deep green," as environmentally friendly as possible. Such buyers were unwilling to accept a partial solution, demanding that the proportion of FSC-certified wood should be close to 100 percent. HLC's other builder-customers, those who built low-cost tract homes, were unwilling to pay a premium for FSC-certified wood. See Exhibit 4.8.

Exhibit 4.8 Hayward Lumber Company Sales by Customer Type ($000s)

Source: Hayward Lumber Corporation

	1998 Actual	1999 Actual	2000 Actual	2001 Actual	2002 Estimate	2003 Budget
Professional Builders	49,765	58,055	62,266	82,017	82,616	83,219
Owner/Builder	2,135	2,982	4,353	5,134	4,610	6,420
Green Builders	0	0	0	1,277	1,159	1,389
CI/Gov	4,100	5,838	6,415	6,404	7,096	7,833
Concrete Contractors	0	0	0	631	2,171	2,066
Retail Customer	8,627	10,119	11,078	15,172	16,420	16,499
Employee	154	162	165	216	274	406
Total Sales	64,781	77,156	84,276	110,851	114,346	117,832

Luxury homes required premium wood products. Unfortunately, the local FSC-certi-fied mill was not equipped to consistently meet premium standards for accuracy and surface finish. Too often, quality problems with the FSC-certified wood led to delay, waste, and dissatisfied customers (builders and home buyers).

Nevertheless, Hayward chose to stock FSC-certified lumber, dedicating one acre of land in the Salinas lumberyard to this purpose. Given the lead-time of approximately three months to obtain FSC-certified lumber from the mill, HLC needed to hold inven-tory in order to deliver the wood to builders in the traditional manner: pre-cut, load stacked, and with a short lead-time. By making it convenient to obtain FSC-certified wood, HLC hoped to attract new customers: green builders from all over California, and in particular, those constructing large public buildings to LEED specifications. Based on its best estimate of demand over the next three months, HLC initially pur-chased $500,000 of FSC-certified lumber at $4.00 per board foot.[8] This was 20 percent greater than the cost of $3.20 per board foot for non-certified lumber. See Exhibit 4.9.

None of HLC's competitors in central California carried FSC-certified lumber. In this vacuum, HLC decided to sell the FSC-certified lumber for $4.20 per board foot. HLC

---

8   One board foot is a piece of lumber that is 1 foot wide, 1 foot long and 1 inch thick, or its volumetric equivalent.

Exhibit 4.9 Lumber Prices in $ per 100 board feet, 1992–2002

Source: "Yearbook Features,' Random Lengths, http://www.randomlengths.com/pdf/yb_sample.pdf,
http://www.randomlengths.com/base.asp?s1=Books_and_Directories&s2=Yearbook&s3=Features

Douglas Fir, Green
2x4 Std&btr, Random
(Prices net of f.o.b. Mill, Portland Rate)

Monthly Averages

	Jan	Feb	Mar	Apr	May	Jun	Jul	Aug	Sep	Oct	Nov	Dec	Yearly Avg
1992	236	263	270	266	243	239	250	269	263	250	289	297	261
1993	336	384	466	440	366	349	323	347	357	342	406	464	382
1994	467	452	414	347	374	347	334	341	315	324	324	308	362
1995	318	323	310	294	281	278	292	310	336	311	322	334	309
1996	317	346	355	350	390	407	413	457	413	398	408	403	388
1997	409	425	414	424	397	399	368	353	325	351	365	333	380
1998	326	326	327	312	268	308	338	371	303	287	304	296	314
1999	349	350	368	356	382	459	505	394	385	343	376	360	385
2000	369	360	362	329	310	300	279	280	291	288	308	287	314
2001	286	292	297	308	366	321	303	309	286	258	258	271	296
2002	289	313	324	303	290	282	277	283	284	281	273	278	290

FSC Douglas Fir, Green
2x4 Std&btr, Random
(Prices net of f.o.b. Mill, Portland Rate)

FSC Monthly Averages

	Jan	Feb	Mar	Apr	May	Jun	Jul	Aug	Sep	Oct	Nov	Dec	Yearly Avg
1992	326	309	294	293	303	326	329	327	300	331	320	295	313
1993	454	477	489	476	416	485	457	454	481	430	439	468	461
1994	435	467	440	451	392	445	465	420	433	400	437	447	436
1995	345	382	404	395	369	374	368	362	341	393	345	356	369
1996	440	497	447	462	474	444	511	505	439	458	450	456	465
1997	413	435	458	461	480	464	468	456	464	426	415	489	452
1998	370	406	393	359	381	352	406	347	352	345	366	342	368
1999	457	476	423	439	472	485	443	506	474	501	436	480	466
2000	406	381	414	370	372	407	359	384	371	402	392	395	388
2001	375	349	385	380	376	332	362	374	334	322	327	371	357
2002	379	361	320	339	363	372	356	333	369	324	341	336	349

also used a five percent mark-up with non-certified lumber, buying at $3.20 and selling at $3.35 per board foot. After two months, HLC had sold 80 percent of the inventory of FSC-certified wood. Rather than allow the remainder to dry out and warp, HLC removed the eco-label and sold the FSC-certified lumber as regular lumber at the regular price of $3.35 per board foot. Fortunately, the FSC-certified wood was physically indistinguishable from other wood.

Building Green and Selling Whole Systems: Expanding the Environmental Strategy

In an April 2000 document that became known as "Hayward's Green Manifesto," Bill Hayward outlined his three-part environmental strategy. The first part of the strategy was to provide a comprehensive selection of environmentally friendly building materials with a short and reliable lead-time. HLC would continue to supply FSC-certified lumber on a just-in-time basis as well as extend into higher-margin green building materials such as nontoxic adhesives, no- and low-VOC paints,[9] formaldehyde-free insulation, FSC-certified or recycled cabinets, counters and floors, and energy-efficient doors and windows. HLC sought substitutes for toxic or environmentally harmful products. For example, in 2000, the company replaced arsenic-treated wood, a very common product in the lumber industry, with arsenic-free wood. (In February of 2002 the Environmental Protection Agency announced that arsenic-treated wood would not be permitted for use in residential buildings after December 2003.) Arsenic preserved wood but poses severe health threats to construction workers who touch it often and potentially to residents of the home. Because many vendors of green building materials were small startup organizations, HLC could add great value by aggregating these products in one place, easing each builder's procurement process.

The second part of the environmental strategy was to stimulate demand through education. Specifically, HLC invited key decision makers such as architects, inspectors, engineers, appraisers, city officials, and influential homeowners, to daylong seminars on green building. HLC created a toolkit for assessing the costs and benefits of building green and an extensive web catalog of green building materials, even listing products that HLC did not carry in stock. In addition, HLC garnered media attention by donating FSC-certified building materials to celebrity-endorsed, charitable construction projects by Habitat for Humanity in Hollywood.

The third part was to change the culture of the company, incorporating environmental values in all decisions and activities. Green builders and their customers were idealistic, preferring to do business with those that shared their values. HLC implemented an internal recycling and waste diversion plan, changed its procurement policies to buy green products for internal use, and made a commitment to build all new Hayward construction projects to the LEED standard. In so doing, they would gain valuable knowledge about green building.

---

9   No/low-VOC paints do not contain, or contain very, few volatile organic compounds, which are known hazards to human health.

Ultimately, Hayward planned to use the company's experiential knowledge and leadership position to become the trusted one-stop shop for green builders. Incremental environmental upgrades were always costly. With a whole-system approach, however, increased capital costs could be recouped through operational savings. For example, a builder had to tighten the entire building envelope to achieve energy efficiency—premiums paid for highly efficient doors and windows would be lost as heat waste if the walls and ceilings were not similarly insulated. Because of these interdependencies, an integrated product offering was particularly attractive to green builders. With intellectual capital garnered through building and buying green, HLC would offer comprehensive, environmentally sound systems.

Hayward added an external sales team. He instructed them to prepare detailed cost/benefit analyses for the green systems, centering on energy efficiency, and identifying rebates, operational cost savings, and payback periods. The sales team was also trained to focus on coordinated sales, building relationships with customers, gathering information about potential building projects, and forecasting demand.

Green Opportunities

As part of his green strategy, Bill Hayward had identified three potential opportunities for HLC to pursue. The first was a truss plant. (A truss is two-dimensional frame to support the roof or floor of a house. See Exhibit 4.10.) Frustrated with the glacial pace of innovation in construction, Hayward aimed to "be the change" by manufacturing wood structures with 20 percent less lumber in one of the first industrial production facilities to meet the LEED Gold standard. The facility would manufacture wall panels in addition to trusses. Roof trusses were common elements in both custom and tract housing and floor trusses were established though much less common. However, prefabricated wall panels were innovative in this market. The truss plant would be located in Santa Maria to serve both the San Luis Obispo and Santa Barbara counties.

The truss plant would specialize in "advance framing:" cutting and assembling lumber with careful design to avoid waste. For example, by using 2 × 6 inch slats spaced further apart than the standard 2 × 4 inch slats, HLC could build a common roof truss[10] with only 16 board feet of lumber instead of the standard 20. (A common roof truss would sell for approximately $140 in central California, with ten copies required to support the roof of a two-car garage.) Essentially, advance framing substituted engineering design effort for wood (approximately eight hours of analysis by a civil engineer for a simple roof truss system). HLC expected to be most competitive on a high-volume job, e.g. 10 copies of the same roof truss system for tract housing, in which the design cost would be spread over many units. A roof truss system would sell for $4,000 for a typical home and $6,000–$10,000 for a complex custom home.

To provide a roof truss, HLC would need to collaborate with the builder in the very early stages of a project. Due to recent earthquakes, the building code required tract builders to commit to the roof structure—and hence to the truss plant—60 days in advance of construction. However, builders of individual, custom homes could cancel an order at any time.

---

10   With a span of 30 feet.

EXHIBIT 4.10   Roof TrussA01 and Overview of Roof Truss System for Fruaslo Residence

Source: Hayward Lumber Company

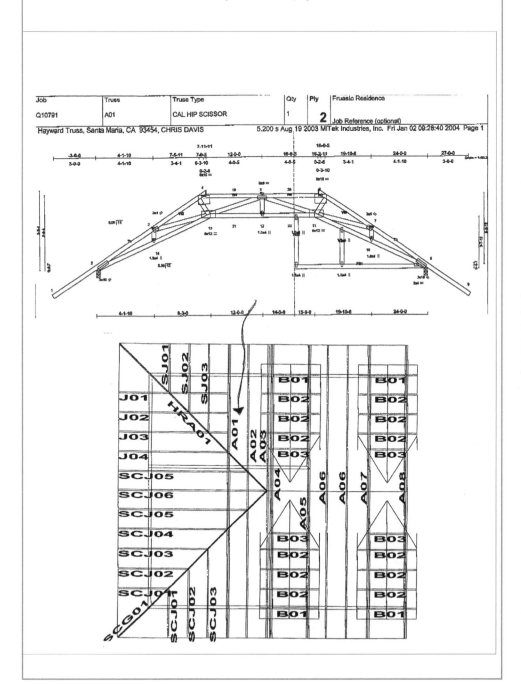

To support a mix of one-off custom jobs with high-volume tract jobs, HLC would invest $600,000 in fast, flexible equipment. This included a computer numerically controlled saw, which performed changeovers in seconds rather than tens of minutes, ergonomically designed elevated assembly tables, and a Gantry press which could quickly secure the framing beams in a truss.

HLC would build an indoor facility to protect this equipment, as well as workers and materials, from the elements. Most truss plants in California (including Hayward's only competitor in Santa Maria, Truss Pro) were open-air facilities, which shut down operations when it rained. The Hayward facility would be designed to maximize water and energy efficiency, with day lighting and 20,000 square feet of solar panels (100 kW) to power the production process.

The sizing of the truss plant was a challenge—demand would be seasonal and dependent on regional growth and the competitor Truss Pro might add capacity. Hayward planned to invest a total of $2.5 million for the land, building, and equipment. With an ideal product mix and current prices, the facility would have capacity to generate revenues of $12 million in roof trusses and $12 million in wall panels annually. In recent years, Truss Pro had generated revenues of approximately $8 million annually on roof trusses, with a gross margin of 35 percent. It was successful in landing approximately 75 percent of the roof truss jobs for which it provided a quote.

The second proposition under consideration was a design center to serve the rapidly growing green building market in Santa Barbara. The design center would provide a lush showcase for premium doors, windows, kitchen cabinets, knobs and pulls, and hardwood flooring. The plan included renovating an existing structure and, in the process, greening the building and surrounding landscape. Plans included 12 operable skylights for natural light and air flow in lieu of air-conditioning, a south-facing ivy trestle to further cool the building, an underground cistern for onsite water reclamation, permeably paved parking, photovoltaic power generation, FSC lumber engineered for advanced framing, and the use of 20–30 percent recycled materials. Estimates for the cost to build the design center totaled $2 million. Hayward projected sales of $5.5 million for its first year of operation, $7.5 million for the second, and $10 million for the third. The Santa Barbara location seemed ideal because it was three blocks from an existing HLC lumberyard and the number of high-end housing starts in the market was growing rapidly. Further, an organization of environmentally focused builders and architects called the Green Alliance was very active in the Santa Barbara market.

Lastly, Bill Hayward was also considering buying Eco Timber, a company created in 1992 that offered ecologically sound wood flooring. Eco Timber products included flooring from FSC-certified forests, reclaimed flooring, and innovative wood alternatives like bamboo flooring. Eco Timber was located in San Rafael, California, but had a national sales force and distribution partners. EcoTimber total flooring sales from 1999 to 2002 were $3,400,000 with annual growth of 40 percent and margins between 17 and 28 percent depending on the type of customer. Architects and their environmentally aware clients were the primary sources of demand for EcoTimber products. These clients ranged from national accounts and corporations, to commercial and high-end residential developers, to affluent homeowners. Customers included Nike, Disney, Pottery Barn, Patagonia, and Whole Foods Market. EcoTimber marketed its brand to architects and their clients and sold directly to contractors as well as to dealers who serviced contractors. They also sold to affluent, progressive consumers through their web site, flooring dealer network, and eco-focused publications.

EcoTimber positioned itself as selling green flooring products at competitive prices. It differentiated itself as the only comprehensive line of eco-friendly flooring products for a "one-stop shop." The emerging competition was still specialized, offering only one green product (certified, bamboo, reclaimed, etc.). In addition, EcoTimber was also actively establishing partnerships with other FSC suppliers (non-flooring) to offer "whole project" solutions for architects and clients.

Conclusion

Bill Hayward looked across the window at the piles of FSC-certified wood lying on its lumberyard. He wondered whether his grandfather would have approved of the new direction he was taking the company. Did it make business sense to sell FSC lumber? How should HLC prioritize and focus its efforts and growth? Should he invest in any of these new ventures (the truss plant, the design center, and EcoTimber)? Were there synergies between all these propositions and HLC's core business? Although Bill Hayward was very excited about these opportunities, he was concerned that HLC's managerial and financial resources might be overly stretched if HLC pursued all of them.

Teaching notes for this case are available from Greenleaf Publishing. These are free of charge and are available only to teaching staff. They can be requested by going to:
http://www.greenleaf-publishing.com/oikos_notes

Part 3
Innovative
Partnership Models

CASE 5

Transforming the Global Fishing Industry
The Marine Stewardship Council at Full Sail?

Alexander Nick[1]

IMD Lausanne, Switzerland

Early on a cloudy March morning in 2006, Rupert Howes, CEO of the Marine Stewardship Council (MSC) was on a conference call with Will Martin, the chairman of the board. Howes had been appointed in 2004, and had previously worked with the sustainable development think-tank, the Forum for the Future. Howes and Martin were discussing recent developments: the first Norwegian fishery had entered the assessment process, and Wal-Mart had committed to sell only MSC-certified fish in the next three to five years. Both men felt that momentum was building. More than 300 seafood products in 24 countries now bore the MSC eco-label. In this buoyant atmosphere, Martin raised the question of whether they really were in safe waters. Had they learned their lessons and implemented all the necessary changes?

Since the MSC was established in 1997, it had faced tough opposition. Tensions with the conservation community, mistrust and opposition from industry and national governments, questionable management decisions and financial crises had made it difficult for the organization to meet its key challenge: setting up a global certification

1 CSM Research Associate Alexander Nick prepared this case, with assistance from Research Associate Oliver Salzmann, under the supervision of Professor Ulrich Steger and CSM Program Manager Aileen Ionescu-Somers as a basis for class discussion rather than to illustrate either effective or ineffective handling of a business situation.

Copyright © 2006 by IMD—International Institute for Management Development, Lausanne, Switzerland. Not to be used or reproduced without written permission directly from IMD.

scheme for sustainable fisheries. It was a huge challenge to circumvent the vicious circle: no supply meant no market, and no market meant no supply.

Although the future seemed bright, Howes and Martin wondered if the MSC would finally manage to satisfy all of its diverse stakeholders. Several NGOs (including local ones) felt attacked on their own turf. Some were arguing for stricter standards. Others seriously felt that the MSC's ambitious venture would be better undertaken by government bodies with more resources. Fisheries and industry along the supply chain called for less strict criteria. For them, certification was too costly and time-intensive. Overall interest from consumers, and hence retailers, was still disappointing. The MSC was short of money and lacked long-term financial stability. Would it really be able to reverse the decline of global fish stocks?

Overcoming the Tragedy of the Commons:[2]
The Need for New Solutions

The Global Crisis of the Fishing Industry

According to the United Nations Food and Agriculture Organization (FAO) in 2004, it was estimated that about three-quarters of the world's commercial marine stocks were

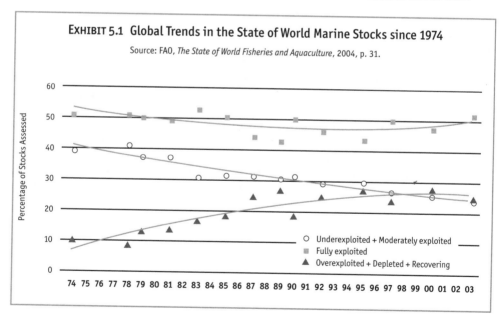

EXHIBIT 5.1 Global Trends in the State of World Marine Stocks since 1974

Source: FAO, *The State of World Fisheries and Aquaculture*, 2004, p. 31.

---

2   An expression coined by ecologist Garett Hardin in 1968 to describe the problems resulting from property owned in common. With human nature being to go for immediate benefit at the expense of less tangible long-term values, common property, e.g. the seas or land, is fast destroyed by uncontrolled use.

fully exploited, overexploited, depleted or recovering and in need of rebuilding (refer to Exhibit 5.1 for global trends in the state of world marine stocks). While marine ecosystems were degrading, demand was on the rise. The rapid expansion of commercial fishing had changed livelihoods and local cultures, forcing fishing communities with hundred years of tradition into turmoil.

Catch as Much as You Can: The Tragedy of the Commons

Here was the problem: fish in the sea was publicly owned and could be exploited free of charge. Hence, governments and fisheries had a clear incentive to catch as much as possible—before their "neighbor" got it. Since the "neighbor" was doing the same thing, the depletion of fish stocks was only a matter of time. To overcome this so-called Tragedy of the Commons, governments defined property rights and set fishing quotas. Next to sound regulation and enforcement of rules in an international context, market-based approaches, such as the MSC's certification scheme, were also possible options.[3]

The Launch of the Marine Stewardship Council

In 1997 two institutions took on the challenge of reversing the decline in global fish stocks: Unilever, the world's largest purchaser of frozen seafood, and WWF, the international conservation organization with the well-known panda bear logo. They had different motives for collaborating, but their common goal was to secure the long-term health and productivity of the oceans. Unilever was driven by a long-term vision of enduring success for its business using renewable resources. WWF wanted to explore the potential of market-based incentives to deliver real improvements in marine conservation and chose to cooperate with industry to achieve this.

They set up the Marine Stewardship Council (MSC) to establish a credible seafood certification and eco-labeling program, to accredit independent certifiers who assessed fisheries against its standard. Once certified, companies wishing to use MSC products underwent a chain of custody certification that guaranteed traceability of MSC-labeled seafood, ensuring that these were separated from non-certified products at every stage of production—from the boat to the plate. In 1999 the MSC became fully independent of its parents. Its "Principles and Criteria for Sustainable Fishing" were based on the FAO's "Code of Conduct for Responsible Fisheries" (refer to Exhibit 5.2 for the MSC's Principles for Sustainable Fishing).

---

3   For more details, see Steger, Ulrich and Rädler, George. *The Marine Stewardship Council (A): Is a Joint Venture Possible between "Suits and Sandals"?* IMD case no. IMD-2-0080, 2000.

EXHIBIT 5.2 MSC Principles for Sustainable Fishing

PRINCIPLE 1

A fishery must be conducted in a manner that does not lead to over-fishing or depletion of the exploited populations and, for those populations that are depleted, the fishery must be conducted in a manner that demonstrably leads to their recovery.

PRINCIPLE 2

Fishing operations should allow for the maintenance of the structure, productivity, function and diversity of the ecosystem (including habitat and associated dependent and ecologically related species) on which the fishery depends.

PRINCIPLE 3

The fishery is subject to an effective management system that respects local, national and international laws and standards and incorporates institutional and operational frameworks that require use of the resource to be responsible and sustainable.

Source: The MSC

Start-up

No Market, No Supply

Transforming the global fishing industry into a more sustainable one was a formidable task for a small, unknown organization like the MSC. Governments, industries, and NGOs all doubted its potential to be truly effective. One of the biggest concerns was to overcome the "chicken and egg" problem: no supply meant no market, and no market meant no supply. Howes remembered the struggle:

> In the early years, a lot of people felt that the MSC was a fantastic idea, but the organization very much suffered from the problem that there was no real supply. It has to take care of two sides of the coin—sustainable production and sustainable consumption. The MSC worked very hard with very limited resources to achieve fisheries and commercial outreach.

In 1996 Unilever announced its objective of buying fish only from sustainable sources by 2005. Dierk Peters, international marketing manager at Unilever, established a "traffic light system" to assess the sustainability of fisheries in order to tackle the problem of lack of supply. He commented:

> We introduced this system simultaneously to the MSC because we knew that we could not certify all our fish in a few years. We needed to identify fisheries that could become possible candidates for the MSC certification process.

Different Stakeholders—Conflicting Demands

Well known for its activist approach and rigorous positions, Greenpeace was skeptical about the MSC's "promise" to promote and certify sustainable fishing. While supporting the idea initially, it later criticized some aspects of the MSC's approach: weak criteria, a governance structure dominated by industry and a lack of stakeholder engagement. Blake Lee-Harwood, campaigns director at Greenpeace, commented on the situation at the time:

> We disagree fundamentally with MSC's claim to certify sustainable fisheries. We believe that it is nearly impossible to claim that a fishery is sustainable. You need so much data to make that claim. And most fisheries do not have that data. They might have some evidence that they manage the fish stock in a way that it hasn't gone down. But that is not sustainability as we see it, namely managing a stock within a whole ecosystem and wanting the whole ecosystem to restore.

Other conservation organizations also called for a stricter interpretation of sustainability. Obviously, as a co-founder, WWF had a different opinion on the legitimacy of the MSC's sustainability claim. As Katherine Short, fishery officer at WWF's Global Marine Programme, noted:

> There has been a lot of debate about the word "sustainable" in the last fifteen years. Almost everyone you speak to has a different interpretation. Improving the management of the world's fisheries cannot be done by imposing any new "quick-fix" system, shifting to effective ecosystem-based management requires as much change culturally as it does in technical or policy terms. Within the first five years of any MSC certification, WWF would expect to see adoption of best practice in mitigating impacts on the marine environment and much greater understanding of the implications of adopting a full ecosystem-based management approach.

Industry—retailers in particular—was primarily concerned about costs and duration of certification processes. Katrin Gruber, head of engagement at Migros in Switzerland, observed:

> Our experiences with the MSC are that the processes, from the very first audit until the final certification, are too long, too complicated and too expensive. This also applies to the certification of the whole chain of custody and the renewal of certificates every one to two years. We need to adopt working flows, forms and IT systems.

The MSC also faced resistance from governments, especially in Scandinavian countries. In their view, a labeling scheme such as that of the MSC should be introduced and led by governments rather than by an NGO.

Exhibit 5.3 Excerpts from "Crisis of Credibility for 'Green' Fisheries"

Drastic reforms urged to save watchdog from collapse

The world's only label to certify sustainable and well managed fisheries, the London based Marine Stewardship Council, lacks credibility and will collapse unless drastically reformed, say confidential reports compiled for its funding organisations.

[. . .]

Fish from across the world sold in British supermarkets carry the MSC logo, but claims that the fisheries it certifies are sustainable should be dropped because consumers are being duped, say the reports obtained by the *Guardian*.

The investigation into the MSC was ordered by five large US foundations that fund conservation work. They were concerned that despite the MSC's high-profile support from the Prince of Wales and Queen Noor of Jordan, the certification given to some fisheries was unjustified.

Four special investigations into fisheries the MSC has certified were carried out and researchers said none was flawless.

[. . .]

The most stinging criticism comes from an independent Wildhavens consultancy, which interviewed conservation groups, the fishing industry, retailers and MSC staff.

Its main recommendation is that the board of trustees should recognise it had reached a "critical tipping point" and must act speedily "to restore its credibility and prevent the organisation's failure". The burden of proof to show that certification will enhance the marine environment was with the MSC and it must show that it did not provide an undeserved "green shield" for inadequate fisheries management.

The report also called for management changes, including Mr Gummer handing over the chairmanship, although it suggests he stays on the organisation's board. There are also criticisms of staff leadership, which is regarded as an attack on the chief executive, Brendan May.

[. . .]

Source: Brown, Paul. "Crisis of Credibility for 'Green' Fisheries." *Guardian Unlimited*, February 21, 2004.

Crisis and Reforms

Crisis Triggered in the US

On February 21, 2004, the *Guardian* reported a "crisis of credibility for 'green' fisheries" (refer to Exhibit 5.3 for excerpts from the article). The article argued that the MSC lacked credibility and would collapse unless drastically reformed:

> The burden of proof to show that certification will enhance the marine environment was with the MSC and it must show that it did not provide an undeserved "green shield" for inadequate fisheries management.

It also described a significant crisis of confidence in the MSC in 2003 and 2004. The crisis started following criticism from several conservation organizations in the US about the possible certification of two fisheries that they had been campaigning against for years, the South Georgia Patagonian Toothfish Longline Fishery and the Bering Sea and Aleutian Islands Pollock Fishery. Consequently, some of the MSC's key US donors commissioned two external reports to evaluate the council and its certification program. These reports, the Bridgespan and Wildhavens Reports, made some 47 recommendations for the future direction of the organization.

Reform and Change in Leadership

The MSC reacted by setting up a reform program. The organization also underwent a significant change in leadership. Howes joined as CEO; Will Martin, an American businessman and a senior fellow for WWF-US, became the new chairman of the board. Howes assessed the situation:

> Many of our supporters stopped funding us when the reports came out. Our credibility was damaged. Unsurprisingly, we then entered a financial crisis. We lost a third of our workforce and were under-resourced. Following this, external expectations about the Reform Agenda were huge. On top of that we had to cope with our "daily" business: outreach to fisheries and retailers, standards and policies, etc.

Howes focused on the following priority action points:

- **Governance and transparency**. An executive committee of the board was formed to support and oversee the CEO, Howes, who embarked on setting up face-to-face meetings with many NGOs and other stakeholders all over the world to improve communication and understanding of underlying issues.

- **Consistency and quality of fishery certifications.** In April 2004 a new fisheries certification methodology was released to ensure consistent interpretation of the MSC's environmental standards. It also included new requirements for local stakeholder consultation.

- **Environmental performance and sustainability.** To better back up its claim of certifying sustainable fisheries, Howes initiated research projects to investigate the environmental benefits of MSC certification. The MSC's advisory bodies reviewed the questioned sustainability claim and proposed that the Board of Trustees should maintain the MSC's sustainability claim. Howes was confident:

> We are trying to improve the long-term productivity of the marine environment and we do that by using a certification label program to create incentives for better environmental performance. It is a shame when things get polarized because of a definition issue, and when people don't look at the bigger issue of what we are trying to achieve. There is also a commercial aspect to this. We are a market program, not an advocacy group. The sustainability claim is important to anybody we speak to. We cannot say, "We are nearly sustainable."

●   **Financial stability and future growth.** Howes also concentrated on diversifying and securing the funding base.

Bluer Skies

At the beginning of 2005, after four years of assessment, the Bering Sea and Aleutian Islands Pollock Fishery—one of the world's biggest white fish fisheries—became certified. This fishery had had average annual landings of about 1.1 million metric tons for about 20 years and accounted for approximately 30% (by weight) of all fish landed in the US.

Throughout 2005, the MSC achieved a lot of momentum: It teamed up with Brakes, the largest supplier of school lunch meals in the UK, to bring sustainable seafood into school meal programs. Retail giant Tesco launched MSC products on its fresh fish counters. The list of MSC-certified fisheries was growing. At the beginning of 2006, 5% to 6% of the total wild edible capture groups were certified against the MSC standard. MSC-labeled products had steadily grown to over 300 (refer to Exhibit 5.4 for MSC-labeled products). For some of the most popular species groups, the ratio was considerable: 25% of prime white fish[4] and 33% of wild salmon carried the MSC logo. These numbers were quite significant when compared with the fact that organic food, for example, generally only accounted for 1% to 2% of total food sales worldwide.

The MSC had developed further in several areas: By this time, it was mainly financed by charitable grants (84%) and its independence was thus assured (refer to Exhibit 5.5

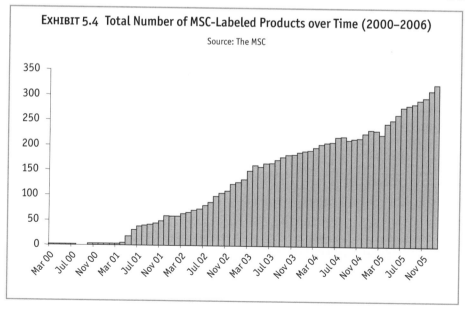

EXHIBIT 5.4 Total Number of MSC-Labeled Products over Time (2000–2006)

Source: The MSC

---

4   Oceanic deep-water fish, particularly cod, whiting, haddock, hake, and pollock.

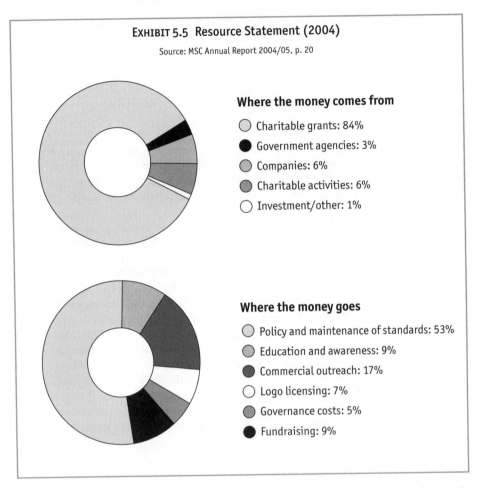

EXHIBIT 5.5 Resource Statement (2004)

Source: MSC Annual Report 2004/05, p. 20

Where the money comes from

○ Charitable grants: 84%

● Government agencies: 3%

◐ Companies: 6%

◑ Charitable activities: 6%

○ Investment/other: 1%

Where the money goes

○ Policy and maintenance of standards: 53%

◐ Education and awareness: 9%

◑ Commercial outreach: 17%

○ Logo licensing: 7%

◐ Governance costs: 5%

● Fundraising: 9%

for some financial facts). Its standard incorporated additional criteria (by then, 22), which were further broken down into performance indicators. The governance structure had been reviewed and changed (refer to Exhibit 5.6 for the governance structure): Besides the MSC board, it included a stakeholder council (40 self-selected members), a stakeholder council steering group (to strengthen the stakeholder council's effectiveness and ability to advise), an accreditation committee[5] that ratified accreditation decisions made by the MSC, and a technical advisory board to advise the main board on all relevant matters including the setup and review of the MSC standard. Howes remarked:

> The MSC puts more into its governance structure than any other organization I have worked for. We expanded again to a staff of over 25 people over the last 15 months. Our process is now incredibly transparent. Stakeholders are now involved from the very beginning. We have a strong stakeholder council and

5   Called the approvals committee in Exhibit 5.6.

EXHIBIT 5.6 MSC Governance Structure

Source: The MSC

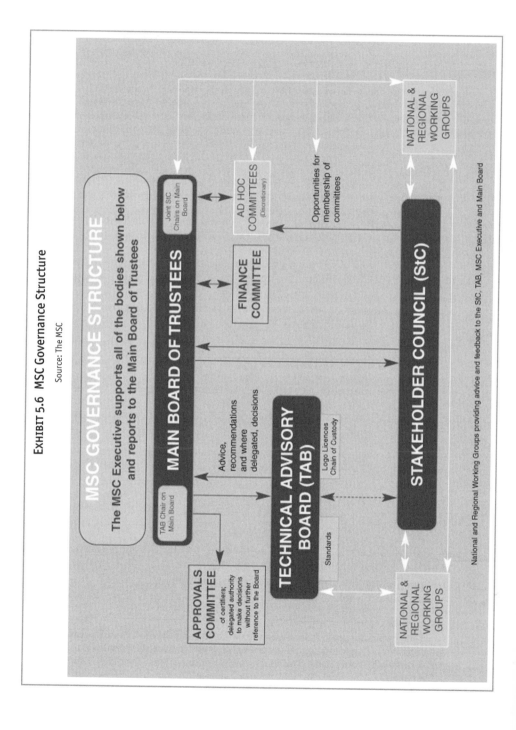

an experienced Technical Advisory Group. All these bodies are essential for maintaining credibility.

WWF was also pleased with the developments at MSC. Short remarked:

> It has been very useful that other major environmental NGOs such as Greenpeace have kept their critique of the MSC out of the public arena over recent years. The debate between the MSC, Greenpeace, other NGOs and the MSC's technical advisory body is very robust and has resulted in the MSC system being strengthened. This type of constructive criticism behind closed doors is critical whilst the MSC is still relatively young, to give it the opportunity to develop into a very rigorous standard. We all know that if this criticism were to get into the public domain it would damage the MSC and put at risk the potential for this fisheries eco-labeling program to really make a difference in the oceans. Clearly, if in the next five years there isn't a big change in the fisheries that are now being reassessed, then making the debate more public would be justifiable. But there have been so many learning opportunities in the first years . . . The current period is really the "make it or break it" test of all the lessons that have been learned.

In March 2005 the UN FAO issued guidelines on minimum requirements for marine eco-labeling and certification, pointing to several cornerstones such as independence, transparency and stakeholder engagement. The guidelines basically mirrored the MSC's principles. Howes saw this as a major opportunity for his organization, since any new serious guidelines would have to adopt criteria as demanding as those used by the MSC.

> The adoption of the FAO guidelines for eco-labeling sends out a message to the global industry. Anybody else who wanted to develop another label would have to realize that it would be a very hard thing to replicate our label.

Seeing that the MSC business model was working, Scandinavian governments and fisheries reduced their opposition. In February 2006 the first Norwegian fishery entered the assessment.

Challenges Ahead

In 2005 Unilever ascertained that 50% of its European fish business (accounting for 75% to 80% of its entire fish business) was MSC-certified and, according to Unilever's own assessment, another 10% was produced in a sustainable manner. However, the company had not been able to meet its initial goal (to source only from sustainable fisheries by 2005). According to Peters, there were two reasons for this:

> When we set our goal in 1996, we were optimistic that the MSC would certify a number of fisheries and that governments would change their fishing policies as well. Unfortunately, although this would have been desirable, it did not happen. Therefore the "flow" of raw material coming in from MSC-certified fisheries was less than all expected. However, I strongly believe that the big leap forward we made anyway would not have happened without the

ambitious commitment of our company and the personal dedication of our chairman.

In 2006 Unilever was still very much behind the idea of the MSC, as Peters underlined:

> We are convinced that only products from sustainable fish sources will be tradable in the long run. And those fisheries that want to stay in business with us and other companies committed to sustainability like we are need to become certified sooner or later.

The price pressure that food manufacturers were under could not be underestimated. By early 2006, Unilever's frozen fish business was under severe pressure mainly owing to competition from retailers' own brands. Consumers were increasingly showing preference for "chilled" as opposed to frozen food in supermarkets. The chilled food market was dominated by retailers and they could also produce frozen foods at cheaper prices than branded competitors. Unilever was finding it extremely difficult to grow its fish business and, by the end of 2005, had put the Bird's Eye and Findus frozen fish business under review. Other food processors, such as Heinz (John West), were having similar problems.

By March 2006, most of Unilever's fish business was also for sale, and it looked as if one of MSC's principal supporting stakeholders would soon no longer be a main player. Would the support from newly certified fisheries and Wal-Mart be able to compensate for this gap?

In addition, the MSC had to meet the following challenges:

- **Growth**. Howes expected various new products on the market in 2006. Additional funding was imperative to be able to keep up with the organization's success, e.g. to double the organization's human resources (primarily) by 2007.

- **Emergence of weaker labels**. For example, the Carrefour Group, leading distributor of seafood products in France, expanded its own "Responsible Fishing Code" in September 2005.

- **Frustration from retailers.** Some retailers that supported the MSC were not totally convinced of its ultimate effectiveness. For example, Gruber, from Migros, suggested that a further (or full) rollout of certified sustainable fishing would require involvement from governments.

    > Additional costs incur in the whole value chain which can only be realized with public support in the long run. There are many parties with different interests involved and there is the need for a superior instance to coordinate and pay. Governments can take on this role more easily than a private institution particularly as they already maintain relations with all parties.

- **Ongoing critique from NGOs.** There was still pressure from some conservation organizations. For Greenpeace's Lee-Harwood, 2006 was the "year of truth":

    > By the end of the year, we need to decide whether the reforms we are seeking have been achieved or whether they have not been achieved.

And then, we need to make a conclusion on how we wish to respond. In 2004 the MSC only issued a rough memo in response to the critique. We still have not received a detailed proposal about how they intend to implement the changes, which they intend to adopt and which changes to reject.

● **Consumer habits.** Price and taste took precedence over environmental concerns for most consumers. For example, in the UK, Unilever had begun to make fish fingers from MSC-certified hoki in 2002. They underestimated the entrenched strong preference for other species, such as cod, and finally—in 2005—abandoned their hoki products. This experience did not augur well for the long term in particular, since most of the favored fish species were in decline.

● **Paradoxical signals on stock availability.** Unilever had tried to keep the price of hoki similar to or even cheaper than cod. In 2005 competition between supermarkets on cod fish fingers had driven shelf prices in the UK down compared with hoki, the certified alternative. This undermined the credibility of the argument that cod stocks were in danger. Communicating the realities of declining fish stocks to consumers was a major challenge[6] and retailers balked at engaging in difficult and expensive marketing campaigns when supply was not yet assured.

*   *   *

In Howes' view, the depletion of fish stocks was the world's second largest environmental challenge after climate change. After putting down the phone, he reflected on his conversation with the chairman. He had spent more than 15 years working in NGOs, and from that experience he knew that there was still a long way to go. He began to jot down some notes capturing the weak spots they had just discussed.

Teaching notes for this case are available from Greenleaf Publishing. These are free of charge and are available only to teaching staff. They can be requested by going to:
http://www.greenleaf-publishing.com/oikos_notes

---

6   While cod was being fished out in the North Sea, for example, stocks were healthy off the coast of Iceland.

CASE 6
Purchasing Strategies and Sustainability
The Migros Palm Oil Case[1]

Jens Hamprecht   ***Daniel Corsten***

ETH Zurich, Switzerland   London Business School, UK

Section A: 1999–2001

Introduction

In the headquarters of Switzerland's largest retailer, Migros, a meeting room was booked on a long Friday night in April 2001. Fausta Borsani, the head of environmental and ethical projects at Migros, and Dr Robert Keller, a senior R&D manager, were pondering over the further pursuit of the project they had initiated almost two years ago: purchasing sustainable palm oil for Migros' products. Previously, Migros had already succeeded in many project phases. It had ensured the support of a major NGO. Jointly, they had established draft criteria for sustainable palm oil. First talks with suppliers had already taken place, too. Now, the NGO recommended to have a second NGO join the project. Was this an advice Migros should follow? Wouldn't it render the entire project too complicated? Moreover, how should Migros communicate its palm oil project to the public? How to ensure that not only the environment but also Migros benefited from the project? The Migros board had already invested significant sums. By Monday morning, it demanded to be informed on the further project steps.

How the project had begun

During a short lunch break on November 10th, 1999, Dr Robert Keller was scanning the newspaper headlines. He had only few minutes left prior to a meeting with his senior R&D staff at the MIFA AG, Migros' manufacturer of fats and detergents. Yet, when Keller was about to put the newspaper aside, he noticed an article that struck his interest.

In this article, Andreas Bänziger, a journalist researching news for the *Tages Anzeiger* in Asia, reported on the hardship of the native people of Borneo, the Penen people. The journalist wrote:

> Back in 1881, the Norwegian scientist and adventurer Carl Bock still described Borneo as an island that the monkeys could traverse by swinging from tree to tree, without ever placing a foot on the ground. Today, however, the native people of Borneo note that the monkeys have changed their habits. Rather than swinging from treetop to treetop, they now walk on the ground.

> Who or what is to blame for this change? Certainly "the company", the corporation with the licence to clear 700 000 hectares of rain forest in Borneo, an area equalling one sixth of the area of Switzerland. [ ].

> For months, the Penan have tried to stop the encroachment of the bulldozers, they have tried to fight for their right of living in the forest—until they were chased away by the police with teargas.[2]

Yet, as the journalist further explained, placing the blame on the timber industry and its global customers only meant taking a myopic stance. There was a second player whose resource demands continued to threaten the rainforest: the palm oil industry. Large producers of palm oil awaited the clearing of the rainforest by "the company," then bought the ground and set up palm tree plantations. This link between palm oil plantations and deforestation of the rainforest, however, was largely unknown in Europe. Thus, the journalist further wrote:

> The unsuspecting consumers are in Europe. The very same environmentally conscious citizens who demand an import boycott of tropic woods originating from an unsustainable production enjoy the rainforest for breakfast. They put it on their lips and use it for keeping their hands tender.

Dr Keller quickly understood the allusion of this closing sentence. Holding a PhD in chemical engineering, he was very well aware of the various uses of palm oil. At the MIFA AG, where he headed the Research & Development department, palm oil was used for the manufacturing of various products, including margarine. Other Migros-owned factories made use of palm oil in cosmetics products. However, while Keller was

---

2   Bänziger, A. 1999. Statt Tropenholz liefert Borneo Margarine. *Tages Anzeiger*. November 22.

an expert in the industrial applications of palm oil, the *ecological problems* associated with the production of this raw material were new to him.[3]

Robert Keller took the article aside and prepared for the R&D meeting. Yet he was unsettled by the news. How would the Swiss consumers respond to such an article? Could it put the reputation of the retailer Migros at risk? After all, Switzerland's largest retailer wholly owned the MIFA AG.

Migros

Migros was founded as a cooperative by Gottlieb Duttweiler in 1925. At that time, a significant share of the Swiss working class was suffering from malnutrition. Duttweiler envisioned providing the market with products that would be more affordable. Given that Migros' retail prices were substantially below the market average, the consumer goods industry initially refused to deliver products to Migros. Duttweiler therefore set up his own factories, supplying the retail outlets with fresh food products, packaged food, as well as cosmetics articles, and washing powder.

Today, nine out of ten products sold by the retailer are manufactured by its own factories.[4] The business is still structured as a cooperative, cf. Exhibit 6.1. In its mission statement, Migros continues to highlight that it seeks to take on a role model in the management of social and ecological issues. The orange "M" symbolizing Migros (see Exhibit 6.2) is commonly judged as the most popular brand in Switzerland.[5] Migros prints a weekly magazine (*Migrosmagazin*) which is distributed free of charge to all 1.96 m members of the Migros cooperative. The magazine thus reaches about 27% of the Swiss population.

With revenues of about 20bn Swiss Francs and 81.600 employees (2003) the cooperative is the largest retailer operating in Switzerland. Retailing makes up 70% of Migros' business today. While maintaining its focus on the Swiss market, it has particularly diversified into consumer markets such as petrol stations ("Migrol") and travel agencies ("Hotelplan"); cf. Exhibit 6.3.

The MIFA AG, one of the 16 Migros-owned manufacturers, employs about 300 people; cf. Exhibit 6.4. Its revenues of CHF 167 m (2003), make it Switzerland's largest producer of washing agents and margarines. Activities of MIFA and the other factories are supervised by a board member of Migros.

Migros' market in Switzerland is characterized by affluent consumers valuing fair trade and protection of the environment.[6] Migros and it main competitor Coop enjoy significant market shares, jointly they account for over 50% of food retailing in Switzerland. Following the market entry of Lidl and Aldi in 2005, the retailers will need to defend these market shares.

---

3   Studer, R. 2003. Interview with Dr Robert Keller. Nachhaltigkeitsmarketing am Beispiel Palmöl. University of St Gallen.

4   Migros 2005. Die Industriebrochüre. http://www.migros.ch/Migros_DE/Content/UeberMigros/MigrosKonzern, retrieved on August 2nd, 2005.

5   Wiegand, M. 2005. Schweizer planen Abwehrkampf gegen Aldi. *Financial Times Deutschland*. June 28.

6   Euromonitor 2004. Retailing in Switzerland. Market analysis.

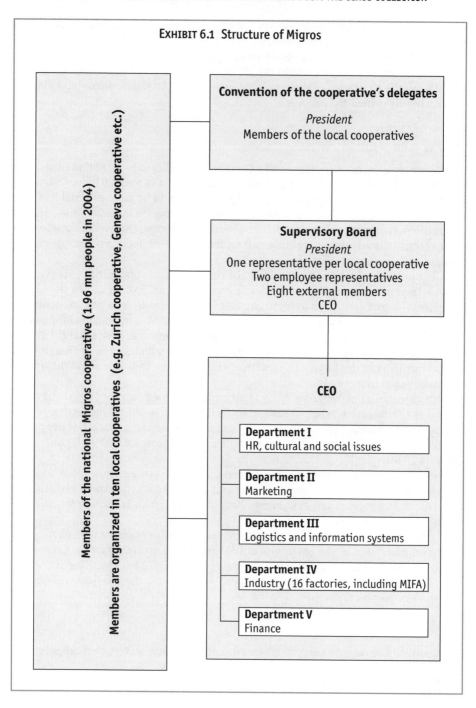

EXHIBIT 6.1 Structure of Migros

EXHIBIT 6.2 Migros M

The orange M of Migros. The painting (oil on canvas) is titled "M". In this artwork, on display in the Migrosmuseum Zürich since 1986, the Swiss artist Jean-Frédéric Schnyder has embedded the retailer's logo in a green background.

Palm Oil

At Migros, palm oil is primarily processed by the MIFA AG and the retailer's bakery, Jowa. For the global consumer goods industry, palm oil is the second most important vegetable oil, second only to soybean oil. Worldwide, the production of palm oil reached 31.6 million metric tonnes in 2004; cf. Exhibit 6.5. The commodity thus made up a 30% share of the worldwide production of vegetable oils.

Palm fruits provide the basis for two different types of oil: palm oil and palm kernel oil. The palm trees grow in tropic regions. Malaysia and Indonesia alone account for 80% of the global palm oil production. The production costs for palm oil vary from country to country but Indonesia is typically regarded as the lowest-cost producer. Direct economic comparisons of palm oil with soybean oil are not straightforward as the oil of soybeans only is a byproduct of soybeans prepared for meals. The production costs for producing soybean oil are about 50% above those for producing palm oil.[7] The extent to which palm oil contributes to deforestation is subject of an academic debate, the social relevance of palm oil plantations, however, is rarely challenged; cf. Exhibit 6.6.

Migros responds to the newspaper article

Returning from the R&D meeting, Robert Keller researched further on the palm oil story. He learned that throughout 1997, vast, uncontrolled fires had swept through the rainforests of Indonesia and Malaysia. There was evidence that these fires had been

7   Corley, R. 2003. Oil palm: a major tropical crop. Burotrop. February.

EXHIBIT 6.3 Migros Key Figures 2003

Figures in Swiss Francs (millions)

Sources: Migros Annual Report 2004

Revenues	20,013
Revenues (Retailing)	14,298
EBITDA	1,290
EBIT	484
Earnings	372
Cashflow	1,005
Free Cashflow	-162
Investments	1,319
Total Assets	16,588
Equity Capital	8,394
Employees	81,600

Net revenues of Migros by business sector

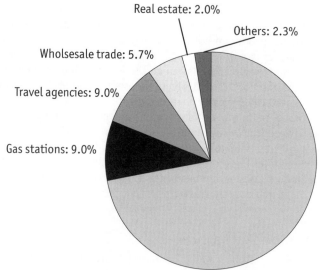

Real estate: 2.0%

Others: 2.3%

Wholsesale trade: 5.7%

Travel agencies: 9.0%

Gas stations: 9.0%

Retail business: 72.0%

Exhibit 6.4 MIFA Key Figures 2003

CHF = Swiss Francs

Source: Migros Annual Report 2004

Net Revenues (m CHF)	167
thereof Migros outlets (m CHF)	143
thereof national customers (m CHF)	1.8
thereof export (m CHF)	22.1
Assortment (products)	272
No. of innovations (products)	108
Employees	315

Exhibit 6.5 Relevance of Palm Oil

Source: Palm World Annual 2004

World Vegetable Oil Consumption 2004

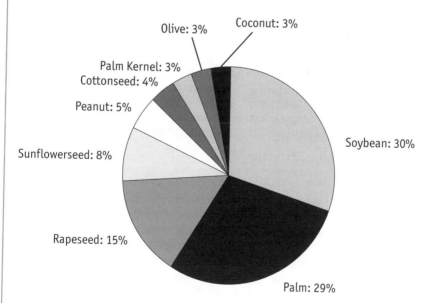

Olive: 3%
Coconut: 3%
Palm Kernel: 3%
Cottonseed: 4%
Peanut: 5%
Sunflowerseed: 8%
Soybean: 30%
Rapeseed: 15%
Palm: 29%

Worldwide, palm oil is the second most important vegetable oil. Taken together, palm oil and palm kernel oil (both gained from the same plant) are even more important for the consumer goods industry than soybean oil.

Exhibit 6.6 Sustainability of Palm Oil Production

RHV Corley, a consultant in plantation crops, characterizes the importance of palm oil in sustainable development as follows:[8]

> In recent years various pressure groups have targeted the palm oil industry as responsible for a major part of the destruction of tropical forests. For example, the WWF recently stated on its web-site that "WWF research shows that together with illegal logging, forest conversion to palm oil is now the major threat to tropical rainforests in Indonesia". Such claims do not stand up to rational scrutiny, though.
>
> - In 1993, FAO estimated that 1.2 Mha of forest was being cleared annually in Indonesia; at that time, the oil palm area was expanding by less than 100 000 ha/year.
> - Over the last twenty years, the oil palm area has increased by about 2.5 Mha, equivalent to about 2% of the total forest area in Indonesia (based on the National Forest Inventory, 1996).
>
> It is clear from these figures that palm oil cannot be classed as a "major threat" to the Indonesian forest. It has been postulated that the demand for palm oil would double by 2020. If yields remain the same, this would require the present global area under palm oil of 6.5 Mha to be doubled. This possible expansion amounts to less than 3% of the expected forest loss. [. . .]
>
> It is important not to lose sight of the fact that a perennial crop such as the oil palm can play a key role in sustainable development in many parts of the tropics. Because it is highly productive, oil palm can provide a family with a decent living from a smaller area of land than most other crops. [In Indonesia, it has been found that subsistence cultivation requires] about 37 ha per household of agricultural land and managed forest. [. . .] By contrast, an oil plantation employs about one worker per 8 ha, so 8 ha of intensively managed oil palms will comfortably support the worker and his family (and make a profit for his employer).

fuelled by corporations that had bought licences for crop cultivation in the pristine rainforests.[9,10] In response, WWF International had triggered a pilot campaign in Europe. Robert Keller realized that WWF Switzerland had set up a webpage in the spring of 1998, already.[11] Designed as an information platform, this website provided the Swiss consumers with information on how they could approach retailers and manufacturers for demanding a certified origin of palm oil. To Robert Keller, it only appeared as a matter of time until this internet platform, in combination with the cov-

8 Corley, R. 2003. Oil palm: a major tropical crop. Burotrop. February.
9 Aditjondro, G. 2000. The Driving Force of Indonesia's Catastrophic Forest Fires. *Eco-Politics Journal*, 1(1): 1-7.
10 Gittngs, J. 1997. Smoke to choke Asia for months. *The Guardian*. September 23.
11 http://www.checkyouroil.org, retrieved on April 21, 2005.

erage in the *Tages Anzeiger*, would fuel inquiries of Migros' consumers regarding the provenance of the retailer's palm oil.

Robert Keller felt compelled to respond. Eleven days after the publication of the article in the *Tages Anzeiger*, he submitted a letter to the editor of the newspaper.[12] While acknowledging that the article on Borneo had addressed an issue of vital importance, Keller pointed out that the palm oil exports to European consumer goods manufacturers did not contribute significantly to the ongoing deforestation of the rainforest. He wrote in his letter to the editor:

> European consumption [of palm oil] only accounts for a small share of the global palm oil demands. In fact, the European consumption of vegetable oils, such as palm oil and palm kernel oil, has dropped throughout the last years.[13]

Nevertheless, while the above statement helped Migros to calm things down, the question remained whether a defensive approach was appropriate as the long-term strategy for answering demands for sustainable palm oil supply chains. Reflecting on this strategic choice, Keller says:

> We had two alternatives at hand: either to pursuit a defensive strategy or to get active. We decided to choose the latter.[14]

Keller had already provided a hint of the pursuit of the "active approach" in his letter to the *Tages Anzeiger* in 1999. In the closing line, he indicated:

> The destruction of the rainforest can only be averted by utilizing [its resources] in a sustainable manner. The cultivation of palm oil must be allowed. Nevertheless, we require more sustainable cultivation methods.[15]

Yet what where those "more sustainable" cultivation methods? How should Migros pursue the "active approach" of changing its current palm supplies? Keller recalls the situation as follows:

> At that time, it was clear that MIFA did not intend to boycott palm oil as a raw material since it represents a vital source of income for the producing countries. Furthermore, a boycott by MIFA or even by the entire Swiss consumer goods industry would not make a difference. The total palm oil imports to Switzerland only add up to 10,000 tons annually—a small figure in comparison to the 23 million tons of annual palm oil production worldwide.[16]

Clearly, Migros was looking for another solution than a boycott of palm oil.

12   Keller, R. 1999. Nicht Palmölexport gefährdet Tropenholz. *Tages Anzeiger*. November 22.
13   Ibid.
14   Studer, R. 2003. Interview with Dr Robert Keller. Nachhaltigkeitsmarketing am Beispiel Palmöl. University of St Gallen.
15   Keller, R. 1999. Nicht Palmölexport gefährdet Tropenholz. *Tages Anzeiger*. November 22.
16   Studer, R. 2003. Interview with Dr Robert Keller. Nachhaltigkeitsmarketing am Beispiel Palmöl. University of St Gallen.

Migros searches for a non-governmental organization (NGO) as a partner

In the *Tages Anzeiger* article, the journalist had mentioned the Bruno Manser Fonds, a Swiss non-governmental organization. The founder of this NGO had been living with the Penans and had supported their interests. Peter Keller decided to contact this NGO in order to explore the options of Migros in sourcing sustainable palm oil. This contact, however, did not result in a long-term collaboration.

Yet Migros did want to collaborate with an external partner in addressing the palm oil problem. As Fausta Borsani notes:

> The way we commonly work at Migros [regarding issues of sustainability] is that we identify a problem or an issue, then we identify partners to address the problem, we build up trust, experience, and a partnership.[17]

Collaboration with an external partner clearly was in line with Migros' culture. Yet which party other than the Bruno Manser Fonds could support Migros in this context? Peter Keller contacted managers at Migros who regularly worked on issues regarding sustainability. He learnt that Migros had been collaborating closely with the World Wide Fund (WWF) since 1997, when Migros began purchasing wood products certified by the Forest Stewardship Council. Back then, Migros had been a founding member of the WWF Wood Group Switzerland.[18]

Migros thus contacted the WWF Switzerland in early 2000 in order to explore the possibility of a partnership for the creation of a sustainable palm oil supply chain. By establishing contact with the WWF, Migros entered discussions with a partner that was highly respected in Swiss society. WWF International is based in Switzerland. In the past, the top managers of the WWF have frequently had Swiss nationality.

Developing a sustainable palm oil supply chain

On May 11th, 2000, a first meeting of Migros and WWF managers was held in Zurich.[19] Robert Keller of Migros was joined by Willi Eisele, Migros' purchasing manager for vegetable oils, and Andrea Ries, a member of the board of WWF Switzerland.

Prior to the meeting, Willi Eisele and Robert Keller felt slightly uneasy. They did not really know whether Migros and WWF Switzerland could find a common understanding of the palm oil problem. Robert Keller describes these feelings as follows:

> [If you are not experienced in working with NGOs], then you tend to think of them as organizations that fight the industry and its supporting lobbies.[20]

---

17   Interview with Fausta Borsani. February 18, 2005.
18   http://www.miosphere.ch/d/newsapp/index.php3?id=308, retrieved on April 22, 2005.
19   Meeting protocol of Migros. May 11, 2000.
20   Studer, R. 2003. Interview with Dr Robert Keller. Nachhaltigkeitsmarketing am Beispiel Palmöl. University of St Gallen.

Were these judgements justified? Would WWF Switzerland indeed take a confrontational posture during the meeting with Migros? As the meeting took off, the concerns quickly vanished. The Migros managers learnt from the WWF that no NGO had developed criteria regarding the certification of sustainable palm oil to that date. In the meeting, the WWF openly acknowledged that no NGO really was in a position to tell the industry *how* they should cultivate palm trees in order to ensure their sustainability. A standard for the purchasing of palm oil (similar to the well-known Forest Stewardship Council) still had to be designed.

Robert Keller and Willi Eisele became interested in collaborating with the WWF on the palm oil issue. They agreed on another meeting with WWF's Andrea Ries in July 2000—this time the meeting was to be held in the offices of the WWF. The relief and the confidence that Migros' managers felt after the meeting of May 11th, 2000 can be grasped in the meeting protocol of Migros. Summarizing the outcome of the meeting, Migros' managers noted:

> We were surprised how cooperative the WWF is. They are seeking for a solution, they want to achieve a change, and they are not interested in a confrontation.

Motivated by the outcome of the first meeting, Robert Keller and Willi Eisele requested from Migros' senior management the go ahead for collaboration on a joint project on sustainable purchasing of palm oil with the WWF.

In this very period, Migros also was in the process of redesigning the organization as well as the communication of its efforts in the management of social and environmental issues. On May 9th, 2000, Migros had launched the miosphere.ch webpage, a central access point for information on the retailer's social and environmental projects.[21] A position for a head of environmental and ethical projects had been set up in the Corporate Communications department. Fausta Borsani, who was an agricultural engineer by training, gained the appointment to this position. Fausta Borsani brought along extensive experience in the work of NGOs. Prior to joining Migros, she had worked for five years for the Stiftung für Konsumentenschutz, a Swiss NGO advocating consumer rights. Thus, she was very experienced in the culture and strategy of NGOs.

Fausta Borsani, Peter Keller, and Willi Eisele formed the team for the palm oil project. Their skills seemed to fit one another perfectly. Keller provided the long-term experience in senior management and R&D at Migros, Willi Eisele was knowledgeable about the palm oil purchases of Migros, and Fausta Borsani had a very good understanding of the thinking of NGOs.

Internally, the team gained support from the Marketing department for collaboration with the WWF. On July 4th, 2000, in a meeting with the WWF, Robert Keller officially confirmed to Andrea Ries that Migros' senior management had approved the collaboration with the WWF. Following the meeting, Andrea Ries began to inform her peers on the boards of other WWF country groups that a joint project on palm oil was initiated in Switzerland. For Andrea Ries and her colleagues, the Swiss market was to be become a test-market for the implementation of a global standard for sustainable purchasing of palm oil.

---

21   The webpage was later renamed engagement.ch.

Migros' members of the palm oil team devised a budget for the single project phases, including the development of the criteria and the identification of suppliers. The development of the criteria then dominated the work of Migros and the WWF throughout the following months. It was a very challenging process as the criteria ultimately had to be applicable and relevant to the palm oil production in several countries. As no standards on sustainable palm oil production existed worldwide, the project members had to consult various sources to develop an integral standard.

Still, by early November 2000, Migros and the WWF had jointly established a draft list of seven criteria for palm oil production. Now, the viability of these criteria had to be assessed in practice. Migros thus asked its two palm oil suppliers to join Migros and the WWF in their next meeting.

Migros negotiates prices for sustainable palm oil with its suppliers

Migros first invited both of its palm oil suppliers at the same time and asked them whether they could adhere to the criteria for sustainable palm oil production. Both suppliers suggested that they could, but they calculated that they would need to raise their prices for a ton of palm oil by 30%.[22,23]

Given these figures, Migros noted that it might simply be too costly to purchase palm oil complying with all seven criteria from the outset. Fausta Borsani said that

> [our] objective has to be to render palm oil sourcing more socially and environmentally responsible while keep it affordable (thus: sustainable).[24]

In order to facilitate further price negotiations, Migros decided to conduct the subsequent talks with the two suppliers separately. Furthermore, the second tiers, the owners of palm oil plantations, were directly included in these talks.

On a business fair in Nuremberg on February 16th, 2001, Fausta Borsani thus had a meeting with one of the palm oil suppliers as well as the second tier, two brothers owning a palm oil plantation in Colombia. Fausta Borsani told the brothers that Migros would be willing to pay a surcharge for palm oil from their plantation even though the cultivation methods of the brothers did not fulfill all seven criteria, yet. In exchange for the surcharge, the brothers agreed to achieve an alignment of their operations to all seven criteria within the next three years. However, it was agreed that once the plantation of the brothers would fulfill all criteria, no further surcharge would arise to Migros.

Based on this business model, the three parties could agree on a surcharge that was already significantly smaller: thereof, the brothers were granted a 65% share. The remaining 35% of the surcharge resulted from increased logistics costs as the "sustainable" palm oil had to be separated from the produce of other plantations during transport and storage. Similar supply contracts were subsequently established with Migros' second palm oil supplier and plantations in Ghana and Brazil.

---

22   Meeting protocol of Migros. November 16, 2000.
23   Meeting protocol of Migros. December 14, 2000.
24   Meeting protocol of Migros. February 16, 2001.

Migros minimizes the costs for purchasing sustainable palm oil

At $230, the overall surcharge had now been lowered to a range that was more tolerable for Migros. As Migros had no intent to lower its margins, the retailer began to pursuit two strategies to balance the increased purchasing costs.[25]

First, Migros raised the prices of margarine manufactured by MIFA. Hereby, care was taken to maintain price leadership. Consequently, the price of some product groups was raised significantly while the price of other margarine products was maintained, depending on the price gap between Migros products and those of competitors.

Second, Migros drew on the Research & Development skills of its food engineers and redesigned several product recipes. Wherever possible, palm oil was being replaced by sunflower oil. Yet great care had to be taken as sunflower oil demands different processing technologies than palm oil. Because sunflower oil needs to be hardened for processing in food products it could not substitute all palm oil supplies to Migros.

These steps allowed Migros to reduce its purchasing volume of palm oil by one-third. Nevertheless, the extra costs for purchasing sustainable palm oil were still significant. The product demanded separate handling on the plantations and along the supply chain. In a retailing environment increasingly threatened by the market entry of low-cost retailers, this was an unnerving thought. In the long run, it was unpredictable whether Migros could afford to pay surcharges that did not occur to other food manufacturers.[26]

The Migros board expected to be informed how the costs for purchasing sustainable palm oil could be further reduced in subsequent years. Hence, Fausta Borsani and Dr Robert Keller were pondering whether they should improve the economies of scale in the palm oil supply chain and include further industry players in the project. While it would help them to reduce the costs, it might put Migros' potential differentiation with the palm oil project in question.

The decision was complicated by a request the WWF had made in a meeting this morning. The WWF suggested that an independent assessor should join the palm oil project to control that palm oil producers were complying with the new standard. The WWF did not have the resources to take on this responsibility. Fausta Borsani and Dr Robert Keller now had to decide whether assessment by another NGO was in the interest of Migros. While the expected extra costs seemed acceptable, Migros had to consider whether it sought this additional collaboration.

In summary, Fausta Borsani and Dr Robert Keller had to consider whether they should include further partners in the project. By Monday morning, the two Migros managers had to present the further pursuit of the project to the Migros board. By then, they also needed to make propositions on how to communicate the project to the Swiss market. The time was pressing. It was unknown whether Migros' main competitor in the Swiss market had already identified the palm oil issue as well and whether he was about to launch a similar project.

---

25   Studer, R. 2003. Interview with Fausta Borsani. Nachhaltigkeitsmarketing am Beispiel Palmöl. University of St Gallen.
26   Studer, R. 2003. Interview with Dr Robert Keller. Nachhaltigkeitsmarketing am Beispiel Palmöl. University of St Gallen.

Section B: 2001–2005

Collaborating with an independent assessor

Migros agreed to have an independent assessor control the compliance with the new palm oil production standard. This approach was pursuit as Migros sought to ensure that its project could not be criticized as "greenwashing" by competitors, NGOs, or journalists. Furthermore, ensuring a critical control of ecological and social aspects was well in line with Migros mission. Fausta Borsani pointed out that

> . . . at Migros, we do not engage in ethical projects for the sake of publicity; instead we get active, because we want to have a good conscience.[27]

Hence, Migros gave the WWF the go-ahead to identify an independent assessor. With the help of WWF UK, a suitable assessor, the Oxford based NGO Proforest, could be gained as an assessor of the palm oil plantations. By July 2001, MIFA could order the first supplies of sustainable palm oil that had been assessed by Proforest.

Communicating Migros' project

Migros followed three major approaches in communicating the palm oil project to the public. First, Migros granted the WWF and other NGOs permission to present its palm oil project as a role model for other businesses and to demonstrate its leadership role in the issue:

On April 6th, 2001, the WWF informed Migros on the plan of three global NGOs (the WWF, Greenpeace, and Friends of the Earth) to conduct a joint campaign on the deforestation of the rainforests.[28] One focus of that campaign was the role of palm oil in the "life cycle of deforestation". Two further foci were placed on the link between paper production and deforestation and the "role of the Swiss banks in financing the ongoing deforestation".[29]

While some Swiss businesses were soon to find themselves the target of that campaign, the Migros project could be presented as a best-practice example. Thus, while the campaign raised the pressure on Migros' competitors, it increased the strategic value of Migros' new palm oil purchasing policy.

From the start of the campaign of the three NGOs onwards, Migros' palm oil project gained widespread acknowledgement. The praise that Migros earned for the project culminated in an award that the retailer received at the Johannesburg Summit of the United Nations in August 2002.

27   Interview with Fausta Borsani. February 18, 2005.
28   Meeting protocol of Migros. April 6, 2001.
29   Ibid.

Backed by the public recognition that Migros now enjoyed for the palm oil project, Migros engaged in a second, more active approach to communicating the project: it reported about it in its own media.

To illustrate, in its annual report 2002, Migros published the account of a journey to the palm oil plantation in Ghana that was now supplying Migros. In the introductory paragraph of this account, the author first established the linkage between palm tree cultivation and the threat of deforestation in simple words; cf. the right-hand side of Exhibit 6.7. That article was structured in a similar manner as the *Tages Anzeiger* article from 1999; cf. the left-hand side of Exhibit 6.7. and p. 1.

EXHIBIT 6.7 A Comparison of Two Texts[30,31]

Tages Anzeiger article, 1999	Migros annual report, 2002
The very same environmentally conscious citizens who demand an import boycott of tropic woods originating from an unsustainable production enjoy the rainforest for breakfast. They put it on their lips and use it for keeping their hands tender. ...	We brush our teeth and the Orang-Utan dies. We enjoy an ice cream for dessert and the Sumatra-tiger is deprived of his habitat. We rub cream onto our skin and lead elephants and rhinoceros to misery...

In the following paragraphs, however, Migros' annual report did not only amplify the demands that the *Tages Anzeiger* article had raised. Migros also changed the nature of these demands since it added in its annual report how vital palm oil was for the entire consumer goods industry. Further articles in the *Migrosmagazin* also underlined that a sustainable purchasing of palm oil was morally desirable while a boycott of palm oil could not be a solution. Hence, one article in the Migrosmagazin cited workers on a plantation that supplies Migros as saying "without the palm oil plantation we would starve".[32]

Despite the campaign of the three global NGOs and the articles in Migros' own media, Fausta Borsani was well aware that any reputational advantage of Migros could only be short-lived as "people easily forget".[33]

Thus, it was agreed that a national poster campaign would follow. That poster Migros represented Migros' third major approach in communicating the project.

The poster was designed to educate the public. It showed a picture of a cake in front of a rainforest. A large writing on the cake said: "why your dessert protects the rainforest" (Exhibit 6.8). The text underneath explained that palm oil production presented a threat to the rainforest and that Migros margarine did not foster this problem. Dr Robert Keller says that it was also essential to mention the collaboration with the WWF on the posters:

30 Left-hand side of the table: Bänziger, A. 1999. Statt Tropenholz liefert Borneo Margarine. *Tages Anzeiger*. November 22.
31 Right-hand side of the table: *Migros Jahresbericht* 2002: 118.
32 Migros Brückenbauer 2002. January 21: 35.
33 Interview with Fausta Borsani. February 18, 2005.

EXHIBIT 6.8 The Swiss Poster Campaign on Migros' Palm Oil Project

Source: Migros

Being seen as the partner of the WWF is worth gold if you are talking about the credibility of such a project.[34]

Developing a global standard

With the approaches described above, Migros was acknowledged as the pioneer in purchasing sustainable palm oil. Following the award by the UN, the communication of the project in Migros' media and the national poster campaign, efforts focused on gaining the support of further industry partners. Migros sought to develop an industry standard that would be globally applicable. As Fausta Borsani put it:

Ten years from now, a sustainable production of palm oil should be business as usual. We want to achieve a worldwide change of the palm oil production.[35]

Migros investigated several opportunities for letting sustainable palm oil become "business as usual". In early 2003, Willi Eisele, Migros' purchasing manager for palm oil, began to contact Swiss food manufacturers in order to discuss joint palm oil supplies. Furthermore, he and Dr Robert Keller contacted Swiss industry organizations in order to suggest that their members jointly purchase sustainable palm oil, too.[36] On an international scale, Migros ensured that the sustainability of palm oil was put on the agenda of businesses and federations. Today, Migros is still "striving to win over other processors or producers of palm oil within the Food Business Forum, an independent global food business network, whose current chairman is Claude Hanser, the President of the Migros Board of Management."[37]

However, Migros' key strategy for developing an industry standard for sustainable palm oil remains the "Round Table on Sustainable Palm Oil" (RSPO).

Development of the Round Table on Sustainable Palm Oil (RSPO)

In the summer of 2002, the WWF and Migros began preparations for an international roundtable of organizations interested in developing an industry standard. While both Migros and the WWF approached potential partners on an individual base as well as on conferences, care was taken not to let the preparatory roundtable appear as an event staged by Migros and the WWF. Instead, the roundtable was set up by an independent

---

34   Studer, R. 2003. Interview with Dr Robert Keller. Nachhaltigkeitsmarketing am Beispiel Palmöl. University of St Gallen.
35   Interview with Fausta Borsani. February 18, 2005.
36   Meeting protocol of Migros. February 6, 2003.
37   RSPO Annual Announcement of Progress, April 5, 2005, http://www.sustainable-palmoil.org.

EXHIBIT 6.9 RSPO Members

Source: www.rspo.org

Roundtable on Sustainable Palm Oil

- Migros
- Cadbury Schweppes
- Ferrero
- Unilever
- Danisco
- Nutriswiss
- Fuji Oil
- The Body Shop
- Rabobank

The exhibit shows some of the 68 members of the Roundtable on Sustainable Palm Oil. RSPO is further supported by social advocacy NGOs such as Oxfam as well as NGOs advocating ecological issues, e.g. WWF.

consultant, Reinier de Man, who also succeeded in gaining the support of Unilever, a major trader (Cargill) and a bank (Rabobank). These "new players" held joint meetings with WWF Switzerland, ProForest and Migros in September and December 2002. On these occasions, the logos of WWF and Migros did not appear prominently. The two organizations did not suggest that they had already developed the one standard that all other companies should now adopt, too. Instead, Migros simply presented its palm oil project, its standards, and the experiences it had gained to date.[38] Following the proposal of Reinier de Man, the participants of the preparatory round table agreed that the first meeting of an international roundtable should take place in August 2003. That round table was also to include governmental bodies, palm oil producers and traders, as well as further NGOs, retailers, and manufacturers. Two working groups were set up for the preparation of this roundtable. In both working groups, Dr Ruth Nussbaum from ProForest took on the role of an expert advisor.[39] An organizing committee was set up to supervise the work of the roundtable. Fausta Borsani of Migros was elected as its treasurer.

In the following months, the parties succeeded in inviting participants from several dozen organizations to the meetings of the RSPO. Each member of the roundtable supported these multiplication efforts.[40] Hence, Migros agreed to contact banks in Switzerland as the retailer enjoyed good relations with them.[41]

---

38 Meeting protocol of the Round Table on Sustainable Palm Oil. September 20, 2002, http://www.sustainable-palmoil.org.

39 Meeting protocol of the Round Table on Sustainable Palm Oil. December 17, 2002, http://www.sustainable-palmoil.org.

40 By May 2005, RSPO comprised 59 ordinary members and 20 affiliate members.

41 Meeting protocol of the Round Table on Sustainable Palm Oil. January 19, 2004, http://www.sustainable-palmoil.org.

Exhibit 6.10 Coop Switzerland

With revenues of 14 bn Swiss Francs in 2004, Coop Switzerland is the second largest retailer in Switzerland. In 2004, the retailer generated a Cashflow (EBITDA) of 1.17 bn Swiss Francs and earnings of 300 mn Swiss Francs. Of the retailer's total revenues, 69% are generated in the traditional retail segment. The other revenues are generated by Coop's DIY outlets, petrol stations and a chain offering consumer electronics. In total, the retailer employs 47.000 people.

Like Migros, Coop is structured as a cooperative. It publishes a weekly journal, *Coop Zeitung*, which is distributed to the 2.3 million members of the cooperative. In the governing structure of Coop, the members of the cooperative are represented in the convention of the cooperative's delegates. This convention complements the supervisory board and the board (as shown in Exhibit 6.1).

While Migros focuses on selling private-label products, Coop offers a larger variety of branded products. On average, the branded products of Coop are 15% more expensive than the private-label products of Migros. Unlike Migros, Coop offers alcoholic beverages and cigarettes, two product groups that Migros traditionally does not sell. Coop prides itself with being a leader in the management of ecological and social issues, too. For example, throughout 2004, Coop only offered Fair Trade bananas in its stores. Migros, however, continued to offer both Fair Trade bananas as well as bananas made by mainstream producers.

On the first meeting of the RSPO in Kuala Lumpur on August 21st–22nd, 2003, a letter of intent was signed by the representatives of numerous stakeholder groups.

Fausta Borsani recalls how she was struck by the reputation that Migros enjoys. When she first met "new" participants of the RSPO in Kuala Lumpur, people typically did not have a precise idea of where Switzerland was on the globe; "Migros" and "Migros criteria", however, were notions that were familiar to them.[42]

Fausta Borsani thought it very helpful that Migros had already gained experience in purchasing sustainable palm oil when engaging in talks with other businesses at the RSPO. Due to Migros' experiences, she was in a position to tell other managers that

> [products manufactured with sustainable palm oil] are in our stores, now. We are not talking about possibilities but reality instead.
>
> In general, I think it is *very* important to demonstrate the feasibility of our propositions. You cannot keep talks [of the roundtable] on an abstract level. You need to demonstrate that [your propositions] can be realized.[43] (Emphasis in original)

Still, Fausta Borsani underlines that the work of the RSPO is based on consensus. All participants have to agree on the wordings of the criteria and any comment needs to be considered.[44] Indeed, the comments concerning a first draft of the criteria for sustainable palm oil production have been numerous to date, thus hinting to the accep-

42   Interview with Fausta Borsani. February 18, 2005.
43   Ibid.
44   Ibid.

tance of the RSPO as a legitimate institution. In January 2005, the participants of the RSPO posted a first draft of the criteria on the webpage of the roundtable. Over 800 comments regarding this draft were received throughout the following weeks. The participants of the roundtable considered each of these in turn, deciding either to ignore the comment or to change the draft accordingly.

Throughout 2005, hundreds of comments regarding the draft of the criteria have been considered. On November 23rd, 2005, the members of the Roundtable on Sustainable Palm Oil "adopted the Principles and Criteria for Sustainable Palm Oil Production with an overwhelming majority".[45] The final version of the RSPO criteria has maintained a similarity to those criteria that WWF Switzerland, Migros and ProForest had already developed.

As Fausta Borsani points out:

> [The RSPO standard] is something like a development of the Migros standard. Migros standards are at the basis of all of this.[46]

Teaching notes for this case are available from Greenleaf Publishing. These are free of charge and are available only to teaching staff. They can be requested by going to:
http://www.greenleaf-publishing.com/oikos_notes

---

45   Press release of the Roundtable on Sustainable Palm Oil, November 23, 2005.
46   Interview with Fausta Borsani. February 18, 2005.

Part 4
Sustainability Strategies in the South

CASE 7
Hindustan Lever[1]

Aileen Ionescu-Somers, Ulrich Steger and Wolfgang Amann

IMD Lausanne, Switzerland

Section A: Leaping a Millennium

MUMBAI, INDIA: JULY 5, 2005, 13:54. Sharat Dhall, the project manager of "Project Shakti,"
Hindustan Lever Ltd's (HLL) initiative that had been running for four years, was about
to meet with senior colleagues to deliver a progress report on his project. As a sequel to
Project Millennium,[2] HLL had brought together a team to help implement this daring
new growth blueprint. It consisted of seven new business initiatives that would drive
the company's ambition to continue to double its turnover every four years.

Project Shakti was an ambitious plan to stimulate new demand at the lower end of
the market by creating a self-sustaining cycle of "business growth through people

Corprrate Sustainability Management.

1 CSM Program Manager Aileen Ionescu-Somers and Research Fellow Wolfgang Amann prepared
   this case under the supervision of Professor Ulrich Steger as a basis for class discussion rather than
   to illustrate either effective or ineffective handling of a business situation.
       This case series won the first prize in the 2006 oikos Sustainability Case Writing Competition
   organized by the oikos Foundation for Economy and Ecology.
2 An ambitious plan to create new business growth areas by exploiting business-to-business opportunities along the company's extended supply chain.

growth." The team had planned a win-win partnership with rural self-help groups (SHGs) by helping them to access micro-credit, buy HLL products and sell them in their villages. If successful, the initiative would create hundreds of jobs, train new entrepreneurs and extend HLL's distribution reach to even the most inaccessible rural villages in India.

Sharat's predecessors had known that such a promising, if daring, innovation would not be a stroll in the park. Penetrating the informal sector in this way was, first of all, a potentially risky endeavor. Was it, moreover, really the company's role to develop rural areas? At first, the management had been concerned about potential channel conflicts with the existing, successful distribution network. Coordinating with governmental and NGO partners would also be a key success factor, which would bring its own complexities. Training mostly illiterate women in sales and promotion techniques was another major challenge. However, the payback in terms of new markets and wealth creation was potentially enormous.

Sharat wondered if HLL had thoroughly thought through everything that would be required for a successful rollout.

Unilever's Background: The Multi-Local Multinational

Unilever, a *Fortune* 500 transnational company, has a worldwide turnover of € 39 billion, operates in 150 countries and has over 223,000 employees. This Anglo-Dutch multinational, a global giant in food, home and personal care products, was formidably placed in 2005. It had a total of 1,600 brands, some of which, for example Knorr, Rexona, Langnese, Dove, Lipton, and Hellmann's, showed substantial brand value. But, in a "path-to-growth" strategy that would concentrate innovation and development on a portfolio of 400 core brands, Unilever was poised to scrap many of the less promising ones.

Unilever and Local Communities

Back in the 19th century, one of the company founders, William Hesketh Lever, built a reputation as a social reformer, promoting a shorter workday, employee savings plans and health benefits for his employees. He laid the foundation stone of the strong corporate responsibility leadership that later became inherent in Unilever's culture. By 2005, Unilever had evolved into what it called a "multi-local multinational." Its management held the view that the company's long-term sustainability depended on looking after consumer needs and improving local communities' quality of life. Being an integral part of local communities and markets gave Unilever invaluable perspectives; it could anticipate market opportunities, develop strategies and levels of investment tailored to particular needs, and anticipate changes in consumer tastes. Unilever produced global brands, but it knew there was no such thing as a global consumer.

EXHIBIT 7.1 Unilever's Corporate Purpose Statement
When Launching Shakti

Source: company information

At the heart of the corporate purpose, which guides us in our approach to doing business, is the drive to serve consumers in a unique and effective way. This purpose has been communicated to all employees worldwide.

Our purpose in Unilever is to meet the everyday needs of people everywhere—to anticipate the aspirations of our consumers and customers and to respond creatively and competitively with branded products and services which raise the quality of life.

Our deep roots in local cultures and markets around the world are our unparalleled inheritance and the foundation for our future growth. We will bring our wealth of knowledge and international expertise to the service of local consumers— a truly multi-local, multinational.

Our long-term success requires a total commitment to exceptional standards of performance and productivity, to working together effectively and to a willingness to embrace new ideas and learn continuously.

We believe that to succeed requires the highest standards of corporate behaviour towards our employees, consumers and the societies and world in which we live. This is Unilever's road to sustainable, profitable growth for our business and long-term value creation for our shareholders and employees.

Unilever's "Gateway to India"

When Unilever first became engaged in India in the 1930s, the opportunity to conquer unexplored markets was enormous. The company broke ground by establishing the first edible oil, soap and personal product companies in India: The Hindustan Vanaspati Manufacturing Company (edible oil), Lever Brothers India Limited (soaps), and United Traders (personal products) were all founded between 1931 and 1935. The three Unilever companies merged in 1956 to form Hindustan Lever Ltd (HLL).

By the 1990s, HLL was the sole representative of Unilever's business in India. Given its long-standing presence there, it had become a uniquely Indian company and was perceived by Indian people as a local company and not a multinational. The company made painstaking efforts to make its mark on people's hearts and minds by showing that it cared about local communities. Its corporate mission statement noted that "to succeed requires the highest standards of corporate behavior towards our employees, consumers and the societies in which we live" (refer to Exhibit 7.1). HLL had several ongoing projects that focused on rural development, education, health, community welfare, resource conservation, sustainable development, and the national heritage in art and culture.

By 2005, HLL was one of India's largest fast-moving consumer goods companies—with market leadership in home and personal care products—and one of its seven largest exporters. HLL had over 100 manufacturing facilities across the country, as well as several third-party manufacturing arrangements. It was one of the most desired employers for Indian graduates in management and marketing. A job at HLL would endow their careers with a unique starting position and experience.

The HLL Distribution Network

In 2005 India was one of the fastest-growing economies in the world, as its population of more than one billion could clearly drive large sales volumes. It was therefore a key target for Unilever's global strategy for growth. However, of the potential total of 3,800 towns and 627,000 villages, the existing distribution network only reached 300,000 villages. HLL's dilemma was how to extend its network to the remaining villages in inaccessible rural areas.

HLL had a tried and tested distribution network for consumer products in India. It was not only one of the widest and most efficient distribution networks, but also a recognized key strength. The company's products were distributed through a network of about 7,500 redistribution stockists (RS) who sold to shops in urban areas and to villages accessible by vehicle and with a population of more than 2,000 (refer to Exhibit 7.2 for an illustration of HLL's rural distribution model). Its supply chain was supported by a satellite-based communication system, the first of its kind in the fast-moving consumer goods industry. This sophisticated network with its voice and data communication facilities linked more than 200 locations all over the country, including the head office, branch offices, factories, depots and the key redistribution stockists.

However, penetrating new markets would be a challenge, not only because of their inaccessibility, but also because the consumers needed to be educated in both personal and oral hygiene matters—HLL products would be entirely new to these rural communities' lifestyle.

Operation Streamline

Operation Streamline, one of HLL's growth engine initiatives to penetrate rural markets that could not be reached by vehicle, had already been launched in 1997. With the help of local stockists, distribution was extended to villages with fewer than 2,000 people, thus doubling the rural reach. Through this new conduit, goods were distributed from the HLL agents to redistributors, who then passed them to "Star Sellers" in local communities. In turn, the Star Sellers sold the brands—everything from detergents to personal products—to retail outlets (refer to Exhibit 7.3 for an illustration of the HLL distribution model under Operation Streamline).

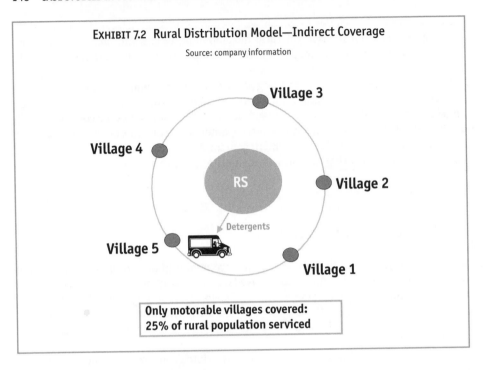

EXHIBIT 7.2 Rural Distribution Model—Indirect Coverage

Source: company information

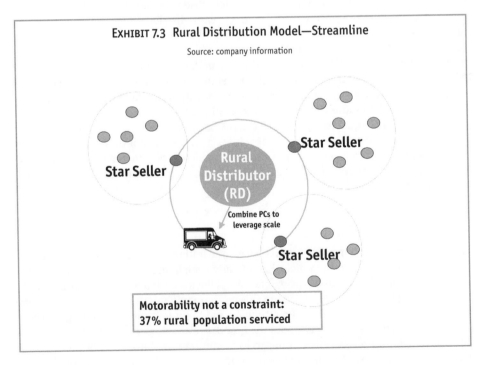

EXHIBIT 7.3 Rural Distribution Model—Streamline

Source: company information

However, HLL wanted to penetrate these local communities even further and work deep within the villages. A profound knowledge of Indian rural communities would give HLL an unbeatable market advantage. Sharat's predecessors had seen one ingenious solution—to work with the rural SHGs.

Self-Help Groups and Micro-Finance

In the early 1970s, access to credit was a major problem for the poor in India, as well as in many other developing countries. The poor did not have access to capital to purchase land, housing and other assets, and banks were reluctant to lend even very small sums without any tangible security. The only solution for many Indians below the poverty line was to borrow from a moneylender at extortionate rates. The poor were under particular financial pressure to borrow from such moneylenders as inviting the whole village to celebrate births and weddings is a social tradition and expectation.

A solution to counteract the power of the moneylender in rural Indian areas was found with the successful Grameen Bank initiative,[3] launched in Bangladesh in 1976, that had more than proved that commercial banking for the poor without collateral was no pipedream. The initiative proved that it was possible to:

- Encourage banks to extend their facilities to the rural poor

- Eliminate the use of moneylenders in rural communities

- Create self-employment opportunities for the unemployed rural poor

- Create and organize an effective savings system, which people (mainly women) from the poorest households could easily manage themselves.

The Grameen Bank initiative set up, organized and trained homogenous affinity groups of between 12 and 20 women living below the poverty line (families earning less than Rs 750[4] per month) in local communities. Members of these SHGs were encouraged to meet and save regularly and to pool the savings in a group savings account, thereby giving them access to credit based on "group" savings (refer to Exhibit 7.4 for the traditional micro-credit model) and allowing the group to use the interest gained for "group" projects. Members of the group could take out loans for consumption (a wedding, birth in the family) and production requirements (purchase of animals or grinding mills), as well as to finance micro-enterprises such as cycle rentals/repairs, retail outlets or tea stalls. Peer pressure proved to be an extraordinarily powerful mechanism to ensure that debtors made their repayments.

The 95% repayment rates that Grameen experienced were more than the banking community could have dared to hope for, since this had never been achieved in normal commercial operations. In the 1980s, the Indian government started vigorously promoting economy at grass-roots level, working with NGOs to create more and more SHGs. By 2000, India had a rich tradition of financial SHGs. Making credit available for

3   Set up by Professor Muhammad Yunus, head of the Rural Economics Program at the University of Chittagong, this action research project examined the possibility of designing a credit delivery system to provide banking services targeted at the rural poor.
4   Rs 56 = € 1

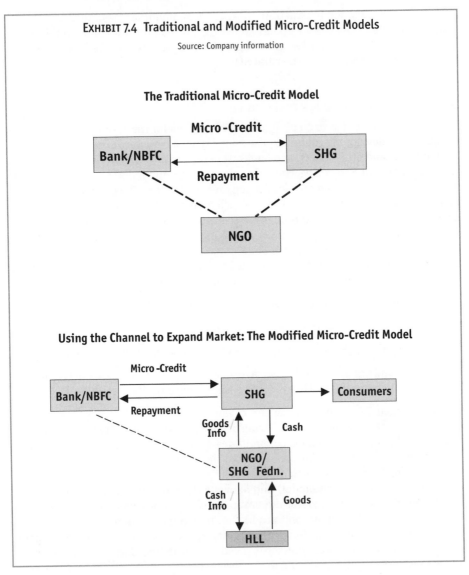

EXHIBIT 7.4 Traditional and Modified Micro-Credit Models
Source: Company information

micro-enterprises had had surprising results, activating, as it did, the innate entrepreneurial spirit within the country. The creation of sustainable livelihoods was the basis of the micro-credit schemes. In fact, micro-finance—as it was called—became increasingly important as a tool for alleviating poverty in the development process.

A Macro Opportunity Based on a Micro Model

HLL's growth strategy was to ask SHGs to operate as "rural direct-to-home" teams of saleswomen, who would accomplish several tasks by raising awareness and educating

EXHIBIT 7.5   Places Where HLL Reaches Out to Rural Consumers

Source: company information (in conjunction with Ogilvy and Mather)

The *Haat* or Market

Religious Festival

people about HLL products as well as selling the products directly within their communities. The idea was for the women to not only act as salespeople, but also as veritable brand promoters, often physically demonstrating products, such as shampoo, by offering hair washes at religious festivals, or at the *haat*, the local village market (refer to Exhibit 7.5 for photos of these events), or by performing hand-washing experiments to compare washing with soap to simply washing with water.

Apart from selling, the women would work on changing people's mindset by, for example, convincing them that a simple wash with water did not guarantee hygiene, or that shampoo could be used as a grooming product for the hair instead of just using soap to clean it. These rural consumers did not have access to television or radio, but by demonstrating and promoting HLL products at the *haat*, the Star Sellers made up for this lack of audiovisual brand advertising.

HLL's challenge was to test whether this organized, potentially major direct sales force available in the local communities could help achieve its business strategy objectives of "meeting the everyday needs of people everywhere" while creating wealth in the community. The existence of a ready-made network of SHGs was a great opportunity.

HLL established a committed project team to help it plan a strategy to achieve this. Kthalli Srinivas—called Srini by his colleagues—was the business manager of the New Ventures Unit (now called "New Adventures" by HLL's staff), and brought many years of sales experience to the team. Pratik Pota was taken on as marketing manager. At the time, both doubted whether engaging untrained groups of women to become micro-entrepreneurs was an attainable objective. They were, nevertheless, convinced that only new and innovative solutions, such as tapping into high-growth markets, would help HLL substantially increase its distribution in India. And although it was true that, per capita, rural consumers in developing markets used smaller quantities of products, a huge rural population also meant a huge market that, even at modest profit levels, was well worth entering.

HLL had the credibility to negotiate with the banks and convince them that the company could provide the local women with a meaningful income-generating activity. The new micro-entrepreneurs would thus be able to access micro-credit and use it to stimulate both demand and consumption at the local level. This could be a win-win situation that could modify the traditional micro-credit model, but without making the model overly complex (refer back to Exhibit 7.4 for the modified micro-credit model under HLL). As Pratik observed:

> We feel as if we are "writing the book" on micro-entrepreneurship. This is a groundbreaking initiative. The problems are many, but the ultimate pay-offs in terms of wealth creation within India and new markets for Unilever could be enormous.

Because their products could clearly offer health benefits, HLL established partnerships with UNESCO and NGOs, working with small theater groups to stage dramas that helped to build the local rural people's health awareness.

HLL had recognized that lending the local population a helping hand rather than giving handouts, would meet its own business strategy and provide opportunities for new distribution channels for its products, as well as contribute to a more stable and prosperous society. HLL felt that if micro-credit were available to local people, it would be possible to build and develop established SHG networks to become direct-to-home HLL distributors in rural markets. This would help create desperately needed new jobs and lead to an improvement in the living standard and prosperity in India. This new direct sales model nevertheless signified a major change from HLL's traditional model of formal sector distribution channels and professional sales representatives—and carried with it an inevitable element of risk.

"Project Shakti": HLL's Rural Initiative

A pilot initiative was set up in the Nalgonda district of Andhra Pradesh in November 2000, with 50 SHGs in 50 villages and between 1,000 and 2,000 inhabitants participating. The kick-off meeting on November 28, 2000 was initially sparsely attended, but as the morning progressed, women who had traveled long distances began to arrive. A discussion involving 150 women, all members of SHGs who ran micro-credit operations, ensued.

The initiative was facilitated by the DRDA in Nalgonda—a body under the authority of the Andhra Pradesh government with a mandate to promote and develop SHGs. As P. Shylinapo, representative of the DRDA at that time remarked:

> The women were looking for ways of capitalizing on their savings. The idea
> of buying HLL products at cost and making a profit on sales was exciting to
> them. They also realized that the direct sales training provided would serve
> them well.

Together with an organization called MART (Marketing and Research Team), a consulting agency specializing in rural marketing and micro-business promotion in rural areas, the DRDA worked towards promoting micro-enterprises in the district of Nalgonda. MART was responsible for coordinating the HLL–SHG business partnership and would also provide formal training in micro-entrepreneurship to the direct-to-home sellers. Once fine-tuned, the model would be scaled upward to cover more than 150,000 villages in India. This HLL–SHG business partnership initiative was called Project Shakti, meaning "strength" or "power" (refer to Exhibit 7.6 for the project logo).

EXHIBIT 7.6 Project Shakti Logo

Source: company information

Making It with MACTs

As part of the Shakti Project, HLL also worked with Mutually Aided Cooperative and Thrift Societies (MACTs) in the Nalgonda District. The MACTs were federations of 20 SHGs with up to 400 members that elected a representative committee to facilitate decision-making (refer to Exhibit 7.7 for the Shakti structure of operations). The MACTs often acted as financing agents for SHGs and, given their membership volume, were in a position to offer a higher loan. They also made decisions on investments to benefit the community, for example, investing in a school or setting up a supermarket. These MACTs were fostered by the same NGOs that had earlier been conduits for finance and advisory services to SHGs. The NGOs later handed over supervision of the MACTs to the SHGs themselves, which could clearly better identify with the basic issues and problems facing their members.

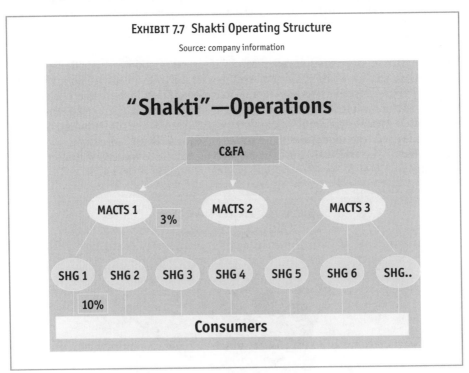

EXHIBIT 7.7 Shakti Operating Structure

Source: company information

In a bid to encourage fledgling entrepreneurs, the Indian government offered successful MACTs incentives, sometimes donating infrastructure, such as buildings, to facilitate further development. The MACTs in Nalgonda opened 14 supermarkets (called "bazaars") across the district in order to further encourage entrepreneurship amongst the members. HLL even envisaged the MACTs becoming distribution stockists for the SHGs. This would keep the distribution costs low and allow HLL to create a commercial system parallel with the Star Seller system. Srini commented:

> The question was: why would people buy from an SHG instead of a retailer? What incentives would there be? We soon realized that shopping for the best

deal would still be more important to the village people than their resolve to promote their SHG in the joint struggle against moneylenders. We thus needed to keep costs down so that there would be a cost incentive, or offer other value-added services.

The challenge of maintaining a different price for rural consumers purchasing from the SHG sales representative was more important for HLL than the scalability of this model. However, HLL also knew that having a system of two channels of the same company competing on price would, unless carefully managed, have its problems. Undermining local retailers would not be a solution, as this would be a real threat to the initiative's success.

The First Reality Check

By the beginning of 2002, the project team had already reached the entire Nalgonda District and more than 400 villages with no sign of this momentum slowing down. This project had the potential of giving the company a lasting superior understanding of rural consumers, which would ensure that the sales and marketing team had a favorable position in future. With the Shakti initiative within Project Millennium, HLL was profiling itself as a sustainability leader. Shakti had also attracted the media's attention, therefore the risk to the company's credibility if the project should fail was high indeed.

Looking back on all the innovations, related troubles and problems of which HLL was now aware, Sharat asked himself whether HLL should have entered the informal sector in the first place. There were substantive opportunities as well as risks for the various stakeholders involved. What were the true drivers of success that could be transferred to other initiatives? What could HLL have done to lower the risk of a channel conflict, and could one have foreseen that it would develop the way it had? Looking back, Sharat wondered if HLL had done all it could to ensure success.

Section B: The Reality Check

MUMBAI, INDIA: JULY 5, 2005, 14:10. Sharat Dhall was bringing his senior colleagues up to date on Project Shakti. He outlined the results obtained so far and detailed the challenges. He had been a brand manager at Hindustan Lever Ltd (HLL) before taking over from the former manager, Kthalli Srinivas, in February 2002. At that time, the project was in serious trouble since the women were earning little and consequently dropping out of the scheme. HLL was, however, able to learn more about the situation in the remoter villages. For example, Vijay Laxmi from the village of Aregudem near Hyderabad was one of the new direct-to-home sellers. She often hosted her SHG group's meetings, in which she took a leadership role, at her home. She kept the HLL products neatly stored in a corner of her sitting room. Her daughter, who was more literate with numbers, did her bookkeeping. Pratik Pota commented:

> When I started with this project, I thought that the problem of training these women was practically insurmountable. Many seemed timid, and none had ever done anything like this before. For example, it is quite amazing to see how confident Vijay Laxmi has become, given the practice.

Vijay Laxmi, however, commented:

> I am delighted to have had this training, but the amount of income generated from this is almost not worth the effort: between Rs 100 and Rs 150 a month. Given a choice, I would prefer HLL to set up a production unit in our area that would give jobs to our children and us.

In another village, the local schoolteacher's wife also sold HLL products, which were clearly on display for any visitor to see. She remarked:

> It all started off well in November, but now that we are in May and it is harvest time, people do not have time to think about HLL products. And neither do I have the time to travel very far to find new customers or to stock up at the MACT. The only way of doing it is to go on foot.

The fluctuation in SHG sales throughout the year was an element of concern for HLL (refer to Exhibit 7.8 for a typical sales pattern). With these fluctuations and low level of transactions, it was difficult to see how the company could scale up quickly. There had to be strong rational reasons for villagers to purchase from SHGs and that meant reducing the margins so that the group could compete with the local retailer. Increasing the overall number of individual transactions was indeed a challenge. There was also a stigma attached to door-to-door selling, so the women waited until the SHG got together to sell the products. Besides, there was no transport for door-to-door selling—it had to be done on foot.

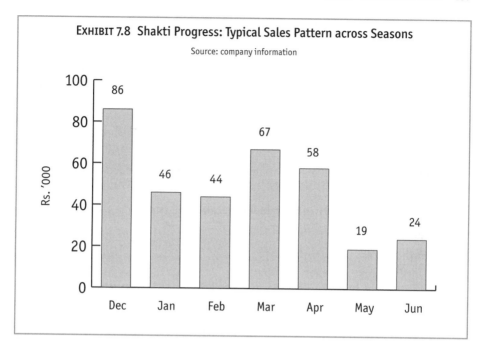

EXHIBIT 7.8 Shakti Progress: Typical Sales Pattern across Seasons

Source: company information

Glimpses of Hope

The good news was that a few months into the experiment the retailers had not noticed a decrease in their business as a result of the SHGs' new involvement in selling HLL products, but it was an important aspect to monitor. Although the retailers had not as yet objected, most probably due to the low level of transactions, what would happen if the transactions increased? The overall impact on HLL sales was undoubtedly positive. The consumption of HLL brands in the district had increased by 17% in six months. Simultaneously, the local consumers showed a dramatic increase in awareness of several brands that were previously almost unknown to them. For example, Red Label Tea, for which awareness had increased from 0% to 35%.

Continuing with this momentum presented a challenge, since the SHG women, who devoted only part of their time to selling HLL products (and wove or farmed the rest of the day), did not have the time to do the type of brand awareness building and hygiene education that the Star Sellers could do in the traditional system.

Changing the System or Giving it Time to Take Off?

It was clear to Sharat and his predecessors that the success of the model depended on being able to create significant enough earnings for the women to retain their interest and grow through their involvement and effort. In order to overcome the obstacles and increase the women's earnings, one or both of the following steps had to be taken: (a) increase overall sales, and/or (b) increase margins.

An analysis of the low sales showed that selling directly to consumers was difficult and was taking time to become established. The reasons for this were:

1. Consumers were used to purchasing from retailers and needed a good reason to change;

2. Consumers preferred to go to retailers because they stocked a greater range of products;

3. Self-employed women (SEs) were reluctant to go to consumers' homes to sell the products.

It was clear that the bulk of purchases in the village took place at retail shops. Yet the model, as it stood then, did not allow sales to the retail trade, because the MACTs, as an intermediary, received 3%. This prevented the SHGs from selling to the retail trade. As a concept, MACTs were not prevalent in most parts of the country—there were some in Andhra Pradesh where the project was launched—so it did not make sense to keep them as part of the broader Shakti model. But should the MACTS be discarded from the value chain? After all, they fulfilled a necessary service role. Or did they?

Removal of the MACTs could result in an additional margin being available for the SEs, which could increase their earnings as well, since theoretically they could earn a higher margin on the same turnover. But, once again, weren't MACTs valued for their support and didn't they contribute to the development of the local community as well? Did HLL really need to expect resistance? Or further setbacks? What other means were available to HLL to revamp the business model? Or did the company just have to wait patiently until the new system took off of its own accord, since all innovative projects take some time before they start flying?

Section C: Delivering the Desired Results

MUMBAI, INDIA: JULY 2005, 15:15. After outlining the challenges and options to his senior colleagues, Sharat expressed the belief that Project Shakti was taking off in a positive manner. By 2005, Shakti had already been extended to about 50,000 villages in 12 states—Andhra Pradesh, Karnataka, Gujarat, Madhya Pradesh, Tamil Nadu, Chattisgarh, Uttar Pradesh, Orissa, Punjab, Rajasthan, Maharashtra, and West Bengal. It had about 13,000 women entrepreneurs in its fold, reaching no less than 15 million people in rural areas. The project was undoubtedly creating opportunities for rural women to improve their living conditions and, most likely, their self-esteem, while changing their families' overall standard of living for the better.

Alterations to the supply model were, however, deemed necessary, so HLL modified it so that the rural distributors could sell directly to the SHGs. This freed them of the MACTs' 3% margin and enabled the SHGs to sell to the retail trade as well, which boosted their overall sales significantly, ensured increased retention rates and gave them a breathing space to start creating a direct customer base in the villages. No conflict of interest was involved because it meant that the retailers would not have to travel to purchase stock, and that the SEs were there to service them. The retailers did not have to buy in bulk to the same extent and many of them actually had no other sources of supply.

Further changes took place; stocks were no longer sent from the C&FA (cash & forwarding agent) but from the rural distributor (RD). This ensured faster and more frequent servicing of orders. Small orders—like those typically placed by the SEs—were easily serviced by the RD, whereas they would have caused problems for the C&FA that specialized in processing bulk orders. Furthermore, no SHG Fed/NGO was involved in the process. Stocks were sent directly to the SHG group/individual (products were delivered to the SE's doorstep by the RD) and cash was paid on delivery. The bank linkage was set up by HLL as it also facilitated the loan process.

As home-to-home selling posed a serious challenge to the initiative, HLL started a large campaign in which a company representative accompanied an SE when she approached the homes of potential clients. This was a crucial step, as it ensured the legitimization of the activity in the eyes of both the SEs and the village community. After the first few home visits, the HLL team were pleased to observe that the SEs participated enthusiastically and were keen to get on with it. The ice had been broken, and the SE was on her way to becoming a door-to-door vendor. HLL still makes sure that its reps make home calls as a part of their daily routine, since it really does help the SE to break through.

Over the following months, HLL realized that the then current level of interaction with and supervision of the rural sales promoters was clearly too high. The company wanted to reduce the supervisory visits from two to one a month. Sharat reported that the project employed 31 managers with 600 outsourced personnel to handle 20 to 25 entrepreneurs each. HLL decided to scale up while maintaining the same number of outsourced personnel.

The key motivator for the women was obviously profit, which made recognition important. HLL therefore developed a reward recognition program—a "consumer silver card holder." There would be several grades of entrepreneurs who would be entitled to different benefits. HLL also felt that there was still too much slack in the system, which had to become more cost-effective and efficient. Consequently, it decided to drive the recruiting and training aspects much harder as economies of scale were essential. The resulting challenge resided in increasing the home sales. HLL presented a number of brand-centric activities to enhance brand loyalty and increase the number of homes reached. It also established a new target of 80 homes per village per person, as well as an incentive system to encourage brand loyalty.

Economically, HLL had experienced challenging times in the form of intense local competition. But the project objectives were not abandoned, nor were the levels of investment decreased. This included financial resources, but also top management attention. There had been tremendous support for the initiative from the top management. In fact, the investment had increased 20-fold from what it had been in 2001. The local populations were also very supportive of Project Shakti.

Not Resting On Its Laurels

Shakti Vani and iShakti were, among others, new initiatives that were subsequently added. They both significantly increased the Shakti footprint in the communities. Shakti Vani was a communication program that spread awareness of best practices in health and hygiene. Local women were appointed as Vanis, and trained in matters relating to health & hygiene. They used specially designed communication material, such as pictorial literature, and spread awareness at SHG meetings, school contact programs and other social events.

iShakti distributed education modules among the children of the village and gave the community, particularly the youth, an opportunity to learn to use a computer. The monthly income that an SHG representative could expect had increased greatly from an average of about Rs 150 to about Rs 750 per month. This represented nothing less than a doubling of the representatives' household earnings and far more than they could possibly achieve through any other vocation in their villages. As other opportunities did not abound for women, the SEs were very happy.

When the project was extended from Andhra Pradesh to 12 other states, the SHGs received varying degrees of support from the different state governments. Where the support was limited, HLL developed a direct contact model for recruitment which involved directly reaching out to women in villages and presenting a proposition for a stable, low-risk income. This proposition also enjoyed the support of the local NGOs.

In turn, HLL also benefited, possibly creating a true win-win situation: the company obtained a vehicle that increased its distribution reach by over 50%—an additional 50,000 villages were now covered. The project covered more than 1 million homes every month—a phenomenal outreach for a brand that had been and continued to be interested in doing trials or communicating with a large rural audience. HLL had a unique one-to-one, interactive communication channel that built brands in media-poor villages. It succeeded in building significant goodwill in communities by providing opportunities to earn a livelihood as well as communication programs such as Shakti Vani/iShakti. Consequently, there were substantial market share and consumption gains in these villages. HLL's studies have shown that there was a 17% increase in the consumption of HLL products across various categories in the Shakti villages. This was achieved by selling regular HLL brands by means of this channel, as no customized products have as yet been developed. There is therefore room for future opportunities.

The Future of Project Shakti

Despite the SE's success, the company envisages the project dynamism accelerating rather than slowing down. HLL has a daring vision for 2010: 100,000 SEs covering 500,000 villages and benefiting 500 million people. Sharat is confident that the future is bright and after his convincing presentation, his senior colleagues shared this view.

Teaching notes for this case are available from Greenleaf Publishing. These are free of charge and are available only to teaching staff. They can be requested by going to:
http://www.greenleaf-publishing.com/oikos_notes

CASE 8
Building a Sustainable Venture
The Mountain Institute's Earth Brick Machine[1]

John Buffington
University of Michigan, USA

Ted London
The University of North Carolina at Chapel Hill, Kenan-Flagler Business School, USA

Introduction

In the Spring of 2002, Elsie Walker of The Mountain Institute (TMI) visited a leading business school in the United States in search of an entrepreneurial, graduating MBA student. TMI, an international non-profit organization, wanted to investigate launching a for-profit entity to promote a machine for which it had recently received a patent. Using dirt as the main ingredient, this machine makes high-quality building blocks (or bricks) appropriate for construction of homes and other one- and two-story dwellings. Walker and TMI believed the machine was ideal for construction in developing countries, particularly for poor populations, who are often accustomed to using earth in home building. Relative to other technologies serving this market, TMI believed that its compressed earth block (CEB) machine was price-competitive, allowed for low-cost construction, and was environmentally friendly.

Focused on environmental protection and community development, TMI hoped that someone with a business school education would be able to determine if these advan-

---

tages and other market factors would support a for-profit venture. If so, a for-profit venture could be free of the need to constantly find new grant money and, perhaps, could be a better tool for fostering economic development for developing-country populations, a key objective of TMI.

At the time of Walker's visit to the business school, TMI had been field-testing this technology in the Tibet Autonomous Region of China (Tibet) for more than two years. After successfully building two small guest cottages and training a number of Tibetan builders in use of this technology, TMI was preparing to launch its CEB machine on a wider scale in Tibet. This experience would form the first real market test of TMI's specific machine design and approach.

Soon after Walker's visit, TMI hired graduating MBA student John Buffington. Specifically, Buffington was to assist with continuing Tibetan efforts, develop a business plan for further promotion of the machine in Tibet, and, most importantly, investigate global opportunities. Provided he maintained the support of TMI's staff and board of directors, it had been suggested that Buffington would be offered the lead for any new, formal initiative to promote this machine, whether it became a stand-alone for-profit or developed into a full-fledged program within the non-profit, an option that also offered certain advantages.

After ten months on the job, Buffington had concluded that designing a long-term strategy for this project was not going to be as easy as he had originally anticipated, especially since progress in Tibet had been fairly slow and offered limited guidance on possibilities in other markets. Buffington's initial excitement with the apparent value proposition of the machine had become tempered with the identification of a growing number of challenges facing wide-scale promotion and expansion in the developing world.

Expecting a full report in two weeks, Walker poked her head in the doorway to Buffington's office. "What do you think?" she said. "Are we still going into the brick machine business?"

The Mountain Institute (TMI)

TMI (www.mountain.org) works to improve environmental conditions and the quality of life for local communities in mountainous regions throughout the world. Specifically, TMI has program offices in the Himalayas, the Andes, and the Appalachians, working on full-time projects in at least seven countries with additional work in another four countries. TMI's annual budget is roughly $3 million. Funding comes from the US and foreign governments and private foundations.

Over the past three years, TMI had begun experimenting with business development efforts in both its Himalayan and Andean programs. Aside from the CEB machine effort, the office in Tibet is also investigating opportunities for economic development through the transfer of dairy processing know-how and promotion of eco-tourism. For these projects, TMI hired outside business consultants to perform market research and venture planning.

For his investigation of CEB machine opportunities, Buffington was also hired as an independent consultant. Throughout his time at TMI, his reporting requirements have remained fairly loose. For initial work involving Tibet, Buffington reported to both Elsie Walker, Director of the Peak Enterprise Program (which oversees all TMI activities in Tibet) and Gamesman Balachander, Director of TMI's Asia/Himalayan Program. For exploration of machine use in other geographies, Buffington reports to TMI's President and CEO, Catherine Nixon Cooke (see Exhibit 8.1 for TMI's organization chart). Meetings for this purpose, however, were infrequent and sporadic.

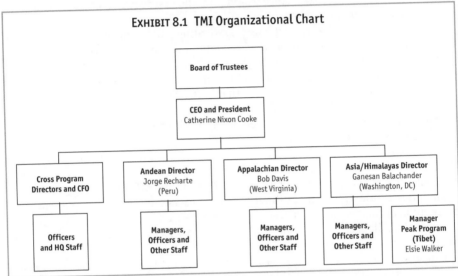

Since Buffington began work for TMI, expenditures for promotion of the CEB machine have been limited to ongoing work in Tibet and Buffington's compensation. As of Spring 2003, Buffington's compensation remained the only substantial expense involving the machine effort. This compensation was taken from limited, general funds that have not been earmarked for other specific purposes. It was anticipated that new funds would need to be found by the end of 2003 to continue work with the CEB machine. Buffington, who works out of TMI's Washington headquarters, is free to seek input from other TMI employees. Buffington, however, is the only person dedicated to machine promotion.

Overview of Earth Building

The use of earth in construction has been significant throughout human history. In addition to the creation of simple shelters, many of the world's great feats of construction involved the use of mud or dirt. The Great Wall of China (246–209 BC) was built of earth along most of its route. Hannibal's watchtowers, built with compressed earth in Europe in 300 BC, stood for more than 600 years.

In both ancient times and today in many developing countries, builders have relied on two primary earth-building techniques. One, commonly referred to as "slip-form," involves the building of walls in place using frames. Mud is packed into a long rectangular form to create a section of wall. Once it dries and becomes hard, the form is used again to place another section of wall on top of it. In this manner, the structure is built from the bottom up in a series of two- to three-foot high sections. The horizontal lines left by this approach are clearly visible in housing throughout the world. A second technique involves the use of forms to make individual blocks, which harden and are then stacked into place once construction begins. Due to the low cost and the fact that these techniques lend themselves well to building by the homeowner, these types of mud construction have remained popular in many parts of the developing world. It has been estimated that half of the developing world lives in houses that rely on mud during construction.

Earth building was significantly advanced in the 1950s with the mechanization of block production. These compressed earth block machines (or CEB machines) are either manually operated or engine driven, and rely on high pressure for block making. Manual machines utilize a large lever that can be pulled by one or two people to compress blocks. The CinvaRam was the first manual machine and has been used in Central and South America as a low-cost way to build higher-quality structures than previously used earth building techniques.

Engine-driven machines use a hydraulic ram for block compression. The high pressure improves the strength and durability of the bricks and the structures they create. Before the 1980s, however, engine-driven machines were not used as widely as manual machines due to cost and the frequency of machine breakdown.

The CinvaRam Manual Machine	The Hydraform M7

Source: TMI

In the 1980s and 1990s, several higher-quality engine-driven CEB machines were introduced to the market. Some involved a novel feature that reduced construction time and lowered costs. Bricks created with these machines were interlocking, containing "tongues" and "grooves" that allowed the blocks to slide into one another. This feature allows builders to eliminate mortar between rows of blocks. Elimination of mortar can reduce the building costs for simple structures by an estimated 5 to 25 percent in developing countries where labor costs are low. Operations in at least three countries developed improved interlocking block making machines. The most well known is Hydraform in South Africa, which developed not only a durable machine, but also obtained certification of their blocks under South Africa's National Building Regulations, increasing credibility and world-wide acceptance.

Nearly all CEB machine producers have central manufacturing operations that ship machines to their international customers. Today, the most basic engine-driven machines typically retail from between $10,000 and $15,000, not including the shipping price. Manual machine can retail anywhere from $375 to $2,000, depending upon the quality of the machine and the size of the block that the machine creates.

Typically, earth building uses soil at the site of construction, eliminating many of the material and shipping costs that occur with other building techniques. In addition, building with earth block requires less skill than most other building techniques, further lowering costs.

Since the introduction of mechanized machines, most manufacturers have recommended the use of a "stabilizer" in the block production process. A stabilizer improves block strength and resistance to water damage. The most common stabilizer is Portland cement, which can typically be purchased even in remote developing country settings. Additional stabilizers include fly-ash (a byproduct of burning coal and other industrial processes) and lime. A stabilized block will contain 5 to 15% of stabilizer, by weight. Although the use of machines and stabilizers increases costs compared to traditional earth building methods, modern CEB construction still keeps costs low relative to other building techniques and it greatly increases the durability of structures built with earth.

TMI Reinvents the CEB Machine

In February of 2002, TMI received a US patent for its machine, designed by TMI board member Jim Underwood. Like many other machines, TMI's machine produces interlocking tongue and groove blocks. Unlike other machines, TMI's is intended for manufacture in simple, developing-country machine shops. When he designed the TMI machine, Underwood believed that existing machines, particularly engine-driven machines, were not appropriate for the populations that needed them the most. They were "unnecessarily complicated and difficult to repair in places without appropriate materials or training." Of his design, Underwood said the following:

> Our machine resulted from an effort to design an interlocking block machine that was safer, lighter, more portable, ergonomic in use, less expensive, adaptable to local power sources, and capable of local manufacture and repair. In essence, this machine was specifically designed for use in developing countries, with an emphasis on simplicity and engagement of local populations (see Exhibits 8.2 and 8.3 for more background on TMI's Compressed Earth Block Machine).

EXHIBIT 8.2 TMI's Machine Information Brochure

TMI's Compressed Earth Block Machine

The Mountain Institute (TMI) offers the ideal machine for creating affordable, environmentally-sensitive building material for the developing country setting. Unlike other machines, our patented rammed earth machine was specifically designed for developing country challenges—low incomes, rugged environments and a deficit of skilled labor. Its secret is simplicity! With a minimal number of parts, our machines are low-cost, easy to use and easy to transport. Using dirt as its primary ingredient, compressed earth block keeps building costs low and can replace other building materials whose ingredients may harm local environments.

Source: TMI

Aside from offering affordable, reliable housing to communities, use of our machine serves as a tool for economic development. Through partnering, TMI will transfer the ability to make this machine to local enterprises, empowering a new generation of entrepreneurs and employees.

The machine's primary components are a steel mainframe with a ramming chamber and two sets of hydraulics. With engine, axle, and wheels included, the machine weighs roughly 500 kg. It can be operated by six or seven workers, of which two should be skilled or semi-skilled. One person operates the machine controls; two or three people mix soil for block making; one person monitors the hopper (where the soil is placed in the machine for block making) to ensure that the soil mix falls into the ramming chamber consistently and appropriately; and two more people remove blocks from the machine and stack them for curing. The tongue and groove blocks made by TMI's machine can be stacked directly into the structure being built, saving time and labor cost.

EXHIBIT 8.3 TMI Marketing Brochure on Machine Specifics

The TMI Compressed Earth Block Machine

- Interlocking tongue and groove feature on blocks allows for "dry stacking," greatly reducing the need for mortar and costs
- Makes 120 blocks/hour
- Requires 6 to 8 workers, only 1 or 2 need to be skilled
- Weighs ~500 kg and is readily disassembled and transported
- Hydraulic pressure can be easily adjusted to allow for highest quality brick production and flexibility with various soil types
- Designed to provide worker comfort and encourage efficiency
- Blocks meet Universal Building Code standards, with a compressive strength of 4 to 5 Mpa for blocks with 5% cement
- Can be readily coupled with local power supplies; simple design allows for local production and minimizes servicing
- Block size: 220 mm (width) x 115 mm (height) x 50 to 240 mm (length)

First machine produced in Lhasa, The Tibet Autonomous Region, China

Source: TMI

Soil is mixed with cement and water either on the ground or in a large metal tumbler. Depending upon the specific characteristics of the soil used and the particular inclination of the builder, 1 part of cement is used for every 11 to 15 parts soil. The bricks achieve 70 percent of their total strength after a week of curing, the chemical process by which cement becomes hard. Interlocking CEB blocks may, however, be stacked into a wall directly from the machine. Bricks reach their full strength after four weeks of curing. After curing, blocks weigh roughly 10 kg and are 220 mm wide × 115 mm high × 50 to 240 mm long, making them equivalent to three to five traditional clay bricks.

When asked why he decided to design an engine-driven machine rather than a manual machine, TMI's Jim Underwood sited the following: (1) manual machines do not achieve the compression strength and, therefore, block quality as engine-driven machines; (2) Tibetan builders did not want to buy manual machines; (3) the per block production speed is typically two to three times slower than engine-driven machines; and (4) the blocks produced are half to a third the size of blocks produced by an engine-driven machine.

A number of staff members at TMI's Washington office felt that TMI's new CEB machine could potentially support a stand-alone, self-sustaining enterprise. The argument was based on the apparent value proposition that the machine would offer to any manufacturing partner and customers who would use this machine for building projects.

The Market for CEB Machines

While some interest has been shown in the United States in the use of CEB (and other alternative or green building techniques) in the past few years, the need for and familiarity with low cost, earth building appears far greater in developing countries. In the developing world, the United Nations Centre for Human Settlements (UNCHS) has estimated that 1.1 billion people are living in inadequate housing conditions in urban areas alone. UNCHS also estimated that approximately 21 million new housing units are required each year in developing countries to accommodate the expected growth in new households during the time from 2000 to 2010. An additional 14 million units would be required each year to end the existing housing deficit by the year 2020.

To date, stabilized CEB has gained only a very small percentage (far less than 1%) of the housing market. Worldwide, CEB machine sales are estimated at less than 3,000 per year.[2] Market resistance to CEB is expected in certain developing-country regions due to its association with low-quality, traditional adobe. In Peru, for instance, build-

---

2   Due to the difficulty in obtaining information on sales in developing countries and the need to aggregate estimates from a number of different sources, these sales figures rely heavily on anecdotal information and educated guesses from people in the field. In India, the current market for CEB machines is estimated at roughly 250 to 300 machines per year and growing from 25 to 40 percent a year, according to Development Alternatives, a nonprofit organization that promotes use of sustainable technologies. In Mexico, the market for CEB machines has been estimated at 150 machines per year with a growth rate of roughly 30 to 40 percent, according to Ital Mexicana (a manufacturer of CEB machines).

Examination of Low-Cost Housing Markets for India and Mexico

In preparation for promotion of its machine outside of Tibet, TMI has investigated opportunities in both the Indian and Mexican markets. According to the 1991 Census for India, 3.41 million households are without shelter and 10.31 million households are living in "unserviceable" houses. Thus, the total housing shortage was 13.72 million in 1991. It has also been estimated that another 10.75 million houses would be needed to cover the population growth from 1991–2002, an annual growth rate of 0.89 million homes. By extrapolation from the available data, it can be estimated that there is a deficit of 24.5 million homes in 2002.

According to the *State of Mexico's Housing*, a report by the Joint Center for Housing Studies at Harvard University, during the 1990s, the total number of new households in Mexico grew by more than 3% per year. This figure does not include replacement or repair of existing homes, which could push the percentage of new home construction sites as high as 6 to 10% of the total number of houses. The majority of growth in Mexico was focused on low-cost building materials of higher quality, a movement fueled largely by the increase in total wealth of Mexican populations over the last 30 years. During the period from 1970 to 1995 the share of houses constructed of block, brick or stone rose from 44.2% of the total housing stock to 75.7%. The share of adobe (traditional earth) houses fell from 30.1% to less than 15%.

ing materials are classified into "noble" and "non-noble" categories. Noble materials include stone, concrete and brick. Adobe (non-stabilized earth) is in the non-noble group of materials. Anecdotal experience suggests that, without significant market education, stabilized CEB would be treated as a non-noble material even though its quality and even its appearance may lead one to think it deserves noble distinction. In Tibet, builders exposed to stabilized CEB initially assumed that it was of lower strength than concrete block, although this has not been determined scientifically and any minor differences in laboratory strength may not be meaningful in actual use.

The following groups have purchased CEB machines:

- **Nonprofit organizations.** Although the total percentage has not been calculated, nonprofit organizations are thought to purchase a large proportion of CEB machines sold. They may purchase directly for their own development projects or may purchase on behalf of local operations, helping to encourage local development and entrepreneurship.

- **Local Developers/Construction Companies.** As is expected to be the case with other developing countries, the Indian and Mexican markets have a large population of small and medium-sized builders. Typically, these builders use oven-fired clay brick or cement block, but have expressed some interest in CEB machines.

- **Governments (Local, National and International).** Government bodies have also purchased a number of CEB machines, particularly in response to natural disasters, such as after earthquakes in India. In Tibet and mainland China, TMI has received significant interest from a number of government entities concerned with housing. TMI expects the rammed earth effort in Tibet will also benefit significantly from China's interest in modernizing the region.

- **Development Agencies.** Several development agencies have used CEB machines for assistance projects, such as the United Nations Development Program in India. Other organizations that have expressed an interest in the technology include the Asian Development Bank, the Inter American Development Bank, and the World Bank.

Sales of machinery that make building material for low-income housing are typically driven by machine price, cost of use in the construction process, interest of the housing market in the material produced, and ability to service the machine. Significant resistance has been shown over the last twenty years against manual machines, which builders and homeowners assume are lower quality than engine-driven machines.

TMI expects its machine will be priced between $4,000 and $6,000. Buffington's research suggested that this price range is competitive with other engine-driven CEB machines as well as with equipment used for most other mainstream building materials, such as concrete block and clay brick.

Competition with Other CEB Machines

TMI's new machine will compete against a number of for-profit and nonprofit CEB manufacturers (see Exhibit 8.4 for a comparison of key competitors). Like other machines, TMI's machine makes blocks out of dirt (which can be taken directly from the building site), water and a stabilizing agent (such as Portland cement, industrial fly-ash, or lime). Even in countries where use of CEB machines has been greatest, it has been estimated that no company or organization selling this product has captured more than one percent of the total market for construction of low-cost housing.

Hydraform

Hydraform, a privately held company based in Johannesburg, South Africa, is likely the most well-known and largest producer of machines that make stabilized earth blocks. Hydraform machines have been sold in Argentina, India, South Africa, and several other African countries. Like other companies serving the market for engine-driven CEB machines, Hydraform manufactures at two central location and then ships, often internationally. In 1995, Hydraform launched a manufacturing operation in India. According to Development Alternatives, a nonprofit organization that promotes the use of appropriate technologies, Hydraform India sells roughly a dozen machines a year at a price of roughly $9,000. Hydraform appears to market largely on the social benefits of the machine. Of its customer and operations, Hydraform India has said the following:

EXHIBIT 8.4 Table of Competitors

Organization/ Company	Price	Power	Output Blocks/hr	Tongue and Groove	Local Manufacture	Axle w/ wheels standard	Engine Used
Private Companies							
Hydraform	$9,000 to $13,000	Hydraulic/ Engine-Driven	180	Yes	No (plants in South Africa and India)	Yes	High quality, may not be locally available
Ital Mexicana	$6,000 to $20,000	Hydraulic/ Engine-Driven	75 to 190	No	No	Yes	High quality, may not be locally available
Foxfire	~$12,000	Hydraulic/ Engine-Driven	180	Yes	No	Yes	High quality, may not be locally available
Eco Brick Systems	$14,250 to $12,375[3]	Hydraulic/ Engine-Driven	300	Yes	No	No	High quality, may not be locally available
Nonprofit Organization or Academic Institution							
Auroville Building Center (Academic Institution)	$1,000/ machine + $300 to $900 each for molds	Manual	90 to 180[4]	No	No	NA	NA
ApproTec (Nonprofit Organization)	$350 (in Africa)	Manual	90[4]	No	NA	NA	NA

Note: Several of the entries listed here have a number of machine types. If only one price is quoted, then the information refers to the organization or company's most commonly sold machine. If a range of prices is presented, then the information for that entry refers to two or more machines or, as in the case of Hydraform, represents geographic pricing differences.

3   Eco Brick Systems' prices decrease to a floor of $12,375 depending upon quantity ordered.

4   Size of manual machine blocks may be 2 to 3 times smaller than engine-driven machine blocks.

Hydraform works in tandem with international/multilateral aid and development bodies who consistently look for effective, efficient and professional organizations to work as channel, technical, and implementation partners for various rehabilitation, shelter, employment and social/economic empowerment programs.

Development Alternatives has estimated that a builder using the Hydraform machine can make roughly $6,500 in profits per year (not including the initial cost of the machine), allowing for capital payback in the second or third year of use. Although this profit seems attractive, Development Alternatives has suggested that the initial price tag severely limits Hydraform's ability to sell machines to homebuilders in the Indian market. The high price tag could be particularly burdensome for small and medium-sized builders.

Ital Mexicana, S.A.

Located in Mexico City, Ital Mexicana is a manufacturer and distributor of building equipment, primarily concrete block machines. Ital Mexicana began to sell hydraulic CEB machines in the late 1990s. Since 2000, the company has sold roughly 150 machines, primarily to projects focused on creating social interest housing. CEB sales represent a very small percentage of Ital Mexicana's total sales. The more high-end of the two machines, which makes upwards of 1,500 blocks/day, sells for roughly $20,000. For many social projects, however, this machine has been sold at a discount of 30%. A low-end machine, which makes roughly 600 blocks/day, sells for roughly $6,000.

Auroville Building Centre

The Earth Unit at Auroville Building Centre, located in Madras, India, sells a number of manual CEB presses. As with other CEB machine manufacturers, the vast majority of these sales go to humanitarian organizations, particularly for rebuilding of disaster areas. Auroville machines have sold on a limited basis in other parts of Asia, Africa and Europe. These machines have interchangeable molds that allow for a wide variety of block shapes and sizes. Auroville sells the basic frame for roughly $1,000 and then the individual molds for anywhere from $300 to $900 apiece. Although the Auroville machines have made some headway, selling as many as 100 units a year, Development Alternatives says that builders have a strong bias against manual presses in India. The primary reason for this bias is the poor quality associated with the machine, real or perceived. This bias also exists in the Mexican market, according to Ital Mexicana.

ApproTec

The nonprofit organization ApproTec sells a manual machine in sub-Saharan Africa called the Action Pack for $375. Four workers can make roughly one block per minute using the machine. Blocks made using this machine do not include a tongue and groove feature, so mortar must be used between rows of bricks for construction.

Alternative Low-Cost Construction Technologies and Techniques

In addition to other CEB manufacturers, TMI will be competing against a number of traditional machines and methodologies for production of low-cost, high-quality building material, such as concrete block and oven-fired clay brick. Although these technologies have tremendous popularity throughout the developing world, CEB appears to offer an equal or greater profit margin in most developing-country construction sites and it has a far more attractive environmental profile. For example, builders in Tibet estimated that profits could be as much as 10 to 30% higher using CEB as opposed to other building materials. Similar figures were found after analysis of conditions in Mexico and India.

Adobe (Traditional Earth Building)

Adobe (or molded mud), produced by a variety of methods, is commonly used throughout the developing world. Unlike compressed earth, adobe does not use a stabilizing agent such as cement. Typically, adobe is made in block-form (similar to stabilized CEB) or using the slip-form technique (where forms or frames are placed atop a building's foundation and mud is smashed in-place from above to form walls). Adobe blocks made by machine are typically considered of higher quality than adobe made by slip-form or some other technique involving frames.

Adobe machines sell for roughly $500 in Tibet, which appears comparable with prices in India and Mexico. In both India and Mexico, adobe machines are sold by large equipment manufacturers for the commercial construction industry and by smaller, local operations (which often imitate machine designs of the larger equipment manufacturers). Compared to stabilized CEB, adobe has a lower density and lesser resistance to water. Thus, adobe is more susceptible to damage from flooding and weathering, and typically requires frequent repair. Adobe is predominantly used by small, rural construction companies or individuals building their own home. Construction companies tend to favor machines; individuals forced to build their own homes typically must rely on the use of forms. In Tibet, manufacture of an adobe block (using a machine) costs roughly half of what it costs to manufacture a compressed earth block, due primarily to the cost of cement. Five laborers are typically required to operate an adobe block machine. Due to the quality limitations of adobe, most developing-country builders and homeowners tend to consider it an inferior product. Those who can afford another material typically do not buy adobe.

Theoretically, handmade adobe can be stabilized with Portland cement. However, the process is very difficult and tends to produce low-quality blocks. The problem with stabilization of traditional adobe lies with the difficulty in thoroughly hand-mixing the cement and mud, which must contain significant moisture in the absence of the high compression strength offered by a CEB machine. To avoid this problem, mud and cement can be mixed by machine. However, mixing machines can cost several thousand dollars. With a CEB machine, the soil is relatively dry and easy to mix with cement.

Clay Brick

Oven-fired clay brick is used extensively throughout the developing world for affordable construction. Brick making in both India and Mexico is a traditional, unorganized industry, generally confined to rural and suburban areas. Like CEB, clay brick can be used for simple construction with little or no need for reinforcement in areas that are not seismically active. Brick is also commonly used for non-load-bearing walls in apartment buildings and other larger construction projects. Although individual bricks are more likely to cost less than CEBs, a number of factors affect the total cost comparison. For example, a single clay brick occupies roughly $\frac{1}{3}$ the wall space of a single block from the TMI machine. In addition, clay bricks are usually created at a specific location, requiring transportation to the building site.

According to Ignacio Landa, a developer in Monterrey, Mexico, once these factors are considered, stabilized CEB can be cost-competitive with or even cheaper than brick. According to TMI's building contacts in Tibet and Jack Blanchette, Coordinator for Construction and Appropriate Technology at Habitat for Humanity Asia, building with CEB will typically be cheaper than building with brick. Total costs for use of brick, however, will vary widely from market to market.

Throughout the world, clay brick is also under fire for its poor environmental performance. In developing countries, the ovens used for baking bricks typically burn highly polluting fuels, such as high-sulfur coal, industrial waste, and wood. This contributes to local air pollution and total amount of greenhouse gases in the atmosphere. A number of regions in China are now banning the use of oven-fired clay brick due to environmental concerns. Several other local and national governments have discussed adopting similar regulations or manufacturing restrictions.

Concrete Block

Concrete block is widely used in construction of affordable dwellings throughout the developing world, particularly Africa and Latin America. According to Chumpe Tsering, one of TMI's development contacts in Tibet, concrete block construction is slightly stronger than CEB construction. Dan Brundage, an engineer who works on building issues for TMI, feels that CEB construction is the stronger technique. Brundage believes Tsering's statement to be an assumption based on knowledge of adobe. Nevertheless, any small difference in strength between the technologies appears to have no structural significance, says Brundage, particularly in non-seismic areas.

According to Tsering, after factoring in the costs of materials in Tibet, building with CEB could offer a larger margin than building with concrete block. A separate building contact in Tibet, Wang Du, offered a cost comparison between CEB and concrete block in terms of the total construction cost divided by square meters of development. According to Du, concrete block construction costs US$148 per square meter, while CEB construction costs US$86 per square meter. In Mexico, concrete block machines sell for between $400 (for the simplest units that produce roughly 500 blocks/day) and $2,500 (which can produce as many as 1,200 blocks/day). The Mexican figures for machine cost and output appear fairly consistent with figures for Indian machines.

Like clay brick, concrete block has significant environmental impacts. Cement manufacture is very energy-intensive, resulting in local air pollution and high greenhouse gas emissions. Cement also requires mining of limestone and other materials used as raw ingredients and mining of coal for fuel use. Mining occupies valuable land and harms local ecosystems. Jim Underwood, the designer of TMI's machine, has estimated that use of CEB that is stabilized with cement reduces total cement use by 50% compared to use of concrete block.

The Tibetan Test Case

TMI began testing use of the machine in Tibet in 2000. Early efforts involved three prototype machines manufactured in the US and shipped to Lhasa. The machines were used for the construction of two cottages in Tibet's second largest city, Shigatse. This construction served as training for 10 to 15 small and medium-sized developers interested in learning about building with CEB. After the training, the machines were loaned to two of the developers who attended. Since the initial building, several additional structures have been built by these developers (see Exhibit 8.5).

In August of 2002, TMI transferred the ability to manufacture and sell the machine to a small machine shop in Lhasa. This operation expects to be able to expand its business with this new capability. Under a three-year licensing agreement (to be reviewed in 2005), the machine shop has full liberty to set its own price and primary responsibility for generating new sales leads. For each sale, TMI will be paid a fee of 10 percent of the total sales price. Buffington sees this fee as somewhat high, but feels it is a necessary charge to help cover both the technology development and assistance with market development. TMI offers connections and know how that can help drive initial machine shop sales to other nonprofit organizations operating in Tibet.

Due to concerns over market potential and political sensitivities in Tibet, this operation will remain part of TMI's nonprofit activities. TMI has a number of projects in Tibet that would be affected if any one program offended local authorities. For this reason, TMI's policy in Tibet is to avoid confrontation in order to preserve program development. Therefore, the arrangement with the Lhasa machine shop will only concern TMI's for-profit aspirations to the extent it can inform new sites for manufacture and promotion.

Manufacturing cost for the machine shop in Lhasa, including the cost and shipping of hydraulics and attachment of a trailer and diesel engine, for the first few machines was roughly 17,200 RMB ($2,100). The labor portion of this cost (just under 20% of the total) is expected to fall as much as 25% as workers gain experience. The machine shop has decided to make inclusion of the Chinese-made diesel engine and an axle with wheels and a trailer hitch standard with each machine. This adds a total cost of roughly $400 to each machine ($125 for the axle and $275 for the engine), which is recognized in the $2,100 figure above. Although readily available and extremely cheap compared to diesel engines available in developed countries, the Chinese engine can break down frequently requiring repair or replacement.

For the Tibetan effort, the hydraulics for the machines are being purchased from Chengdu in mainland China (see Exhibit 8.6 for a map of TMI's operations in and related to Tibet). TMI was not able to identify a hydraulics manufacturer in Lhasa capa-

Exhibit 8.5 Building Pictures

Source: TMI

Chumpe Tsering in front of house he built using TMI's CEB machine (Shigatse, Tibet, China)

EXHIBIT 8.6 TMI's CEB Machine Operations in China

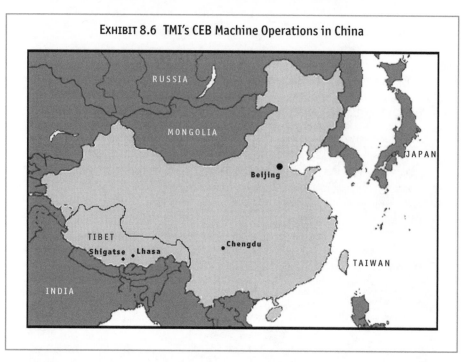

ble of producing the high-quality hydraulics selected for use in the machine. A TMI volunteer, who covered all of his own travel expenses, spent several days with this hydraulics manufacturer to ensure that the new products met the intended specifications.

To attract interest, the machine shop has agreed to offer a two-year warranty on the sale of its first dozen machines. This warranty does not cover the engine and will not cover instances where it has been determined that damage occurred from improper use or abuse of the machine, which can often be detected by inspection. The hydraulics, the most expensive item covered under the warranty, have an estimated useful life of 5 to 7 years.

To transfer the manufacturing capacity and set up the necessary business arrangements, TMI relied on a team of several employees and key members of its strategic partner in Lhasa, the Tibet Federation of Industry and Commerce (ICF), a Chinese government agency that oversees development efforts in Tibet. Foreign operation in Tibet cannot occur without the approval and involvement of ICF. All but one of TMI's employees involved in the effort are based in the United States. TMI's local employee, Chris LaDue, acted as liaison for all efforts and was instrumental in selecting the machine shop.

Jim Underwood, the machine's inventor, trained machine shop workers on manufacturer. Buffington arranged the formal agreement between the machine shop, TMI and ICF and began initial sales efforts. One other TMI employee and another TMI volunteer were also involved in the effort. Now that initial experience has been gained in the technology transfer process, Buffington would not expect to use so many different parties to set up any new site for machine manufacture.

Chris LaDue, program manager of TMI's Tibetan program, forecasts sales for the machine shop as follows: 70 machines in Year 2, 110 machines in Year 3, 150 machines in Year 4 and 190 machines in Year 5. These estimates are based on the market for building in Tibet alone. After several months of research on the market in Tibet, Buffington has since concluded that these estimates are probably aggressive. However, having limited marketing data available and no capital for detailed market research, Buffington cannot confidently offer a more "realistic" projection. The machine shop's current capacity is roughly 50 machines per year, and LaDue felt that additional capacity could be added as demand increased.

In Tibet, TMI has focused initial sales efforts on small and medium-sized developers and foreign nonprofit organizations. According to information from the Tibet Federation of Industry and Commerce, there are approximately 300 construction companies in Tibet. The majority of these are small and medium-sized enterprises. For the year 2000, total revenue for construction companies in Tibet was estimated at 668,737,000 RMB (US$82.6 million) and total profit was estimated at 86,810,000 RMB (US$10.7 million). The construction industry has grown by roughly 10% per year in Tibet for the past five years. This level of growth is expected to be maintained or increased due to China's "Develop and Open the West" policy, which calls for massive infrastructure development in Tibet over the next 10 years.

If necessary, TMI may choose to use local distributors for product promotion. At least in China, these distributors are little more than independent stores that have been established as the place for certain types of goods. A store that sells construction equipment in China typically seeks a mark-up of roughly 30%.

At the machine shop in Lhasa, machines are made to order and shipped directly to the customer. The customer will be expected to cover the cost of shipment, both in-country or abroad. With its strong spring-loaded axle, this machine can be pulled behind a vehicle (for local transport) or set in the back of a truck for long distance transport. In order to grow total sales and seed interest in the machine in other regions, TMI has begun talks with several interested parties throughout Asia. International shipment, however, should only be necessary for unusual events or in advance of setting up a new manufacturing operation. In these cases, TMI may choose to cover the shipping costs.

Challenges for TMI's CEB Venture

Armed with the experience in Tibet, Buffington now needed to make decisions regarding the future promotion of the CEB machine. He realized that TMI's work in Tibet provided important lessons on key challenges that must be addressed in order to successfully expand this venture to other locations.

Production

As of late January, 2003, TMI's sales activities in Tibet were on hold while the machine shop works to solve technical glitches with the first few machines produced. The machines have been working well enough to build a few small structures, including a dairy processing plant, but not well enough for the machine shop to comfortably provide warranty support. Problems have included slower than expected block production and overheating, for which improper installation or maintenance of the hydraulics have been suspected as the likely culprit.

Underwood, TMI's machine inventor, and Dan Brundage, a retired naval engineer who volunteers time to TMI, have assured Buffington that these issues are only "small bugs expected with any start-up manufacturing operation" that can easily be solved and avoided in the future. "We should have budgeted for more time to spend with the machine shop working actively with them to solve these problems and to make sure that they could competently train customers on how to maintain their machines in good health," says Underwood. For future instances of manufacturing training, he has recommended an extra month on the ground for debugging. "Unfortunately, our Tibetan partners are not exactly used to self-empowerment. This means that small, solvable problems can take a long time to fix."

Promotion

Looking to borrow wisdom on the challenges facing promotion of "appropriate technologies," Buffington has consulted a number of organizations in the field. One insightful correspondence was with Martin Fisher, cofounder of ApproTec, which sells manual earth block machines, micro-irrigation systems and other relatively inexpensive products in sub-Saharan Africa. When asked why he does not operate as a for-profit, Fisher said that the products he sells require far too much hands-on marketing and training for the relatively small profit per unit he achieves.

Since ApproTec's products are intended for use by entrepreneurial individuals (rather than an existing business or some other intermediary, as would be done for the rammed earth machine), it focuses on technologies that will retail for $300 or less. Once a technology has been designed, ApproTec teaches a local machine shop or small factory how to make the technology. This manufacturer is typically located in the largest city of a given sales region. ApproTec then buys the product leaving a profit margin of roughly 25 to 30% for the manufacturer. ApproTec then sells the product at a mark-up of 35% to any of a number of retail outlets, which have been educated by ApproTec on marketing and selling the product. These retailers are rural "general stores" that sell a wide variety of products to local markets. These stores typically receive a margin of 16% on the sale of ApproTec products. Fisher says that his organization can spend up to two to three times what they make in revenue on marketing for a given product.

Piracy

Those involved with the machine effort at TMI have worried that the simplicity of the design leaves it vulnerable to copying by would-be competitors, particularly in the developing-country regions where TMI intends to have the technology manufactured and distributed. Buffington also discussed this subject with Martin Fisher of ApproTec. Fisher explained that when a product is novel and unproven to the local population, the marketing burden is high and there is little incentive for someone to try to pirate the technology. As it catches on, however, copiers are expected to emerge. Fisher seemed unconcerned about this. In fact, if the ultimate goal is market development, piracy and increased competition could serve as a measure of success for his nonprofit organization's activities.

Licensing Agreement

TMI expects that its licensing arrangements could create an incentive for a local TMI-selected manufacturer or distributor to try to eliminate TMI from sales involvement after initial manufacturing hurdles have been cleared and demand was growing. Buffington hoped TMI could discourage this by building machine shop loyalty and engaging government entities in technology transfer and market development activities. Along with technology transfer, TMI also has the opportunity to improve business practices at the machine shops. Machine shop employees, including managers, typically have little or no formal business training, and may not even have much basic education. These operations could benefit greatly from extending their knowledge on operations, finance, marketing, and other business concerns that are more familiar in developed countries. In past projects, TMI had successfully leveraged participation from government agencies, which have a special interest in assuring that the projects they are involved with run smoothly so as not to lose face.

Managing from Afar

The CEB venture will be headquartered in TMI's Washington DC office, an ideal location for networking with socially motivated nonprofits, government entities and international organizations (see Exhibit 8.7 for a project budget submitted by TMI to the US Department of State for work in Afghanistan). To the extent possible, Buffington is aiming to utilize resources on the ground in developing countries to meet its operational needs, minimizing staff and activities at headquarters. While strategic decision-making and general venture direction would come from TMI's headquarters, machine manufacture, shipment, training, and distribution would occur in the specific markets of interest.

Lack of a significant local presence, however, could reduce TMI's ability to coordinate with appropriate players. Francesco Piazzesi of Ital Mexicana, which produces CEB machines for the Mexican market, stressed the importance of having relationships with industry, government officials and mortgage loan providers. With several decades of operations, Ital Mexican has built these relationships. For this reason, Buffington thought he might initially focus on those geographies where TMI operations already exist. TMI currently has formal operations in India, Nepal, Peru and the United States and coordinates on efforts in a number of other countries. Relationships with national authorities, industry leaders and other organizations are probably most developed in Peru, where TMI has been working closely with government officials and a number of mining operations.

EXHIBIT 8.7 Afghan Project Budget (Proposal to the US State Department's Bureau of Population, Refugees and Migration)

Project Management and Facilitation	
John Buffington's Salary (3 Full Months of Project Management)	13,500
Travel-Related Expenses	
Airfare (roundtrip)	2,500
Per-diem and Lodging ($65/day for 20 days)	1,300
Translator ($25/day for 15 days)	375
Ground Transportation	200
Coordinator for Women's Inclusion in Project (airfare, lodging, per-diem, translator)	7,200
Total	25,075
In-country Manufacturing Training and Machine Shop Marketing Assistance	
Manufacturing Expert (Jim Underwood)	
Airfare (roundtrip)	2,500
Salary ($200/day for 30 days in the field)	6,000
Per-diem and Lodging ($65/day for 30 days in the field)	1,950
Translator ($25/day for 25 days of use)	625
Ground Transportation	200
Shipment of Existing Machine to Serve as a Template	5,000
Material and Labor for Four Initial Machines	10,000
Translation of Machine Blueprints	1,000
Development of Local Language Marketing Brochures	1,000
Correspondence with NGO and Relief Efforts for Machine Promotion	500
Other Machine Promotion Efforts	5,000
Total	33,775

(continued opposite)

(from previous page)

In-country Building Training	
Building Expert (Jim Underwood)	
Airfare (cited in Manufacturing Training)	
Salary ($200/day for 60 days in the field)	12,000
Per-diem and Lodging ($65/day for 60 days in the field)	3,900
Translator ($25/day for 50 days of use)	1,250
User Manual Development/Translation	1,000
Building Expenses (estimates considered conservative, based on info from contacts)	
Labor ($5/person/day for 20 people for 50 days)	5,000
Cement ($6/50 kg bag at 10 bags/building for 15 buildings)	900
Fuel ($10/full machine day of operation for 4 machines for 16 full days)	640
Roofing, Doors, Foundation Material and Other ($500/building for 15 buildings)	7500
Total	**32,190**
Office Materials and Supplies	**200**
Legal Fees (currently pro-bono)	
Total Direct Costs	**91,240**
General and Administrative (15% of Total Direct Costs)	**13,686**
Total Costs	**$104,926**
In-Kind Contributions to Project	
Dan Brundage's Airfare, Per-diem, and Lodging	7,200
Machine Donated by TMI for use in Training	5,000
Total Contributions	**12,200**

The Path Ahead

The marketability of CEB machines is greatly enhanced by their potential to contribute to sustainable development. This may be particularly true with the TMI machine. Based on its experience manufacturing and using the machine in Tibet, TMI has estimated that each of its machines, over an estimated useful life of 10 years, could result in $2,600 in profit (assuming no additional costs for marketing) for a manufacturing partner; the construction of 225 homes; and 1,125 people living in these homes.

TMI's simple machine design also allows for manufacture in developing countries, where technical skills may be relatively low and sophisticated machine components may not be readily available. Local manufacture will create jobs for local populations and greatly reduce machine cost for customers. Currently, TMI has made no attempts to quantify environmental benefits or the impact on the local economy, but believes both to be significant.

Looking across his desk at Elsie Walker, Buffington reflected back on what that he had learned over the past 10 months. He still was not sure what the best approach was for TMI. He knew, though, that he had only a few more weeks to put together a plan that charted the path forward for the CEB venture.

Teaching notes for this case are available from Greenleaf Publishing. These are free of charge and are available only to teaching staff. They can be requested by going to:
http://www.greenleaf-publishing.com/oikos_notes

Richard Ivey School of Business
The University of Western Ontario

CASE 9
City Water Tanzania[1]

Kevin McKague   *Oana Branzei*

York University, Canada   Ivey School of Business, Canada

Section A: Water Partnerships for Dar es Salaam

Introduction

The spring of 2002 brought new hope for improved water services to the inhabitants of Tanzania's largest city, Dar es Salaam. Led by the World Bank, a cohort of multilateral

1   Kevin McKague and Professor Oana Branzei wrote this case solely to provide material for class discussion. The authors do not intend to illustrate either effective or ineffective handling of a managerial situation. The authors may have disguised certain names and other identifying information to protect confidentiality.

Ivey Management Services prohibits any form of reproduction, storage or transmittal without its written permission. Reproduction of this material is not covered under authorization by any reproduction rights organization. To order copies or request permission to reproduce materials, contact Ivey Publishing, Ivey Management Services, c/o Richard Ivey School of Business, The University of Western Ontario, London, Ontario, Canada, N6A 3K7; phone (519) 661-3208; fax (519) 661-3882; e-mail cases@ivey.uwo.ca.

Copyright © 2007, Ivey Management Services. Version: (A) 2007-06-07.

The Richard Ivey School of Business gratefully acknowledges the generous support of the Schulich School of Business and the Erivan K. Haub Program in Business and Sustainability in the development of these learning materials.

financial institutions proposed a US$165 million project to rehabilitate Dar es Salaam's water and sewerage system. The project cost was to be financed by the World Bank (US$61.5 million), the African Development Bank (US$48 million), the European Investment Bank (US$34 million), the Government of Tanzania (US$12.6 million) and by a prospective private operating company (US$8.5 million). The loan was offered to the Tanzanian government to:

- Rehabilitate existing water treatment, transmission, storage and distribution facilities

- Expand piped water-supply systems to unserviced areas

- Reduce physical water losses

- Develop and implement a community water supply and sanitation program for low-income communities that were not currently served by the utility's piped water network

- Upgrade and sustain the water utility's commercial operations, reduce illegal tapping and improve the collection of water and sewerage bills

Following a pattern repeated in many other cities in Africa, Asia and Latin America (see Exhibit 9.1), Dar es Salaam's water and sewerage infrastructure had deteriorated significantly over the last 30 years to a state of considerable disrepair that required a huge rehabilitation effort. Even the current $165 million would only be the first stage of investment that would be needed in the longer term. Currently, the government estimated that 27 per cent of the city's 3.5 million residents did not have access to safe water (see Exhibit 9.2). In reality, this figure was a significant underestimate. Cholera epidemics were a regular occurrence, especially in the city's sprawling low-income areas. However, with the active support of the government, the current proposal was seen as an important opportunity to begin to rehabilitate and expand the system to meet the needs of the city's rapidly growing population, including the poor.

The next challenge was to identify a reputable international water company willing to partner with the Tanzanian government to aid the rehabilitation of Dar es Salaam's crumbling water infrastructure. A successful private–public partnership could not only fulfill immediate water provision needs by infusing capital and capabilities but might also send signals that Tanzania was on course for improved social and economic development. Tanzania's Minister of Water, Edward Lowassa, looked back at the regulatory changes that had gradually made the water sector more attractive to private investors. He wondered whether the Tanzanian government should accept the World Bank loan and how the water ministry could attract and select the right private operator.

The Intention: Free Water for All

The government of Tanzania had centralized water services soon after the country's independence in 1961. In 1967, Tanzania's first president, Julius Nyerere, had issued the Arusha Declaration on Socialism and Self-Reliance, ushering in a socialist model of

EXHIBIT 9.1 How Water Utility Performance Declines

Source: *New Designs for Water and Sanitation Transactions: Making Private Sector Participation Work for the Poor,* published by the Water and Sanitation Program and the Public–Private Infrastructure Advisory Facility, Washington, DC, 2002. http://www.wsp.org/publications/global_newdesigns.pdf, accessed February 1, 2007.

Water utility performance can take a downward spiral in the absence of a supportive regulatory environment, lack of cost recovery mechanisms and reduced maintenance and investment as described in the diagram below:

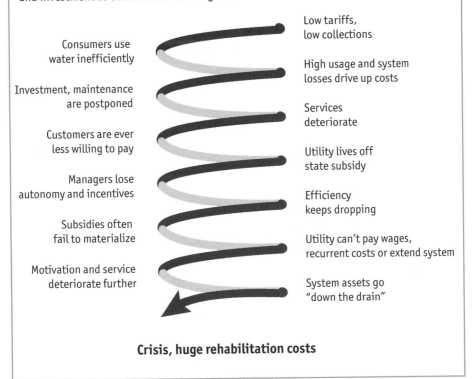

Consumers use water inefficiently

Low tariffs, low collections

High usage and system losses drive up costs

Investment, maintenance are postponed

Services deteriorate

Customers are ever less willing to pay

Utility lives off state subsidy

Managers lose autonomy and incentives

Efficiency keeps dropping

Subsidies often fail to materialize

Utility can't pay wages, recurrent costs or extend system

Motivation and service deteriorate further

System assets go "down the drain"

Crisis, huge rehabilitation costs

national development. Businesses were nationalized, and the government began to move people into collective villages and farms. The government initiated large-scale centralized projects to provide basic services, such as water, health, and education. By 1969, the Tanzanian government had taken on the responsibility for financing the operation of the existing water systems and was responsible for investing in their maintenance and expansion. Only a handful of very rich households in Dar es Salaam were required to pay for water; for everyone else in the city (and the rest of the country), the government made water freely available. This was the era of "free water for all." The government believed this approach would be the most effective and equitable way to develop the country and provide water to everyone, especially the poor.

In 1980, the United Nations launched the Water Decade. By this time, the Tanzanian government was still far short of providing safe water for all of its citizens, and it embraced the UN Water Decade wholeheartedly. The government mobilized interna-

EXHIBIT 9.2 Tanzania's Human Development and Economic Indicators

Sources: (1) World Bank Data and Statistics for Tanzania, 2004, available at www.worldbank.org/tz, accessed February 1, 2007; (2) Tanzanian Ministry of Water and Livestock Development, 2006; (3) UNDP Human Development Index, 2003, available at http://hdr.undp.org/statistics/data/cty/cty_f_TZA.html, accessed February 1, 2007.

Tanzania	
Population[1]	37 million
Life expectancy at birth[1]	42.7 years
Infant mortality rate[1]	10%
Population of Dar es Salaam with sustainable access to improved water source[2]	73%
Population with sustainable access to improved sanitation[3]	46%
Adult literacy rate[3]	69.4%
Population living below $1 a day[3]	20%
Population living below $2 a day[3]	60%
Per capita GDP[3]	US$287
Per capita GDP (Purchasing Power Parity)[3]	US$621
Percentage of total government budget dependent on donor funding	42%

Map of Tanzania

Source: authors

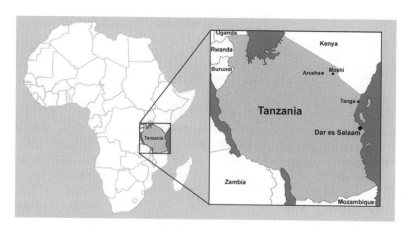

tional donor assistance to prepare regional water master plans and to facilitate the rapid construction of additional water supply schemes. Foreign donors responded favorably. Throughout the decade, however, despite considerable efforts, it was proving very difficult to provide Tanzanians with adequate, safe water. Although significant investments were being made, the rate of system failures exceeded the rate of construction of new systems. Insufficient attention was paid to the operational efficiency and financial sustainability of existing and new water delivery systems. Tanzania's struggle was not unique. In several other African countries, the UN Water Decade came and went without significant improvements in water supply, despite the best efforts of donor agencies, governments, nongovernmental organizations (NGOs) and other stakeholders.

Julius Nyerere's model of national development was crucial in forging a peaceful, unified nation with a strong national identity that valued inclusiveness and cooperation. Nyerere's social legacy would establish a stable and non-violent political culture, which would see a number of subsequent peaceful elections and handovers of political power. However, by the mid-1980s, the country's experiments with centrally planned, state-controlled development had lead to an economic crisis. After Julius Nyerere stepped down from power in 1985, the new government initiated comprehensive economic reforms. Foreign exchange controls were lifted, prices were deregulated and private sector involvement in the economy was enhanced through a privatization program and a new investment code. Business owners, who had left the country when their enterprises had been nationalized, were invited by the Tanzanian government to return. In later years, Nyerere himself admitted that the socialist model of development had not been successful from an economic perspective.

It had become evident to the country's new leadership that although nature provided water freely from the heavens, safely collecting, cleaning and distributing it to millions of households required significant investments of money, technical expertise and management capability. But who should pay for these necessary investments—the government (with its limited resources), donors (with their regional pet projects and strings attached), or users (many of whom were very poor)?

The High Cost of Free Water

In Tanzania, the population had more than tripled from 12 million in 1976 to 37 million in 2004.[2] The population growth rate in the country's largest city, Dar es Salaam, was significantly higher than the national average as people migrated to the city in search of work. The majority of this growth had taken place in the city's large unplanned or informal areas where 75 per cent of Dar es Salaam's population lived.[3]

2   World Bank, *Tanzania Data and Statistics*, 2004, www.worldbank.org/tz, accessed February 1, 2007.
3   Damas Mashauri and Osmo Seppala, Turning to PSP in Water Supply and Sanitation Service. Case Study: Dar es Salaam Water and Sewage Authority, PRINWASS Open Workshop Presentation, http://users.ox.ac.uk/~prinwass/PDFs/Damas04.PDF, accessed February 1, 2007.

Little had been done to upgrade or expand Dar es Salaam's water and sewer systems since the mid-1970s. By 2002, only 50,000 customers were connected to the city's piped water system with a house connection (although it was estimated that an additional 300,000 to one million people sourced their water from neighbors with a house connection).[4] Water utility customers with a house connection were typically middle- or upper-income households, government offices, and businesses. Many received their water through so-called spaghetti lines, small-diameter pipes made of black polyethylene. Some even used electrical conduit polyvinyl chloride, but these PVC pipes were so thin walled that they leaked almost as soon as water was fed into them. The spaghetti lines extended 700 to 2,000 meters from a water main. Because they were typically installed at or near ground level they were highly susceptible to illegal tapping and breakage.

The piped infrastructure that did exist sourced its water mainly from two water treatment plants on the Ruvu River, which flowed east into the Indian Ocean, about 70 kilometers north of Dar es Salaam (see Exhibit 9.3). A smaller water treatment plant at Mtoni also provided some water for the system. Combined, the source capacity of the existing water supply infrastructure was theoretically 270 million liters per day, much less than the estimated demand of 340 million liters per day. Dar es Salaam sat on sandy soil, making it difficult to identify leaks and breaks in the pipe infrastructure. Of the water that was sourced by the utility every day, approximately one-third was lost due to leaks and one-third was lost due to unauthorized use and illegal tapping. The city's water utility collected revenue on the remaining one-third of the water it supplied.[5]

Many customers in Dar es Salaam received water irregularly. Sometimes pipes stayed dry for days. Water pressure was low, and water quality was often questionable. To be safe, it was best not to drink the tap water untreated. It was estimated that household access to drinking water had fallen by seven per cent over the last 10 years, and this estimate applied only to customers with house connections.[6] There were hundreds of thousands of households with no direct water connection at all.

The vast majority of Dar es Salaam residents were not connected to the water utility system and had to rely on other ways of getting water (see Exhibit 9.4 for an illustrative diagram of the sources and distribution channels for water in Dar es Salaam). The government estimated that about 20 private borehole operators had drilled deep wells, or boreholes, and installed pumps; they were selling water to wealthy neighborhood homes through a small piped system or to water tankers and individual hand carters. Even in areas that did have access to the city's piped water system, some people paid for water from a private borehole operator because the water was available 24 hours per day at good pressure. However, some argued that borehole water was not chlori-

4   A note about sewerage and sanitation: Although Dar es Salaam's water utility dealt with sewerage as well as water, this case focuses on the issues surrounding water provision. The authors recognize that increasing access to sanitation, especially for poor families in urban areas, is a crucial part of the development process and an important part of the water treatment and waste-water treatment businesses.

5   Interestingly, in some cases where long-standing leaks had been repaired, residents discovered that what they believed were natural wetland areas were actually marshes created by the leaky water infrastructure.

6   WaterAid Tanzania. http://www.wateraid.org.uk/uk/what_we_do/where_we_work/tanzania, accessed February 1, 2007.

EXHIBIT 9.3 Map of Dar es Salaam's Water Sources and Transmission Pipelines

Source: Damas Mashauri and Osmo Seppala, PRINWASS Interdisciplinary Research Project "Barriers to and Conditions for the Involvement of Private Capital and Enterprise in Water Supply and Sanitation in Latin American and Africa: Seeking Economic Social and Environmental Sustainability," Case Study D13/Tanzania: Water Supply and Sewerage Authority (DAWASA) January 2004, European Commission, Fifth Framework Programme 1998–2002. http://users.ox.ac.uk/~prinwass, accessed February 1, 2007.

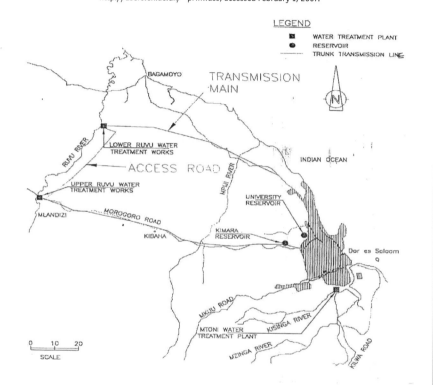

nated and often polluted; ensuring water quality requirements would require investing in chlorination equipment, or even closing down some of the most polluted boreholes.

Most of Dar es Salaam's low-income, unplanned slums were not serviced by the water utility system. Dar es Salaam's largest slum, Temeke, had grown to more than one million residents since the late 1970s. Most residents in Temeke obtained their water from hand carters, community water kiosks, or unprotected shallow wells or streams (see Exhibits 9.4 and 9.5). Some were more than 30 km away from the nearest water source. Hand carters (individual water sellers) filled 12 20-liter plastic jerry cans at private boreholes, community water kiosks, from individuals with a house connection, or stole it from the piped water network and delivered it door-to-door on two-wheeled carts. Residents could also carry their own water from water kiosks that were operated by local water user groups, community organizations, or NGOs. Although these organizations attempted to run their systems effectively, they often struggled to keep the pumps and systems in good working order and to collect enough fees to cover major repairs.

EXHIBIT 9.4 Water Distribution and Prices in Dar es Salaam

Source: Adapted from B. Collignon and M. Vézina (2000). "Independent Water and Sanitation Providers in African Cities: Full Report of a Ten Country Study". Washington, DC: World Bank Water and Sanitation Program, p. 23.

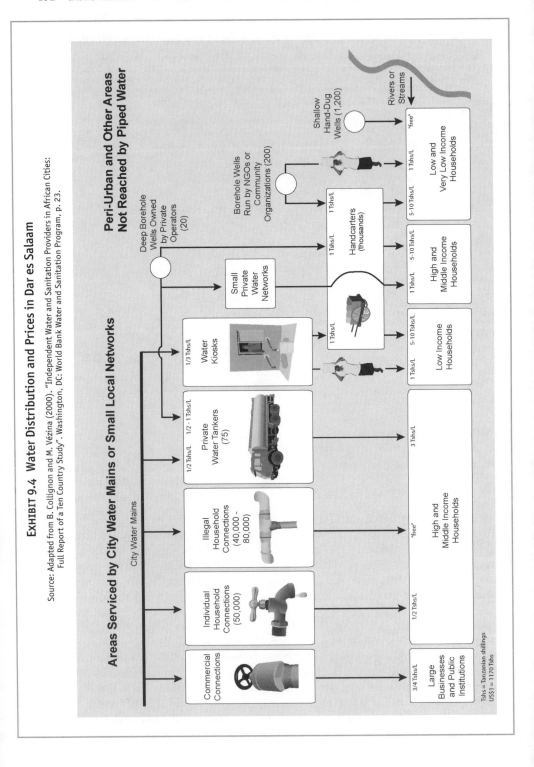

Exhibit 9.5 Hand Carters, Tanker Trucks, and Private Borehole Operators

Hand carters are individual water sellers; they push two-wheeled carts through the streets of the city, delivering yellow plastic jerry cans filled with water to Dar es Salaam's residents. A hand carter makes about four to six trips a day, delivering a dozen 20-liter containers in each trip. They typically buy water from private borehole operators, kiosks, or from households with individual house connections to the water system for 20 Tanzanian shillings ($0.02) per 20-liter container or steal it from the water  distribution system for free. Depending on the distance travelled, they charge water users between 100 and 200 shillings ($0.10 to $0.20) per 20-liter container. Hand carters deliver some of the most expensive water per unit volume in Dar es Salaam, but residents working long hours are often willing to pay for the convenience of home delivery. Even in more affluent neighborhoods, hand carters provide a convenient water delivery service when taps are dry; the time and energy users save by not fetching their water from local pumps compensates for the increased price.

Hand carters are not governmentally regulated; they compete head-to-head with other water carters and with all the other water providers in each neighborhood. Hand carting is subject to market prices; competition among individual carters regulates the price of the service through the market mechanisms of supply and demand. Many water carters seek to stabilize demand by nurturing relationships with their clients. They often offer flexible payment arrangements and credit (a service not provided by the water utility). This is extremely valuable to customers who have unpredictable cash flows and irregular incomes.

Upstream of the hand carters are the private borehole operators. In Dar es Salaam, approximately 20 individuals have drilled their own deep wells and have installed pumps and storage tanks. They sell water to unserved or underserved households and hand carters and supply water through two other channels: tanker delivery trucks and small pipe systems that directly serve local homes. For example,  Faud Mansour operates a registered borehole in the Ubungo area of Dar es Salaam. Some of the water he pumps is bought by individual hand carters. Mr Hmansour also operates tanker trucks and provides house connections and water to 80 houses on his street. Although the City Water pipelines comes to his neighborhood, houses connected to the City Water system only have access to water a couple of times a week. Mr Hmansour offers his customers reliable 24-hour service at an affordable price—he charges every buyer 1 shilling per litre. His father and his brother each run similar businesses in nearby areas.

Private water trucking companies cater to more affluent users who have their own storage tanks and require water at all times, such as hotels, larger businesses, and embassies. Each trucking company operates up to five trucks. Some large users, such

(continued over)

(from previous page)

as embassies and universities, have their own water trucks. Many of the trucks fill at private borehole operators around the city or at the City Water tanker filling point. Since City Water only operates one tanker filling point, trucks wait in line for as long as six hours for a single fill during times of low water pressure in the mains. At the City Water filling station each truck pays 5,000 shillings; the average capacity of a truck is around 10,000 liters. Customers are charged 20,000 to 60,000 shillings per truckload, depending on distance traveled and the water shortages in their neighborhood.

During times of water shortages, the cost of water from hand carters increased, and some of the poorest residents were left to source water from shallow hand-dug wells or open streams, both of which were often polluted. These residents were therefore especially susceptible to water-borne, fecal-related diseases. Flooding periodically contaminated shallow wells from pit latrines, triggering repeated cholera epidemics.[7] Because of unsafe drinking water and inadequate sanitation, the infant mortality rate in these low-income slums was twice as high as the national average.[8]

Reforms

A 1986 conference on the sustainable development of the water sector launched a significant shift in Tanzania's water policy. Policy-makers recognized that the previous approach of "free water for all" had not met its intended objectives. The conference marked the beginning of a process to formulate a radically new water policy, based on the following principles:

- Shifting the role of government from service provider to service regulator

- Decentralizing the planning, implementation, and management of water and sanitation services to the lowest administrative level

- Including the private sector in service delivery

---

7   A 1997 World Bank–sponsored study estimated that water-borne diseases, such as diarrhea and cholera, affected 38,600 people in Tanzania between 1986 and 1992, leading to 4,364 deaths.

8   Damas Mashauri and Osmo Seppala, PRINWASS Interdisciplinary Research Project "Barriers to and Conditions for the Involvement of Private Capital and Enterprise in Water Supply and Sanitation in Latin American and Africa: Seeking Economic Social and Environmental Sustainability," Case Study D13 /Tanzania: Water Supply and Sewerage Authority (DAWASA) January 2004, European Commission, Fifth Framework Programme 1998–2002. http://users.ox.ac.uk/~prinwass, accessed February 1, 2007. p. 18.

- Adopting a philosophy of cost recovery with safety nets for the poor
- Responding to consumer demand, with community ownership and management

The new policy was approved by Parliament in 1991, and was significantly revised and strengthened in 2002. The Minister of Water, Edward Lowassa, and the Tanzanian government hoped that these policy reforms would create a legal and regulatory environment that would help rehabilitate Dar es Salaam's struggling water utility.

In Dar es Salaam, these policy changes had a direct impact on the city's existing water utility, the Dar es Salaam Water and Sewerage Authority (DAWASA). Under the new policy and institutional arrangements, DAWASA would be given a new mandate: to own existing and future water system assets. This asset-holding entity would retain the name DAWASA and remain fully owned by the government. A new organization would be appointed to manage the day-to-day-operation of the water system. The former would remain under governmental control and oversight. The latter could attract international private sector operators who would work to improve the commercial viability, and thus the long-term sustainability, of the city's water utility.

These policy changes were welcomed by major donor agencies. International donors were willing to loan money to fix Dar es Salaam's water utility system, but they were justifiably nervous because they felt that past investments in publicly managed large water utilities had drained large sums of donor financing without delivering significant improvements in water service. Therefore, the World Bank made the $165 million rehabilitation financing package conditional on the Tanzanian government securing the services of an international private water utility operator.

Pros and Cons of Private Sector Participation

Accepting the World Bank's condition required some diligent consideration of the pros and cons of private sector participation in Dar es Salaam's water system. During Tanzania's period of socialism, the government had promised and delivered free water to some of its citizens. At times, it had labeled private sector activity as antisocial. Changing its position now would be a difficult and controversial political act. However, the state of collapse of the system meant that the status quo was no longer a viable option.

Water's relatively unique nature of being essential for life raised complex economic, political, and social implications for its management. Regardless of the mix of public and private participation in management, a water utility operator would have to address the following challenges:[9]

---

9   Adapted from Jacqueline Medalye, *A Study of Public–Private Partnerships in the Water Sector,* unpublished study prepared for David Wheeler, chair, Erivan K. Haub Program in Business and Sustainability, Schulich School of Business, York University, Toronto, Canada, 2004.

- Ensuring water infrastructure is well maintained
  - Reducing leakage and illegal tapping
  - Replacing and expanding the network
  - Improving technology

- Ensuring that various social and political objectives are addressed
  - Public acceptance of the form of utility management
  - Improving service to unserviced and underserviced households
  - Affordability, especially for low-income households

- Ensuring transparency and accountability in operations and decision making
  - Ensuring environmental and health challenges are met
  - Public health and sanitation needs
  - Water conservation

- Ensuring financial decisions are made in the best interests of sustainable water provision
  - Sustainable and equitable tariff rates
  - Effective revenue collection
  - Financing system improvement and expansion

- Ensuring managerial objectives are met
  - Improving efficiency and productivity
  - Capacity building

These were the challenges that any water utility would face, regardless of governance structure and involvement of private sector operators. However, proponents on various sides of the debate argued that either the public or the private sector was better positioned to meet these challenges. The arguments for and against private sector participation in Dar es Salaam's water system took on increasing importance.

Pros

On the one hand, there were several relevant arguments in favor of private sector participation in Dar es Salaam's water system. First, partnering with an international private utility operator would allow the government to mobilize the much-needed investment of $165 million from the World Bank and its partners. In the 1990s, supporters of private sector participation had claimed that private companies would be able to mobilize significant private sources of financing and investment. This significant increase in private investment in the water sector did not materialize for the most part since the risks were seen as too high and the potential returns modest at best. However in Dar es Salaam, under the World Bank proposal, during the initial years of the rehabilitation project an international utility management company would contribute a modest amount of its own financing ($8.5 million) to cover electricity bills, chemical purchases, and new equipment (computers and vehicles).

Second, a private operator would bring technological, operational, and managerial skills and experience to bear on Dar es Salaam's increasingly complex challenges.[10] A private firm would also be able to facilitate the transfer of new technologies and business practices, speeding up the operations and the modernization of the existing system. A private operator would therefore be well positioned to achieve cost savings. More efficient operations could translate into reduced charges to customers and reduced government subsidies (freeing up scarce government resources for other purposes).

Third, the performance and accountability of the water service would be improved because a private sector operator would be subject to a contract with explicit parameters, performance incentives and operational targets. Under some government-run utilities, managers and employees were paid regardless of whether customers received water or not. With the right contract and incentives in place, private sector operators had proven more than willing to improve services to currently unserviced and underserviced customers, both poor and wealthy.

Fourth, it was argued that, in theory, an independent private operator would help reduce political interference in the water sector. In the past, politicians had tended to base water policies on political criteria (e.g. setting water rates below cost recovery) rather than on the financial needs and ultimate long-term sustainability of the system. The intention was that an independent regulator would be established to set water rates fairly and help settle disputes between the private sector company, the customers and the government. Under this arrangement, the government maintained ultimate ownership and control over water resources and infrastructure; it regulated the private sector utility through an independent regulator.

Fifth, introducing a private operator further reinforced the concept of full-cost pricing (with safety nets for the poor) for water services. This pricing model might have been easier for governments to introduce with a private sector partner. Full-cost pricing for water could, in turn, reduce water wastage and overuse for low-value-added activities (e.g. lawn watering and vehicle washing) and improve the conservation of a scarce resource.

Although not directly comparable, some supporters of international private participation in the sector pointed to the thousands of small-scale private water sellers already operating on a purely free market basis in Dar es Salaam. These private sellers included hand carters, private borehole operators and water tanker operators, as well as some people who sold water to their neighbors from their own house connection. These private entrepreneurs were effectively, and some times innovatively, providing water to both rich and poor citizens alike who were not being serviced or were underserviced by the ailing public system. This activity, they claimed, was evidence that the "private sector" had already stepped in to meet an important need efficiently and effectively.

---

10   All domestic consumers were paying a flat rate charge based on an exaggerated estimate of the amount of water supplied. Because DAWASA had not been allowed for some years to increase the unit tariff, it had adjusted the estimated consumption upwards.

Cons

Despite a number of apparent advantages of private sector participation, there was also evidence to oppose this form of utility operation in Dar es Salaam and other cities in the developing world.

First, worldwide, 85 per cent of drinking water provision remained the responsibility of public utilities. In the developed world, most Organisation for Economic Cooperation and Development (OECD) countries opted for public sector provision of water; the United Kingdom and France were the two exceptions where water and waste-water services were provided by the private sector or some form of public–private partnership.[11] Most of the developed countries seemed to believe public provision of water was better. Opponents were also quick to point to the many instances where an international private operator had failed in its attempts to effectively run a water utility in a developing country.

Second, provision of water services in urban areas were a "natural monopoly" due to the efficiencies achieved through economies of scale. Private operators would not face direct competition for the delivery of water services (although competition was introduced through the bidding process for the contract). The success of private sector involvement in utility management in developing countries was often highly dependent on the capacity of the government and the independent regulatory agency established to impartially oversee the operation of the contract, including mediating disputes and setting prices. In the absence of a capable government and regulator, the risks of failure of the private contractor increased as the risks of political interference increased. It was argued that weak public sector capacity was a good argument against private sector participation, rather than for it.

Third, opponents of private sector participation in Dar es Salaam's water utility were alarmed at what some perceived as the transfer of ownership of water resources from public to private hands, shifting the balance of power away from governments toward an international company. They believed that the purpose of private sector companies was to make profits, not to promote the public good, and they warned against "the privatization of water." They emphasized that water was a fundamental human right, essential for life, and they rejected the concept that it should have an economic value to be bought and sold in the marketplace like a common commodity.

Fourth, opponents also objected to the entire thrust of the government's economic reforms to liberalize markets, encourage foreign investment and increase the role of the private sector in the economy. They claimed that these reforms were forced upon developing countries by the World Bank and other external donors. Opponents also argued that local and international opposition to private sector involvement in the water sector was often ignored or repressed and that there was little, if any, meaningful public participation or consultation about water sector reforms.

Fifth, private sector participation was often accompanied by an increase in the price for water since government-managed systems often failed to charge enough to cover basic costs. Opponents believed that private sector participation would make water

---

11   Jacqueline Medalye, *A Study of Public–Private Partnerships in the Water Sector*, unpublished study prepared for David Wheeler, chair, Erivan K. Haub Program in Business and Sustainability, Schulich School of Business, York University, Toronto, Canada, 2004, p. 9. In France, for example, private water concessions had been issued for more than 200 years.

unaffordable for the great majority of the city's poor and that increased water costs would simply generate profits for large international water companies—profits that would not stay in the country. Opponents also questioned the claim that with the right incentives private companies could be motivated to provide and improve service to unserviced and underserviced households. They believed that private operators had a bias towards serving richer populations that represented more attractive markets, rather than low-income populations that often required innovative solutions, incentives and partnerships to serve. There was concern that private sector participation would therefore potentially increase inequalities among the urban population.

Sixth, some also argued that opportunities to develop local talent and expertise would be lost since engineers and managers would be hired from abroad. Opponents were also concerned about loss of jobs and increased job insecurity at the utility as a private company would want to achieve productivity improvements and cost reductions by reducing staff.

Other Models

As Minister Lowassa pondered the decision, he also recalled several recent examples of water systems that had been rehabilitated without involving the private sector in their operations and management. Several of the larger towns in Tanzania, such as Arusha, Tanga and Moshi (with populations between 100,000 and 300,000), had rebuilt their water systems by attracting both grant funding and debt funding from bilateral donors, such as the German aid agency Kreditanstalt für Wiederaufbau (KfW). Water provision in these three towns was governed by local autonomous water authorities with their own Boards (the granting of autonomy had been a precondition for obtaining the last portion of KfW funding).[12] The resulting improvements to water quality, pressure, and availability meant that the water utilities in these towns were now collecting more revenues. There remained, however, some question as to the ultimate viability and sustainability of these systems if donor support were to be withdrawn altogether. Could the government further refine this model or would an international utility management firm be a better choice? Lowassa reminded himself that no single bilateral development agency felt that it could take on a city the size of Dar es Salaam given the amount of money required and the deteriorated state of the existing system.

At the same time, the International Finance Corporation (the private sector arm of the World Bank) was celebrating the success of Manila Water in the Philippines (see

---

12   In theory, but not in practice, Dar es Salaam water supply had had a similar autonomy since the 1970s. At that time it was the Dar es Salaam Water Corporation Sole. In the early '80s, at the World Bank's insistence, the National Urban Water Authority (NUWA) was set up. It initialling included Moshi and Iringa in addition to Dar es Salaam.

   When NUWA took over from the Dar Water Corporation it did not have the required funds to start the implementation. Both Moshi and Iringa had had consultancy designs prepared by Gauff in hopes of World Bank funding of their transition to autonomous operations, but investments did not materialize until KfW came along to support the Moshi project. Iringa is still under consideration for funding by the European Union.

Exhibit 9.6 The Success of Private Operator Manila Water in Rehabilitating the System and Improving Water Provision to the Poor

Source: V.C. Rivera, Manila Water Company, Inc., Presentation at the 3rd World Water Forum: Water and Poverty Initiative Multi-stakeholders Dialogue on Water Services for the Urban Poor, May 29–31, 2002, http://www.adb.org/Documents/Events/2002/Third_Water_Forum/Manila_Water_Presentation.pdf, accessed February 1, 2007, and V. K. Rangan, J. Comeault, D. Wheeler, Manila Water Company, forthcoming, Harvard Business Press (personal communication with the authors).

The water and sanitation system in Manila, Philippines, was taken over by Philippine private companies in 1997 under two separate concession contracts divided into East and West Zones. The Manila Water Company (Manila Water) was one of the two private operators and over the last several years it has been remarkably successful in improving service to customers, including the poor. This has been accomplished in the face of a number of considerable obstacles, including the Asian Financial Crisis of the late 1990s, a severe drought caused by El Niño in 1998 and NGO anti-water privatization activism.

Since it began operations in 1997, Manila Water has expanded service coverage by 71 per cent from 325,000 to 556,000 households. The company also has nearly doubled the volume of water running through its distribution network. Non-revenue water (i.e. water lost due to leakage or illegal tapping) has dropped from 63 per cent (before privatization) to 36 per cent. The percentage of areas that have 24-hour access to water has increased from 26 per cent to 89 per cent. Manila Water has also improved the water quality standard from 91 per cent in 1997 to 99.84 per cent in 2004, exceeding the national benchmark of 95 per cent.

In the highly political environment of Manila, where at least 40 per cent of the population is poor, Manila Water's leadership has recognized the direct connection between "soft" issues such as quality of service, ability to reach the poorest, transparency and stakeholder consultation and the "hard" issue of delivering shareholder value. Manila Water has been able to pull off this successful privatization for a number of reasons, including good operational management and a clear business case for proactive relations with poor communities.

Manila Water has actively developed programs to meet the needs of the city's large low-income population. This includes a "Water for the Community" program which provides safe drinking water to informal settlements, while reducing water losses caused by unregistered connections from these areas. Over the past eight years, this program has served about 820,000 people in 517 low-income communities. The company's target is to serve 100,000 additional people from poor communities every year.

The Water for the Community projects rely on Manila Water's ability to identify or help organize local resident cooperatives that collectively take responsibility for a community water connection and metering scheme. With a community organization in place, Manila Water typically installs a "mother meter" to the whole community and individual sub-meters to serve four or five households each. The whole community is accountable for paying the gross water consumption on the mother meter and each family settles its own bill with a community representative. The program successfully reduces illegal con-

(continued opposite)

(from previous page)

nections while lowering maintenance costs and provides clean water at approximately 5 per cent of the cost that these communities would otherwise pay. As a result of its ability to provide service to the poor as well as its excellent managerial and financial performance, the Manila Water concession is now regarded as one of the most successful public–private partnerships in the world.

EXHIBIT 9.7   A Ugandan Model for Improved Water and Sanitation Provision through Growing Local Private Water Operators

Source: K. Winfred, *Access to Drinking Water and Sanitation: The Role of Local Private Initiatives*, December 1, 2006, OECD Paris, www.oecd.org/dataoecd/50/25/37787617.ppt, accessed February 1, 2006.

The Ugandan government has made the provision of clean water one of its top three priorities (along with health and education). It supports the most effective means of achieving its water provision goals, including involving local private companies.

In December 2003, a group of local Ugandan private sector water utility companies formed the Association of Private Water Operators (APWO) in Uganda. In early 2006, the APWOs eight member companies were responsible for providing water to 50 small urban centres in Uganda. Five other individuals operate water systems in rural growth areas. Each private operator signs a one to three year contract with the local water authority that sets out expected performance targets, prices and expectations.

Private sector involvement in the water sector in Uganda is relatively new and many of APWOs members are also new to the business. But their success has encouraged more small urban centres (those with populations between 5,000 and 15,000) to contract the management of their water systems to local private companies.

The past chairman of APWO, Engineer Mutikanga Harrison, illustrates the potential of this model of private sector participation: "In view of the on-going reforms in the water sector we could probably form companies that may one day be in a position to manage even bigger towns."

With the support of the government, there is momentum from a number of industry stakeholders that private sector participation is the way forward to improve service in the water sector. With appropriate professional support and regulation, many stakeholders in Uganda believe that local private operators are a viable option for small towns today, and could expand to encompass larger urban centers and a greater number of rural areas in the future.

It should be noted that the successful private sector participation in the water sector in Uganda has only materialized after two other unsuccessful attempts to involve private sector actors with different structures and approaches to the one currently being implemented.

Exhibits 9.6 and 9.7). This initiative was seen by some as an extremely successful example of private sector participation in the water and sanitation sector. Manila's crumbling infrastructure had been rehabilitated, several hundred thousand poor city residents in unplanned informal settlements were now receiving clean reliable water at affordable prices, and tens of thousands of households were receiving house connections every year.

Next door to Tanzania in Uganda (see Exhibit 9.6), a group of local Ugandan private water utility operators was beginning to demonstrate the possibility that local firms could efficiently run small-town water systems. They did not have nearly enough capacity to take on the operation of a large city, such as Kampala, Uganda or Dar es Salaam, but perhaps eventually, as they envisioned, the operation of a large city water utility might be possible.

In Dar es Salaam, the role of the international private operator would be limited — the international operator would not own the water resources or the water delivery infrastructure. However, in accordance with Tanzania's recently approved water policy, the international firm would have discretion over, and responsibility for, the day-to-day operation and maintenance of the water delivery system.

Minister Lowassa thought about how much was hanging in the balance. Many countries in Africa did not have a tradition of private sector involvement. Only the francophone countries in West and North Africa had a history of successful private sector participation.[13] Anglophone West African countries, such as Ghana and Nigeria, had recently attempted projects similar to the one Tanzania was now contemplating, but these projects had unleashed significant opposition from the public and from local and international NGOs. In Ghana, fierce protests and accusations of high-level corruption had recently forced the World Bank to withdraw its support for a proposal for a private firm to operate the water utility in the country's capital, Accra. In Nigeria, protesters marched with coffins to demonstrate their anger at what they saw as the water privatization agenda of the government and the World Bank.

Finding reputable and interested private operators might also prove challenging, given that there were only a handful of companies in this industry that were large enough and capable enough to take on the job. In addition, after an initial wave of interest in the late 1990s, many international water companies were now taking a long hard look at potential risks of investing in the water sector on the African continent.

Minister Lowassa knew that Tanzania's decision regarding the provision of water in Dar es Salaam would be watched closely by other governments, financial institutions and donor agencies. Around the world, two billion people still lacked access to safe water sources. The success or failure of Tanzania's attempt to revive its ailing water infrastructure would send a signal to potential investors in the country and would be noted by other stakeholders who were observing the continent's larger efforts to chart a course for improved social and economic development.

---

13   For example, Côte d'Ivoire had entered into a lease contract with the French international water utility operator Saur in 1960. Saur had also been operating lease contracts in Guinea since 1989, in the Central African Republic since 1991, in Senegal since 1996, and in Mali since 2000. The international water utility operator Vivendi had been operating lease contracts in Niger and Gabon since 1997 and management contracts in Chad since 2000 and in Burkina Faso since 2001.

Section B: Privatizing Dar es Salaam's Water Utility

On February 19, 2003, after a competitive bidding process, the Tanzanian government signed a ten-year lease contract which put the operation and maintenance of the Dar es Salaam water utility into private hands. City Water Services, Ltd (a Tanzanian-registered private water operator with UK, German and Tanzania shareholders) was appointed as operator.[14],[15] Two of the prominent figures in the negotiation and implementation of the contract were Edward Lowassa, the Minister of Water[16] for the Tanzanian government, and Cliff Stone, Biwater's former director of sales for Africa, who was in charge of managing the change for City Water.

The parties had considered two other alternatives: a management contract or a concession contract, both of which had previously been used by other governments and private sector operators.[17] The main differences between lease, management and concession contracts concerned the allocation of risks and responsibilities between the public and private sector, the basis on which the private operator is remunerated, the financing mechanism, and the duration of the contract (see Exhibit 9.8). Management contracts were typically short-term agreements (one to five years), and they had the least commercial risk for a private sector operator. Financing of capital investments were the responsibility of the government, which maintained public asset ownership. Concession contracts were typically long-term agreements (20 to 30 years). Although the government maintained asset ownership, the private operator assumed commercial and operational risks by taking responsibility for all operations as well as financing capital investments. A lease contract fell in between management contracts and concession contracts. In lease contracts, the public sector handed responsibility for overall operations and maintenance to the private operator. The private operator bore the commercial risk over the duration of the contract (which was typically eight to 15

---

14 The United Republic of Tanzania, Dar es Salaam Water Supply and Sanitation Project: Project Restructuring (Credit 3771-TA).

15 A ten-year Development Contract was also signed between the United Republic of Tanzania and DAWASA setting out the framework for the development of capital investments. This contract specified the conditions under which the Capital Investment Program was financed by the government of Tanzania (with funding from the World Bank) and implemented by DAWASA.

16 The Ministry Lowassa headed was officially titled the Ministry of Water and Livestock Development after responsibilities for water and livestock were merged in 2001.

17 There were also other types of contracts in addition to those mentioned, including Build, Operate, Transfer (BOT) contracts, which were typical in new infrastructure construction projects (e.g. building a water treatment plant) and complete divestiture contracts, where the private owner assumed ownership of the assets and all responsibility for the operation (although complete divestiture contracts were rare).

EXHIBIT 9.8 Alternative Contractual Arrangements in the Water Sector

Source: Adapted from *New Designs for Water and Sanitation Transactions: Making Private Sector Participation Work for the Poor*, Public Private Infrastructure Advisory Faculty and Water and Sanitation Program, Washington, DC, 2002 and from David Hall et al., *Water Privatisation in Africa*, Public Services International Research Unit, 2002. http://www.psiru.org/reports/2002-12-W-DSAAfricawater.doc, accessed February 1, 2007.

Contract Type	Nature	Responsibility/Risk	Remuneration	Examples
Management	Transfers responsibility for managing operation and maintenance to the private sector.	Only limited operational responsibility given to the private operator.	Fixed fee or fee plus payments, sometimes performance-related.	Johannesburg Gambia Mali Namibia São Tomé and Príncipe Burkina Faso Uganda
Lease	The private operator takes responsibility for operating and maintaining the infrastructure but is not required to fund investment in the system. The operator pays a lease fee to the contracting authority.	Greater responsibility given to the private company, including all technical and commercial management of existing operations. Funding of new capacity investment normally retained by the government. Commercial risk: the operator's revenue is dependent on tariffs.	The private operator collects tariffs into its own account. The operator pays a lease fee to the water authority's account. The balance of the tariff revenue is paid to the private operator. Performance bonuses may be paid related to efficiency.	Dar es Salaam Mozambique Côte d'Ivoire Senegal Niger Guinea DR Congo Central African Republic
Concession	Long-term right to use all utility assets is conferred on private operator, including responsibility for all operation and investment.	Complete responsibility for management and investment transferred to the private operator.	Remuneration for the concessionaire is from the revenue collected. The government receives a concession fee from the concessionaire.	Cameroon Morocco Gabon Nelspruit, South Africa Cape Verde Mozambique

years). The government retained all ownership rights and finances all major capital investments with advice from the private operator.

To select the international private operator, the government of Tanzania followed the international competitive bidding process. Three international water utility firms— Biwater, Vivendi and Saur—participated in a number of successive rounds of bidding. Each round helped align the interests of the government, the international operators and the funding agencies. In the end, the contract went to Biwater,[18] a UK-based water and waste-water treatment company, which had joined forces with Gauff Ingenieure, a German engineering consulting company.[19] At the end of the final round both Vivendi and Saur declined to submit a bid, although they had participated in all the pre-bid meetings and processes. Their decisions surprised both the government and the World Bank. The Biwater–Gauff's bid met all technical and financial requirements, and the DAWASA–City Water alliance was duly awarded a 10-year lease contract.

The lease contract required the international utility firm to form a consortium with a Tanzanian company. During the pre-award negotiation phase, Biwater–Gauff brought on board Superdoll Trailer Manufacture (STM), a Tanzanian company that had successfully taken over two of the country's state-owned sugar companies and turned them into commercially viable firms. STM did not have any previous experience in managing a utility; however, its understanding of the local social and economic context and its involvement in the Tanzanian economy were seen as welcome contributions. The required equity contribution from the Tanzanian partner was 20 per cent; however, STM successfully negotiated with Biwater–Gauff a 49 per cent share. This significantly reduced the equity contribution of the international operator.

Past experience in Africa and elsewhere had shown that an essential element of successful public–private water sector arrangements was the existence of a strong, impartial and effective independent regulator. In Tanzania, a new government regulatory body, the Energy and Water Utility Regulatory Authority (EWURA), was to be set up to regulate the operations of City Water and oversee the ownership rights of DAWASA.[20]

18 Biwater, the leading company in the consortium, specialized in construction and operation of water and waste-water treatment facilities. Biwater also operated water and waste-water treatment concessions in Bournemouth and West Hampshire in the United Kingdom. Biwater was founded in 1968, and had signed its first overseas contract in Nigeria in 1975. Most of Biwater's work in Africa was construction projects, although it was also involved in utility management in South Africa. Although it was not in the same league as large international water utility companies, such as Vivendi and Saur, Biwater was currently working in South Africa, Ghana, Nigeria, Libya, and Algeria. The Dar es Salaam contract was one of the company's largest contracts to date.

19 Gauff had worked in East Africa for 35 years and had been involved in utility management in Kenya and Uganda.

20 However, the regulatory body, EWURA, only became effective in 2006.

The Terms of the Lease

The lease, which came into effect on August 1, 2003,[21] specified that DAWASA (the former operator of the water and sewerage system) would retain full ownership rights of all of the fixed assets of the water utility (i.e. the pipes, pumping stations, meters, and so forth). City Water would be responsible for operating and maintaining DAWASA's water and sewerage infrastructure, employ the utility's 1,400 employees, bill the utility's 50,000 commercial, public sector and household customers at specified rates and be responsible for collecting fees.[22]

DAWASA would be responsible for financing and developing water supply and sanitation facilities in Dar es Salaam. The Tanzanian government (through DAWASA) would retain overall responsibility for financing and rehabilitating Dar es Salaam's water system and would control the $156.5 million loan from the World Bank and its partners. Much of this money would be allocated to construction projects managed by DAWASA, one of which was subcontracted to City Water at a value of about US$35 million. Included in the overall award to City Water were two smaller ($9 million) contracts for the procurement and installation of water meters and for the supply and installation of water plant equipment. These two contracts were an important part of the lease contract and were seen as necessary to enable City Water to generate additional revenues since revenues from water utility customers was not yet near breakeven level. City Water was also responsible for contributing US$8.5 million as working capital to fund equipment regarded as essential for the success of the contract, such as vehicles and computers.

Tariffs and Pricing

During the first year of operation, City Water produced a total of approximately 90 million cubic meters of water and incurred water-related operating costs of TZS16,742 million.[23] However, because physical and commercial losses amounted to two-thirds of total water produced, City Water was only able to generate revenue from approximately 30 million cubic meters of water.

---

21   The contract documents comprised a 120-page main volume and a separate volume with 14 Appendices. A different volume contained the results of all the negotiations and pre-award discussions as well as three smaller contracts that complemented the lease contract and had been signed that same day: a Supply and Installation of Plant and Equipment (SIPE) contract, a Purchase of Goods (POG) contract, and a Government Subloan Agreement. There was also a six-volume Project Operation Manual.

22   The contract included numerous targets which had to be met. There were no financial or other incentives for bettering any target. Failure to meet a target would trigger financial penalties. If a number of key targets were not met the contract could be cancelled. The terms also allowed for a major review by both parties after five years, at which time the Government had the right to terminate the contract.

23   Based on the exchange rate of US$1 = 1,170 Tanzanian shillings (as at January 1, 2006), TZS16,742 was the equivalent to approximately US$15 million.

With the commencement of the lease contract, the price for "lifeline" water services provided by City Water to customers was regulated: the first five cubic meters per month[24] were provided at a reduced rate of TZS322 per cubic meter (about US$0.28).[25] Volumes above five cubic meters per month would be charged at TZS432 (or about US$0.37) per cubic meter of water for domestic use and TZS725 ($0.62) for non-domestic use.[26]

The lease contract specified that City Water would keep TZS322 from each cubic meter of water sold. For volumes exceeding the lifeline amount, City Water would pay the difference of TZS110 per cubic meter to the government, via DAWASA. This arrangement came to be known within City Water as the DAWASA tariff since it was designed to cover DAWASA's expenses, including the debt service on the World Bank loans, DAWASA's overhead costs and funding future capital expenditure programs.

Although these water tariffs were increased slightly in 2003 and 2004 (see Exhibit 9.9), they were still not high enough to generate revenues that would make the system financially self-sufficient. The government and City Water knew that water rates would have to rise further over the life of the 10-year contract, but they also acknowledged that it would be best if rates rose slowly in line with improvements in water and sewerage services so that customers could associate increased rates with improved service.

EXHIBIT 9.9 City Water Tariff Charges for Water Supply, 2002–2004

Source: DAWASA Lease Contract Done, http://www.globalwaterintel.com/index.php?page=articleView&articleId=510, accessed February 1, 2007; and Masebu, Haruna, "Private Public Cooperation in Infrastructure Development and Maintenance," October 20, 2003, http://info.worldbank.org/.../114925/eum/docs/eum/tanzania/ MODULEIVPRIVATEPUBLICCOOPERATIONININFRASTRUCTURE.ppt, accessed February 1, 2007.

Water Supply Charge per m³ of water (TZS)	Aug 2002	Aug 2003	Aug 2004
Lifeline Tariff (to City Water)	322	337	359
Domestic Tariff			
Operator (City Water) Tariff	322	337	359
Lessor (DAWASA) Tariff	110	114	147
Total Domestic Tariff	432	451	506
Non-domestic (Commercial) Tariff	725	725	725

24 The lifeline volumes were equivalent to an individual family member requiring 40 liters of water per day (four liters for drinking, eight liters for cooking, 12 liters for bathing, and 16 liters for sanitation), which, for a family of four, would equal just less than five cubic meters per month.

25 Each cubic meter contained 1,000 liters of water.

26 These tariffs were in place when City Water began operations and were increased to TZS359 (lifeline) and TZS506 (regular tariff) in late 2004, in accordance with the indexation formula agreed in the lease contract.

Implementation Benefits and Challenges

For low-income households, there were many economic and social benefits to being connected to the City Water piped water system since alternative sources of water were often considerably more expensive per unit volume. Houses connected to small private networks supplied by borehole operators paid approximately TZS1,000 per cubic meter, and houses that received water by tanker truck paid about TZS2,000 per cubic meter. In poorer neighborhoods, such as Temeke, residents sourced water from unprotected (and often polluted) streams for free, or paid TZS500 to 1,000 per cubic meter from locally operated community water kiosks or TZS5,000 to 10,000 per cubic meter for water delivered to their door by a hand carter.

Access to piped water from the utility would improve the health of the family by reducing its dependence on polluted stream and well water. It would decrease the amount of time and energy devoted to hauling water (usually the task of women and girls), reduce the family's expenses and provide convenient washing and sanitation. Realistically, however, few expected many low-income households to be provided with individual house connections to the system for many years. In the interim, what could be reasonably hoped for would be for the new water utility to extend the network to low-income areas and install water kiosks from which clean water could be sourced.

However, because the contract was highly complex, City Water and the government could interpret a particular section in a somewhat different way. For example, in the case of determining whether or not a household was eligible for a free first-time connection, the criteria was "three water points." But the contract did not explain what counted as a water point. Was it a tap or a water entry point into a dwelling unit? Such differences in interpretation could slow down the provision of first-time connections.

Overall, City Water regarded the lease contract as a guide to be adhered to as far as practicable but to be negotiated where circumstances were found to make it impracticable. DAWASA, however, regarded it as a bible to be rigidly adhered to and strictly interpreted. This was not a good recipe for an amicable working relationship.

Section C(1): The Private Sector Experiment

On the warm tropical evening of May 1, 2005, Edward Lowassa walked the beach in downtown Dar es Salaam, reflecting on some of his own efforts to improve the water and sewerage services in the city over the last three years.[27] As Minister for Water in the Tanzanian government, he had been involved in updating Tanzania's National Water Policy and had been part of the discussions with the World Bank and other funders regarding the US$165 million project to rehabilitate Dar es Salaam's aging water infrastructure through partnership with an international private sector operator. Minister Lowassa knew that this internationally sponsored project was one of the most ambitious deals in the water sector in Africa. His government hoped that the partnership with City Water would help transform a leaky and antiquated government-run water utility into a commercially viable private company-run enterprise.

Many observers saw Tanzania's move as a flagship test case—politically, socially, and economically. Expectations were high. If this approach succeeded, it could help provide better water and sewerage services to hundreds of thousands of people in Dar es Salaam. Failure had implications for access to safe water locally, but also had larger implications for potential foreign investors in Tanzania and for other international water utility management firms considering doing business in Africa.

The Economic, Social and Political Aftermath of the Privatization Decision

Two years after he had welcomed the initial lease contract with City Water, Minister Lowassa was questioning the performance of the private operator now servicing Dar es Salaam's residents. Lowassa had expected that City Water would have completed equity investments of $8.5 million by this point in the contract. From City Water's perspective, it had invested US$4.1 million in the first 18 months of the project—approximately half the amount in half the time, which was on target for the contribution of $8.5 million over the three-year period specified in the lease agreement. City Water had, however, withheld some of its payments to the Dar es Salaam Water and Sewerage Authority (DAWASA), known as the DAWASA tariff, by an estimated $3.6 million. This was likely intended to bring DAWASA to the negotiating table and put pressure on the local partner, Superdoll Trailer Manufacture (STM), to contribute its share of the equity installment, which it had so far failed to do.

---

27 This scenario was written for teaching purposes. It does not necessarily reflect actual events or actual opinions of the actors and it includes fictitious details.

Lowassa was well aware of the unforeseen difficulties that City Water had encountered since starting operations in August 2003. He knew that there were still tens of thousands of illegal customers in Dar es Salaam who tapped into the water mains and pipes to take water without paying. In addition, many customers who were legitimately connected to the system were not paying their bills. Cliff Stone's predecessor as chief executive officer (CEO) of City Water, Mike O'Leary, had taken legal action against the illegal users and disconnected customers who hadn't paid their water bills. This approach hadn't been particularly successful in decreasing lost water or increasing revenues but it had been successful in attracting the ire of customers, politicians, and civil society. Ultimately, O'Leary was forced to quit because of the negative impact of his actions on City Water's stakeholder relations.

In accordance with contract requirements, City Water declared a six-month amnesty for customers with illegal connections. Stone had hoped that this reprieve would encourage people to legitimize their hook-ups and settle their accounts without penalty; however, out of an estimated 40,000 illegal customers, only 2,500 came forward during the amnesty. Although Lowassa appreciated City Water's attempts to manage in a more inclusive and conciliatory manner, he also believed that this situation was one example of City Water's poor stakeholder relations and lack of sensitivity to the Tanzanian cultural context.

Although Stone and Biwater had some international experience, Lowassa believed that the four expatriate managers at City Water didn't fully understand Tanzanian culture, including its bias towards non-confrontation. Dar es Salaam was not Nairobi, the capital city of neighboring Kenya, where it was typical to take a much more confrontational and aggressive approach to dealing with people. In Tanzania, competition and aggression were treated with mistrust and suspicion.

When Lowassa and other Tanzanian political leaders had asked Tanzanians to accept private sector participation in the water sector (along with the associated principles of cost recovery for services), they were asking for a major shift for citizens. Many people, especially those who came to the city from the country and those who lived in the low-income neighborhoods, still understood water as coming freely from the heavens, and not out of taps that they had to pay for. Decades of socialist leadership by Julius Nyerere had led most people to expect that the government would help people meet their basic needs.

At the same time, Lowassa and the government were only just learning how to deal with foreign investors and large private companies, and were not always sure how they operated or what to expect. The government was much more accustomed to dealing with donors (who contributed 42 per cent of the total government budget). Too often, donors did not impose high levels of accountability on their money. The government had been accustomed to getting away with making mistakes (e.g. the millions of dollars of donor money that had been invested in the Dar es Salaam water system in previous decades without noticeable improvements).

Led by their government, Tanzanians had been optimistic that moving from socialism to a market economy with private investment would improve their well-being. They were willing to give the government the benefit of the doubt and trusted their leadership. Privately, it was believed, the government was having many discussions about how much privatization and economic reform it could undertake, while being able to keep opposition criticism of the downsides of economic reforms and private sector involvement in the economy at bay.

To stay in power, the government had to win the national elections that were scheduled for December of the current year. If the electorate began to believe that privatization and market liberalization were not improving their lives, then these issues could be effective rallying points for the opposition parties. Government opponents could easily point to the clash between the expectations of the foreign investors (i.e. to charge for water, to cut off people who were not paying their bills or to take illegal tappers to court) with the reality of living conditions of the majority of voters who were very poor.

Just a few years previously, private sector involvement in water provision in Cochabamba, Bolivia, had been the tipping point for grievances against the government, sparking violence and riots against the government and the company. Water was one of the most sensitive areas of private sector involvement in the Tanzanian economy. In order to secure re-election, Lowassa and the government would want to avoid voter dissatisfaction over water-related issues at any cost.

International development advocacy organizations exacerbated local tensions. For example, the UK-based organization ActionAid released a report in September 2004 that claimed private sector participation in the sector had increased costs to the poor without improving services. The report also stated that international donors, such as the World Bank, were "using their influence to push poor countries into privatizing basic services such as water, with little concern for the views of the public or poor people's needs."[28] The report argued that donors applied both "hard" pressure, in the form of conditions attached to aid and debt relief, and "soft" pressure, through technical assistance, privatization-friendly consultancies, and other forms of policy advice. The ActionAid report further argued that the privatization process had been conducted with very little meaningful public participation or consultation and limited public debate. City Water did not issue any official statement in response.

The ActionAid report also discounted the company's "pro-poor" measures to establish new water kiosks in slum areas, such as Temeke, as paltry and tokenistic compared to the scale of unmet needs. The report claimed that donor resources and the Tanzanian government's current and future tax revenues were being used to fund a project in which 98 per cent of the money was spent on the richest 20 per cent of the city's population, ignoring the needs of the low-income households in the city's slums who had dim prospects of ever being legally connected to the piped water system. Although Minister Lowassa did not agree with all the points raised by ActionAid, and knew of City Water's efforts to prioritize service to low-income areas, he did know that the report was indicative of a certain segment of international and local opinion.

As the minister responsible for water, Edward Lowassa had provided necessary support to City Water during the first year of the lease contract. He had made favorable comments in the press, encouraging customers to be patient and supportive while they waited for improvements in the system to affect their daily lives. Since February 2005, however, Minister Lowassa seemed to be experiencing a change of heart. In newspaper articles, he began to openly criticize City Water for failing to live up to initial expectations and for falling short of its promised commitments. Was the lease contract doomed

28   "Turning off the Taps: Donor Conditionality and Water Privatization in Dar es Salaam, Tanzania," ActionAid, London, England, 2004.

to failure? He considered this possibility as he watched a water seller pushing a two-wheeled cart of yellow plastic jerry cans along the seaside road, destined for city residents who still had no water connection in their houses. Minister Lowassa knew that new pipes had yet to be installed and he knew that most Dar es Salaam residents had not yet seen clear benefits from private sector involvement in the water system.

As Lowassa continued his journey and prepared to meet Cliff Stone the next morning, he thought about what he would do.

Section C(2): Striking a Deal

On the warm tropical evening of May 1, 2005, Cliff Stone walked the beach in downtown Dar es Salaam, reflecting on some of his own efforts to improve the water and sewerage services in the city over the last three years.[29] Stone was now chief executive officer (CEO) of City Water, the private sector consortium that operated Dar es Salaam's water utility. had come to Tanzania in December 2002, when his UK-based international company, Biwater, had won the contract for operating Dar es Salaam's existing water utility (taking over operations from the public utility, Dar es Salaam Water and Sewerage Authority, or DAWASA). Stone personally believed in the viability of the contract and was committed to making it work. In August 2003, Stone had been present for the handover of operations from DAWASA to City Water. The opening address of his predecessor, Graham Gorrod, City Water's acting CEO when the contract was awarded, had been a vivid reminder of the sense of challenge and shared optimism that marked the beginning of City Water's operations:

> We understand the immediate need for improvements in the system, but unfortunately, the residents of Dar es Salaam will not notice a difference overnight. The problems that affect the water and sewerage systems will take a great deal of work to fix properly. A quick fix will not work. Dar es Salaam needs a long term, reliable and sustainable water and sewerage system and that is what City Water will provide over the 10-year period.[30,31]

Stone, who had taken over from O'Leary as CEO on September 1, 2004, had been a key player in Biwater's internationalization. In the late 1980s, he had been involved in the construction, operation, and maintenance of part of a water supply project in Malaysia, which, at the time, was Biwater's largest overseas project. He had later worked in many countries, including Ghana, Nigeria, Guatemala, Mexico, South Korea, and Indonesia. Just before taking on the CEO role for City Water, Stone had been head of sales for sub-Saharan Africa. In that role he had developed a personal interest in the social as well as economic development of Africa. Although he didn't have any previous experience in Tanzania or in managing a water utility, Stone believed that the City

---

29 This scenario was written for teaching purposes. It does not necessarily reflect actual events or actual opinions of the actors and it includes fictitious details.

30 Adapted from a quote by Mike O'Leary cited by Neil Ford, "Countryfile Tanzania: Water Concession Goes Down the Drain," *African Business*, July 2005, pp. 50-51.

31 In hindsight, this may have been overly ambitious. The initial lease negotiations did not surface a number of concerns that soon came to hinder the implementation of the contract, including the incompleteness of the Data Room Documents regarding the availability of water and the state of the water infrastructure, the hidden costs in the DAWASA accounts, and the expectations of the staff in terms of work hours, work performance, salaries, and disparities in compensation between locals and expatriates.

Water contract held a lot of promise that could bear fruit for both the residents of Dar es Salaam and Biwater's investors over the next 10 years.

Many observers saw Tanzania's move as a flagship test case—politically, socially, and economically. Expectations were high. If this approach succeeded, it could help provide better water and sewerage services to hundreds of thousands of people in Dar es Salaam. Failure had implications on access to safe water locally, but also had larger implications for potential foreign investors in Tanzania and for other international water utility management firms considering doing business in similar countries in Africa.

City Water's Struggle for Commercial Viability

Over the last few years, Stone's biggest concern had been increasing the revenues of the water utility. Actual revenues lagged the initial projections by a significant margin, and this gap was affecting the financial viability of the project. City Water had tried a couple of approaches for reducing illegal water use and collecting the overdue accounts of legal customers; however, both the legal battles and an amnesty for illegal connections had failed to significantly improve revenues. City Water's limited success in collecting overdue accounts actually worsened once rumors spread that the company might be struggling. Customers might have assumed that no one would follow up on their bills, as had been the case before City Water had taken over from DAWASA.

Stone did know that, in contrast to popular perception, City Water had achieved some modest accomplishments in the past two years. City Water had signed up more than 10,000 new customers and had introduced a new billing system. The company had also successfully refurbished some major electrical and mechanical equipment, which, in turn, had improved service reliability, water quality, and water quantity. The utility's existing assets were being operated more efficiently. Designs for nearly 1,000 kilometers of new secondary and tertiary distribution pipelines had been completed, and contractors were already at work on a few small rehabilitation contracts. The first large rehabilitation contract was currently out for tender.

Stone was proud of City Water's plans for installing 600 water kiosks, double the number required by the original contract, to serve the poor in peri-urban areas (areas in transition from being rural to becoming urban), such as much of Temeke. Stone believed that these kiosks would serve low-income neighborhoods as well as help reduce illegal tapping by increasing the availability of safe and affordable water in many poor areas. The kiosks would be run by individual entrepreneurs who would pay City Water the basic lifeline rate for all the water received and then sell the tap water to customers or hand carters. When built, these kiosks would be an intermediate solution for providing water to customers without house connections in areas where previously no water pipelines existed.

Stone took pride in all these important accomplishments, but at the same time he was mindful that few regular customers had so far seen any clear improvements in their water service. Initially, political endorsements had helped to manage expectations and encourage patience, allowing City Water to focus on the important planning and design tasks. Now that politicians were openly questioning City Water's performance, Stone worried about his ability to convince the public that good-faith efforts were being made, and that benefits would be forthcoming if people could remain patient. He was confident that progress would be more self-evident in the next three to five years, and customers in both rich and poor areas would enjoy an improved water supply.

Stone believed that one of the main causes of City Water's poor revenue performance was the unexpectedly dismal state of the existing infrastructure, including crumbling pipelines and widespread leaks and illegal taps. Biwater's initial bid was based mainly on information provided by the Tanzanian government and augmented by a specialist hired by the World Bank. Each international bidder had also done some of its own due diligence. Looking back, Stone now wondered whether the other two more experienced bidders, Vivendi and Saur, which had each decided against making an offer at the last moment, might have caught a glimpse of how grim the situation was.

Once City Water began running the system and realized the level of disrepair, it attempted to revise the technical and revenue terms of its lease contract. DAWASA didn't, however, believe City Water had proven its case, and the matter was left unresolved. The government's privatization reforms had included establishing an independent regulator, the Energy and Water Utility Regulatory Authority (EWURA), to oversee both DAWASA and City Water. At first, Stone was concerned about how long it took to set up the regulatory organization. Then he was dismayed to learn that the regulatory body had not been established. Instead, the Minister of Water was empowered to take on the responsibilities of the regulator. In Stone's view, this arrangement created important conflicts of interest in how the regulator could operate impartially without political interference.

On several occasions, the government insisted on actions which were not, in Stone's opinion, operationally sound. For example, City Water was required to procure and install over 170,000 water meters within three years. At that time, very few residential properties had water meters and, if they did, very few were working. City Water proposed a gradual approach. It would purchase only enough meters to meet annual installation requirements so that the meters wouldn't deteriorate in storage and have their warranties run out after 12 months. This proposal would also allow City Water to learn from the experiences of installing the first meters and take advantages of any improvements in meter technology in the coming years. But the proposal was turned down by the government. The purchased meters (per contract specifications) turned out to be unsuited to the low-pressure and intermittent supply environment that they needed to operate in. Because many of the installed water meters did not work, accurate billing for the water delivered remained a challenge. Similarly, government's insistence on free first-time connections for the urban poor may have been prematurely decided. The lifeline tariff proved problematic for the urban poor. While paying 20 shillings for water after every day's casual employment was possible (if more expensive), few had the ability to make the monthly payment. Most households who took advantage of a free connection failed to pay the first month's bill, and were disconnected; thus, investments in the connection would be wasted, or even increase the likelihood of vandalism and theft unless they were physically removed.

Even more troubling to Stone was the sudden and unexpected withdrawal of support by some key political figures, including the Minister of Water, Edward Lowassa. He knew that the Lowassa was aware that the full rehabilitation and stabilization of

DAWASA were going to be medium- to long-term processes. Given the size of the city, at least five years could pass before the changes would show any clear results. Stone felt that the current improvements, though modest, were the best that could be achieved under the difficult circumstances and that they symbolized City Water's ongoing commitment to improve services as provided for in the lease contract.

Another issue in Stone's mind was the low and declining morale among City Water employees. One of the conditions of City Water's contract was that it would assume all of the employees from the former parastatal organization, DAWASA. This contractual commitment meant that City Water was unable to achieve some operational efficiencies because it couldn't lay off unnecessary staff. Stone was also beginning to hear rumors about grievances regarding discrepancies in salary scales between the four expatriate managers and City Water's local employees. City Water's local partner, STM, also wanted a more active role in managing the company but Stone was concerned that STM lacked experience in utility management.

Stone was hopeful, however, that agreement on most matters could be reached and points of dispute could be resolved amicably. As Stone continued his journey and prepared to meet with Edward Lowassa, Tanzania's Minister for Water, the following morning, he thought about what they could each do next to ensure a renegotiated contract would better meet their ambitious goals.

Section D: Things Fall Apart

On Friday, May 13, 2005, Edward Lowassa entered the government state house for a cabinet meeting. When he emerged, he briskly announced that "the government has terminated the contract with City Water Services effective from today."[32] Lowassa indicated that a new government-owned firm, the Dar es Salaam Water and Sewerage Corporation (DAWASCO), would be formed to take over from City Water. Minister Lowassa stated that City Water had failed to meet revenue collection targets and other performance conditions as described in the contract, including investing less than half of the initially promised equity. Lowassa stated: "The water supply services in Dar es Salaam and in the neighboring places have deteriorated rather than improved since this firm took over some two years ago."[33]

This announcement came as a shock to Cliff Stone, the chief executive officer (CEO) of City Water, who said that he still considered the contract intact and was considering taking legal action to reverse the decision.[34] Stone openly admitted to many of the Lowassa's allegations, including the withholding of money due to DAWASA and there were delays in installing new pipelines, since in most cases these installations were not contracted to City Water. In fact, just a few days earlier on May 9, Stone had proposed to DAWASA that City Water invest a further $5 million over the next year (meeting and exceeding its initial obligation) and borrow an extra $6 million to accelerate the rehabilitation and development process. Stone also pointed out that both the quantity and the quality of Dar es Salaam's water had improved since his company had become involved. The lag in visible progress was due in part to DAWASA's unwillingness to adjust the contract to more accurately reflect the situation on the ground. City Water had expanded the customer base and was implementing fairer water distribution alternatives for low-income neighborhoods, such as Temeke, which had to wait for the new pipelines to reach them. Despite its improved customer reach, City Water was still troubled by delinquent debtors and illegal tapping. Stone felt that both circumstances fell outside City Water's direct control. Stone ended his initial response to the minister by saying "There are clearly no big profits to be made in Africa . . . Our intention was to

32   Bilal Abdul-Aziz, "Tanzania: Government Dumps City Water," *The Guardian*, May 14, 2005, http://www.worldwatercouncil.org/fileadmin/wwc/Sections_for/Journalists/Water_Media_Program/wmp_resources_guardian_14.05.05.pdf, accessed February 1, 2007.

33   Jon Cronin, "Tanzania Ditches Private Water Supplier," *BBC News*, May 18, 2005, http://news.bbc.co.uk/1 /hi/business/4558725.stm, accessed February 1, 2007.

34   As cited by Neil Ford, "Countryfile Tanzania," *African Business*, July 2005. http://www.highbeam.com/doc/1G1-134460831.html, accessed February 1, 2007. John Vidal, "Public Backlash over Private Water Deals," *The Guardian*, May 25, 2005, http://www.guardian.co.uk/hearafrica05/story/0,,1491629,00.html, accessed February 1, 2007.

bring water to the poor. Whatever happens now, the problem of how to provide water for them remains a challenge."[35]

Under the terms of City Water's contract with the Tanzanian government, both parties were required to settle disputes at the London Court of Arbitration. City Water was granted an injunction at the High Court in London to prevent the government from terminating its contract, pending the outcome of arbitration. The Tanzanian government and courts ignored the injunction. On June 1, 2005, the termination of the lease contract ended City Water Services' role as the operator and reassigned this role to DAWASCO. City Water Services' role in the design and supervision of the water mains also ceased on termination. The City Water Services' SIPE and POG contracts were similarly suspended, and on June 2, three senior City Water executives were detained by the Tanzanian police and summarily deported. A month later, Biwater–Gauff instituted arbitration proceedings against the government at the International Center for the Settlement of Investments Disputes. They claimed that the government had broken international law by seizing its investment in City Water and that the government had acted disgracefully towards their staff. Numerous attempts were made to discuss the matter with the government of Tanzania but all efforts were rebuffed. Biwater and Gauff finally dropped their claim in December 2005, when, after Tanzanian parliamentary elections, Edward Lowassa was named the country's new prime minister or more information on the aftermath of the termination of City Water's contract (see Exhibits 9.10 and 9.11).

At the request of the Government of the United Republic of Tanzania following the termination of the lease contract with City Water Services by the government, on May 27, 2003, the World Bank's board of directors approved a revised Dar es Salaam Water Supply and Sanitation Project: a five-year project which comprises a US$164.6 million investment and operational support program co-financed by the International Development Agency (IDA—US$61.5 million); African Development Bank (AfDB—US$48.0 million); European Investment Bank (EIB—US$34.0 million); Private Operator (US$8.5 million in the form of equity in the operating company) and DAWASA Government of Tanzania (US$12.6 million).[36] This was part of a larger commitment of US$250.08 million to support efforts by the Tanzanian government to reduce poverty in the country. The World Bank required that the government had addressed key issues, such as management arrangement, cost recovery and commercial policies, before implementation would start, and stipulated that the partnership going forward would combine private management of the technical and commercial operations by an international professional operator, and public financing of the rehabilitation and extension of the systems.[37] On June 19, 2003, the posted procurement notice[38] called for:

- Major consulting services including the preparation of water resources development plan, water supply and sewerage expansion studies, preparation of

35   John Vidal, "Public Backlash over Private Water Deals," *The Guardian*, May 25, 2005, http://www.guardian.co.uk /hearafrica05/story/0,,1491629,00.html, accessed February 1, 2007.

36   The United Republic of Tanzania, Dar es Salaam Water Supply and Sanitation Project: Project Restructuring (Credit 3771-TA).

37   World Bank, Eric Chinje, *Tanzania: Dar es Salaam Water Supply and Sanitation Project*, http://www.irc.nl/page/2893, June 2, 2003, accessed June 7, 2007.

38   http://english.manshoori.com/eproc/np-notice.do?noticeId=460075, accessed June 7, 2007.

EXHIBIT 9.10 DAWASA Triumphs against City Water

City Water Services Ltd (CWS) has abandoned a case at the International Arbitration Tribunal, where it has been contesting Government of Tanzania's decision to terminate its contract and enlisting the services of Dar es Salaam Water and Sewerage Company (DAWASCO). The legal tussle between CWS and Dar es Salaam Water and Sewerage Authority (DAWASA) was triggered off last year, when the government terminated the service of City Water to manage water supply and sewerage services in the city of Dar es Salaam and Coast regions. "This is a technical knock out, they [City Water Services] have run away from the case. They have no basic claims against DAWASA" said Nimrod Mkono, Managing Partner of Mkono and Co, a legal firm commissioned to represent DAWASA at the international arbitration.

The 10-year contract between the foreign firm on behalf of the UK-based Biwater–Gulf International and DAWASA on behalf of the government, was sealed in August 2003. Two years later—June, 2005—the government unilaterally terminated the contract. Prime Minister, Edward Lowassa who was then Minister for Water and Livestock Development said the decision was made because CWS had failed to meet revenue collection targets and other performance conditions as spelt out in the contract. City Water Services is incorporated by Biwater–Gulf–Tanzania of United Kingdom (51 per cent) and Super Doll Trailer Manufacture Tanzania Ltd (49 per cent). City Water Services then expeditiously filed a request for arbitration at the United Nations Commission on International Trade Law (UNCITRAL) on May 16, 2005, challenging the legality of the decision and demanding compensation. The firm contended that the termination was illegal and demanded compensation of between US$20 m and US$24 m for breach of contract.

Both CWS through London-based Allen & Overy Advocate Company and DAWASA through Mkono & Advocates, picked independent arbitrators Julian Lew and Michael Lee both from UK, as required by international laws, to represent them at the tribunal (UNCITRAL). However, before proceedings began, CWS filed an injunction at the British High Court Justice seeking an order to restrain Tanzanian government from taking over its bond deposit of US$5.2 m at the CRDB-Bank and block implementation of the terminated contract. The application was granted on May 23, 2005 by the UK High Court of Justice. However, the Tanzania High Court declined to enforce the order, saying it was inapplicable locally. Mkono Advocates contested the order at the UK High Court of Justice and had the injunction lifted on June 8, this year.

After the lifting, CWS continued with proceedings at UNCITRAL. William Laurence Graig as an independent arbitrator chaired the proceedings at the tribunal. *The Guardian* has impeccably established that last month, William Laurence Graig directed CWS, Julian Lew, to file its statement of claim and supporting documents within 30 days, elapsing July 14, 2006. Julian Lew acknowledged receipt of the directive from the chairman, but failed to comply as required. This therefore has effectively left CWS out of contention as they have failed to comply with the requirements at the international tribunal. "That is why I am saying this is a technical knock out. That means CWS have no legitimate claim against DAWASA or the government," said Nimrod

(continued over)

(from previous page)

Mkono. In what was viewed as abandoning the case in despair, CWS Attorney Julian Lew wrote to the tribunal saying: "It is with regret that we notify the tribunal that we are no longer able to represent City Water Services in this arbitration." The latest development, according to Nimrod Mkono, paves the way for DAWASA to file its counterclaim, demanding compensation from City Water Services. "The City Water Services, US$5.2 m, which was deposited at the CRDB as a bond, becomes ours automatically. We will demand between US$20 m and US$24 m, as compensation," said Mkono. "Of course, there would be some other costs. We are still compiling and quantifying the cost of the suit. We will announce the exact figures later on," he said.

Source: Tarimo, Judica. "DAWASA triumphs against City Water", *The Guardian*, http://www.ippmedia.com/ipp/guardian/ 2006/07/19/70655.html, accessed February 1, 2007.

strategic sanitation plan, and preparation of a national strategy for urban water supply and sewerage.

- Non-delegated works, including: rehabilitation of three water treatment plants (capacities of 182,000 m³ per day, 90,000 m³ per day, and 9,000 m³ per day); rehabilitation of transmission mains from the three treatment plants); rehabilitation of two reservoirs and construction of a 5,000 m³ reservoir; construction of primary distribution mains (58 km pipes and 180 bulk meters); rehabilitation of nine waste-water stabilization ponds; rehabilitation of sewers, sea outfall, and sewage pumping stations.

- Delegated works: rehabilitation and extension of about 970 km secondary and tertiary distribution pipe network.

- Goods: This includes mainly the supply of about 970 km pipes and fittings.

The revised Dar es Salaam Water Supply and Sanitation Project became effective on July 31, 2003. The new closing date for the project is December 31, 2009, a 12-month extension from the original goal.

EXHIBIT 9.11 Excerpts from World Bank's Project Restructuring Document
(Credit 3771-TA)

"The Operator mobilized in August 2003 and began the take over of operating staff
and assets in the DAWASA designated service area. Within the first 12 months City
Water Services was in breach of many key provisions of the Lease Contract. In
particular, CWS had begun to consistently fail to remit the Lessor tariff to DAWASA and
to deposit the First Time New Domestic Water Supply Connection Fee into the First
Time New Domestic Water Supply Connection Fund on a timely basis. Beginning in July
2004, City Water Services ceased payment of the monthly rental fee to DAWASA.
Initially, City Water Services sought a substantial Operator tariff increase to alleviate
its cash flow difficulties, under the 'material change' provisions of the Lease Contract.
In August 2004, an audit ordered by the Interim Regulator and conducted by
PricewaterhouseCoopers (PwC) to determine whether changes in key assumptions,
such as water available for sale or costs of production, warranted a tariff increase
under the Lease Contract. When PwC found that no 'material changes' had occurred,
City Water Services sought to renegotiate the Lease Contract." (pp. 2-3)

"IDA assisted with the formal renegotiation attempt during April and May 2005 by
funding a regulatory specialist to facilitate the discussions between the parties. The
renegotiation was not successful, however, and DAWASA terminated the Lease on June
1, 2005. Following the termination of the City Water Services Lease Contract, IDA
engaged the Government to ensure continuity in the delivery of water supply and
sewerage services and to maintain the policy framework for the Project. The
Government agreed to an interim arrangement that retained the separation of the
responsibilities between the Operator and DAWASA, as the asset holder, to facilitate
the future transition to private sector participation. A new entity, the Dar es Salaam
Water and Sewerage Corporation (DAWASCO) was formed under the Public
Corporations Act, with capital of TZS 2 billion to be provided by the Government.
DAWASCO took over City Water Services' responsibilities on June 1, 2005, and began
implementing a 100 Day Rescue Plan in July 1, 2005. A new Lease Contract and
Subloan Agreement for $6 million were signed between DAWASA and DAWASCO in
September 2005 both taking effect retroactively as of July 1, 2005. A new
Development Contract was also entered into between the Government and DAWASA."
(p. 3)

"The Project continues to record steady progress in spite of the drawn out and failed
renegotiation process with City Water Services surrounding the Lease contract as well
as delays encountered on some components of the rehabilitation program. Most of the
contracts (rehabilitation of water treatment plant-CP1, rehabilitation of transmission
mains-CP2, rehabilitation of sewerage network-CP5) are under execution;
rehabilitation of sewage treatment ponds-CP4 and rehabilitation of sewage pumping
stations-CP6 are at advanced stages of procurement processing. Progress on Part 1 of
the rehabilitation of the distribution network under the delegated works contract is
encouraging. Disbursements are on track (a little over 30% of IDA financing after
about 24 months of implementation). After falling behind for a number of months,

(continued over)

(from previous page)

DAWASA is currently in compliance with maintenance of minimum balance in the operating account." (p. 3)

"Project Description: The Project components remain substantially unchanged as per the existing Project description. One significant change is the reduced order of meters from 173,000 to the current stock of 100,000. Three new works components are being requested:

1. *Groundwater development.* This involves drilling three deep, large-capacity boreholes to test the water quality and capacity of the large, deep aquifer located under Dar es Salaam (identified by the Future Water Sources Study).

2. *Repair of a breach on Ruvu River at Kidgozero.* Unless corrected this will substantially lessen the water available to the DAWASA water supply system, especially during periods of drought.

3. *Construction of a waste management facility.* This would handle solid waste for the city of Dar es Salaam and allow for disposal of sludge from the wastewater ponds, which is currently being accumulated onsite." (pp. 4-5)

"Re-Allocation of Credit Proceeds: IDA commitment to the Project will remain at the original SDR 45,000,000.00.[39] [. . .] The proposed changes to schedule 1 are as follows:" (p. 5 & Table).

Category	Original	Change Amount	Revised
1. Works	14,250,000	2,450,000	16,700,000
2. Goods	6,300,000	−2,750,000	3,550,000
3. Consulting Services	16,900,000	−1,300,000	15,600,000
4. Training	350,000	350,000	700,000
5. Operating Costs of the Operator	4,000,000	3,600,000	7,600,000
6. Refunding of the Project Preparation Advance	850,000	0	850,000
7. Unallocated	2,350,000	−2,350,000	0
Total	**45,000,000**	**0**	**45,000,000**

"Benefits. There are not anticipated changes in the benefits associated with the Project. Reliability, affordability, and sustainability of the services will improve for the approximately 3.0 million people in the DAWASA designated service area. With the proposed extension of 12 months and adjustment made in the implementation program, the Project outcome of ensuring 80% of the population with access to piped

(continued over)

39   Special Drawing Rights, 1 SDR is equivalent to US$1.52 or TZS1,905.95, http://coinmill.com/ SDR_calculator.html, accessed June 7, 2007.

(from previous page)

water supply and 70% with 24-hour supply will be attained. This will contribute to the attainment of the MDGs for water and sanitation services in DAWASA designated service area specifically and Tanzania in general." (p. 6)

"Risks. The Project risk remains substantial as appraised. Most of anticipated risks associated with the operator (poor performance, inadequate equity injection, withdrawal of the international operator, focus on construction rather than services to customers, etc.) emerged during implementation. The updated Project Implementation Plan takes cognizance of the Government position that the termination of the Lease with City Water Services was one of contract failure, not policy failure, and therefore made the necessary adjustments to ensure that some of the underlying mitigation measures are addressed under the interim arrangements with DAWASCO. The mitigation measures include (i) the calibration of the network through the installation of bulk meters and (ii) the mobilization of the customer database through the introduction of a new billing system is being fast tracked. The two activities are aimed at ensuring a more credible database (technical, financial, and commercial) for maintaining current operations and providing better data for the medium term institutional correction plan which will include the option of exploring the introduction of a potential successor private operator. A new financial model (with a new working capital arrangements and tariff adjustments) aimed at tracking the sustainability of the operation has also been put in place and will be monitored under the enhanced supervision period of 12 months from June 1, 2005." (p. 7).

Source: The United Republic of Tanzania, Dar es Salaam Water Supply and Sanitation Project: Project Restructuring (Credit 3771-TA).

Teaching notes for this case are available from Greenleaf Publishing. These are free of charge and are available only to teaching staff. They can be requested by going to:
www.greenleaf-publishing.com/oikos_notes

Part 5

Sustainable Business Models and Stakeholder Tension

CASE 10
The Body Shop
Social Responsibility or Sustained Greenwashing?[1]

Debapratim Purkayastha and Rajiv Fernando
ICFAI Center for Management Research, Hyderabad, India

> In terms of power and influence, you can forget the church, forget politics. There is no more powerful institution in society than business—I believe it is now more important than ever before for business to assume a moral leadership. The business of business should not be about money, it should be about responsibility. It should be about public good, not private greed.[2]

> —**Dame Anita Roddick, founder of The Body Shop, in her book** *Business as Unusual,* **in 2000**

1   This case was written by Debapratim Purkayastha, under the direction of Rajiv Fernando, ICFAI Center for Management Research (ICMR). It was compiled from published sources, and is intended to be used as a basis for class discussion rather than to illustrate either effective or ineffective handling of a management situation.

2   "Anita Roddick Talk to Benefit Project Censored," http://www.sonoma.edu, December 31, 2000.

It's ironic that a company (The Body Shop) well-known for its anti-animal testing stance should sell-out to one (L'Oréal) that tests on animals and which has yet to show its commitment to any ethical issues at all.[3]

—**Ruth Rosselson,** *Ethical Consumer* **magazine,**[4] **in March 2006**

I do not believe that L'Oréal will compromise the ethics of The Body Shop. That is after all what they are paying for and they are too intelligent to mess with our DNA . . . I want to make things happen, to spread human values wider in business if I possibly can. And this sale gives us the chance to do so.[5]

Dame Anita Roddick, in May 2006

A Controversial Makeover

On March 17, 2006, The Body Shop International Plc (Body Shop), a retailer of natural-based and ethically sourced beauty products, announced that it had agreed to be acquired by the beauty care giant L'Oréal SA[6] (L'Oréal) in a cash deal worth £652 million (US$ 1.14 billion). The deal valued the shares of Body Shop at a premium of 34.2 percent to their price before the acquisition. It was also a major windfall for its founder Dame Anita Roddick (Roddick).

Following this announcement, Body Shop and Roddick came under severe criticism. Body Shop was regarded by many as one of the pioneers of modern corporate social responsibility (CSR). The company was also strongly associated with the social activism of Roddick. Since its inception, the company had endorsed and championed various social issues that complemented its core values—opposition to animal testing, developing community trade, building self-esteem, campaigning for human rights, and protection of the planet. Body Shop was one of the first companies to publish a 'Values Report' in 1996 (refer to Exhibit 10.1 for Body Shop's mission statement and Exhibit 10.2 for its values). Through these initiatives, the company had cultivated a loyal customer base who shared these values of the company.

On the other hand, L'Oréal was viewed by activists as the face of modern consumerism—a company that tested its cosmetics on animals, exploited the sexuality of women, and sold their products by making women feel insecure. Moreover, Nestlé

---

3   "Body Shop's Shares Rise as its Ethical Rating Plummets," http://www.ethicalconsumer.org, March 17, 2006.

4   *Ethical Consumer* is a magazine in the UK that is produced by the Ethical Consumer Research Association (ECRA). ECRA is a not-for-profit consumer organization that seeks to promote human rights, environmental sustainability, animal welfare, and provide information on the social and environmental track record of well-known organizations. (Source: http://www.ethicalconsumer.org/aboutec/aboutus.htm).

5   Mark Goyder, "The Body Shop and L'Oréal: Why Can't Big be Beautiful?" http://www.ethicalcorp.com, May 25, 2006.

6   L'Oréal SA, headquartered in Clichy, France, is the world's leading cosmetics and beauty company. Its portfolio includes various cosmetic brands in segments such as hair color, skin care, sun protection, make-up, perfumes, and hair care. In 2005, L'Oréal's revenue was €14.53 billion and it earned a net income of €1.639 billion. As of December 2005, it employed 52,080 people.

Exhibit 10.1 Body Shop's Mission Statement

- To dedicate our business to the pursuit of social and environmental change.
- To creatively balance the financial and human needs of our stakeholders: employees, customers, franchisees, suppliers and shareholders.
- To courageously ensure that our business is ecologically sustainable: meeting the needs of the present without compromising the future.
- To meaningfully contribute to local, national and international communities in which we trade, by adopting a code of conduct which ensures care, honesty, fairness and respect.
- To passionately campaign for the protection of the environment, human and civil rights, and against animal testing within the cosmetics and toiletries industry.
- To tirelessly work to narrow the gap between principle and practice, whilst making fun, passion and care part of our daily lives

Source: http://www.thebodyshopinternational.com

Exhibit 10.2 Body Shop's Values

AGAINST ANIMAL TESTING **Against animal testing:** We consider testing products or ingredients on animals to be morally and scientifically indefensible.

SUPPORT COMMUNITY TRADE **Support community trade:** We support small producer communities around the world who supply us with accessories and natural ingredients.

ACTIVATE SELF ESTEEM **Activate self esteem:** We know that you're unique, and we'll always treat you like an individual. We like you just the way you are.

DEFEND HUMAN RIGHTS **Defend human rights:** We believe that it is the responsibility of every individual to actively support those who have human rights denied to them.

PROTECT OUR PLANET **Protect our planet:** We believe that a business has the responsibility to protect the environment in which it operates, locally and globally.

Source: http://www.thebodyshopinternational.com

owned 26 percent of L'Oréal. Nestlé was one of the most boycotted companies in the world for its alleged unethical business practices and aggressive promotion of baby milk in developing countries.

Body Shop's critics said that they felt betrayed by the deal as Roddick had previously been quite vocal in her criticism of companies like L'Oréal. They called for a boycott of Body Shop's products as they felt that the company had sold out its values and principles. Body Shop and Roddick defended the deal by saying that L'Oréal would not compromise Body Shop's ethics and that the merger would give Body Shop a chance to spread its values to L'Oréal. L'Oréal also announced that Body Shop's values would not be compromised and that it would continue to operate as an independent unit.

Many analysts were concerned that Body Shop's image would be affected by the acquisition. Some activists felt that Body Shop would not be able to function independently and that an important partner in CSR had been lost. However, they were a few who felt that Body Shop's values would rub in on L'Oréal and believed that the deal had some positives. There were also questions raised about whether L'Oréal was trying to improve its image and buy CSR through this deal. But for Body Shop's staunchest critics, the acquisition by L'Oréal was vindication of their view that Body Shop was nothing more than a greenwasher.

Background Note

In 1970, Roddick (then Anita Perella) and Gordon Roddick (Gordon) were inspired to set up a beauty products store after seeing a store called "The Body Shop" in Berkeley, California, USA, that sold cosmetics like shampoos, lotions, body creams, etc. The California store was run by two entrepreneurs, Jane Saunders (Saunders) and Peggy Short (Short), who sold cosmetics on the "care for the environment" plank.

In March 1976, the Roddicks set up their first Body Shop store at Brighton, UK. The store sold around 15 lines of homemade cosmetics made with natural ingredients such as jojoba oil, rhassoul mud, etc. This store was just next to some undertakers, and two funeral directors threatened to sue Roddick if she used the name "Body Shop." They also filed a complaint to the local council regarding the name of the store and its proximity to their businesses. Anita shot back a letter to the council saying that she was a housewife with kids trying to make a living.[7] She even anonymously phoned the story to *The Argus*.[8] The newspaper published the story as a centrespread, which resulted in plenty of free publicity for Body Shop.

From its very early days, Body Shop was associated with the social activism of Roddick. The windows of Body Shop stores featured bills of local charity and community events. Roddick was also very critical of what she called the environmental insensitivity of industry and called for a change in standard corporate practices.

---

7   At that time Dame Anita was living with her two daughters while her husband was in the US. On his return to UK, he joined the business.
8   *The Argus* is a local newspaper based in Brighton, with editions serving the city of Brighton and Hove and the other parts of both East and West Sussex, UK.

The second store was opened six months after the opening of the first store. A former garage owner Ian McGlinn (McGlinn) helped them open this shop by lending the Roddicks £4,000.[9]

Roddick gave the company's products brand names such as, Tea Tree Oil Facial Wash, Mango Dry Mist, etc. Urine sample bottles, the cheapest packaging available at the time, were used as containers. All labels were hand-written. Unlike other branded cosmetics, the packaging of its products contained detailed descriptions of the ingredients and their properties. The company never "sale"[10]-priced their products but customers who returned product containers for refilling were offered a 15 percent discount. In addition to providing product information, a number of leaflets and posters (on recycled paper) provided information about social causes that the company believed in and encouraged its customers to get involved. Customers were greeted with employees wearing T-shirts bearing a social message. "The politicism of the Body Shop has always been its DNA—the shops became our billboards. I don't give a damn if we were made successful by Mrs Rosie Brown who loved her vitamin E cream. Behind us there was a tacit acceptance of what we were doing,"[11] said Roddick.

Body Shop's core brand identity was its "profits-with-a-principle" philosophy and the brand was closely associated with the social justice agenda. This was a revolutionary idea at the time, and Body Shop developed a loyal customer base. By the late 1970s, it had a number of franchisee stores throughout the UK. Body Shop was growing at a rate of 50 percent annually and was also getting a lot of media attention. Anita hired a PR firm to handle the media. In 1978, Body Shop's first foreign franchisee opened in Brussels, Belgium.

In the 1980s, the Roddicks acquired the US rights to the "Body Shop" name from the two entrepreneurs of Berkeley, who continued to operate a small chain in the San Francisco Bay Area under the new name "Body Time." Some analysts were critical of the Roddicks for having copied the whole business model of these entrepreneurs—from the idea and name, to even the product catalogs and image strategy.

In April 1984, the stock of Body Shop opened for the first time on London's Unlisted Securities Market,[12] at 95 pence. By the time it obtained a full listing on the London Stock Exchange in January 1986, the stock was selling at 820 pence. During this time, there were some concerns among the Body Shop franchisees that the outfit was becoming too political. But despite these concerns, in 1986 the Body Shop formed an alliance with Greenpeace[13] for the "Save the Whales" campaign. Following some disagreements with Greenpeace, Roddick discontinued this relationship and formed an alliance with

---

9   As of December 2006, McGlinn owned 25 percent of the company's shares.

10 An occasion (usually for a brief period) for buying at specially reduced prices.

11 "Dame Anita's Radical Approach," http://www.news.bbc.co.uk, July 17, 2003.

12 The Unlisted Securities Market (1980 to 1996) was a stock exchange set up by the London Stock Exchange to serve the market for shares of companies too small to qualify for a full listing.

13 Greenpeace, with its global headquarters at Vancouver, British Columbia, Canada, is an international environmental organization founded in in 1971. It has a presence in 41 countries. It is known for its various campaigns to stop atmospheric and underground nuclear testing, and for protecting whales. It is also focused on other environmental issues such as bottom trawling, global warming, ancient forest destruction, and genetic engineering.

EXHIBIT 10.3 Awards Won by Anita Roddick*

1984 Veuve Clicquot Business Woman of the Year

1988 Order of the British Empire (OBE)

1991 Center for World Development Education's World Vision Award, USA

1993 Banksia Foundation's Australia Environmental Award

1993 Mexican Environmental Achiever Award 1993—National Audubon Society Medal, USA

1994 Botwinick Prize in Business Ethics, USA

1994 University of Michigan's Annual Business Leadership Award, USA

1995 Women's Business Development Center's First Annual Woman Power Award, USA

1996 Women's Center's Leadership Award, USA

1996 The Gleitsman Foundation's Award of Achievement, USA

1997 United Nations Environment Programme (UNEP), Honouree, Eyes on the Environment

1999 British Environment & Media Award

1999 Chief Wiper-Away of Ogoni Tears, Movement for the Survival of the Ogoni People, Nigeria

2001 International Peace Prayer Day Organisation's Woman of Peace

2003 Dame Commander of the British Empire (DBE)

* The list is not exhaustive.

Source: www.en.wikipedia.org/wiki/Anita_Roddick

Friends of the Earth[14] (FOE) in 1990. It also teamed up with Amnesty International[15] and from the 1990s onwards became very vocal in its support for international human rights. In 1991, Roddick was awarded the World Vision Award for Development Initiative (refer to Exhibit 10.3 for a list of awards received by Anita Roddick).

During the 1980s and 1990s, Body Shop had its share of critics who accused the company of hypocrisy as they felt that it was making profits under the guise of endorsing social equality. On the other hand, some shareholders complained that instead of maximizing profits, the company was diverting money into "social work" projects.

However, the company had shown strong growth through the 1980s and at its height, in 1991, the company was worth £700 million. But then the company faced many challenges. In the early 1990s, problems surfaced for Body Shop as many "me too" retailers

14   Friends of the Earth is an international network of environmental organizations spread across 70 countries. It considers environmental issues in their social, political, and human rights contexts and goes beyond the conservation movement to address the economic and development aspects of sustainability (source: http://www.en.wikipedia.org).

15   Amnesty International is an international non-governmental organization with the stated purpose of promoting human rights. It is one of the leading and most respected human rights organizations in the world.

mushroomed in the UK, running businesses on a similar green agenda. The Boots Group Plc[16] launched the Botanics and Natural Collection ranges that directly competed with Body Shop's product portfolio. Body Shop's international expansion strategy had not achieved much success. In the US, it faced major reverses as Bath & Body Works[17] emerged as a tough competitor. Its new products too failed to take off.

Body Shop published its first *Values Report* in 1996 and its second *Values Report* in 1998. These reports were audit statements of its social, environmental, and animal protection practices. Both reports were given a top rating in a worldwide ranking by SustainAbility[18] for the United Nations on environmental and social reporting.

Though the company continued to grow in size, its market value was on the decline. The board had also got tired of Roddick's radicalism, her combative stance on globalization, and vocal criticism of anti-wrinkle creams. In 1998, Roddick was forced to step down as the CEO and Patrick Gournay (Gournay) replaced her. Her critics felt that her radicalism had done more harm to the company than good and were happy that she had stepped down. Richard Ratner (Ratner), a retail analyst at Seymour Pierce[19] commented: "It's very good news. The less she has to do with the business the better."[20]

In 1999, Gournay initiated a restructuring exercise and decided to concentrate on new products. Body Shop exited manufacturing and wholesaling, and focused on retailing. One-fourth of the product line was trimmed and the company bought out franchises that were not in a sound financial position. In 2000, Roddick announced that she would quit the board in two years. However, she continued to carry out PR functions for Body Shop and also traveled the world in search of new product ideas. In fiscal year 2001, the operating profits of the company had decreased to £18.2 million when compared to £33.0 million in fiscal year 2000. Some management control problems also surfaced in Body Shop's franchise structure. There were also discussions on the possible buyout of Body Shop. Takeover talks with Grupo Omnilife, a Mexican retailer that distributes nutritional supplements, failed as Grupo Omnilife could not back up its £300 (US$500) million offer. A £175 million offer by Lush[21] failed to impress Roddick as she felt that Lush's founder Mark Constantine was not ethical enough.

In 2002, both Anita and Gordon Roddick stepped down as co-chairmen and were replaced by Adrian Bellamy (Bellamy). Gournay also quit as the CEO and was replaced by Peter Saunders (Saunders), who was the CEO of the company's North American operations. The new chairman shelved the idea of selling the company. "We would not enter into [further buyout talks] unless we had very good reason to believe that it was in the best interests of shareholders,"[22] said Bellamy.

---

16   Boots Group Plc is a leading pharmacy chain in the UK. It was founded in 1849.
17   Bath & Body Works is a chain of retail store in the US owned by Limited Brands. It specialized in many fragrant lotions, bath items, and home fragrances. It was founded in 1990 in New Albany, Ohio, USA, and had since expanded across the US.
18   SustainAbility is a strategy consultancy and thinktank.
19   Seymour Pierce, based in London, UK, is a leading provider of corporate broking and corporate finance services.
20   Emma Clark, "The End of Anita's Heyday," http://www.news.bbc.co.uk, February 12, 2002.
21   Lush, based in Poole, Dorset, UK, is a producer and marketer of handmade bath products, soaps, body lotions, and cosmetics.
22   "Body Shop Chief Steps Down," http://www.news.bbc.co.uk, February 12, 2002.

Since 2002, Body Shop started working on repositioning itself to the "masstige"[23] sector of the consumer market. The re-positioning exercise began to bear fruit. For the fiscal year ended February 2003, Body Shop reported that its pre-tax profits were £20.4 million, when compared to £11.6 million in the previous year. The turnaround in its performance was followed by strong growth in the next two years.

For the year ended February 26, 2005, Body Shop announced a 21 percent rise in pre-tax profits to £34.5 million (US$65.6 million). As of March 2006, Body Shop had 2,085 branches around the world, including 304 in the UK. Its brand portfolio consisted of more than 600 products (refer to Exhibit 10.4 for key financials of Body Shop: 2002–2006).

EXHIBIT 10.4 Key Financials of The Body Shop[24]

Adapted from "The Body Shop International Plc Annual Reports and Accounts" 2004-2006, http://www.thebodyshopinternational.com, 2006.

(For the 52 weeks ended February 25, 2006)	2006	2005	2004	2003	2002
Revenue (£ million)	485.8	419.0	381.1	378.2	379.6
Operating Profit (£ million)	41.5	39.2	30.3	24.3	15.2
Net Profit (£ million)	29.2	28.8	21.7	13.6	5.4
EPS					
Basic earnings per ordinary share (pence)	13.6	13.8	10.7	6.8	2.8
Diluted earnings per ordinary share (pence)	13.2	13.3	10.6	6.8	2.8
Number of Stores	2,133	2,045	2,007	1,968	1,954

On March 17, 2006, Body Shop announced that it had agreed to be taken over by L'Oréal in a £652 million (US$ 1.14 billion) deal. L'Oréal offered 300 pence a share, a premium of 34.2 percent to Body Shop's closing share price of 223.5 pence on February 21, 2006. Bellamy said, "For the shareholders, L'Oréal's offer is a significant premium to the share price and I believe provides an opportunity for them to now realize fully the prospects for the group on a stand alone basis."[25]

L'Oréal said that the management team at Body Shop would be retained and it would be allowed to preserve its independent identity. Roddick would also continue to act as a consultant. L'Oréal's chairman and CEO, Lindsay Owen-Jones (Owen-Jones), said, "We have always had great respect for The Body Shop's success and for the strong identity and values created by its outstanding founder, Anita Roddick."[26] He added, "A partnership between our companies makes perfect sense. Combining L'Oréal's expertise and knowledge of international markets with The Body Shop's distinct culture and values will benefit both companies."[27]

23 The term "masstige" (Mass-market combined with prestige) covers relatively low-priced retail goods that are sold under the banner of a prestigious brand name.
24 2002 to 2003 figures are according to UK GAAP (Generally Accepted Accounting Principles). 2004 to 2005 figures are according to IFRS (International Financial Reporting Standards).
25 "Body Shop Agrees L'Oréal Takeover," http://www.news.bbc.co.uk, March 17, 2006.
26 Ibid.
27 "L'Oréal Buys Out Body Shop for $1.4 billion US," http://www.ctv.ca, March 17 2006.

The deal was also a major windfall for the Roddicks, as they would receive £117 million (US$204 million) for their 18 percent stake in the company.

The announcement of the deal had surprised many. Over the years, Anita had been quite vocal in her criticism of L'Oréal. She had vociferously accused the cosmetic industry of making women insecure and particularly criticized L'Oréal for its alleged policy of employing only "sexy" saleswomen on its counters. She had once said, "Does the beauty industry hate women? I've been saying so for years. That L'Oréal is being sued for attempting to fire a saleswoman in California for not being 'hot' enough only confirms it yet again."[28]

On June 1, 2006, the two companies went on with the deal as European Commission[29] (EC) cleared the takeover and said that the takeover would not result in higher prices for cosmetics, nor would it impede competition in the European Union (EU).

The Pioneer in Modern CSR

Body Shop was regarded as one among the first firms in the world to publish a proper report on its social responsibility initiatives.[30] In addition to social activism, internal audit programs were conducted at Body Shop for environmental protection, health and safety at work, and the monitoring of "Against Animal Testing Policy." In 1991, it drafted the EU Eco-Management and Audit Regulation (EMAS),[31] and in 1992, Body Shop published its first environmental statement called *The Green Book*. Till 1994, the company continued to publish its independently verified annual environmental statements. In January 1996, it published its first *Values Report*. The report contained results of a social audit of Body Shop (arrived at through consultation with 5,000 stakeholders) as well as its environmental and animal protection performance. Subsequently, in January 1998, Body Shop published its second *Values Report*. The report included results of Body Shop's integrated internal management systems audit and accounting processes in the area of social, environmental, and animal protection.

The United Nations Environment Programme (UNEP) and SustainAbility ranked both the *Values Reports* highly in their international benchmarking surveys of corporate environmental reports. This firmly established Body Shop as a pioneer in social reporting. Its social reporting coupled with its social activism led many people to consider Body Shop as a pioneer in modern CSR. And Roddick reinforced this association with her statements such as, "My vision, my hope, is simply this: that many business leaders

---

28   Fiona Walsh and Julia Finch, "£600m—Because it's Worth it," http://www.guardian.co.uk, February 24, 2006.

29   The European Commission is the executive body of the European Union, an intergovernmental and supranational union of 25 member states.

30   "Is this the First Ever Corporate Social/Environmental Report?" http://www.mallenbaker.net, February 2003.

31   The Eco-Management and Audit Scheme, is a voluntary initiative designed to improve companies' environmental performance. It was initially established by European Regulation 1836/93. Now this has been replaced by Council Regulation 761/01.

will come to see a primary role of business as incubators of the human spirit, rather than factories for the production of more material goods and services."[32]

Body Shop's CSR Initiatives

Against Animal Testing

Body Shop did not test its cosmetic products on animals and did not commission others to do it on its behalf, as it considered this practice unethical. Along with customers and animal protection groups, Body Shop campaigned for a change in the law on the testing of animals for cosmetics purposes in the UK, Europe, the Netherlands, Germany, and Japan. Its campaigns had some major successes. In 1996, Body Shop presented the EU with a petition signed by over 4,000,000 people, which at the time was the largest petition against animal testing. Body Shop was also instrumental in the UK government's decision in 1998 to ban animal testing for cosmetic products and ingredients. In addition to this, the company's campaigns also resulted in finished product test bans in Germany and the Netherlands. In Japan, Body Shop organized the first major campaign on this issue.

In 1995, Body Shop got its Against Animal Testing supplier monitoring systems independently audited and certified against the ISO 9002 quality assurance standard. It was also one of the few companies that complied with the Humane Cosmetic Standards (HCS).[33] In fact, it was the first international cosmetics company to sign the HCS in 1996. It placed restrictions on its suppliers' use of animal tests and fixed December 31, 1990 as the cut-off date for them to comply with these restrictions. Body Shop said that it would not buy any ingredients that had been tested on animals after the cut-off date. Body Shop also ensured that ingredients derived from animals were suitable for vegetarians and did not cause harm to the animal from which it was derived. In 2004, The Body Shop Foundation (BSF) awarded £20,000 to The Centre for Alternatives to Animal Testing at John Hopkins University to support research into alternatives that could substitute animal testing.

In 2005, the company was awarded the first place in the cosmetics category for "Achieving Higher Standards of Animal Welfare" by the Royal Society for the Protection of Animals, in recognition of its efforts on this issue. The following year it was awarded Europe's first annual Proggy Awards[34] in the "Best Cruelty-Free Cosmetics" category, presented by People for the Ethical Treatment of Animals (PETA). Lauren Bowey of PETA said, "The Body Shop is a driving force in promoting a more humane

---

32   Chrisna du Plessis, "Finding the Tin Man's Heart—Social Responsibility in the Construction Sector," http://www.buildnet.co.za, May 2002.

33   The Humane Cosmetics Standard is a internationally recognized scheme that enables consumers to easily identify and purchase cosmetic and toiletry products that have not been tested on animals (source: http://www.buav.org).

34   The Proggy awards are given by the People for the Ethical Treatment of Animals (PETA) since 2005. PETA, based in Norfolk, Virginia, USA, is the largest animal rights organization in the world. (Source: http://www.en.wikipedia.org).

lifestyle. By renouncing animal tests, The Body Shop has shown beauty doesn't have to have an ugly side."[35] Roddick said: "I'm thrilled that we've won this award in recognition of our Against Animal Testing policy. It was always my vision to offer customers not just great products but an opportunity to demonstrate their ethical purchasing power as well. A recent survey conducted with our customers showed that 84 percent of them shopped with us because they shared our values—a million thanks to them for their support."[36]

Support Community Trade

In the late 1980s, Body Shop purchased its first Community Trade product (CTP). Through CTP, Body Shop sourced products from marginalized communities for a fair price in a sustainable way. For instance, it sourced marula oil from Namibia, bananas from Caribbean, beeswax and honey from traditional beekeepers in Zambia, shea butter from a women's group in Ghana, etc. In Roddick's words, "Our trade with these communities is not just about creating another product or market for The Body Shop. It is about exchange and value, trade and respect, friendship and trust."[37]

Through CTP, Body Shop guaranteed a living wage for its Community Trade suppliers and their workers through a predictable and long-term business relationship. It also supported initiatives in the supplier's community that contributed to sustainable development. Due to its CTP program, Body Shop was also considered a pioneer of fair trade in the cosmetics industry. According to the company, its vision was to present a model for other companies to follow.

To ensure that its CTP relationships would be successful in fulfilling a community's goals, Body Shop developed a set of Fair Trade Guidelines in 1994 (refer to Exhibit 10.5 for Body Shop's Fair Trade Guidelines). It benchmarked its CTP Supplier Guidelines to external standards such as Smallholder Guidelines of the Ethical Trade Initiative and the Fairtrade Labelling Organization.

In addition to this, the company conducted participatory audits, and provided its CTP suppliers with information and feedback to assist them in maximizing long-term benefits. It helped suppliers to reduce their dependence on Body Shop by helping them gain access to wider markets and sharing best practices with them.

As of July 2006, the CTP included 31 communities spread across 24 countries. More than half of Body Shop's core product line contained at least one item sourced through CTP. The company strove to include such ingredients in new product development, gifts and accessories. Even gift packaging was sourced through this program. According to the company, each year it bought over £5 million worth of ingredients, gifts, and accessories through the CTP initiative.

Improve Self-esteem

Body Shop said that it marketed products honestly, did not make misleading claims and product promises. The marketing messages celebrated diversity and did not feature

35   "The Body Shop Captures PETA Europe Prize," http://www.thebodyshopinternational.com, 2006.
36   Ibid.
37   http://www.thebodyshop.com/bodyshop/values/support_community_trade.jsp.

Exhibit 10.5 Body Shop's Fair Trade Guidelines

1. COMMUNITY

We are looking to work with established community organizations which represent the interests of their people.

2. COMMUNITY IN NEED

We target those groups who are disadvantaged in some way, those whose opportunities are limited.

3. BENEFITS

We want the primary producers and their wider community to benefit from the trade—socially as well as economically.

4. COMMERCIAL VIABILITY

It has to make good commercial sense meaning that price, quality, capacity and availability are carefully considered.

5. ENVIRONMENTAL SUSTAINABILITY

The trade has to meet The Body Shop standards for environmental and animal protection.

Source: http://www.thebodyshop.com/bodyshop/values/support_community_trade.jsp.

ultra-thin or very young models, as was the norm in beauty advertising. A statement in Body Shop's website reads, "We will not promise eternal youth, or prey on people's insecurities, but focus instead on products that provide wellbeing and comfort."[38] It promoted diversity, acceptance, and empowerment in its workplace, and maintained equal opportunities standards. Employees were groomed through volunteering, training, and personal development programs.

From its early years, Body Shop had promoted self-esteem as one of its values. It challenged what it called "unrealistic beauty ideal presented by the beauty industry" and claimed that it used language and images that showed respect for women. Its campaigns on self-esteem took off in a big way in 1995, when it ran a "Women's Rights Campaign" during the fourth UN World Conference on Women. As a part of the campaign, it collected more than a million signatures in support of the issue from people in 25 countries. In 1997, it launched a campaign based on "Ruby," a realistic doll which represented real women as opposed to the dolls such as "Barbie." In the same year it supported a debate on self-esteem by the Sophia Institute in Singapore.[39] In addition to this, Body Shop UK sponsored an Oxford University research project that looked at the self-esteem of young women and worked with the UK Guide Association to produce a self-esteem activity pack called "The Can Do Girls." In the following year, Body Shop published and distributed globally "The Body and Self Esteem," to raise awareness of the issue of self-esteem and generate debate on the subject.

In 2003, Body Shop launched a global campaign against domestic violence called "Stop Violence in the Home." From its stores in the UK, the company raised £90,000

38 http://www.thebodyshop.com/bodyshop/values/activate_self_esteem.jsp.
39 Sophia Institute, based in Manchester, UK, one of the few institutions in the world dedicated to promoting self-esteem.

for the charity organization Refuge[40] in less than six months through the sale of badges and the recycling of 18,000 mobile phones. Each of these phones helped raise £2.75 for Refuge and its beneficiaries—women and children affected by domestic violence. In the US, 50,000 mobile phones were donated by customers, raising US$ 80,000 for The National Coalition Against Domestic Violence[41] (NCADV) and The Wireless Foundation.[42] In 2004, Body Shop's customers helped raise over £500,000 through the "Stop Violence in the Home" campaign. Throughout Europe and the Middle East, Body Shop stores recycled mobile phones and sold campaign key rings. In the UK, the campaign funded a pilot program to provide women with reconfigured mobile phones as emergency alarms that could be used in vulnerable situations.

In 2005, Body Shop extended its "Stop Violence in the Home" campaign to 40 countries. In that year, it raised over £500,000 for charities supporting victims of domestic violence. US customers donated over 100,000 old mobile phones to raise funds for the NCADV. In Canada, the campaign raised funds to support the Canadian Women's Foundation.[43] In Singapore, the company launched the campaign with public buses on six important routes carrying "Stop Violence in the Home" advertisements on them. Throughout Europe, a special edition lip care stick was launched to promote the campaign. It became a best seller and customers also donated thousands of products and gifts, which the company distributed to local women's shelters. In the UK, customers donated over 60,000 mobile phones, which were transformed into personal safety alarms for women or recycled to raise funds for "FonesForSafety"[44] initiative.

Defend Human Rights

Defending human rights is another core value of the company as it felt that it is the responsibility of every individual to actively support those whose human rights are denied. It ensured that its products were sourced and produced in regions where human and civil rights were respected and adhered to, as set out in the Universal Declaration of Human Rights.[45] Body Shop conducted and supported many Human Rights campaigns. For instance, in 1998, Body Shop Australia ran a "Thumbs Up for Reconcil-

---

40   Refuge is a national charity for women and children experiencing domestic violence.

41   National Coalition Against Domestic Violence is an non-profit organization with a mission "to organize for collective power by advancing transformative work, thinking and leadership of communities and individuals working to end the violence in our lives" (source: http://www.ncadv. org).

42   The Wireless Foundation is a non-profit organization established in 1991. It oversees philanthropic programs that utilize wireless technology to help American communities (http://www. wirelessfoundation.org).

43   Canadian Women's Foundation is a national public foundation for women and girls in Canada. It raises money and makes grants to help stop violence against women and build economic independence for women and their children.

44   Fonesforsafety is a mobile phone recycling scheme which turns used mobile phones into reconfigured "999 only" phone alarms for victims of domestic violence (source: http://www. fonesforsafety.org.uk).

45   The Universal Declaration of Human Rights is a declaration adopted by the United Nations General Assembly on December 10, 1948 at Paris. It outlined the organization's view on guaranteeing human rights to all people.

iation" campaign in support of reconciliation between black and white Australians. In 2000, Body Shop launched its Human Rights Awards.

In addition to adhering to all relevant international Human Rights Standards in areas such as working conditions, protection of privacy, etc., Body Shop also benchmarked its employee management policies against international standards.

Body Shop was a founding member of the Ethical Trade Initiative (ETI) and strove to ensure that its suppliers complied with the ethical trade standards (refer to Exhibit 10.6 for the Body Shop's ethical trade standards). Suppliers were screened by a buying team who were given "ethical targets" on an annual basis. The team was also provided training in this area. Being a member of Supplier Ethical Data Exchange (SEDEX), Body Shop insisted on and ensured that its suppliers conducted regular ethical assessments. In addition to this, Body Shop worked with other stakeholders at various levels to share best practices and influence national and international policy on ethical trade issues.

EXHIBIT 10.6 Body Shop's Ethical Trade Standards

- Employment is freely chosen
- Freedom of association and the right to collective bargaining are respected
- Working conditions are safe and hygienic
- Child labour is not used
- Living wages are paid
- Working hours are not excessive
- No discrimination is practiced
- Regular employment is provided
- No harsh or inhumane treatment is allowed

Source: http://www.thebodyshopinternational.com

Protect the Planet

Body Shop said that it aimed to be a sustainable business and considered protection of the planet as a key responsibility. In 1986, the company began its campaign for protection of the planet. The company developed its first international environmental policy in 1992.

Body Shop supported materials and technologies that caused minimal harm to the environment and promoted the use of renewable resources and sustainable ingredients. It also strove to minimize wastage by using recycled materials and minimal packaging. In 1993, it stopped using PVC[46] in its packaging, and in 2005, it announced that it would phase out all use of phthalates[47] in its products by the end of 2006. It partnered

46   PVC or polyvinyl chloride is a polymer used for packaging and building and construction industry. There are concerns about the negative impact of PVC on the environment.

47   Phthalates are a group of chemical compounds that are mainly used as substances added to plastics to increase their flexibility. There are concerns about the impact of phthalates on health.

with Friends of the Earth, Greenpeace, WWF US, and the US Campaign for Safe Cosmetics to ensure that its policies for chemicals use were environmentally responsible. The company had also set itself a target of becoming a carbon-neutral retailer by 2010.[48]

Body Shop strove to ensure that its policies and practices regarding wood products were in line with the best sustainability practices. It was a supporter of the Forest Stewardship Council[49] (FSC) certification scheme. It strove to ensure that all its wood products were derived from an FSC source. Body Shop was also a member of the World Wildlife UK Forest and Trade Network.[50]

In 2004, Body Shop committed itself to address social and environmental impacts of palm oil[51] production including deforestation, biodiversity and the rights of indigenous populations, poor labor conditions, etc. As an active member of the Roundtable on Sustainable Palm Oil,[52] Body Shop partnered with NGOs and producers to ensure that customers would be able to choose sustainable palm oil.

Other Initiatives

The company made regular donations to charitable organizations including The Body Shop Foundation (BSF), its charitable trust that was set up in 1990. The trust supported charities working on environmental, animal welfare and human rights issues. As of April 2006, Body Shop had donated over £8 million to BSF.

In 2004, the company donated £1.3 million to charitable organizations, of which £0.7 million was donated to The Body Shop Foundation[53] and £100,000 to the Disaster Emergency Committee for the Asian tsunami[54] victims. The company pledged an additional £100,000 to Children on the Edge[55] to help rebuild the lives of children in Aceh, the Indonesian province that was severely hit by the tsunami in December 2004. Body Shop raised £200,000 for tsunami victims through the contributions of its customers. The company also sold bracelets in the US and Canada to raise US$ 300,000 for HIV/AIDS victims.

---

48   "Protect Our Planet," http://www.thebodyshopinternational.com, 2006.

49   The Forest Stewardship Council (FSC) is a non-profit organization based in Bonn, Germany. FSC's stated mission is "to promote environmentally appropriate, socially beneficial and economically viable management of the world's forests" (source: http://www.en.wikipedia.org).

50   The World Wildlife UK Forest and Trade Network was founded in 1995 by 20 member companies with the stated mission of improving the management of the world's production forests by using the purchasing power of UK businesses.

51   Palm oil is an important ingredient in many toiletry products.

52   Roundtable on Sustainable Palm Oil is a not-for-profit association whose members represent the oil palm growers, palm oil processors and traders, consumer goods manufacturers, retailers, banks and investors, environmental/nature conservation NGOs, and social/development NGOs.

53   The Body Shop Foundation is the charitable trust of Body Shop established in 1990.

54   The Asian Tsunami (a series of waves generated when a body of water, such as an ocean is rapidly displaced on a massive scale) is one of the deadliest disasters in modern history that left a total of 229,866 persons lost, including 186,983 dead and 42,883 missing. The tsunami occurred in the Indian Ocean on December 26, 2004.

55   Children on the Edge is a organization committed to working on behalf of marginalized and vulnerable children especially those orphaned or victims of war.

In 2005, the stores in the UK supported the "Make Poverty History"[56] campaign through the sale of over 200,000 white wristbands, raising in excess of £100,000 for the campaign. In addition to these campaigns, Body Shop was also engaged in causes such as violence against children. The year 2004 saw the return of Body Shop to social reporting as it published its independently verified *Values Report* in 2004 and 2005.

Criticisms

Though the company had a distinguished record as a pioneer of corporate responsibility, it had its fair share of critics. From the 1990s, Body Shop faced increased scrutiny regarding its activities and claims. Business ethics expert Jon Entine (Entine) was one of Body Shop's fiercest critics. Entine accused Body Shop and its founders of being hypocrites, as in his opinion they were preying on the idealism of consumers, while not being any different from other companies in their pursuit of profit. In 1994, Entine reported that Charity Commission for England and Wales[57] records did not show any charitable contributions from the company in its first 11 years of operation. In the subsequent years, its contribution to charity was less than 1.5 percent of pretax profits (which was the average contribution made by US corporates). He also said that the company made false claims that its products were natural. He alleged that there was extensive use of petrochemicals in the preparation of Body Shop's products. He quoted many ex-employees who had claimed that the stories put out to customers about various products were totally fabricated. He even cited the fact that Roddick herself had likened the operations at Body Shop to a "dysfunctional coffin."[58]

In 1998, McSpotlight[59] and Greenpeace UK put forward similar criticisms that Body Shop exploited the public by championing various agendas while it was actually more similar to other corporate entities. They said that Body Shop's products were not natural, but had been synthesized and produced. Though the company claimed that it was against animal testing, its products contained ingredients that had been tested on animals by other companies (refer to Exhibit 10.7 for the leaflet released by McSpotlight and Greenpeace UK).

Critics also dismissed the company's CTP as a mere marketing ploy as it accounted for less than one percent of sales of Body Shop products. Body Shop was also accused of paying exploitative wages and having an anti-trade union stance. Its CTP was also viewed as patronizing and was said to have created tensions and divisions within indigenous communities and undermined self-sufficiency and self-dependence. McSpotlight accused Body Shop of marketing products by making people feel insecure

56 It is the biggest ever anti-poverty movement. It was started in 2005 (source: http://www.makepovertyhistory.org).

57 The Charity Commission is the non-ministerial government department that regulates registered charities in England and Wales.

58 Australian Financial Review, "Body Shop's Packaging Starts to Unravel," http://www.jonentine.com, December 18, 2002.

59 McSpotlight is a website that highlights the alleged exploitation of animals, people, and the environment by the McDonald's fast-food restaurant chain.

EXHIBIT 10.7 Leaflet Released by McSpotlight and Greenpeace UK

WHAT'S WRONG WITH THE BODY SHOP?
—a critique of 'green' consumerism—

The Body Shop has successfully manufactured an image of being a caring company that is helping to protect the environment and indigenous peoples, and preventing the suffering of animals—whilst selling 'natural' products. But behind the green and cuddly image lies the reality—the Body Shop's operations, like those of all multinationals, have a detrimental effect on the environment and the world's poor. They do not help the plight of animals or indigenous peoples (and may be having a harmful effect), and their products are far from what they're cracked up to be. They have put themselves on a pedestal in order to exploit people's idealism—so this leaflet has been written as a necessary response.

Companies like the Body Shop continually hype their products through advertising and marketing, often creating a demand for something where a real need for it does not exist. The message pushed is that the route to happiness is through buying more and more of their products. The increasing domination of multinationals and their standardised products is leading to global cultural conformity. The world's problems will only be tackled by curbing such consumerism—one of the fundamental causes of world poverty, environmental destruction and social alienation.

FUELLING CONSUMPTION AT THE EARTH'S EXPENSE

The Body Shop has over 1,500 stores in 47 countries, and aggressive expansion plans. Their main purpose (like all multinationals) is making lots of money for their rich shareholders. In other words, they are driven by power and greed. But the Body Shop try to conceal this reality by continually pushing the message that by shopping at their stores, rather than elsewhere, people will help solve some of the world's problems. The truth is that nobody can make the world a better place by shopping.

20% of the world's population consumes 80% of its resources. A high standard of living for some people means gross social inequalities and poverty around the world. Also, the mass production, packaging and transportation of huge quantities of goods is using up the world's resources faster than they can be renewed and filling the land, sea and air with dangerous pollution and waste. Those who advocate an ever-increasing level of consumption, and equate such consumption with personal well-being, economic progress and social fulfilment, are creating a recipe for ecological disaster.

Rejecting consumerism does not mean also rejecting our basic needs, our stylishness, our real choices or our quality of life. It is about creating a just, stable and sustainable world, where resources are under the control of local communities and are distributed equally and sparingly—it's about improving everyone's quality of life. Consuming ever more things is an unsatisfying and harmful way to try to be happy and fulfilled. Human happiness is not related to what people buy, but to who we are and how we relate to each other.

continued opposite

from previous page

LET'S CONSUME LESS AND LIVE MORE
MISLEADING THE PUBLIC

Natural products?—The Body Shop gives the impression that their products are made from mostly natural ingredients. In fact like all big cosmetic companies they make wide use of non-renewable petrochemicals, synthetic colours, fragrances and preservatives, and in many of their products they use only tiny amounts of botanical-based ingredients. Some experts have warned about the potential adverse effects on the skin of some of the synthetic ingredients. The Body Shop also regularly irradiate certain products to try to kill microbes—radiation is generated from dangerous non-renewable uranium which cannot be disposed of safely.

Helping animals?—Although the Body Shop maintain that they are against animal testing, they do not always make clear that many of the ingredients in their products have been tested on animals by other companies, causing much pain and suffering to those animals. They accept ingredients tested on animals before 1991, or those tested since then (if they were animal-tested for some purpose other than for cosmetics). There continue to be concerns about the enforcement of their policy. Also, some Body Shop items contain animal products such as gelatine (crushed bone).

Caring for our bodies?—The cosmetics industry, which includes the Body Shop, tries to make women—and increasingly now also men—feel inadequate and insecure about their bodies, and pushes the message that people need 'beautifying'. Women especially are often put under pressure to conform to the impossible physical ideals set by money-oriented industries and the media. Let's appreciate everyone's natural beauty and dignity.

LOW PAY AND AGAINST UNIONS

The Body Shop pay their store workers low wages at or near the expected minimum wage and well below the official European 'decency threshold' for pay. The company is opposed to trade unions, ensuring that they keep labour costs down and that employees are not able to organise to improve their working conditions. None of their workers are unionised so employees are forced to channel their grievances and demands through procedures completely controlled by the company. This isolates workers and denies them collective bargaining power.

EXPLOITING INDIGENOUS PEOPLES

The Body Shop claim to be helping some third world workers and indigenous peoples through so-called 'Trade Not Aid' or 'Community Trade' projects. In fact, these are largely a marketing ploy as less than 1% of sales go to 'Community Trade' producers, and it has been shown that some of these products have been sourced from mainstream commercial markets. One such project, which has been the centrepiece of the company's marketing strategy for years, is with the Kayapo Indians in Brazil. The Body Shop have claimed that by harvesting brazil nut oil (used in hair conditioner), the Indians are able to make sustainable use of the forest thereby preventing its destruction by mining and logging

continued over

from previous page

companies. But only a small number of the Kayapo are involved, creating resentment and internal divisions within the community. As the Body Shop are the sole buyer of the oil, they can set any price they like. The project does nothing to safeguard the Indians' future interests. Furthermore, the company has used them extensively for PR purposes for which they have not been compensated.

Such projects take attention away from the need to oppose the threats to the survival of indigenous peoples. Rather than encouraging them to be tied into the market economy controlled by foreign companies, people should be supporting their freedom to control their own land and resources and therefore their future.

One recent Body Shop advertisement extolled their commitment to indigenous peoples and the American Express card (the ultimate symbol of consumerism). At the time American Express was a major backer of a massive hydroelectric scheme due to flood vast areas of Cree Indian land in Quebec against Cree opposition.

CENSORSHIP

As the Body Shop rely so heavily on their 'green', 'caring' image, they have threatened or brought legal action against some of those who have criticised them, trying to stifle legitimate public discussion. It's vital to stand up to intimidation and to defend free speech.

Source: http://www.mcspotlight.org.

about their looks, in the same way that other firms used to sell their personal care products. McSpotlight cited the company's "Love Your Body" campaign as an example. Some critics pointed out that the visual on the home page of Body Shop was no different from the idealized body images of beauty as projected by the cosmetics industry. The company was also accused of being very aggressive in its response to any form of criticism and allegedly tried to intimidate its critics through invectives and/or lawsuits.

Some analysts suggested that the image projected by the company and its "anti-city" attitude was hypocritical for a company that raised funds by listing on the London Stock Exchange. "It's massively hypocritical. If making money from the City, you've got a nerve criticising the very people you're taking money from,"[60] said Ratner. Critics felt that there was a big gap between the image projected by the company and its actual practice.

Critics also argued that after its lackluster results in 2001 and 2002, the management was more focused on improving its financial position. It was only in 2004 that the company made a comeback to serious social reporting. But analysts felt that even after this gap, the 2005 report was unsatisfactory and failed to answer the criticisms leveled against it in a comprehensive way. The 2005 *Values Report* responded only indirectly to some of the criticisms that had been leveled against Body Shop.

60   "Dame Anita's Radical Approach," http://www.news.bbc.co.uk, July 17, 2003.

Some analysts said that the company's report had not clarified its position on the allegations regarding its CTP. It did not provide any figures as to what proportion of Body Shop's products were sourced through the CTP. Though the company had listed its participation in many stakeholder initiatives, the impact of these initiatives was not touched upon. It was also said that the company's position on workplace issues was not set out clearly and allegations of exploitative working conditions were not refuted properly.

Criticisms of Body Shop intensified after the company announced that it had agreed to be taken over by L'Oréal. L'Oréal did not deny that it used animal testing for cosmetics, something Body Shop founder, Roddick, had opposed throughout the 30 years of her business life. Critics (including Roddick, in the past) had campaigned against L'Oréal's alleged exploitation of the sexuality of women. Also, it was Roddick who had previously criticized L'Oréal for using only "sexy" saleswomen in their stores.

In a statement on its website, Naturewatch said: "We feel that the Body Shop has 'sold out' and is not standing by its principles."[61] There were also several calls to boycott Body Shop's products. John Ruane, director of Naturewatch, said, "She appears to be taking the money and running. Clearly all the money that goes into the till at Body Shop in the future effectively amounts to supporting L'Oréal and, by association, disgusting animal testing. Consumers can make their feelings clear by not shopping at Body Shop."[62]

Another reason why the sale of Body Shop to L'Oréal was criticized was that Nestlé was a large shareholder (26 percent) in L'Oréal. Nestlé had been strongly criticized by activists for several decades for allegedly promoting baby milk powder in the developing world. In January 2005, Nestlé was voted as the 'least responsible company' in an Internet poll. It was also one of the four most boycotted companies in the world and the most boycotted company in the UK.

Anti-animal testing and anti-Nestlé campaigners called for a boycott of Body Shop too. Various protests were organized by animal rights activists and they also began digging deeper behind the marketing strategies and public image of Body Shop. They used a spoof of a 1990s leaflet of Body Shop and urged Body Shop loyalists to send back their Body Shop loyalty cards to register their protests (refer to Exhibit 10.8a and 10.8b for backlash against Body Shop).

In response to the protests, L'Oréal clarified that it had not done any animal testing since 1989. L'Oréal said in a statement, "We have not carried out or commissioned tests of products or ingredients on animals since 1989."[63] But it added that it could not guarantee that all ingredients bought from other firms had not been tested on animals. Its spokeswoman said that some ingredients still had to be tested under European health and safety rules. However, it did not stop the flow of criticism and demonstrations in front of various Body Shop stores.

On June 26, 2006, Naturewatch organized a protest at the Body Shop headquarters in Littlehampton, West Sussex, UK. The protest included "Lilly Lapin," a bunny mascot adopted for this campaign, while one supporter wore a dress made out of Body Shop's

61   Heather Tyler, "Mixed Reaction to Body Shop Takeover," http://www.stuff.co.nz, March 21, 2006.
62   Sean Poulter, "Roddick Sells the Body Shop for £652m," http://www.dailymail.co.uk, March 18, 2006.
63   "Body Shop Row Over Animal Testing," http://www.news.bbc.co.uk, June 26, 2006.

EXHIBIT 10.8a Backlash against Body Shop

Source: http://www.naturewatch.org.

loyalty cards that were sent to Naturewatch by customers unhappy with the L'Oréal deal. Ruane said that the campaign was getting a lot of support. "It's been very good with tremendous support from everybody passing, the horns are hooting all over the place and we think it's been successful,"[64] he said.

Many Body Shop loyalists were taken aback by the deal. Some of them said that they felt betrayed and vowed never to shop at Body Shop again. A consumer said, "The Body Shop used to be my high street 'safe-house,' a place where I could walk into and know that what I bought was okay, that people were actually benefiting from my purchase. Now the people benefiting are the overpaid, underworked 'fat-cat' CEOs of animal-testing L'Oréal and baby-milk-selling Nestlé. By buying from the Body Shop, you are now no longer supporting ethical consumerism. If I want legitimate fair-trade, non-animal tested products, I can find them easily, at the same price, elsewhere."[65]

Several anti-animal cruelty organisations struck Body Shop off from their ethical shopping lists. *Ethical Consumer* downgraded its ethical rating of Body Shop from 11/20 (average), to 2.5/20 (very poor), on "ethiscore."[66] As per the BrandIndex,[67] within three weeks of the announcement of the deal, Body Shop's "satisfaction" rating had dropped by 11 points to 14, its "buzz" rating fell by 10 points to −4, and its "general impression" fell by three points to 19.

64   "Body Shop Row over Animal Testing," http://www.news.bbc.co.uk, June 26, 2006.

65   "Has the Body Shop Sold Out?" http://www.newconsumer.org, April 2006.

66   Ethiscore is a numerical rating (out of 20) designed to allow consumers to compare companies across a range of corporate responsibility issues, including the environment, human and animal rights. The higher the score, the better a company's ethical record. Scores between 0 and 4 signifies "very poor."

67   BrandIndex is a daily measure of public perception of more than 1,100 consumer brands across 32 sectors, measured on a 7-point profile: general impression, "buzz," quality, value, corporate image, customer satisfaction, and whether respondents would recommend the brand to a friend (source: http://www.brandindex.com).

EXHIBIT 10.8b Backlash against Body Shop

Source: http://www.stopanimalcruelty.co.uk.

WHY BOYCOTT THE BODY SHOP? ☠

As you may have recently heard the body shop is to be sold to French cosmetics giant L'Oreal. So what does this mean for the Body Shop? What you might not know is that there are three companies involved in this situation. Body Shop may be a part of L'Oreal but who are L'Oreal owned by? The answer is Nestle, the worlds most campaigned against multi national company. Below are some issues which we hope might give you reason to not support the once ethical Body Shop.

AGAINST ANIMAL TESTING - NOT TRUE

L'Oreal claim to have stopped testing their products on animals in 1989
EU Legislation states that new chemical formulas must be tested on animals.
3% of L'Oreals annual turnover goes to Research and Development.
L'Oreal develop over 4000 new chemical formulas every year

L'Oreal products as a finished formula have most probably not been tested on animals but the ingredients which go into L'Oreal products have been tested on animals. These experiments require one small animal (usually a rabbit) and one large animal (usually a cat or dog). Nestlé openly admit animal experimentation.

DEFEND HUMAN RIGHTS - NOT TRUE

Demanding money from a war torn Iraq
Sued by human rights group over child labour
Demanding money from a famine stricken Ethiopia

It may sound far fetched but these are facts. Nestlé doesnt seem to have the interests of fellow humans on its list of priorities.

SUPPORT COMMUNITY TRADE - FALSE

Operations in oppressive regimes
The Nestle union leader was assasinated
Colombian union workers recieve death threats

Nestlé majority owners of L'Oreal and now the body shop have a very murky past when we delve into the workings of overseas, particularlly 3rd world and developing country activities.

ACTIVATE SELF ESTEEM - FALSE

Dame Anita actually has lashed out in the past against L'Oreal of all people! Anita Roddick criticised L'Oreal for its treatment of female staff and internal policies to fire employees whom they considered un-attractive.

For more information or to view our sources for information please visit our website at the below address or email us info@boycottbodyshop.co.uk
Why not write or email the Body Shop and tell them how you feel about L'Oreal and Nestlé?

PROTECT OUR PLANET - FALSE

Nestlé Disregard of palm oil environmental threat
Nestlé knowingly sold contaminated baby milk formula
Mislabelling of Nestlé products with GM ingredients
Use of nanotechnology in Nestlé food production

Please sign the pledge to boycott the Body Shop at
WWW.BOYCOTTBODYSHOP.CO.UK

Mike Brady (Brady), Campaigns and Networking Coordinator at Baby Milk Action commented: "The strength of feeling seems to have taken Body Shop and Dame Anita Roddick by surprise—they still do not have a statement on the Nestlé link."[68]

Body Shop's Response

Body Shop clarified that the acquisition by L'Oréal would not dilute its ethical stance and that it would continue its position on anti-animal testing. Body Shop spokesman Bill Eyres said, "It has been agreed that all our values are ring-fenced and we will continue to apply our animal testing policy."[69]

Roddick justified the deal by saying that L'Oréal wanted to learn from Body Shop's commitment to the environment and human rights in business. She also denied that she had sold out and maintained that the company's values would not change. She said, "I don't see it as selling out. L'Oréal has displayed visionary leadership in wanting to be an authentic advocate and supporter of our values."[70] She added, "The campaigning, the being maverick, changing the rules of business—it's all there, protected. And it's not going to change. That's part of our DNA. But having L'Oréal come in and say we like you, we like your ethics, we want to be part of you, we want you to teach us things, it's a gift. I'm ecstatic about it. So I don't see it as selling out."[71]

Roddick argued that if at all she had sold out, it was by going to the stock market in 1984 and putting Body Shop in the hands of people who were contemptuous of the values of Body Shop. "We then became 'owned' by people who were happy to downgrade our stock at the merest whiff of community trade, who believed that pioneering an end to animal testing in cosmetics was a threat to our share price . . . That was, I now realise, selling out,"[72] she said. She added that Body Shop would be better off in the hands of L'Oréal who had publicly committed itself to upholding the values of Body Shop. "They [L'Oréal] understand what a maverick The Body Shop was in the business world and how we helped change the language of business, incorporating the action of social change, especially in human rights, animal welfare, the environment and community trade,"[73] said Dame Roddick.

Owen-Jones acknowledged that L'Oréal would not be able to stop animal testing overnight, but this issue was a part of its long-term plan. He said, "I can't overnight use the Body Shop approach in all of the L'Oréal companies, but our long-term commitment is to join Body Shop on this issue. I cannot be clearer than that."[74]

68 "Body Shop Will Lose Support of 99% of Nestlé Boycott Supporters Initial Survey Results Reveal," http://www.babymilkaction.org, March 28, 2006.
69 Robert Booth, "Activists Call Body Shop Boycott," http://www.guardian.co.uk, March 17, 2006.
70 "L'Oréal Buys Out Body Shop for $1.4 billion US," http://www.ctv.ca, March 17, 2006.
71 David Teather, "Roddick Nets £130m from Body Shop sale," http://www.business.guardian.co.uk, March 18, 2006.
72 Anita Roddick, "Every Body Grows Strong," http://www.anitaroddick.com, March 21, 2006.
73 "L'Oréal to Buy the Body Shop," http://abc.net.au, March 17, 2006.
74 David Teather, "Roddick Nets £130m from Body Shop sale," http://www.business.guardian.co.uk, March 18, 2006.

Roddick agreed that she had an issue with L'Oréal over animal testing earlier, but she was now convinced that L'Oréal was sincere in its commitment to this issue. She said, "So yes, I have criticised the cosmetics industry for their fantasies in the past. I'm not going to stop doing so now, but that does not mean I'm going to be satisfied with a splendid but pure isolation . . . I have not worked all these years to be satisfied to have pioneered a new way of doing business that nobody else ever tries."[75]

With regard to the allegations that Body Shop marketed its products by making people feel insecure, Body Shop stated: "We do not promise eternal youth in our advertising, or prey on women's insecurities, but focus instead on products which provide well-being and comfort." It also said that it was committed to not using ingredients in its cosmetics that had been tested on animals for cosmetic purposes after December 31, 1990. It further pointed out that most of the ingredients used in cosmetic and toiletry products had been animal-tested for some purpose at some time in their history, and it would be almost impossible to sell products whose ingredients had never been tested on animals.

L'Oréal Buying CSR?

Some analysts felt that the acquisition was an attempt by L'Oréal to buy CSR. They cited other instances when major multinational corporations bought up smaller, model ethical corporations such as Unilever's acquisition of Ben & Jerry's, The Coca-Cola Company's buyout of Odwalla, Colgate-Palmolive Company's takeover of Tom's of Maine, and Dean Foods' acquisition of Horizon Organics. Critics argued that these "model" corporations would find it difficult to continue the good work under their new parent.

The economic viability of an acquisition for such a reason is also a question mark as, generally, there is a public backlash after such acquisitions. As L'Oréal was not perceived to share the principles of Body Shop, Body Shop's association with L'Oréal raised questions about the ethical standards of Body Shop itself. Its customer base was also affected. A spokeswoman of *Ethical Consumer*, Mary Rayner, said, "This deal would have a seriously negative impact on the Body Shop. It has built itself up on the principle of not testing on animals, but in one fell swoop this would completely ruin its reputation."[76] ABN AMRO[77] too said that it was unconvinced by the deal. It commented: "We have some concerns that L'Oréal's mere ownership will deter some of Body Shop's existing customers, while management's presentation was relatively short on detail as to how it will seek to grow the business going forward."[78]

Critics felt that if a company is serious about CSR and ethical issues, it could cultivate this in their own organization rather than buy out a company that is considered a model organization. Ruth Rosselson (Rosselson) of *Ethical Consumer* said, "If L'Oréal is

75   "The Body Shop Sold Out," http://www.choosecrueltyfree.org.au, 2006.

76   Jim Armitage, "L'Oréal Mulls £600m Body Shop Takeover," http://www.thisismoney.co.uk, February 23, 2006.

77   ABN AMRO is the largest bank in the Netherlands and has operations all over the world.

78   "ABN Amro Unconvinced by L'Oréal Body Shop Buy," http://www.newratings.com, March 20, 2006.

really concerned about ethical issues, it can start taking them more seriously within L'Oréal itself."[79]

Outlook

Some analysts felt that L'Oréal did not share the principles of Body Shop and that this acquisition had removed the biggest supporter of ethically sourced beauty care products from the market. Despite the assurance to the contrary, Body Shop might not be able to function autonomously. They pointed out that already five members of the board, namely Peggy Bruzelius, Howard Mann, Jack Keenan, Irene Miller, and Gordon, had resigned, and were replaced by former L'Oréal UK chief Tom Vyner and current L'Oréal CEO Jean-Paul Agon, along with four others.[80] Brady said that the Body Shop brand had been badly damaged by linking itself to an allegedly unethical company like Nestlé. Rosselson said, "I for one will certainly not be shopping at Body Shop again. L'Oréal has yet to show its commitment to any ethical issues at all."[81] It was reported that many consumers too had similar views.

Though many people were concerned by the deal, some were more optimistic of the merger. Save Animals From Exploitation[82] (SAFE) campaign director Hans Criek said, "Hopefully the Body Shop will continue to grow the message as the company expands with its new owners. We would like to see the Body Shop's ethics rub off on L'Oréal— not the other way around."[83] The Royal Society for the Prevention of Cruelty to Animals[84] (RSPCA) felt that the match was "odd" but urged L'Oréal to take up the Body Shop's ethical stance on animal testing. It said, "The Body Shop has proved that an ethical approach to trading can be a huge high street success—an approach which it must be allowed to maintain."[85] Analysts felt that L'Oréal's interest would be well served if it kept its word of not interfering with the integrity of the Body Shop brand in any way that might have an adverse impact on Body Shop's public image. According to Euromonitor, if L'Oréal kept its distance, it would convince the consumers to get back to their previous buying habits.

Body Shop claimed that, despite some public unhappiness over the deal, its business was not hurt in the period after the acquisition. It announced that sales in the eight weeks to April 22, 2006, were up 5 percent as compared to the corresponding period of 2005. Sales for the quarter (July to September) were £116 million, a growth of 8.8 per-

79   *Ethical Consumer*, Press Release, http://www.ethicalconsumer.org, March 17, 2006.

80   "L'Oréal Takes Over Body Shop," http://www.naturewatch.org, June 15, 2006.

81   David Teather, "Roddick Nets £130m from Body Shop sale," http://www.business.guardian.co.uk, March 18, 2006.

82   Save Animals From Exploitation, based in Chirstcurch, New Zealand, is a non-profit animal welfare and rights organization in New Zealand. It was founded in 1930.

83   Heather Tyler, "Mixed Reaction to Body Shop Takeover," http://www.stuff.co.nz, March 21, 2006.

84   The Royal Society for the Prevention of Cruelty to Animals (RSPCA) is a charity in England and Wales that promotes animal welfare. It is funded by voluntary donations and is one of the largest charities in the UK (source: http://www.en.wikipedia.org).

85   Sean Poulter, "Roddick Sells the Body Shop for £652m," http://www.dailymail.co.uk, March 18, 2006.

cent over the corresponding period of 2005.[86] The company also announced that it was looking forward to launching a number of innovative products in the fiscal year 2007, including a major new-look make-up collection and a skin care range using aloe vera sourced through its CTP.

However, some of Body Shop's critics maintained that Body Shop was merely continuing its earlier unethical ways and that it was no different from any other company. It had smartly leveraged on the growth in ethical consumerism. There was a huge gap between the image projected by the company and its actual practice. For long, these critics had dismissed all talk of sustainability by Roddick as empty rhetoric. They now saw the Body Shop's decision to be taken over by L'Oréal as a vindication of their view that Body Shop had always been a greenwasher.

Suggested Questions for Discussion

1. The Oxford English Dictionary defines greenwashing as "disinformation disseminated by an organization so as to present an environmentally responsible public image." Do you believe that The Body Shop was guilty of greenwashing, under the leadership of Dame Anita Roddick? Justify.

2. The Body Shop was considered a pioneer in modern corporate social responsibility. Can its sale to L'Oréal be considered a sellout of its values and principles? Or is it an attempt to "to spread human values wider in business"? Or has it just found a strategic partner to help its products reach a larger market?

3. Discuss the importance of CSR and brand values as factors that need to be considered during mergers and acquisitions vis-à-vis financial parameters. Some critics opine that many multinationals are keen to acquire an ethical company with the hope that it may influence how the parent company is perceived. Do you agree with the critics that L'Oréal was trying to buy CSR through its acquisition of The Body Shop? Discuss.

> Teaching notes for this case are available from Greenleaf Publishing. These are free of charge and are available only to teaching staff. They can be requested by going to:
> **www.greenleaf-publishing.com/oikos_notes**

---

86 Nick Bevens, "Body Shop Defies Green Critics," http://www.scotsman.com, October 14, 2006.

CASE 11
Mobility Car-sharing[1]

Kai Hockerts

Copenhagen Business School, Denmark

Section A: From Ecopreneurial Start-up to Commercial Venture

Learning to Drive a Co-operative

> If you buy a lawnmower with three neighbours, this does not mean that you want to set up a business for lawnmower sharing. You think: "I need a lawn mower and that's it." As the model works others come and want to join as well. (Heusi, 2002, interview)

The Vierwaldstädtersee situated in the heart of Switzerland is probably one of the most beautiful and serene lakes of Europe. However, Peter Muheim was not able to appreciate the magnificent landscape in the summer of 1993. Sitting on his balcony he was immersed in a discussion with Rolf Fischer and Conrad Wagner. Together the three constituted the management of *ATG • AutoTeilet Genossenschaft* one of Switzerland's two car-sharing co-operatives. With about 80 cars (that were jointly used by 1,500 clients) the organization was no longer the hobby it had been when Wagner and Fischer started it six years back. Wagner, the managing director, and Fischer, the head of administration, had come to meet Muheim, in charge of car fleet management, to

debate the possibility of a merger with ShareCom, Switzerland's only other car-sharing co-operative.

While the three from ATG were sitting together Charles Nufer was looking unseeing over another expanse of water—the lake Zürich. Nufer had founded ShareCom in the same year ATG started and his co-operative was now roughly the same size. Both organizations were complementary in the area they covered. ShareCom was mainly present in Zürich and its surroundings, while ATG had its clients in smaller cities in the countryside. However, as car-sharing became more popular, their territories began to overlap. St Gallen in the western part of Switzerland, for example, was served by both organizations. Combining the two fleets would considerably extend the network and thus increase the attractiveness.

How Car-sharing Works

> We keep [durable goods] by us even if we do not want them at the moment.
> But their utility will of course increase the more often we use them. So it is
> often better to hire, or to buy and sell, or to make various arrangements for
> common usership. (Jevons, [1871] 1965)

Private car ownership can be a costly form of individual mobility (see Exhibit 11.1). It binds a substantial amount of capital and causes the owner recurring annual costs for taxes, insurance, and maintenance. However, most of the time cars sit around idle taking up scarce parking space. When used they cause air pollution, noise, traffic congestion, and accidents. Nonetheless, cars are the preferred choice of transportation in most parts of the developed world. Automobiles dominate the planning of inner cities. Even when promoted by policy makers, public transport struggles to compete with car ownership.

EXHIBIT 11.1 Total Cost of Mobility

Source: Mobility CarSharing Schweiz, 2003

	100% Own car	100% CS	50% CS + 50% PT	25% CS + 75% PT	100% PT
5,000 km	6,300.00	4,300.00	2,700.00	1,800.00	950.00
7,500 km	6,800.00	6,400.00	3,800.00	2,600.00	1,400.00
10,000 km	7,300.00	8,500.00	5,200.00	3,600.00	1,900.00
15,000 km	8,100.00	12,800.00	7,800.00	5,300.00	2,850.00
20,000 km	9,000.00	17,000.00	10,300.00	7,100.00	2,850.00

The table compares different alternatives for meeting mobility needs either through car ownership, car-sharing (CS) or public transport (PT) or a mix of CS and PT. The calculation assumes CHF 6,000 (~€3,600) p.a. fixed cost for a compact car (parking, taxes, insurance, depreciation).

However, in the 1980s the automobile finally began to choke on its own success. With the cost of car ownership increasing and parking space in inner cities decreasing, demand emerged for more efficient solutions, linking sporadic car use with public transport. Car rental—the traditional alternative to car ownership—was not well suited to meet this demand. Most people did not live close enough to car rental outlets to make rental a viable everyday solution. Furthermore, given their cost structure, most rental firms did not find short-term rental to be profitable. In fact most car-rental firms made money through long-term rentals, offering one-day hire as a loss-leader to complement their program. Accordingly, traditional car rental was primarily aimed at multi-day business clients and holiday travel. It was not an option for the occasional trip to the supermarket or picking up the kids from school. Car-sharing emerged as a way to meet demand for occasional short-term car usage that could not be satisfied through traditional car rental.

The **unique attributes of car-sharing** were accordingly a focus for short-term rental (cars were available for as short a time as 30 minutes), and decentralized availability of cars (most clients had a vehicle within walking distance of their home). The operational details differed from one car-sharing organization to another. However, many car-sharing schemes include the following elements:

● **To join,** clients bought a share in a co-operative (which they could sell back to the organization when leaving the scheme) or they paid a recurring annual fee. Most car-sharing organizations offered shares for between €500 and €700, or charged between €70 and €150 for an annual membership.

● **Cars were located** in central places such as train stations or in residential areas. The number of cars in given locations ranged from one or two to a dozen or more in prime locations such as the train station. Most clients lived within walking distance of at least one location.

● The actual **rental cost** depended on duration (about €1.5–2.0/hour) and distance traveled (about €0.2–0.5/km). Thus for occasional short-term requirements car-sharing was cheaper than car rental or car ownership. For trips of more than 200 kilometers car rental was more cost-efficient. The economic break-even between car-sharing and an own car was at 9,000 km per year. The average car-sharing client usually drove about 800 km per year.

● In the early days of car-sharing the **reservation system** was very informal. Each car had an administrator whom members could call to book a trip. They would retrieve the car key from a safe deposit box near the car. Each member had a key that opened all deposit boxes. After each trip they returned the car and noted in the board book the distance and time of their journey.

ATG and ShareCom Invent Car-sharing in Switzerland

Joint ownership of cars is not a new invention. For decades cars have been used jointly by family members or friends when no money was available to afford several cars. However, such informal solutions were not without problems. One car-sharing pioneer recalls his experiences as follows:

> Jointly using a car among neighbors can easily strain the relationship when problems arise. For example, when the car breaks down the owner often has unrealistic expectations as to the residual value of the car. So I did not hesitate to join [a formal car-sharing group] when it became available.

In 1987 two car-sharing co-operatives were founded independently of each other in Switzerland. The "**ATG • AutoTeilet Genossenschaft**" grew out of an informal car-sharing scheme in Stans (Kanton Lucerne). Rolf Fischer, one of the original eight founders, recalled:

> From the outset there was both an ecological and an economic motivation. On the one hand we were critical about car ownership from an ecological point of view. Thus car-sharing allowed us to meet an occasional need without having to actually own a car. On the other hand some among us were attracted to car-sharing because they would not have been able to afford a car by themselves. (Fischer, 2002, interview)

Conrad Wagner (Wagner, 2002, interview), another ATG founder, added that he was attracted by the flexibility of a sharing system. Rather than having only one type of vehicle ATG offered him access to a compact car, a van, as well as a cabriolet.

The co-operative "**ShareCom**" was also motivated by ecological reasons. Charles Nufer described the ShareCom philosophy as follows:

> Our approach was motivated by the environmental crisis of the early '80s. The desire to own more and more things was increasingly causing environmental problems. I felt that we could solve these [problems] only by separating ownership and usage, hence our motto "Use it—but don't own it!" (*Nutzen statt Besitzen*). (Nufer, 2002, interview)

ShareCom differed from ATG in two aspects. Firstly, it offered to share all kinds of durable goods (not only cars), and secondly was deeply rooted in the idea of mutual self-help. Accordingly ShareCom relied strongly on voluntary work by members. By spreading the responsibility for product maintenance, Nufer hoped to motivate members to look after the products as they would look after their own goods (Nufer, 2002, interview). The ShareCom system consisted of "user groups." Members of each group knew each other well and also often interacted outside the ShareCom system. This social interaction component became an important element of ShareCom's philosophy. The position of user group administrator was rotated on an annual basis and members would take weekly turns to wash a car and clean the interior. "The co-operative was about sharing and not rental," summarised Nufer (2002, interview) the ShareCom approach.

Both co-operatives quickly realized that their offers struck a nerve with many people. In the first six years they doubled their size nearly every year, although they spent hardly anything on **communication**. Co-operative members attracted new users by word of mouth alone. This was supplemented by a considerable amount of media attention both at the national and local level (each time a user group was founded).

Very quickly other players remarked the potential of car-sharing. In 1989 the **Verkehrsclub der Schweiz (VCS)**, Switzerland's "alternative" traffic club, began to systematically support car-sharing. It promoted the two co-operatives among its members, who were naturally predisposed to be interested in an offer like car-sharing. Probably the most important contribution of the VCS was its role in initiating a co-operation between ATG, ShareCom, and the Bundesamt für Energie (BFE), the Swiss Federal Office of Energy. In 1991, the BFE had launched **Energie2000**, a program aimed at promoting energy efficiency and renewable energy sources so as to reduce the amount of CO_2 emissions caused from fossil fuel consumption. The VCS proposed car-sharing as one of the projects funded under the program and offered to act as project manager between the BFE and the two co-operatives. One outcome of this project was the first systematic analyses of car-sharing (Muheim and Inderbitzin, 1992).

Joining Forces?

Inevitably the close co-operation under the Energie2000 program and a constant prodding by Monika Tschannen in charge of car-sharing at VCS led to discussions about **merging the two co-operatives**. However, these talks quickly became stuck due to philosophical and personal difficulties. Conrad Wagner and Charles Nufer both recalled these discussions as very problematic.

ShareCom felt that its central contribution lay in a neighborly self-help philosophy that encouraged people to freely share goods. Cars were the most successful item. But the organization also offered to share electrical equipment, sports gear, and holiday houses. Its mission was to form small groups of users who would share many things in a communal alternative to the all-pervasive consumer society. Cross-usage from one group to another was very rare. Only a few vehicles in the city center were actually used by all members. Nufer was afraid that "by losing the voluntary element, we would just become another car rental firm" (Nufer, 2002, interview).

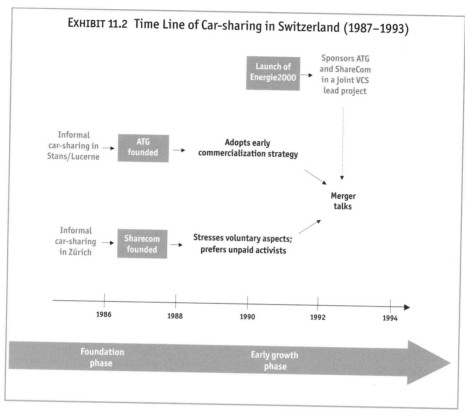

EXHIBIT 11.2 Time Line of Car-sharing in Switzerland (1987–1993)

Wagner and the ATG team on the other hand were clearly committed to commercialization and positioned ATG as a car-sharing service provider. They saw self-help as a form of self-exploitation (Muheim, 2002, interview). Although ATG had initially relied on voluntary contributions by all members, the organization quickly decided to appoint professionals to take care of cars and over time moved towards a system whereby these persons were paid and employed by ATG. Obviously these costs had to be covered by the users, thus driving ATG's user costs up.

As the sun vanished behind the mountains Muheim's balcony fell into shadows. He wondered: should the two co-operatives join forces? Looking at other countries did not seem to make a merger the logical choice. Both the Netherlands and Germany (the only two other countries with noteworthy car-sharing activities at the time) had a largely fragmented market. In Germany, independent co-operatives existed in many large cities. And although some had co-operation agreements members rarely used cars in another city. After all, car-sharing seemed to be a primarily local need.

References

Fischer, R. 2002. Personal interview with the author. 29 April 2002. Mobility CarSharing Schweiz: Luzern.

Heusi, K. 2002. Personal interview with the author. 24 April 2002. Mobility CarSharing Schweiz: Luzern.

Jevons, S.W. [1871] 1965. *Theory of Political Economy*. Kelley: New York [originally published in 1871 in London].

Muheim, P. 2002. Personal interview with the author. 29 April 2002. Mobility CarSharing Schweiz: Luzern.

Muheim, P., Inderbitzin J. 1992. *Das Energiesparpotential des gemeinschaftlichen Gebrauchs von Motorfahrzeugen als Alternative zum Besitz eines eigenen Autos. Eine Untersuchung am Beispiel ATG Auto Teilet Genossenschaft, Forschungsprogramm "Rationelle Energienutzung im Verkehr."* BEW: Bern.

Nufer, C. 2002. Personal interview with the author. 13 June 2002: Zürich.

Wagner, C. 2002. Personal interview with the author. 29 April 2002. CarLink Portland: Luzern.

Section B: Confrontation Swiss-Style

Confrontation: ATG's Encirclement of ShareCom

In the summer of 1994, Peter Muheim was feeling restless. Over the past 12 months ATG and ShareCom, Switzerland's two car-sharing co-operatives, had actively explored possibilities for combining their two organizations. A merger it was hoped would build Europe's first car-sharing champion and pave the ground for further professionalization and growth of decentralized short-term rental.

After heated discussions the merger talks finally broke down in 1994. The philosophical and personal differences turned out to be too much. The ATG management team of Conrad Wagner, Ralf Fischer, and Peter Muheim was deeply disappointed. Without a merger they felt car-sharing would remain a regional product for a small group of committed self-help activists. Exasperated Wagner left ATG and moved to the US where he launched one of America's first car-sharing companies, CarLink in Portland. Fischer also decided that it was time to quit. He started his own company offering accounting and auditing services. However, ATG being one of his clients, he remained somewhat close to the organization.

Meanwhile, Muheim and ATG's new CEO, Reiner Langendorf, decided to adopt a more aggressive strategy towards ShareCom. "At the outset of this confrontation we were in a disadvantaged position," recalled Peter Muheim (2002, interview). "ShareCom was well established in the Kanton Zurich and thus controlled one of the largest and most profitable market segments in Switzerland." Muheim, an enthusiastic player of the strategy board game "Go," described the situation as a constant uphill game. "Luckily for us ShareCom did not realize that they were playing a game until it was too late for them" (Muheim, 2002, interview). He engaged ATG in the planned **"encirclement" of ShareCom** in Zürich, so as to cut off ShareCom from its hinterland and thus hamper its growth outside Zürich.

An analysis of the growth patterns (Harms and Truffer, 1998: 19-20) of both organizations illustrates ATG's strategy. In 1991, both had roughly the same number of clients (about 500) and cars (about 30) and were present in the same number of communities (about 20). Over the next five years both grew at the same rate (50–70% annually) in terms of members and cars. However, while ShareCom was present in only 70 communities by 1995, ATG had cars in twice as many locations.

Two elements explain the **difference in network size**. Firstly, ATG was actively using marketing to grow its network, while ShareCom was relying on bottom-up growth through its grass-roots system (Harms and Truffer, 1998). More importantly, ATG consciously adopted an expansion strategy to quickly cover all communities around Zürich. However, ATG's encirclement strategy came at a price. By expanding its network faster, ATG had a lower density in the communities it served. This was a risky approach for a business in which higher density meant more variety and choice for clients as well as increased operating efficiency. Furthermore, ATG's insistence on trumping ShareCom sometimes led to the opening of a new location that turned out to unprofitable (Schwager, 2002, interview).

In 1995, ATG's assault finally yielded a response. The management team of Share-Com decided to found a commercial subsidiary, the **CarSharingCompany (CSC)**. The idea behind CSC was to keep up the voluntary system of ShareCom, but still to offer a commercial alternative to those clients who were not interested in a self-help system. However, CSC turned out to be too little and too late. While the two incumbents continued to grow at staggering rates, the newcomer CSC could report only 100 members by the end of 1996.

What held CSC back was the unwillingness of ShareCom to allow CSC access to its own fleet. ShareCom was afraid that the "commercial" CSC clients would unduly benefit from the voluntary work of its members, thus eroding the basis for the self-help system. After all, it was this voluntary contribution which had allowed ShareCom to maintain prices of 10–30% below ATG's (Nufer, 2002, interview). Only after tedious negotiations between CSC and ShareCom did the two sister organisations decide to pool their fleets. However, now pioneer members of ShareCom were complaining that too many users were free-riding on their voluntary contribution. If it wanted to save the self-help character of the co-operative, ShareCom had to maintain the high degree of social control in the user groups. This meant keeping the number of users in check who were using cars outside their own user groups, so as not to frustrate the members who were eventually responsible for cleaning and maintenance. Critics at ATG quickly rephrased ShareCom's slogan from "Use it—but don't own it!" (*Nutzen statt besitzen*) to "Clean it—but don't use it!" (*Putzen statt nutzen*) (Muheim, 2002, interview).

Ultimately two developments consolidated ATG's position and sealed ShareCom's fate: the failure of CopAuto and the decision of ZüriMobil to choose the outsider ATG as its partner rather than ShareCom. **CopAuto** had been founded in 1993, in Geneva, as the first car-sharing organization in the French-speaking part of Switzerland. The managers of CopAuto decided that a voluntary self-help system would not hold in the Romandie and thus chose a more commercial service approach. An important element of this strategy was CopAuto's intention to develop its own onboard computer system to increase the ease of usage and also reduce abuse. However, CopAuto failed after just two years in operation. Its heavy investments in the development of an onboard computer had overstretched its financial abilities, while clients had been attracted much slower than hoped for initially. After some soul-searching ATG decided to take over CopAuto's clients, who, however, lost their deposits in the process. Suddenly ATG had graduated from regional patchwork provider to national champion.

An even more important development came in 1996. A year earlier Zürich's public transport provider, the Verkehrsbetriebe Zürich (VBZ) had launched **ZüriMobil**, an integrated mobility service, together with Energie2000, several taxi organizations and Europcar, a car-rental firm. However, by 1996, the offer bundling an annual subscription to the public transport with cheaper taxi and car rental access had gained only 300 clients (Baumann, 2002, interview). The VBZ thus decided to bring in either Share-Com/CSC or ATG to increase the attractiveness of ZüriMobil. Given the fact that Share-Com/CSC had 160 cars in the canton of Zürich as opposed to ATG's 11 cars, the decision seemed a forgone conclusion. However, to the surprise of all concerned, VBZ chose the weak outsider rather than strong local boy preferring ATG's professional profile. The ZüriMobil partnership brought ATG a mass of free advertising in Zürich. Furthermore, ATG memberships could now be purchased at each of the VBZ's points of sale thus increasing ATG's "presence" dramatically.

As a result of the CopAuto takeover and the ZüriMobil co-operation, ATG's growth outpaced that of ShareCom for the first time. In the summer of 1995, both groups had had roughly 3,000 members (Harms and Truffer, 1998). However, by the end of 1996 ATG reported 6,900 clients as opposed to ShareCom's 5,200 members. In 1997, the co-operation between ATG and ZüriMobil alone attracted 3,000 new clients in just six months (ZVV, 2002).

At the same time the gulf between ShareCom's traditionalists (advocating voluntary self-help) and the modernist faction (pushing for more commercialization) had been growing. Among other things the modernists were once again advocating the idea of a merger with ATG. By fall 1996 the smoldering conflict resulted in a **challenge of ShareCom's leadership**. In the end the modernist faction ousted the old guard and took control of ShareCom. Nufer (2002) believed that "the self-help system had become a victim of its own success." He concluded that there might be an upper limit of members beyond which a meaningful sharing of goods through a self-help system cannot work. Disappointed with the new, purely commercial course, a group around Charles Nufer left the co-operative and founded a new organization ProShare, based in Winterthur. Today, ProShare has revived the original spirit of ShareCom albeit with less ambitious growth intentions (Nufer, 2002, interview).

Once the leadership struggle at ShareCom was resolved, it did not take long for ATG and ShareCom to launch a new round of merger talks. Starting in September 1996, the two co-operatives quickly found common ground, leading to a first draft of the merger contract by the end of the year. Members from both co-operatives ratified the merger in spring 1997 at two extraordinary general assemblies with 97% (ATG) and 78% (ShareCom) of the delegates voting in favour (Langendorf, 2002, interview). The result of the merger was launched only a few months later under the name of **Mobility Car-Sharing Switzerland (MCS)**. A group of three managing directors jointly ran the new organization under the overall leadership of Reiner Langendorf (ex-ATG), with Christian Vonarburg as head of marketing (ex-ATG) and Lorenzo Martinoni as head of IT and administration (ex-ShareCom). Hans-Rudolf Galliker (ex-ShareCom) became president of the board.

In the wake of the merger Peter Muheim took a seat on the board of the new co-operative. Now outside the day-to-day management he had time to consider what car-sharing had actually achieved in the first decade of its existence. True, recent years had seen the ATG business model move from strength to strength. But could they sustain these growth rates? As he was heading for Mobility's head office, Muheim reviewed the key findings of a **market study** he had just finished for the Energie2000 project (Muheim, 1998). In this study he analyzed the prerequisites for participating in a car-sharing scheme.

Potential users had to:

- Possess a driver's license for a passenger car

- Live in the developed zones of municipalities with more than 2,000 inhabitants

- Public transport alternatives to get to work had to be acceptable (i.e. it should not increase the daily journey to work by more than 30 minutes).

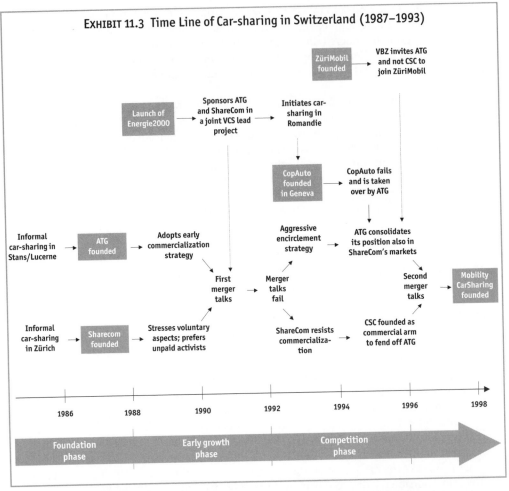

EXHIBIT 11.3 Time Line of Car-sharing in Switzerland (1987–1993)

Muheim found that out of the 7 million Swiss citizens only 25% satisfied these criteria. Car-sharing could thus expect a maximum of 1.7 million potential customers in Switzerland. Based on a representative survey of 3,150 people Muheim had found that a third of these potential users were "fairly" or "very" interested in the idea of car-sharing. This corresponded to about 600,000 potential users. So far Mobility had just above 20,000 members. Yet to tap into the larger client pool Mobility would have to change its positioning. The key for success Muheim decided would be in the hands of Christian Vonarburg, who had joined ATG in 1996, after having worked in the marketing of food products for ten years (Vonarburg, 2000, interview). Now as vice-CEO and head of marketing for Mobility Vonarburg's main challenge would be to define a new marketing strategy for Mobility. Given his virtually non-existing marketing budget Vonarburg would have to be creative. Nearing Mobility's head office on the Mühlenplatz (placed right in Lucerne's historic center) Muheim wondered how Vonarburg should approach the issue.

References

Baumann, K. 2002. Personal interview with the author. 2 May 2002. ZVV/VBZ: Zürich.

Harms, S., Truffer B. 1998. *The Emergence of A Nation-Wide Carsharing Co-operative in Switzerland*. EAWAG: Dübendorf.

Langendorf, R. 2002. Personal interview with the author. 2 May 2002. Mobility CarSharing Schweiz: Luzern.

Muheim, P. 1998. *Car-Sharing: The Key to Combined Mobility, Synthesis Document*. Energie Schweiz: Bern.

Muheim, P. 2002. Personal interview with the author. 29 April 2002. Mobility CarSharing Schweiz: Luzern.

Nufer, C. 2002. Personal interview with the author. 13 June 2002: Zürich.

Schwager, T. 2002. Personal interview with the author. 30 April 2002. Mobility CarSharing Schweiz: St Gallen.

Vonarburg, C. 2000. Personal interview with the author. 22 August 2000. Mobility CarSharing Schweiz: Luzern.

ZVV. 2002. Kombinierte Mobilität im ZVV. PPT presentation of the Zürcher Verkehrsverbund (ZVV) released in a press conference on 24 April 2002.

Section C: Growing Out of its Roots?

The Web of Partnership

After the formation of Mobility CarSharing (the result of a merger between ATG and ShareCom) in 1988, the main challenge of the new co-operative was to replicate the ZüriMobil model in other regions (Vonarburg, 2000, interview). Given the extraordinary success among the clients of VBZ (the local provider of public transport in Zürich), many other communities decided to offer similar partnerships between their **local public transport providers** and Mobility. By 2001, Mobility had eleven such co-operations in place. For a young and small organization these partnerships were priceless for two reasons. Firstly, given his virtually non-existing advertising budget Christian Vonarburg, Mobility's marketing manager, wouldn't have been able to advertise on his own. More importantly, by reaching out to the clients of public transport providers Mobility was able to target a segment of the Swiss population that was particularly likely to be interested in Mobility.

But Vonarburg's most important coup was to persuade the Schweizerische Bundesbahnen—**SBB, the Swiss railway**—to join in a marketing co-operation. Both ATG and ShareCom had been in close co-operation with the SBB's department for real estate as a supplier for parking space near the railway stations. However, they had never worked with SBB's marketing department (Lütolf, 2000, interview). By drawing on research funded by Energie2000, Mobility was able to demonstrate that the SBB had much to gain from an increased car-sharing penetration (Muheim, 1998): clients who switched from owning a car to car-sharing usually increased the amount they spent on public transport (PT). Stressing this indirect "PT rent" Mobility succeeded in persuading the SBB to advertise car-sharing among its clients. By offering the possibility to link the annual and monthly renewal of its subscription with a Mobility membership, the SBB particularly allowed Mobility to target the SBB core clients who were most likely to join a car-sharing scheme.

Another opportunity for co-operation materialised when Armin Eberle (2002, interview) became head of environmental management at **Migros**, Switzerland's largest retailer in early 1999. During his studies in the early '90s, Eberle had been a member of ShareCom's board. Thus he was delighted to find that Migros was already an occasional client of Mobility at its headquarters. By extending these first contacts, Eberle turned Migros into Mobility's first showcase client for **business car-sharing**. As part of this offer Mobility allowed business clients to book cars for their staff through the Mobility system. Most firms maintained their own fleets of cars for business trips of their employees. Apart from reducing the need for such a fleet, the new Mobility product helped firms to reduce administrative cost and hassle of fleet management. Mobility's advanced booking and billing system finally allowed them to track every single business trip and to book the full cost effortlessly to the correct budget (Langendorf, 2002, interview). From Mobility's point of view business car-sharing was an excellent extension of its product range. Most private clients needed a car in the evening or over

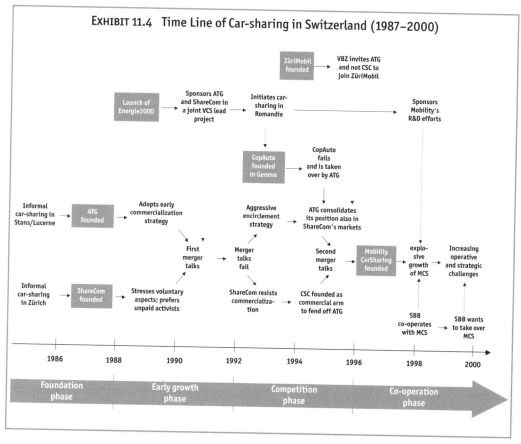

EXHIBIT 11.4   Time Line of Car-sharing in Switzerland (1987–2000)

the weekend, while businesses usually needed cars during office hours only. Thus business and private car-sharing supplemented each other, helping Mobility to further increase the efficiency of its fleet.

Other examples of the **Migros/Mobility co-operation** included five Mobility transporters that were block-booked by Migros during the day to allow clients to transport bulky goods home (Eberle, 2002, interview). The co-operation went further after Volkswagen had launched the Lupo, a new car specifically designed to consume less than 3 liters per 100 km. Although the Lupo consumed less fuel its higher sales price made it financially unattractive. Migros, therefore, decided to help Mobility by sponsoring the cost differential between the Lupo and the traditional vehicles used by Mobility. As a consequence 75 Lupos were made available at 75 Migros sites across Switzerland. The most recent co-operation launched in the summer of 2002 opened Migros' discount system for Mobility clients, who could now receive "Cumulus" discount points for every Mobility mile traveled.

Apart from striking new co-operations, Mobility also continued to leverage its relationship with **Energie2000** (which in 2001 was renamed SwissEnergy). Although the program's financial contributions were never very high in absolute terms, they nonetheless had important consequences by enabling Mobility to make investments outside its day-to-day business. Support from Energie2000 took four forms (Scherrer, 2002, interview): public awareness and credibility building, support of selected events, research and development grants for technological innovations, and pilot demonstration grants to prove the economic viability.

Projects included research into how car-sharing usage could be further simplified (instant access, open-end usage), an improved coverage of residential areas, an integration of third-party fleets, and the further development of business car-sharing. However, the key project sponsored by Energie2000 was the development of an **onboard computer** system (Cunz, 2002, interview). This ambitious R&D project had grown out of ShareCom and was managed by Lorenzo Martinoni, Mobility's head of IT and administration. In the early days, Mobility clients had gotten access to the key of a car by opening a safe, which was installed close to the parking lot. At the end of a trip they noted the distance traveled in the car's board book. Once per month Mobility employees collected the board books and communicated the details to the billing department in Lucerne. The system was inefficient and accident-prone: bills took two months to be delivered; clients tended to take the wrong car or made mistakes in the board book; and finally Mobility had no way to control abuse of the system. This last point became more of a problem as cars were increasingly stolen and shipped out of the country.

The new onboard computers solved these problems Mobility because they linked cars to Mobility's headquarters via the mobile telephone network using a short messaging system (SMS). Every client now could access cars through a smart card that identified him to the board computer. Car doors opened automatically only if a valid reservation has been made via telephone or internet. At the end of a trip the computer automatically transmitted all relevant data to the Mobility headquarters. Furthermore, Mobility could localize the position of every car via a global positioning system (GPS) thus making theft and abuse more difficult. The onboard computer was supplemented by Mobility's award-winning **call centre** (*Mobility Journal*, 2001/1). This key element of Mobility's operations handled 1,250 calls every day (*Mobility Journal*, 2000/4) for Mobility. Peter Muheim (2002, interview) stressed that without excellent systems and processes a density of a hundred calls per hour at peak times (equalling one call every 36 seconds) would not be manageable.

Another important partner of Mobility was actually a would-be competitor—the **car-rental firm Hertz**. The European headquarters in the UK had asked Hertz Switzerland to explore the possibilities of car-sharing (Langendorf, 2002, interview). As early as 1995, an ATG user group in Lenzburg had struck a deal with Hertz, allowing its members cheaper access to Hertz cars. After initial doubts about the motives of Hertz in this unusual co-operation, Vonarburg negotiated an extension of the program giving all Mobility members a 30% reduction on the standard rates of Hertz, and allowing Mobility clients to book Hertz cars via the Mobility call center. This unlikely co-operation was useful for both sides. Mobility's own business model was geared primarily towards short-term and short-distance usage. By offering the link with Hertz Mobility clients had an economically attractive alternative if they needed a car for several days in a row or if they wanted to drive more than 200 kilometers. Hertz in turn was able to increase the efficiency of its fleet, which was mainly used by business clients during office hours (Florin, 2002, interview). Mobility clients on the other hand needed cars usually over the weekend or in the evening. The success of the program was demonstrated by the fact that over time Mobility had become the largest client of Hertz Switzerland, with a turnover of CHF 2 million in 2001 (Langendorf, 2002, interview).

An End to the Co-operative Structure?

Mobility's strong growth in the post-merger phase (see Exhibit 11.5) was seen as a **vindication of ATG's strategy of professionalization**. Although the merger was publicized as a union of equals, it was in reality a takeover of ShareCom. ATG management was clearly in the driver's seat: the joint headquarters were located in Lucerne; the prevailing management philosophy was one of commercialization; and when two years after the merger Martinoni decided to quit, he left the effective management of Mobility fully in the hands of the ATG "dream team" Langendorf/Vonarburg. The two brought in a group of young engineers from Switzerland's top university ETH Zurich, to help them run the organization more and more like a for-profit business.

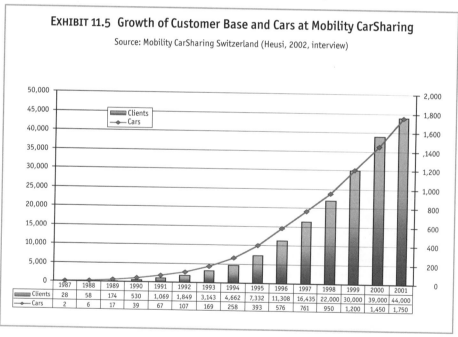

EXHIBIT 11.5 Growth of Customer Base and Cars at Mobility CarSharing

Source: Mobility CarSharing Switzerland (Heusi, 2002, interview)

	1987	1988	1989	1990	1991	1992	1993	1994	1995	1996	1997	1998	1999	2000	2001
Clients	28	58	174	530	1,069	1,849	3,143	4,662	7,332	11,308	16,435	22,000	30,000	39,000	44,000
Cars	2	6	17	39	67	107	169	258	393	576	761	950	1,200	1,450	1,750

An important ambition of Langendorf and Vonarburg was the **growth of Mobility abroad,** leading to several joint ventures in Germany and Italy. When the oldest car-sharing organization in Germany, StattAuto Berlin, experienced serious financial problems in 2000, Mobility even offered to take over StattAuto (Vonarburg, 2000, interview). Although nothing came of this proposal (the ailing StattAuto decided to look for a German solution to its problems) the discussions had whetted Mobility's appetite for international growth.

The organization's enduring growth (30–40% p.a.) strengthened Langendorf and Vonarburg. Under their leadership **Mobility had moved further away from its self-help roots** than ever before. As Mobility started to communicate more on price and quality, the ecological motivation of car-sharing became much less dominant (Belz, 2001). While Vonarburg agreed that grass-roots activists had been crucial in the early years, he did not expect them to play a role in the future:

> Today we are a service organization with clients who expect good quality. This does not fit with a voluntary self-help system. *Commenting on the role of the co-operative system he added*: We have neutralized the co-operative system to a maximum. Today the management team can run Mobility as it sees fit. The annual delegate assembly has been marginalized as far as legally possible. (Vonarburg, 2000, interview)

However, as Mobility thrived frustration and disaffection among the traditional grass-roots activists grew. Although professional Mobility employees serviced a considerable part of the fleet, volunteers were still looking after cars in many rural settings (where a commercial solution was not financially viable). These activists were also still represented at the co-operative's annual assembly where they challenged the expansion plans of Langendorf and Vonarburg concerned that Mobility was becoming just another rental company.

Christian Vonarburg began to suspect that the activist model might have run its course and that the co-operative structure was no longer an asset (Vonarburg, 2000, interview). He wanted to run Mobility as a pure for-profit business and dissociate it from the fundamental past. Rather than being helped by its activists, he believed that disappointed pioneers and cumbersome proposals at the annual assembly held the organization back.

Caught in the Web? A Partner Turning Unfriendly

Entrepreneurs like to fret that nobody takes due notice of their achievements—until the day someone does. On 22 March 2000, a very concerned Hans-Ruedi Galliker called the other members of Mobility's board of directors (Muheim, 2002, interview). Earlier that day Galliker as president of the board had met with Paul Blumenthal, head of passenger transportation of the Swiss railways (SBB). Blumenthal had been plain (Belz, 2002): he was delighted by the successful co-operation between Mobility and the SBB. In fact he was so delighted that he wanted to transform the SBB into an integrated mobility supplier including an SBB car-sharing product. He shared the optimism of the Energie2000 study (Muheim, 1998) as to the market potential for car-sharing as well as the secondary benefits for public transport. However, he felt that Mobility was not growing as fast as it might. By integrating car-sharing as a new business unit into the overall structure of the SBB, Blumenthal expected to realize this untapped potential faster as well as achieving overall efficiency gains.

He, therefore, offered to **take over Mobility**. If this was not possible then the Swiss railway would have to build up its own car-sharing offer, while at the same time canceling all existing contracts with Mobility, including the parking lots (Belz, 2002). Although Mobility had expected threats from potential competitors some day, nobody had foreseen such an early challenge with so much at stake. The SBB had both the marketing and financial muscle to build up a viable network of car-sharing locations across Switzerland. Furthermore, Mobility would face problems in quickly replacing the roughly 20% of its parking lots currently rented from the SBB.

Preparing for Action

As he considered the months ahead, Peter Muheim mused about the challenges they faced:

- Should Mobility change its organizational form from a co-operative into a public company quoted on the stock market?

- What should he think about Langendorf's and Vonarburg's international ambition?

- Most urgently the board had to come up with a reply to the SBB takeover offer. In this it had to consider the interests of co-operative members, the preservation of the by now over 140 jobs in Lucerne, and the consequences a takeover would have for the long-term success of the car-sharing idea.

References

Belz, F.M. 2001. *Integratives Öko-Marketing: Erfolgreiche Vermarktung von ökologischen Produkten und Leistungen im Konsumbereich, Habilitation*. Gabler: Wiesbaden.

Belz, F.M. 2002. *Integrationsfallstudie Mobility CarSharing*. IWÖ-HSG: St Gallen.

Cunz, P. 2002. Personal interview with the author. 1 May 2002. Energie Schweiz: Bern.

Eberle, A. 2002. Personal interview with the author. 3 May 2002. Migros: Zürich.

Florin, S. 2002. Telephone interview with the author. 14 May 2002. Hertz Germany

Heusi, K. 2002. Personal interview with the author. 24 April 2002. Mobility CarSharing Schweiz: Luzern.

Langendorf, R. 2002. Personal interview with the author. 2 May 2002. Mobility CarSharing Schweiz: Luzern.

Lütolf, T. 2000. Personal interview with the author. 22 August 2000. Mobility CarSharing Schweiz: Luzern.

Mobility Journal. 2000/4. Das modernste Call Centre der Schweiz. *Mobility Journal*. 2000(4): 1-2.

Mobility Journal. 2001/1. Call Centre Award für Mobility. *Mobility Journal*. 2001(1): 4.

Muheim, P. 1998. Car-Sharing: The Key to Combined Mobility, Synthesis Document. Energie Schweiz: Bern.

Muheim, P. 2002. Personal interview with the author. 29 April 2002. Mobility CarSharing Schweiz: Luzern.

Scherrer, H. 2002. Personal interview with the author. 1 May 2002. Energie Schweiz: Bern.

Vonarburg, C. 2000. Personal interview with the author. 22 August 2000. Mobility CarSharing Schweiz: Luzern.

Section D: Showdown in Lucerne

The Fontana Effect

In the Spring of 2000, the board of Mobility CarSharing was at its wits' ends. Galliker and the other board members (including the ATG entrepreneur Peter Muheim and the former VCS lobbyist Monika Tschannen) were car-sharing pioneers. None had experience in how to lead negotiations over a hostile takeover bid. Anticipating a tough confrontation, they started looking for someone who could help develop the board's strategy in difficult times. Mobility approached **Giatgen-Peder Fontana**, a former CEO of Rivella (a Swiss soft drinks company) and an experienced manager who was a member of several boards of directors in Switzerland.

Soon after Fontana started working with Mobility, the board realized that its challenges were much broader. The directors accordingly invited Fontana to join the board and become its president for the time it would take him to sort out the problems (*Mobility Journal*, 2001/2). Mobility had reported a modest operating profit since 1998. However, in 2000, the organization was heading for **operating losses** of CHF 1.2 million (*Mobility Annual Report*, 2000). Although it had increased its revenues from CHF 21.4 million to CHF 27 million, the organization had let its costs spiral out of control even faster: in just 12 months the personnel cost had grown by CHF 2.5 million, necessitating the hiring of new offices to house the call center; the marketing budget had tripled to CHF 1.2 million; and what pushed Mobility eventually into the red was an extraordinary investment which came from Mobility's decision to equip its 1,500-strong fleet with onboard computers (not negligible at CHF 1,500 apiece).

As the board started to reassert itself, an **increasing rift** became apparent between directors and management. Having been used to running the organization quite independently, the management team thought that the board was far removed from the day-to-day business. The board on the other hand felt that it was not properly informed and even suspected having been sidelined on purpose on some strategic decisions (Tschannen-Süess, 2002, interview). The resulting struggle between board and management was finally resolved when the board decided to look for a new CEO. As a result Vonarburg quit Mobility, while Langendorf became head of the newly formed Mobility Support AG (*Mobility Annual Report*, 2000), now responsible for developing Mobility's services abroad. To tackle the immediate problems Fontana was appointed **interim CEO** during 10 months.

Mobility CarSharing's organizational growing pains were also impacting its **organizational culture**. Traditionally, the management team had encouraged open debate. "Shortly after the merger we had management team meetings with as many as 30 participants," recalls Thomas Lütolf (Lütolf, 2002, interview), who joined Mobility in 1998 to head its network marketing. Such a consensus-based approach cost a lot of time. On the other hand, the quick pace of development required the duo Langendorf/Vonarburg to take decisions informally on the spot. The resulting organizational uncertainty had worked fine for a tightly knit team of 30 employees. However, as Mobility approached a staff of 140 the old processes proved to be incompatible. "The new mass business requires more traditional (one might even say boring) management skills less the old visionary leadership," concludes Lütolf (2002, interview).

During his short stint at the helm of Mobility Fontana steered an austerity course, including a hiring freeze and a 50% cut in the marketing budget. As a result Mobility was once again able to report an operating profit for 2001 of CHF 327,606. Other measures included the development of a management information system, and a formalization of the formerly fluid and non-transparent decision processes.

> As is often the case in young organizations, the willingness to change at Mobility was very high even among the more fundamentally oriented members. It is much more difficult to initiate these kinds of changes at a traditional organization where people are deeply opposed to change. Change in a young organization is easier because that is a normal part of its activities. (Fontana, 2002, interview)

Most members of the Mobility family agreed that the radical changes that happened in 2001 were necessary and positive. However, a certain nostalgia for the early days remained in some cases:

> The contact between Lucerne and the activists was closer in the beginning. After the merger this relationship became more anonymous as the onboard computer reduced the need for interaction with Lucerne or among the users here in St Gallen. The first new cars for St Gallen were still driven here by Reiner Langendorf personally. Today we have a different management generation in Lucerne. (Schwager, 2002, interview)

RailLink—Extending the Mobility Model

While the leadership struggle unfolded at Mobility, the board was also engaged in its discussions with the SBB. In these tough negotiations the onboard computer and software systems of Mobility proved decisive. For the SBB to develop its own system would have taken up to two years, and without the onboard computer the SBB would not have been competitive against Mobility (Cunz, 2002, interview). Realizing that a confrontational course would be detrimental for both sides, the two organizations finally agreed to form a new company, **RailLink**, which was owned jointly by SBB (55%), Mobility (25%), and DaimlerChrysler (20%). Under the RailLink agreement SBB placed 75 additional Smarts at SBB train stations (*Mobility Journal*, 2001/3). Mobility provided the onboard computer system and the RailLink call center service.

The idea was that RailLink and Mobility would serve two different markets. Exhibit 11.6 illustrates the key difference between RailLink and Mobility. Mobility clients usually do not own a car and use car-sharing as an independent element of their mobility needs. "However, this is not an option for all citizens," explains Stephan Schneider (2002, interview), head of marketing for RailLink.

> For example, I could not imagine giving up my own car and sharing one with several others. Nonetheless, when taking the train I still face the challenge to get to my final destination from the train station. RailLink has been particu-

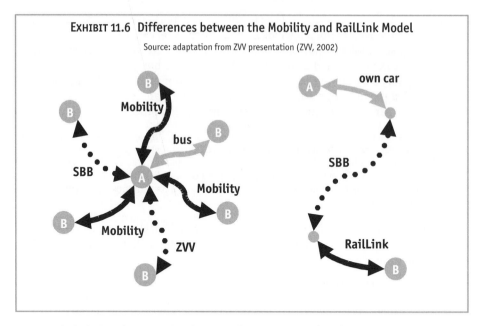

EXHIBIT 11.6 Differences between the Mobility and RailLink Model

Source: adaptation from ZVV presentation (ZVV, 2002)

larly designed to cover this "last mile" for SBB clients. (Schneider, 2002, interview)

Thus while 93% of all Mobility trips started from the location nearest to the place of residence (Tschannen-Süess, 2002, interview), RailLink planed to serve those clients who had a transportation need at the end of a train trip. It remained to be seen just how such a segmentation of clients would actually work out, or whether both offers would not in the end vie for the same clients.

In any case, RailLink constituted an important step for Mobility. It was the first time the organisation has been able to sell its technology and support to another car-sharing supplier. Reiner Langendorf (Langendorf, 2002, interview) hoped that this kind of service would become a profitable option for the Mobility Support AG to expand across Europe without actually having to take over fleet management and local marketing. Whether RailLink would actually realize the ambitious growth targets set by Blumenthal (i.e. 10,000 new clients per year) remained to be seen. In June 2002, nine months after its introduction, RailLink was still struggling to increase its subscriber base.

The RailLink experience could be interpreted as a sign that Mobility had saturated the market niche for car-sharing. This conclusion was also supported by the declining growth in Mobility users. While Mobility had grown more than 30% in the late 1990s, this rate dropped to a mere 16% in 2001. However, the Mobility management remained optimistic that it could continue to grow substantially (Lütolf, 2002, interview). Peter Muheim pointed out that Mobility had so far tapped into only 8% of the potential 600,000 Swiss citizens that could be interested in car-sharing (Muheim, 1998). Furthermore, Mobility had only just begun to explore the lucrative market for business car-sharing and fleet management.

To reach its full potential Mobility was also reviving old partnerships. In June 2002, Mobility relaunched its partnership with the VBZ, extending the offer of joint Mobility membership and public transport subscription to the **Zürcher Verkehrsverbund (ZVV)** and thus the public transport in the whole of Kanton Zürich and not just the city center as had earlier been the case with the VBZ (Baumann, 2002, interview). By marketing this offer with its roughly 200,000 annual and monthly subscribers, the ZVV provided Mobility with a direct link to this attractive market segment. Within the first month this relaunch of an old partnership alone attracted 380 new clients (Lütolf, 2002, interview).

The Role of Grass-roots Activists

As Mobility grew in size, it evolved to a point where the old management team had seen no more value in maintaining its **entrepreneurial activist structure**. This position was vehemently rejected by Monika Tschannen (Tschannen-Süess, 2002, interview), member of the Mobility board and former VCS lobbyist. She saw in this stance a proof of Mobility's growing arrogance, feeling that the co-operative was about to squander its most valuable resources. Following the leadership struggle the new management team adopted a more differentiated approach towards its activists (Fischer, 2002, interview). Professionalization remained the ultimate goal (and if anything it has even increased under Fontana). However, the Mobility management once again stressed the "high importance" (Fischer, 2002, interview) of its activists.

> The contribution of our over 850 activists and 350 sections is crucial for the functioning of the co-operative Mobility. [. . .] In rural regions the maintenance could never be guaranteed centrally from Lucerne. Furthermore, the attraction of new members has to be supported by activists on the ground. [Their work was] essential for the positive development of sections, [with 31 new sections founded in 2001]. Furthermore, the co-operative benefits from interested activists, who are willing to participate as delegates and to give important impulses for the development of the organisation. (*Mobility Annual Report*, 2001: 7)

The consequence is a **dual strategy** that aims at operating as a service-oriented for-profit business, while at the same time maintaining the high identification and feeling of ownership among its members. Although the core is run like a business, Mobility wants to sustain its large number of motivated and voluntary activists.

> The strategy must be developed here [in Lucerne]. It is wrong to say that the co-operative members make strategy. That was never the idea. However, we take [the activists] very seriously. In the delegate assembly we received a number of very good proposals as well as some cumbersome ones. However, we owe the [members] accountability. Considering the hours we have taken to respond to these proposals, I can say that we do take them very seriously. (Heusi, 2002, interview)

A dedicated customer base was also permanently spreading news about Mobility by word of mouth. Even in times when Mobility was not running active marketing campaigns or advertisements (such as in 2001), these members allowed Mobility to continue its growth (Muheim, 2002, interview).

> What every book-club dreams of—current clients attract new clients by word of mouth—that is built into the Mobility system. [. . .] This is very important—economically and emotionally. [. . .] Accordingly the system has a very high self-sustaining dynamic. I have a high regard for this. (Fontana, 2002, interview)

The annual delegate assemblies and user feedback during the year provided a regular feedback mechanism, allowing Mobility to stay in touch with customer needs as well as to identify options for further innovation, thus effectively saving immense cost for market research.

> The members [. . .] force us to take up difficult topics. Many constructive proposals are submitted via the internet. It is fantastic that the users tell us, for example, how we have to design our webpage so that it is easier for them to work with. (Heusi, 2002, interview)

The fact that the 2002, delegate assembly had more participants than ever and yielded a large number of proposals ranging from fleet management, through price structure, to general business strategy was seen by Mobility management as prove for the vitality of the grass-roots system (Lütolf, 2002, interview).

Financing Growth—The Choice of Organisational Form

Mobility new management also backpedaled on the question of its co-operative form. Karl Heusi, who took over the position of CEO in 2002 stressed that the co-operative structure turned out to be an important cornerstone for its financial success.

> The self-help groups did something very clever. They founded co-operatives in which every user had to buy a share of CHF 1,000. This has financed the whole growth until today. "Financing for growth" has never even been a topic. Even today 50% of our customers are members of the co-operative. In traditional enterprises more clients mean more investments and more working capital needs, leading eventually to a liquidity problem. We have never had such a problem; our financing has always been ingeniously solved. (Heusi, 2002, interview)

This puts the Mobility CFO in the comfortable position of having an equity rate of 40% (*Mobility Annual Report*, 2000). The co-operative form has also turned out to be a useful tool for reconciling the profit motivation and non-profit goals.

Apart from the requirement to maintain the co-operative's capital and to pay dividends (in the form of lower prices), its statutes also required Mobility to support ecological goals and the general development of car-sharing in particular (Fontana, 2002, interview). With half of its users being co-owners, it was easier to maintain the dual strategy of professionalization and an activist network. Co-operative members, for example, helped to identify and obtain new vehicle locations at reasonable prices. And because they were also co-owners they even made proposals that in some cases lead to *increased* rates. It is for example due to the insistence of the delegate assembly that Mobility introduced a cancellation fee or the night tariff. (Muheim, 2002, interview)

Up until now the co-operative has been godsend. I have never seen anything like this—that owners of an enterprise are also intensive users. That is sensational! I will probably never encounter a similar situation, in which people feel so implicated in a company. Mobility is not simply a supplier for its customers—the customers are a part of Mobility. [. . .] Many a company wants to better understand its customers. [. . .] Everybody talks about customer focus, often without ever having met a customer face to face. With us this is different. At the section and delegate assemblies we are confronted with the customers. And [between assemblies] many write and give active feedback. (Heusi, 2002, interview)

The Road Ahead

In the process of developing RailLink Mobility had actually discovered a new activity field. By selling its services it could make revenues without having to take on local fleet management or client acquisition. Rather than setting up car-sharing services abroad Mobility decided that it would offer its core capabilities to interested parties, while leaving the on-the-ground responsibility to its partners. In 2002, Hertz Germany, for example, began offering business car-sharing with the help of the newly founded Mobility Support AG. In this pilot venture Hertz took care of fleet management and client management, while Mobility provided its technology and call center support for day-to-day operations (Langendorf, 2002, interview). This solution had also the added bonus that Mobility could expand without having to abandon its co-operative form which it cherished more than ever.

How would Mobility develop over **the coming years**? Looking into the future Giatgen Fontana saw Mobility's potential particularly in the linking of different car fleets rather than the single-minded growth of the Mobility fleet, and at the same time underlined the ideological shift that Mobility had undergone over the past decade:

Mobility has the goal to operate (either by itself or through partners) different car fleets in a similar way through the "Mobility model," while allowing migration between the fleets. We don't think that all cars on the road should be red [the standard color of all Mobility cars], but that cars should be used rather than taking up parking space. Private users should be able to use cars from a business fleet [during the weekend], while businesses should be able to use the Mobility fleet [when their mobility needs peak]. Mobility's mission is not to fight private car ownership. [The decision to own a car or use car-sharing] is a question of efficiency depending on the specific mobility needs of each person. [Car-sharing] is one element of many mobility options. (Fontana, 2002, interview)

References

Baumann, K. 2002. Personal interview with the author. 2 May 2002. ZVV/VBZ: Zürich.

Cunz, P. 2002. Personal interview with the author. 1 May 2002. Energie Schweiz: Bern.

Fischer, R. 2002. Personal interview with the author. 29 April 2002. Mobility CarSharing Schweiz: Luzern.

Fontana, G.-P. 2002. Personal interview with the author. 23 April 2002. President and former CEO, Mobility CarSharing Schweiz: Bern.

Heusi, K. 2002. Personal interview with the author. 24 April 2002. Mobility CarSharing Schweiz: Luzern.

Langendorf, R. 2002. Personal interview with the author. 2 May 2002. Mobility CarSharing Schweiz: Luzern.

Lütolf, T. 2002. Personal interview with the author. 13 June 2002. Mobility CarSharing Schweiz: Luzern.

Mobility Annual Report. 2000. *Mobility Geschäftsbericht 2000*. Mobility CarSharing Schweiz: Luzern.

Mobility Annual Report. 2001. *Mobility Geschäftsbericht 2001*. Mobility CarSharing Schweiz: Luzern.

Mobility Journal. 2001/2. Die neue Geschäftsleitung. *Mobility Journal*. 2001(2): 3.

Mobility Journal. 2001/3. RailLink - Operated by Mobility. *Mobility Journal*. 2001(3): 1.

Muheim, P. 1998. *Car-Sharing: The Key to Combined Mobility, Synthesis Document*. Energie Schweiz: Bern.

Muheim, P. 2002. Personal interview with the author. 29 April 2002. Mobility CarSharing Schweiz: Luzern.

Schneider, S. 2002. Personal interview with the author. 1 May 2002. RailLink–SBB: Bern.

Schwager, T. 2002. Personal interview with the author. 30 April 2002. Mobility CarSharing Schweiz: St Gallen.

Tschannen-Süess, M. 2002. Telephone interview with the author. 21 June 2002. Mobility CarSharing Schweiz: St Gallen.

ZVV. 2002. Kombinierte Mobilität im ZVV. PPT presentation of the Zürcher Verkehrsverbund (ZVV) released in a press conference on 24 April 2002.

> Teaching notes for this case are available from Greenleaf Publishing. These are free of charge and are available only to teaching staff. They can be requested by going to:
> **www.greenleaf-publishing.com/oikos_notes**

CASE 12

Catamount Energy and the Glebe Mountain Wind Farm
Clean Energy versus NIMBY[1]

Robert Letovsky

St Michael's College, USA

During the summer and fall of 2004, officials of Catamount Energy Corporation (CEC), headquartered in Rutland, Vermont, faced a challenging public relations situation. The company was seeking regulatory approval for the development of a 27-turbine wind farm to produce wind-generated electricity (WGE) atop Glebe Mountain, in south-central Vermont. The project promised to add a considerable amount of "clean" energy to the state's electricity grid, as well as bring considerable economic spin-offs to the area. However, a number of local residents were actively opposed to the project, fearing that it would harm the area's scenic beauty as well as threaten the state's lucrative tourist trade. Both opponents and supporters of WGE from across the state had weighed in on the proposed project, and as of the spring of 2004, the company faced a long and arduous process to gain approval of the project from Vermont's Public Service Board. With opinion in the community and across the state divided as to the relative merits of WGE and of the Glebe Mountain project in particular, company officials had to map out their next steps in building increased support and gaining ultimate approval for the project.

History of Wind Power

The earliest instance of man harnessing wind power through windmills can be traced to 2000 BC in ancient Babylon, and involved grinding of grain and pumping water. Over the next thousand years, windmill usage to grind grain spread throughout the Islamic world, as well as to China and India. Windmill use for grain grinding only came to the Western world in early medieval times. Windmills were being adapted for use in pumping irrigation canals. During the 19th century, steam-based railway systems used windmills to pump water into train engines. In fact, windmills were Europe's primary energy source until the introduction of the steam engine in the early 19th century. In the United States, between 1850 and 1970, over six million mechanical output small wind machines were installed, mainly in farms, to power water pumping and provide water for farmhouses. By the early–mid 1950s, however, government efforts to extend the central power grid to nearly every American household basically ended the market for these machines.

The first usage of a large windmill to generate electricity was built in Cleveland, Ohio, in 1888 by Charles F. Brush. The Brush windmill was moderately successful, and operated for over 20 years, though its output was puny by modern standards. In 1891, a Dane, Pou La Court developed the first wind machine for producing electricity based on the aerodynamic principles of the large, European windmill towers. By the end of the First World War, windmills generating electricity had spread throughout Denmark, though they were subsequently driven out of business by fossil-fueled power plants.

The 1930s saw a renaissance of WGE, with construction of experimental wind farms focused on electricity production in Denmark, Germany, France, Britain and the US. The most significant of these experiments in the US was actually in the state of Vermont, where Palmer Putnam installed a 1.25 megawatt turbine featuring a 175-foot diameter 16-ton stainless steel rotor. However, the size of the Putnam turbine exceeded the strength of existing materials, and one of the blades broke off in 1945 after only several hundred hours of irregular operation. The failure of the Putnam turbine system marked the end of ongoing WGE developments n the United States until the mid 1970s (see below). However, in Europe temporary shortages of oil and gas following the end of WW II spurred ongoing developments in WGE technologies.

The sharp run-up in prices that accompanied the Organization of Petroleum Exporting Countries' (OPEC) 1973 oil embargo gave WGE a major boost in both the United States and Europe, on two levels: electricity buyers began considering alternatives to generating electricity through fossil-fueled power plants. Meanwhile, governments in Europe and North America, panicked by the prospect of a cutoff in energy supplies, introduced a number of tax incentives to promote WGE.

However, this stimulus proved to be short-lived. The 1980s saw the phasing-out of a number of these incentives. Meanwhile, economies in the industrialized world adjusted to higher oil prices by adopting various technologies to increase their energy efficiency. Interest in WGE declined through the decade, and only picked up in the 1990s as environmental concerns, mainly about climate change, began to mount around the world. In 1995, the United States reintroduced tax incentives for renewable energy, which further stimulated a WGE upsurge in the country.

Wind Power around the world

As of 2004, Germany, the United States, Spain and Denmark were the world leaders in installed WGE capacity (see Exhibit 12.1). However, when expressed as a share of total system electricity capacity, WGE is far more important in Europe than the United States.[2] For example, in western Denmark, the utility ELTRA gets 100% of its electricity from WGE during low-demand periods of the year. In fact, WGE represents over half of ELTRA's required system capacity.[3]

Exhibit 12.1 Leading Countries Installed WGE Capacity (December, 2003)

Source: American Wind energy Association (http://www.awea.org/faq/tutorial/wwt_statistics.html)

Country	WGE Capacity (MW)
Germany	14,609
United States	6,374
Spain	6,202
Denmark	3,110
India	2,110
Netherlands	912
Italy	904
Japan	686
United Kingdom	649
China	568

The European WGE industry has been driven by extensive government support. For example, the German WGE industry has been driven by generous tax incentives, estimated at between US$1.5 and $1.8 billion, to promote construction of wind turbines.[4] These construction incentives have been supplemented with a high minimum guaranteed selling price of 11.5 cents/kW-hour (almost $2\frac{1}{2}$ times the prevailing market price of 4.5 cents/kW-hour as of 2004).[5]

In the United Kingdom, the government announced a goal of obtaining ten percent of the nation's electricity supplies from renewable sources by 2010, with this percentage increasing to 20% by 2020. These goals were set in the context of the British government's commitment to reduce the country's carbon dioxide (CO_2) emissions by 60% by the middle of the 21st century. In late 2001, the British government announced two major offshore WGE projects that would triple the country's WGE capacity from about

2   UK wind industry to take the plunge; the UK plans to become a world leader in wind technology through the development of offshore resources (2003). *Power Engineering International* 11(7) (August).

3   Ibid.

4   Ferguson, N. (2004, July 24). War of the winds. *National Post*, p. A12.

5   Ibid.

500 MW to almost 1.5 GW. In late 2003 the government announced plans for another expansion of offshore WGE turbines, adding another 6 GW of capacity at a cost of up to £6 billion (approximately US$9 billion).[6]

In the United States, WGE accounted for less than 1% of total energy production as of 2003, but output of WGE was rising rapidly since the late 1990s. Between 2003 and 2008 installed WGE capacity was expected to increase from 6,374 MW in 2003 to almost 9,500 MW.[7] The US Department of Energy announced a goal of having WGE produce 5% of total American energy capacity by 2020, though industry groups were predicting that at, current growth rates, WGE would constitute 6% of total American energy output by that year.[8]

Two of the main drivers of WGE capacity installation and demand for WGE in the US have been federal and state tax incentives, and state-level mandates on utilities to acquire a stipulated percentage of their energy from renewable energy sources. The federal tax incentives promoting renewable energy originated with the Energy Tax Act of 1978. This statute offered income tax credits to businesses and consumers who purchased renewable energy equipment. In the 1980s, the US government broadened the terms of the credits and the types of equipment that qualified for credits. In 1992, the Energy Policy Act introduced a 1.5 cent/kW-hour production tax credit (PTC) to WGE produced by privately owned facilities. The PTC was subsequently changed to make it a 10 year 1.8 cents/kW-hour credit (with an inflation allowance) for large-scale WGE projects that go online before December 31, 2003. As of that date, the PTC officially expired, though efforts were under way in the US Congress to extend the PTC through to the end of 2008.

In addition to the federal incentives, numerous states have introduced tax credit/rebate schemes at the state level to promote WGE investment. Finally, at least a dozen states had, by 2004, adopted some version of a mandated renewable energy portfolio for utilities in their jurisdictions. These mandates range from relatively low levels (e.g. Arizona's regulated utilities must purchase 1.1% of their power from renewables in the five years between 2007 and 2012) to the ambitious (e.g. 20% of California utilities electricity must be derived from renewable sources by 2017).[9]

A number of states were emerging as leaders in the American WGE scene Their positions in the industry reflected a combination of unique topographical/geographical features and state tax incentives.

California

As of the end of 2003, California had the most installed wge capacity in the US, with some 2,043 MW. The state had been the leader among all American states in introducing WGE in the early 1980's. The first large-scale wind farms in California reflected its unique topography, with large numbers of wind turbines packed into various mountain

6   Ibid.
7   American Wind Energy Association (http://www.awea.org/faq/tutorial/wwt_statistics.html).
8   Fischbach, Amy F. (2002, February). Wind biz: High voltage electrical contractors are installing electrical infrastructure for large-scale wind farms. *Electrical Wholesaling* 83(2).
9   Renewable energy power purchase agreements: A reflection of the carrot-and-stick approach to renewable energy legislation (2003, March). *Journal of Structured and Project Finance* 9(1).

passes throughout the state. The early 1980s turbines were far smaller yet less efficient and cost-effective than the newer versions that emerged in the marketplace in the late 1990s. So, beginning in 1998, a number of WGE operators in the state began "repowering" the older wind farms, tearing down the 1980s vintage turbines and replacing them with the newer technologies. For example, a farm with 100 40 kW turbines would be replaced with six 700 kW turbines, resulting in fewer turbines but higher output.[10] However, wind farm repowering projects in the state have been stalled as a result of the electrical energy crisis of 1998–99, and the subsequent deregulation of California's electricity industry. A by-product of the crisis was the bankruptcy of the state's largest utility (PG&I) and the near bankruptcy of another (Southern California Edison). Both firms were forced to cancel large-scale wind farm repowering projects.

Despite these developments though, the WGE scene in California was not all gloomy as of 2004. The state began offering a 50% state tax credit to homeowners and businesses who installed WGE turbines. There was also the possibility that the state would offer an additional state tax credit of 30% on installation costs. Some industry observers predicted that the tax credit program would lead to an explosion in WGE usage and capacity in the state.[11]

Texas

WGE capacity in the state has risen dramatically since 1999. In that year, the state legislature adopted a requirement that 3% of the state's electricity be produced by renewable sources by 2009. This mandate and accompanying state tax credits added impetus to a federal energy tax credit (see above). Another key factor promoting WGE in the state has been its vast expanse of flat, wind-swept, sparsely populated cattle-grazing lands. A prolonged drought, which began in the late 1990s, has brought economic hardship to many of the state's cattle ranches, and their owners have discovered a much-needed source of revenues by selling rights to situate wind turbines on otherwise unused grazing lands. By 2003, a number of leading American energy firms had invested over $1 billion in wind farms in the state, resulting in approximately 1,200 MW of installed capacity.[12] This represents over 20% of the US total, and made Texas the second largest state in terms of WGE capacity.

Iowa

Iowa, the third largest WGE producer in the United States, was one of the early leaders in the American industry. In 1983, the state legislature had enacted a mandate that investor-owned utilities operating in Iowa had to source at least 2% of their energy from renewables. Two out-of-state utilities came in and each built large wind farms to serve Iowa's utilities. To stimulate demand for WGE, the state also introduced a unique zero interest loan program in encourage homeowners and businesses to install wind tur-

10   Wind biz: High voltage elect contractors are installing electrical infrastructure for large-scale wind farms. Op cit.
11   Ibid.
12   Herrick, Thaddeus (2002, September 28). The new Texas wind rush. *The Wall Street Journal*, pp. B1, B5.

bines. The state even began offering low-interest loans to schools in the state to install WGE turbines. WGE in Iowa has also benefited from the state's topography which, like Texas, is characterized by vast expanses of open plains.

The World Supply of Oil

One of the justifications for WGE was that the world faced considerable uncertainty in terms of its future supplies of fossil fuels, notably oil, and that this uncertainty would directly impact utilities' ability to meet future demands for electricity. There have been dramatic changes in the world oil market over the past three decades. 1973 saw the world's first oil crisis, as the Arab nations who belonged to the Organization of Petroleum Exporting Countries (OPEC), initiated a boycott on exports to the United States and some of its allies. At that time, there were just over 3.5 billion people on earth, and total global consumption was approximately 35 million barrels per day (bbd). At the time of the Arab embargo, there were still substantial sources of untapped oil, both within the United States and around the world. The rapid increase in petroleum prices which this first energy crisis created spurred dramatic increases in exploration and development of new oil fields. At the same time, the industrialized countries of the world found themselves having to confront the issue of energy efficiency for the first time. Businesses and governments in these countries responded with a number of new products, services and policies that greatly increased energy efficiency in many sectors of the economy and society.

By the year 2000, however, the long-term outlook for world oil supplies was again uncertain. It was estimated that at the start of the industrial age, the total amount of oil beneath the earth's crust which could be economically recovered was between 1,800 and 2,200 billion barrels. As of 2000, about 880 billion of these resources had been consumed.[13] Meanwhile, world population and global oil consumption both doubled from their 1973 levels, to 6 billion people, and 80 million bbd. By 2004, global daily oil consumption had increased to some 88 million barrels, reflecting increased economic activity in China and India, the two most populous countries on earth. However, discoveries of new sources of oil slowed significantly, with some 90% of global oil supplies in the year 2000 coming from fields found before 1980.[14] Furthermore, most major discoveries made since 1990 were considered to be quite small by traditional standards.[15] Compounding the uncertainty in the world's oil market was political instability and violence in several of the world's leading producing countries, including Nigeria, Iraq, and Venezuela. As a result of these developments, crude oil future prices of a 50 gallon barrel of oil rose from just over $30 in late 2003 to over $52/barrel in October 2004, an increase of practically 66% in just over a year.

With increased consumption and a slowdown in discoveries of new oil fields, many industry experts have predicted that global oil production would peak some time

13   The coming energy crisis. *The Vermont Sierran*, 24(2), June 2000, pp. 6-7.
14   Phillips, W.G. Are we really running out of oil? *Popular Science*, May 2000, p. 56.
15   Ibid.

between 2006 and 2015, then fall steadily to the point where the world ran out of oil some time between 2050 and 2090.[16] However, this scenario is not universally accepted, and there are observers who feel that it is too pessimistic. These observers base their arguments on the fact that increasing prices generally stimulate even more exploration which will ultimately yield new supplies.[17] At the same time, the oil supply optimists point to advances in drilling technology, which should permit the industry to increase the yield of existing oilfields above the present-day figure of about 20%.[18] Finally, they point to energy efficiency gains which have been made in the industrialized world over the past 30 years, a trend these observers say will only be further stimulated by higher oil prices. As proof, they point to the dramatic improvements in automobile gas efficiency since 1973, and to the fact that developed economies such as the US and the UK have increased the amount of GDP produced per unit of energy by almost 500% since the 19th century.[19]

Pros of Wind Power

WGE proponents present it as a clean, reliable and economically efficient source of power. The motivation for moving to WGE from other forms of electricity generation— notably burning fossil fuels—is based on three elements:

Environmental

WGE backers stress that unlike fossil fuel-burning energy plants, wind farms do not generate any air or water emissions. Unlike nuclear power plants, wind farms do not produce hazardous waste. Finally, in contrast to hydroelectric plants, wind farms do not require major impacts on rivers.

In terms of emissions of pollutants into the air, WGE backers note that fossil-fueled power plants in the United States were responsible for almost 70% of sulfur dioxide (SO_2), 33% of nitrogen oxide (NO), 28% of particulate matter and 23% of toxic heavy metals released into the air as of 1997.[20] SO_2 and NO and oxide are blamed for a phenomenon known as acid rain, where the acidic content of rain kills all living things in lakes, rivers, and streams. Acid rain is particularly acute in the northeast United States, where many bodies of water have been impacted by SO_2 and NO emissions from coal-fired power plants in the American Midwest states.

16   Ibid.
17   Lomborg, B. (2001). *The skeptical environmentalist: Measuring the real state of the world.* Cambridge, UK: Cambridge University Press, p. 125.
18   Ibid.
19   Ibid.
20   American Wind Energy Association (http://www.awea.org/faq/tutorial/wwt_environmental. html).

Concerns about global warming/climate change basically come down to concern about human activities that generate so-called greenhouse gases (GHGs), the most prominent of which is CO_2. According to scientists involved in the climate change debate, GHGs emitted into the air rise to the earth's stratosphere, where they form a layer which traps heat escaping from the earth. This so-called greenhouse effect is begin blamed by many scientists for what appears to be a slight warming of the earth's temperatures over the past 20 years. The policy debate on climate change focuses on the question of whether or not the warming is a natural evolution in the planet's climate, or if it is the result of this greenhouse effect. If it is indeed the latter and if human activities—notably the burning of fossil fuels—are the reason GHGs are released in the environment, then some reduction in GHG emissions is called for to prevent a potentially catastrophic rise in temperatures on earth.

A significant amount of GHGs, mainly CO_2, are emitted when fossil fuels—primarily coal, oil, and natural gas—are burnt to power turbines which generate electricity. Proponents of WGE say it offers an alternative to fossil fuel burning, thus directly addressing climate change concerns. For example, a 1 MW wind turbine generating about 3.1 million kW-hours of electricity would eliminate 1,500 tons of CO_2 emissions if the turbine replaced a natural gas-fired turbine.[21] This figure goes up, to almost 2,100 tons of CO_2 emitted, if one were to assume that the electricity generated by the wind turbine had replaced a "typical" portfolio of 85% natural gas-fired and 15% oil-fired turbine generated electricity.[22] Finally, if one assumes that some of the electricity generated by the WGE turbine had replaced power generated from a coal-fired plant, the figure of CO_2 emissions saved is higher still.

The concerns about GHG emissions are particularly important in the US, given that the country produces over 36% of all GHG emissions from industrialized countries. Moreover, according to 2002 data from the Environmental Protection Agency (EPA), emissions of CO_2 from electricity generation in the US amounted to over 2.25 billion metric tons per year, more than double the amount released by motor vehicles in that year.[23]

Economic

Another major argument employed by WGE proponents is the idea that since wind is free, the cost of WGE is stable and predictable, once installation costs have been accounted for. As Dr Linn Draper, Chief Executive of the largest utility in the United States noted at the American Wind Energy Association's 2003 annual meeting:

> Any renewables added to our generation mix reduces some of the volatility in the overall cost of fuel for our power plants . . . We've seen natural gas prices rise from about $3/thousand cubic feet in late 2001 to as much as $9/thousand cubic feet this year. We like the idea that the cost of fuel for a wind turbine is totally predictable.[24]

21   Boucher, T. and Stoddard, T. (2003, October 12). Do you prefer wind or coal? *The Burlington Free Press*, p. A12.
22   Ibid.
23   As Kyoto protocol comes alive, so do pollution permit markets (2004, November 8). *The Wall Street Journal*, p. A2.
24   Regulators vow that change is in the wind (2003, July). *Power Engineering* 107(7).

WGE supporters also point to the economic benefits of siting wind turbines. They argue that wind farms represent critical additions to local and state tax bases, and through the lease payments wind farms pay for land use rights, represent a crucial revenue for property owners across the country. In Texas, for example, a landowner can earn about $3,200 per turbine installed each year, with turbines placed every 25 acres.[25] A proposed 200 turbine farm in Grant County, Virginia is expected to pay over $500,000 per year in local taxes, making it the fifth largest taxpayer in the county. The company developing the facility has also entered into a partnership with two local schools, who will earn royalties of $75,000 per year from the farm. Landowners in the county, an area hard hit by coal mine closures over the years, will receive between $2,000 and $4,000 per acre to lease the almost 8,000 acres needed for the facility. Finally, installation of the turbines will create 200 construction jobs for up to one year, and 15 permanent servicing jobs in the county.[26]

Finally, WGE supporters claim that with current improvements in turbine technology, electricity generated by wind turbines is economically competitive with power produced through burning of fossil fuels. Factoring in installation costs, operations and maintenance costs, and cost of fuel, one WGE firm estimates electricity costs of between $0.05 and $0.10 per kW-hour for wind, versus $0.06–$0.08 for natural gas-fired engines.[27] These technological improvements have focused on making the turbines quieter, more reliable, and more powerful, all at a lower cost. A spokesperson for a leading manufacturer of wind turbines noted that turbine efficiency has gone up by 5% per year every year since the late 1990s.[28]

Criticisms of Wind Power

WGE has attracted opposition from a wide and sometimes surprising range of groups and interests. These opponents base their opposition on the following areas:

Variability/reliability

Critics of WGE point to its variability. Simply put, the wind on any given day cannot be too weak, since it will not turn the turbines. However, winds that are too strong can force a shutdown of the turbines to prevent possible toppling. Wind's efficiency is usually estimated at between 30 and 40%. Critics of WGE charge that this means every WGE facility needs an equivalent power backup source, usually from traditional fossil fuel-fired plants, thus negating much of the "savings" which WGE supporters claim.

25   Thaddeus, op cit.

26   Seelye, Katharine Q. (2003, June 5). Windmills sow dissent for environmentalists: An energy source's impact is debated. *The New York Times*, p. 28.

27   Northern Power Systems (2003). *On site power systems deliver cost savings and emission reductions*. Waitsfield, VT: Author.

28   Kirsner, Scott. (2003, August 28). A high tech update makes windmills more efficient, changing the energy equation. But inconspicuous they're not. *The New York Times*, pp. G1, G4.

The WGE industry's response is that wind is only part of a constantly shifting electricity generating portfolio. As described by one WGE proponent:

> . . . electricity demand is a constantly moving target. The more accurate picture is one of a number of generating plants moving on and off line throughout the day to meet a steadily shifting load. At any one time, only some 15% of the total generating capacity is consciously "dispatched" to keep load and generation in balance. Obviously a variable generating source fits into this latter picture much more readily.[29]

WGE supporters stress that most fossil fuel electricity plants are able to be operated on a variable basis to accommodate changes in wind conditions. They also point out that that wind turbines typically generate most of their output at night, when electricity usage is low and fossil fuel plants are used less, if at all. Better forecasting of wind conditions, together with more available WGE, will allow operators to scale back use of fossil-fueled plants even further.[30]

Cost

Another serious charge levied against WGE is cost. Critics claim that while wind turbines cost between $1,000 and $1,500 per kW to install, natural gas-powered plants of equivalent scale cost between $400 and $650 per kW.[31] Critics of WGE concede that wind is essentially a free input, while traditional plants must pay for fossil fuel. However, they contend that the combination of wind's relatively low efficiency and the higher installation cost of turbines mean that WGE is invariably more costly. For example, the Royal Academy of Engineering in Britain has estimated that coal, gas, and nuclear plants in the UK produce power for about 6 cents/kW hour, versus over 13 cents for land-based turbines.[32] This gap is even higher in the case of offshore turbines, whose higher installation, service and transmission costs push the price of their electricity to over 18 cents/kW-hour.[33]

Critics of WGE's economics note that wherever it is used, it is accompanied by massive state subsidies. Referring to Denmark's WGE experience, one American-based critic claimed that the Danish Energy Commission subsidizes nearly 30% of the true cost of producing wind power in that country.[34] In the case of Germany, a British WGE opponent stated that the industry has received tax concessions worth about $1.8 billion simply for installation costs.[35] On top of that, the German industry, according to this observer, has been guaranteed a price of 11.5 cents/kW-hour, almost triple prevailing market prices of 4.5 cents/kW-hour.[36]

---

29   Rising wind—time to take a second look (2003, September). *Power Engineering* 107(9).
30   Bouchard and Stoddard, op cit.
31   Mazur, Frank. (2003, October 12). Wind power not practical. *The Burlington Free Press*, p. 8A.
32   Ferguson, op cit.
33   Ibid.
34   McGrath, Kevin. (2003, December 17). Facts and fictions on wind power. *The Burlington Free Press*, p. 7A.
35   Ferguson, op cit.
36   Ibid.

Here too, WGE proponents have a counterargument. They maintain that the energy market is filled with various subsidies to other fuel producers. For example, they point to the over $30 billion which the US government has paid out over several decades to cover medical expenses for coal miners who developed "black lung" disease as a result of working in the coal mines, the federal government's role as an insurer of last resort in the case of a major accident at any American nuclear power facility, and the billions of dollars in military expenditures which the US government incurs to ensure shipping lanes from the oilfields of the Middle East are kept open.[37]

Environmental

A somewhat unintended consequence of WGE has been its impact on migratory birds. In areas with high levels of bird migration, the rotary turbines have caused thousands of bird deaths. This is particularly true of the older, 1980s generation turbines. For example, the Altamont Pass wind farm in California, built in the early 1980s, is in an area with one of the world's largest populations of breeding pairs of golden eagles. The farm is the world's largest, in terms of the number of turbines. Each fall, the eagles as well as thousands of red tail hawks fly through the pass on their way to winter homes in central California. According to the California Energy Commission, some 22,000 birds have been killed by the Altamont windmills, including between 400 and 800 golden eagles.[38]

As the wind farm applied to renew its permits in late 2003, a number of environmental groups actually opposed renewal. As a spokesman for one of the groups, Californians for Renewable Energy, stated that ". . . renewing these permits without addressing the impacts of wind energy on migratory birds, especially raptor species, will give a black eye to wind power."[39]

The WGE industry has responded to the criticism by referring to the Altamont wind farm as an "anomaly." More importantly, they content that lessons learned at Altamont have been applied to other wind farms in migratory bird routes, significantly reducing bird deaths.[40] An industry-funded study conducted in 2001 found that the number of birds killed annually in the US by wind turbines (between 10,000 and 14,000) paled in comparison to the number killed in collisions with cars (60 million), building windows (98 million) and satellite/radio towers (4 million).[41]

The main environmental objection to WGE concerns aesthetics. Besides the visual impacts which may be caused by road building and site clearance needed for wind farms, the turbines themselves represent what one critic called "visual pollution." As a resident of Thomas, West Virginia whose home is near a wind farm of over 40 228-foot-tall wind turbines lamented

> I can't believe how large and hideous they are. When you hear the word "windmill" you think Holland and Don Quixote. That's wrong. They [the turbines] look like alien monsters coming out of the ground.[42]

37   American Wind Energy Association (http://www.awea.org/faq/tutorial/wwt_costs.html).
38   Tempest, Rone (2003, December 22). Bird lovers blast wind farms. *The Detroit News*, p. 7A.
39   Ibid.
40   Ibid.
41   Ibid.
42   Seelye, Katherine Q., op cit.

Robert F. Kennedy Jr, son of the late senator and one of the country's leading environmental activists, explained his opposition to a major WGE project off the coast of Cape Cod, on similar lines:

> There are appropriate places for everything. You would not want a wind farm in Yosemite [a famous national park in Montana] and you wouldn't want one in Central Park [New York City's central green space].[43]

Another celebrity who has shared Kennedy's opposition to the Cape Cod project, which calls for 130 turbines to be built seven miles off the coast of Nantucket Island, is the legendary American journalist Walter Cronkite. Cited in opinion polls as the most trusted man in America, Cronkite was quoted in the *New York Times* as saying " . . . our national treasures should be off limits to industrialization."[44]

Echoing this notion that wind farms represent industrialization of previously pristine vistas, Wayne Kurker, the founder of a group formed to oppose the Nantucket project, stated:

> A good portion of us who migrated to Cape Cod came to enjoy Nantucket Sound . . . and if Nantucket Sound becomes an industrial electrical generation area, then it's no longer the national treasure that people currently feel it is. We look at this as our wilderness, our national park.[45]

Community members' objections to the aesthetic impact of wind farms have developed in several American states where WGE projects were being proposed. For example, in the late 1990s, a proposal for relatively small (three turbine) wind farm on Long Island, NY was dropped following community member objections that the area's view of a lighthouse would be marred.[46]

The phenomenon of residents of an area where a WGE project was being proposed objecting to its proximity to their homes while simultaneously supporting the notion of renewable energy had even acquired a moniker in the press: NIMBY ("not in my back yard").

WGE supporters vigorously dispute the notion that siting of a wind farm destroys views and harms the tourist appeal of an area. For example, a 2002 survey of tourists in the Argyll region of Scotland found that 91% said the presence of wind farms there would have no impact on their decision to revisit the area.[47] About one-fifth of the respondents had actually seen one of the three wind farms in the region, and whereas 55% of these people felt that the wind farms contributed to a "generally or completely positive" perception of the region, only 8% said the turbines created a "negative" impression of the Argyll area.[48]

---

43   Ibid.

44   Burkett, Elinor (2003, June 15). A mighty wind. *The New York Times Magazine*, pp. 48-51.

45   Ziner, Karen Lee (2002, April 6). Offshore harvest of wind s proposed for Cape Cod. *The New York Times*, p. F3.

46   Belluck, Pam (2003, March 2). Travel Advisory: Correspondent's report; a wind power plan stirs debate in Massachusetts. *The New York Times*.

47   American Wind Energy Association (http://www.awea.org/faq/tutorial/wwt_environmental.html).

48   British Wind Energy Association (http://www.bwea.com/media/news/tourism.html).

In fact, WGE backers claim that wind farms actually help tourism. They cite data showing that in scenic areas in both the US and Denmark where wind farms have been built, tourism has actually gone up, with local tourist promotion boards actively marketing the presence of the facilities to potential visitors. The Argyll, Scotland survey noted above found that twice as many people would return to an area because of the presence of a wind farm than would stay away.[49]

Electricity supply and demand in Vermont

Vermont is one of the smallest states in the United States, ranking 43rd in area (24,903 square km or 9,615 square miles) and 48th in population (approximately 620,000). Exhibit 12.2 shows the location of the state as well as the site of the proposed Glebe Mountain project. The state consumes about 6 million MWh of electricity per year.[50] Average load is about 600 MW but can rise as high as 1,000 MW.[51] Though the state has a small population and a relatively small industrial base, the extremely cold winters

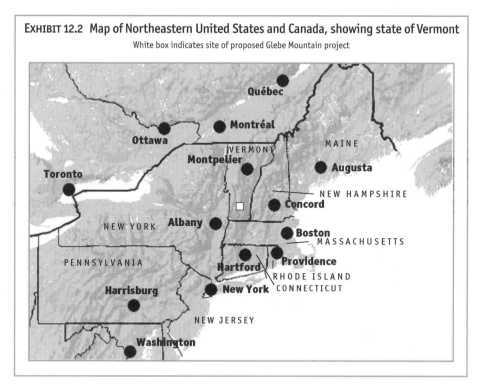

EXHIBIT 12.2 Map of Northeastern United States and Canada, showing state of Vermont
White box indicates site of proposed Glebe Mountain project

49   Ibid.
50   Glebe Mountain Group (2004). Power Information, State of Vermont [on-line]. Available http://www.glebemountaingroup.org/q_&_a.htm.
51   Ibid.

constitute an important driver for electricity demand. The state's utilities rely on long-term contracts for almost 85% of Vermont's needs. The most important of these are with Hydro-Quebec, the provincial government owned utility in nearby Quebec, which supplies hydroelectric power to the state, and with Vermont Yankee, an investor-owned nuclear plant located in southern Vermont. Vermont is actually the "cleanest" consumer of electricity in the United States, ranking first in the nation in terms of having the least amount of sulfur dioxide and carbon dioxide emissions arising from its electricity purchases, and second in the nation in terms of having the lowest level of nitrogen oxide emissions.[52] Moreover, the state is ranked 9th in the country in terms of the percentage of renewable energy in its total energy mix.[53] As of 2004, its mix of energy for electricity production was as shown in Exhibit 12.3.

EXHIBIT 12.3 Energy Sources for Vermont Electricity Production, 2004

Source: Green Mountain Power (http://www.gmpvt.com/whoweare/green.shtml)

Fuel	Percentage
Renewables:	
Hydro	39.4
Wood	3.5
Wind	0.5
Nuclear	37.4
Market Purchases	19.2
Gas	1.3
Oil	2.7

Vermont has typically had among the highest electricity rates in the country, averaging just under 12 cents/kWh as of 2004. Retail electric prices are regulated by a state government appointed authority, the Vermont Public Service Board.

Vermont is not considered an ideal state for WGE siting, ranking 32nd in the country in terms of wind resources.[54] Given the state's mountainous terrain, wind turbines have to be situation atop mountain ridgelines to capture prevailing westerly winds. However, only ridgelines between 2,000 feet and 3,400 feet vertical rise are suitable for wind turbines. Below 2,000 feet, prevailing winds are not sufficiently strong for turbines. Above 3,400 feet, fragile mountain ecosystems and abnormal cold which could ice the turbines inhibit WGE project siting. There are between 600 and 700 miles of ridgeline in the state which lie in this desired zone, but up to 85% of these lands are owned by the state or federal governments, and usually carry provisions barring devel-

52   Green Mountain Power (2004). Who we are. [on-line] Available http://www.gmpvt.com/whoweare/green.shtml.
53   Ibid.
54   American Wind Energy Association (http://www.awea.org/faq/tutorial/wwt_potential.html).

opment.[55] This means that only 100–150 miles of ridgeline in Vermont is amenable to turbine siting.[56]

As of 2004, the only wind farm operating in the state was the 11 turbine Searsburg projected, owned and operated by Green Mountain Power, the second largest utility in Vermont. Opened in 1997, this wind farm was, as of 2004, the largest WGE facility in the eastern United States. It features relatively short towers (193 feet) and no 24-hour lighting for aircraft safety (though a proposal has been made to the US Forest Service to add 20 more turbines, each over 330 feet tall, requiring 24-hour lighting). The topography of the Searsburg project is such that there are a number of adjacent ridgelines and mountain peaks which reduce the overall impact of the wind farm on the scenic views in the area.[57]

In the fall of 2003, East Haven Windfarm announced plans to build four 1.5 megawatt wind turbines atop East Mountain, the site of a former US Air Force radar base in northeast Vermont. The project was presented to the local community as a demonstration project, aimed at showing the community what a wind farm would look like and how it could benefit the area. The local utility, Lyndonville Electric Department, had agreed to purchase the WGE output of the project at discounted rates. East Haven Windfarm announced that their ultimate goal was to build up to 50 turbines in the area. Each of the four initial turbines would be about 220 feet tall. The company held a series of informational hearings in the area in the fall of 2003. It also released a survey of area residents which showed that over 80 per cent were in favor of the project.[58] The town's Selectboard also gave its approval to the project, noting that the project would generate almost $70,000 per year in additional property taxes.[59] The company originally planned to have the project running as of the fall of 2004, but as of November, 2004 the project was still under regulatory review.

Tourism in Vermont

With an overall impact of about US$4.2 billion per year, tourism is the second largest contributor to the economy of the state of Vermont. Tourism-related expenditure supported almost 64,000 jobs in the state, representing over 20% of total employment in 2001.[60] Tourism accounts for approximately one-quarter of all business tax revenues for the state's government.[61]

55   Glebe Mountain Group (2004). Why Glebe Mountain? [on-line]. Available http://www. glebemountaingroup.org.
56   Ibid.
57   Glebe Mountain Group (2004). Wind turbines are not magic [on-line]. Available http://www. glebemountaingroup.org.
58   Survey: Residents back wind project (2003, October 9). *The Burlington Free Press*, p. 3B.
59   Board backs wind farm (2003, October 17). *The Burlington Free Press*, p. 3B.
60   Vermont Tourism Data Center (2002). The Vermont visitor 2001 [on-line]. Available http://www.uvm.edu/~snrvtde.
61   Kelley, K. (2002, October). Conference facilities expand at tourist venues. *Vermont Business Magazine*, 33-34.

Winter is the most important season for the state's tourism industry, with its hundreds of alpine and Nordic ski centers generating almost US$1.6 billion per year. However, summer ($1.23 billion) and fall ($1.06 billion) fall closely behind in terms of economic importance.[62] For these latter two seasons, Vermont's attraction is based on the natural beauty of its forested mountains (the state name "Vermont" is translated from the French "Green Mountain"), and the tranquility of its mainly rural makeup. As an official in charge of marketing the northeast portion of Vermont to out of state tourists has noted:

> People just love the peacefulness of Vermont . . . Peaceful is the one word you hear over and over. People want to get back to earth, back to nature. Maybe their whole soul needs to be at peace . . .[63]

The positioning of the state as an oasis of rural tranquility is particularly important given its proximity to the crowded urban areas of the American northeast. The state is within driving distance of some fifty million residents of the Boston–New York–Washington urban corridor, and it aggressively promotes itself as a place of pastoral peace, clean air and unspoiled views.

The company

Catamount Energy Corporation (CEC) was formed in 1986 as a non regulated subsidiary of Central Vermont Public Service (CVPS), the largest utility in Vermont. The original mission of CEC was to invest in a wide range of renewable energy projects including wind, hydroelectric, natural gas, and wood waste. However, in 2001 the company altered its mission from being a passive investor in renewable energy to becoming an active developer, operator, and owner of WGE projects. As the company website explains, "Catamount believes that wind power will maintain the highest growth rate in the global energy market in the decades ahead."[64]

Since undertaking its strategic redirection, CEC had by 2004 an operating portfolio of over 450 MW and a short-term development pipeline of over 400 MW.[65] The company's main focus has been WGE projects in the US, UK, and Germany.

In May 2004, CEC announced a new WGE partnership with Marubeni Corp., a giant Japanese industrial conglomerate. The agreement with Marubeni, owner of a global renewable energy portfolio of over 500 MW, represented a major boost in resources available to CEC as it attempted to build its WGE presence.[66]

62 Vermont Tourism Data Center (2002). Vermont tourism data 2001 [on-line]. Available http://www.uvm.edu/~snrvtde.

63 Marcel, Joyce (2002, October). After 9/11: Domestic tourism thrived, international waned. *Vermont Business Magazine*, 31-32.

64 Catamount Energy Corporation (2004). What is our vision? [on-line]. Available http://www.catenergy.com/culture_values.html.

65 Ibid.

66 CVPS plans wind power expansion: Unveils link with Japanese power company (2004, May 6). *The Burlington Free Press*, p. 8A.

The Glebe Mountain Project

In 2003, CEC proposed a 27-turbine wind farm atop Glebe Mountain, in the southeastern corner of Vermont. The $58 million project would have a generating capacity of 50 MW, or just under 10% of total demand in the state (in comparison, the state's only nuclear plant, Vermont Yankee, has a capacity of 550 MW). The project as proposed would spread of 3.5 miles of ridgeline, with each of the turbines spaced approximately 500 feet apart. The land for the proposed project is privately owned by two individuals, both of whom reside outside the state.[67] CEC was proposing to lease between 2,000 and 3,000 acres, though the turbines themselves would only occupy about 100 acres. In addition to land cleared for the turbines, the Glebe Mountain wind farm would require a four-lane access roadway as well as connections to power substations in the nearby town of South Londonderry.

CEC selected Glebe Mountain since, at just over 2,923 feet elevation, it is in the ideal range for mountaintop turbine siting (see above). As well, the mountain has a favorable north–south alignment to take advantage of prevailing wind flows. Another factor favoring Glebe Mountain is the fact that one end of its ridgeline has already been developed as a ski area, known as Magic Mountain.

The company predicted the $58 million spent on the project would include almost $15 million disbursed in Vermont, resulting in some $10 million in direct and indirect wages for Vermonters. Though construction would only take about 12 months, CEC forecast that the total development period for the project would last between two and three years, and create some 260 jobs. Finally, the company forecast that over the estimated 20-year life of the Glebe Mountain project, some $650,000 would be added to Vermont's economy each year.[68]

The Glebe Mountain project differed considerably from the state's existing wind farm at Searsburg (see above). The 27 turbines proposed for Glebe Mountain would each be some 330 feet tall, almost 140 feet taller than the Searsburg turbines and some 25 feet taller than the Statue of Liberty in New York. In addition to having a significantly greater degree of visibility due to their height, the turbines would be subject to US Federal Aviation Administration (FAA) regulations on lighting. These rules mandated that all structures over 200 feet tall had to be fitted with aircraft warning navigation lights. Though the FAA had not issued detailed instructions for the Glebe Mountain facility as of 2004, it was known that among the possible requirements for the turbines would be red lights, flashing strobe lights (up to 40 times/minute, 24 hours/day), or selective lighting of only some of the turbines. In contrast, the Searsburg turbines, being under the 200-foot threshold, did not have to be lit.

According to critics of the project, both the town of Londonderry's development plan and the Regional Plan make specific mention of the area's scenic beauty and the need to protect ridgelines in the area. The town plan includes a reference to the need for "protection of ridgelines from development which adversely affects scenic values."[69]

67   Glebe Mountain Group (2004). Wind turbines are not magic [on-line]. Available http://www. glebemountaingroup.org.

68   Catamount Energy Corporation (2003). An open letter to the community [on-line]. Available http://www.catenergy.com/glebe_mtn_documents.htm.

69   Glebe Mountain Group (2004). Wind turbines are not magic [on-line]. Available http://www.glebemountaingroup.org.

Shortly after CEC announced plans for the Glebe Mountain wind farm, a number of residents and property owners in the nearby town of Londonderry formed the Glebe Mountain Group to block the project. The group, led by former state legislator and former chairman of the Vermont House Natural Resources Committee Sam Lloyd, based its opposition on the aesthetic impact of the project. These concerns focused on the height of the proposed turbines, the probable FAA mandate for lighting the towers, and the potential impact of the development on wildlife habitats along the ridgeline. As Lloyd stated in an interview with *The Burlington Free Press*, "we'd be giving up something that is quite precious in Vermont—what you might call the purity of Vermont's ridgelines."[70] Though not opposed to renewable energy, Lloyd went on to say in the same interview that it appeared WGE was better suited to areas in the western US where population density was lower than in the northeast. As stated on its web site, the Glebe Mountain group asked if the limited putative benefits of WGE warranted the aesthetic impacts of projects like Glebe Mountain:

> The commercial development of Vermont's mountain ridgelines for wind power is contrary to decades of Vermont public policy designed to protect fragile high elevation areas, preserve important scenic resources, promote tourism and maintain Vermont's special reputation as a place of unparalleled beauty. Glebe Mountain Group believes that wind power must be placed in perspective and analyzed in the Vermont context . . . wind power developers should have the burden to demonstrate that there is a compelling reason to sacrifice mountain ridgelines for an energy source of limited potential . . .[71]

However, not everyone in Londonderry was opposed to the project. In late 2003, a small group of environmentalists led by local cross-country ski center manager Rob Roy Macgregor and architect Keith Dewey formed Fairwinds Vermont. The group's aim, according to Macgregor, was to offer facts ". . . in the face of misinformation coming from the wind opponents."[72] The group was motivated by concerns about the impact of continued fossil fuel burning to generate electricity. As Dewey noted, "what trumps all of the aesthetic conversations is the fact that we're doing some very nasty things to the planet."[73] As for the notion that Glebe Mountain offered too little energy to really address serious environmental issues such as climate change, Macgregor was emphatic that the project was ". . . like baby steps. If Vermont doesn't have the social and political vision to take their first steps, what is the incentive for another state to do it?"[74] Speaking about the benefits of WGE, Macgregor was equally emphatic: "The wind, it blows and it's free. That's got to be better than sending people to Iraq to preserve our access to the oil."[75]

70   Allen, Anne W. (2004, February 1). Wind turbine project stirs Londonderry: Glebe Mountain debate focuses on environment.

71   Glebe Mountain Group (2004). Welcome to the Glebe Mountain Group web site [on-line]. Available http://www.glebemountaingroup.org.

72   Allen, Anne W. op cit.

73   Ibid.

74   Ibid.

75   Ibid.

The Regulatory and Consultative Process

Vermont is the only state in the United States to have a state-government-level approval process for development projects. The statute under which the state regulates development projects, Act 250, was enacted in the early 1970s to protect Vermont's rural character and tourist appeal. Electric generating projects are exempt from Act 250. Instead, such projects must seek approval from the state's Public Service Board (PSB), under Act 248. However, the PSB is required to evaluate projects using a number of criteria which closely mirror Act 250 priorities, such as giving "due consideration" to development plans of towns and regions. That said, the PSB is authorized to approve electricity generation projects even if they are contrary to local objections and plans if the project in question is deemed "for the public good."

CEC began its efforts at building support for the Glebe Mountain project with a presentation to the Select Board (an elected council which functions as a local governing body) and the Planning Board of the town of Londonderry in November, 2002.[76] In March of 2003, the company issued an open letter to the community of Londonderry to solicit support for the Glebe Mountain project.[77] During the spring of 2003, CEC hired an outside consultant, David van Wie, to organize and lead a series of meetings in and around Londonderry to bring property owners, local officials, environmentalists, residents, and company representatives together. The aim of the meetings was to try to respond to as many of the concerns being raised as possible, before CEC began the formal process to obtain Act 248 approval from the PSB. However, from the outset it was clear that both opponents and supporters of the Glebe Mountain project were so polarized that there was little, if any, middle ground between them. Speaking for the Glebe Mountain Group, Sam Lloyd stated that ". . . there's little to negotiate in the matter . . . there's either a wind farm or there isn't."[78] As for Fairwinds Vermont, leader Rob Roy Macgregor stated flatly ". . . there's no way any information is going to come out of this process that is going to convince Glebe Mountain Group to do anything but try to stop it tooth and nail."[79]

Opposition builds and the Process Breaks Down

In late 2003, the first rumblings of wider opposition to WGE began to emerge in Vermont. A spokesman for one of the state's leading hunting and fishing groups, HAT (Hunters Anglers Trappers of Vermont), spoke out at a WGE forum in favor of a moratorium on all wind project construction until the state could determine a new policy on the issue. In early February, the moratorium call was echoed by several other outdoorsmen's groups led by the Vermont Federation of Sportsman's Clubs. A spokesman for the Federation express concerns about how large-scale WGE projects could restrict

76   Go to http://www.catenergy.com/glebe_mtn_documents.htm for presentation.
77   Go to http://www.catenergy.com/glebe_mtn_documents.htm for letter.
78   Allen, Anne W. op cit.
79   Ibid.

access for hunters and hikers on certain mountaintops, as well as negatively impact high-altitude species, notably bear and moose.[80]

In February, 2004, *The Burlington Free Press*, the largest daily newspaper in the state, issued a scathing editorial against WGE. Calling the siting of wind turbines ". . . a serious threat to Vermont's natural beauty . . . ," the editorial went on to warn that such projects represented a form of "visual pollution" that ". . . would be devastating" to a state so dependent on the tourism industry.[81]

In early May 2004, the Glebe Mountain Group gathered over 900 signatures from residents of the towns surrounding Glebe Mountain for a petition sent to Vermont's governor, James Douglas. The petition called for a moratorium on all WGE projects in the state, pending a comprehensive review of all potential economic, environmental, and "quality of life" impacts (see Appendices 2 and 3). Finally, in late May 2004, the Group notified David van Wie via a letter and email that it was formally withdrawing from the collaborative planning process which CEC had begun the previous year. In the letter, James Wilbur, the group's co-chairman and longtime Londonderry resident, stated

> Catamount has consistently stated its intent to proceed with a massively scaled project even though necessary studies have not yet been carried out, and seemingly without any regard for the views of other participants.[82]

Sam Lloyd, for his part, stated simply that the Glebe Mountain Group had felt for some time that the collaborative process would yield nothing from their point of view. "There's really not that much to negotiate," he told *The Rutland Herald*, ". . . they [CEC] have done their arithmetic to reveal that for it to be profitable, they've got to have that number of towers in that location."[83]

Lloyd went on to suggest that the Glebe Mountain Group could be drawn back into the process by some kind of concession from CEC, such as offering to reduce the height of the Glebe Mountain turbines below 200 feet, thus eliminating the need for lighting. However, Lloyd then said ". . . I didn't feel they [CEC] would make any retreat."[84] For now, Lloyd said that opponents of the Glebe Mountain project would focus their efforts at blocking the project in the Act 248 approval process.

Teaching notes for this case are available from Greenleaf Publishing. These are free of charge and are available only to teaching staff. They can be requested by going to:
www.greenleaf-publishing.com/oikos_notes

---

80 Crawford, Matt. (2004, February 1). Outdoors folks wary of wind development. *The Burlington Free Press*, p. 7C.

81 The high cost of wind (2004, February, 18). *The Burlington Free Press*, p. 6A.

82 Smallheer, Susan (2004, May 19). Group pulls out of wind planning. *Rutland Herald*, p. 1.

83 Ibid.

84 Ibid.

Appendix 1: Glossary

i. Measuring Electricity

Watts: A measure of electricity

- Kilowatts: 1,000 watts

- Megawatts: 1 million watts

- Gigawatt: 1 billion watts

Kilowatt-hours (kWh): 1,000 watts of electricity produced or consumed for one hour. The most commonly used measure of electricity production and consumption.

An average household in the United States uses about 10,000 kWh of electricity per year. One megawatt of wind energy can produce between 2.4 million and 3 million kWh of electricity per year. So, one megawatt of wind energy can supply the needs of between 240 and 300 households. The proposed Glebe Mountain project, producing up to 131,400 MWh, could supply up to 18,700 households.

ii. Wind Turbine

A propeller-like blade connected to a generator to produce electricity. Wind turbines can have two or three blades, mounted on a tower to capture stronger winds at heights of 100 feet (30 meters) or more above ground. Under force of the wind, wind turbines begin to spin. The turbines are connected to a turning shaft which spins a generator to produce electricity. Wind turbines currently produced have power ratings from 250 watts to 2.0 megawatts. A 2.0 MW wind turbine can produce over 5 million kW-hour per year. Wind turbines range in size (in terms of diameter) from 8 meters (24 feet) or less for small residential systems, to between 50 and 90 meters (150–270 feet) in diameter for utility-scale turbines.

Wind turbines can be used as stand-alone generating systems, usually used for pumping water or to generate electricity for local structures. Alternatively, they can be connected to a utility power grid. When grouped together to produce electricity for a grid, turbines are referred to as wind farm.

Appendix 2: Letter

May 6, 2004

Governor James Douglas
109 State Street, Pavilion Office Building
Montpelier, VT 05609-0101

Dear Governor Douglas,

Enclosed are more than 900 signatures of residents and landowners of the Mountain-Valley/Glebe Mountain Region, including the towns of Londonderry, So. Londonderry, Windham/West Townshend, Peru, Stratton, Weston, Langrove, Andover, Chester, Jamaica, and Bondville, supporting a closer study of wind generation.

These signatures have been collected one-by-one, over the past 6 weeks, at town meetings, through phone calls, letters, neighbor visits, and emails.

Each person has expressed strong support for a careful review of the impact of large-scale wind turbines on the ridgelines of Vermont, especially at or above 2500', regardless of whether the land ownership is Federal, State, Land Trust, or private.

We believe that the Administration, the Legislature, and the people of Vermont should have the opportunity to review the potential environmental, economic, safety, and quality of life impact on the State of Vermont, and to weigh the costs and benefits of the installation of the modern large-scale 330" wind turbines on Vermont's pristine ridgelines. A comprehensive study would give us all the opportunity to better understand this complicated subject, and to participate in this important issue that will so profoundly affect Vermont's future.

As more wind factories are developed throughout the world, the unintended negative impacts of wind energy production have become more evident. While wind power appears to be an attractive source of renewable energy, it may come at considerable risk to many of the things that make Vermont a special place to live and to visit.

Governor Douglas, we greatly appreciate your support for a commission to study wind turbines and their appropriateness for the State of Vermont. The construction of massive wind power plants along Vermont's mountaintops has the potential to severely impact the beauty of the State in exchange for a small amount of energy. Let us not rush into industrial wind power before a thorough study of its effects on Vermont's environment, economy, and quality of life.

Sincerely,

Residents and landowners of the Mountain-Valley/Glebe Mountain Region

Contact:
Judith Mir
P.O. Box 1058
Chester, VT. 05143

Appendix 3: Petition

SUPPORT A MORATORIUM ON
WIND POWER PROJECT CONSTRUCTION

We, the residents and landowners of the Mountain-Valley/Glebe Mountain region, including the towns of Londonderry, Windham, Peru, Weston, Landgrove, Andover, Chester, and Jamaica, hereby urge our Governor and State Legislature to immediately pass legislation that will impose a <u>three-year moratorium</u> on the construction of large scale wind turbine projects on protected (at or above 2500') ridgelines of Vermont, regardless of whether the land ownership is Federal, State, land trust, or private.

We need time to:

* Study the many environmental, economic, health, safety, wildlife, and other impacts that would profoundly affect the area.

* Develop a statewide industrial wind policy.

* Resolve inconsistencies between land use issues and protections (Act 250) and electric power issues and regulations ("Act" 248.)

* Weigh the costs and benefits of putting large-scale wind projects on Vermont's ridgelines.

We now have an excess of power. A three-year moratorium would give us time to better understand this complicated subject and participate in this important issue affecting Vermont's future.

If you would like to add your name to a request for time to consider Vermont's future, please sign and return to the address below. You can also send an email, telephone message or fax indicating your support (see below.) *Please encourage others who would like to sign this petition to sign below or get in touch with us.*

Name(s):	_____	Phone	_____
Address:	_____	Email:	_____
	_____	Other:	_____
Name(s):	_____	Phone	_____
Address:	_____	Email:	_____
	_____	Other:	_____
Name(s):	_____	Phone	_____
Address:	_____	Email:	_____
	_____	Other:	_____

Please sign & return to: The Glebe Mountain Group, PO Box 2087, S. Londonderry, VT 05155 or indicate your support by Tel/Fax: 802-824-4493 or e-mail postmaster@glebemountaingroup.org

(Please use the back of this sheet for additional names)

Part 6
Resources

Writing cases need not be an art. In fact, it is primarily a handicraft and there are a lot of helpful resources available—both on- and offline—that could help any writer to develop an excellent case. The following information is selected from a variety of sources and does not necessarily cover the whole picture. If Internet links are broken we recommend to check the resources via keyword search in search engines such as Google. We welcome your comments on errors or additions: write to case@ oikosinternational.org.

6.1
Guidelines for Case Writing

PennState University: Case Writing Guide

Opinions vary about what constitutes a good case. Jill L. Lane from PennState University's Schreyer Institute for Teaching Excellence offers a fine seven-page synopsis of guidelines for case writing. An excellent introduction.

http://www.schreyerinstitute.psu.edu/pdf/CaseWritingGuide.pdf

The Case Method Institute at Babson College

The Case Method Institute at Babson College at Babson College offers a number of excellent online resources ranging from a three-page primer on "What is a Good Case and Teaching Note?" to "Merchandising Your Case: A Last Step in Publishing." The site also contains very informative links to other Internet resources.

http://www.casewriting.org

http://faculty.babson.edu/wylie/CWA_Resources

The European Case Clearing House (ECCH)

The European Case Clearing House (ECCH) is an independent, non-profit, membership-based organization dedicated to promoting the case method of learning. The ECCH case collection of management case studies and journal article reprints is the largest in the world. It is a unique and accessible resource for business school and university teachers worldwide. ECCH provides valuable online resources on how to write cases and how to use them in class.

http://www.ecch.com/about/completed-projects.cfm

6.2

International Case Writing Competitions

oikos Case Writing Competition (Switzerland)

The oikos Case Writing Competition aims to promote the development of new, high-quality case studies in the field of sustainability management and strategy. Launched in 2003, it attracts submissions from leading management schools throughout the world. Apart from a substantial prize money (first prize: 5,000 swiss francs) the competition provides qualitative feedbacks for each case contributor within a double-blind case evaluation process.

http://www.oikos-foundation.unisg.ch/homepage/case.htm

European Foundation for Management Development (EFMD) Case Writing Competition (Belgium)

EFMD organizes an annual case competition with different categories, among them a category on corporate social responsibility, sponsored by the Spanish Business School Instituto de Empresa, Madrid. Case contributors may also submit cases in other mainstream categories such as entrepreneurship, family business, managing risk, and marketing. Each category winner is awarded with a prize money of € 2000. Cases are reviewed within a double-blind process. No feedback is given to case contributors. Winners are invited to the annual EFMD conference.

http://www.efmd.org

Dark Side Case Competition (Canada)

The Critical Management Studies (CMS) Interest Group and the Management Education Division (MED) of the Academy of Management are sponsors of the annual Dark Side Case Writing Competition. The competition is designed to encourage and acknowledge case writing that addresses the dark side of contemporary capitalism. The goal is to encourage the development of first-rate classroom materials that generate discussion around the darker issues of contemporary business. According to the organizers, the award will go to the best case study—not to the worst offender.

http://group.aomonline.org/cms/competions.htm

CEEMAN: Central and East European Management Development Association (Slovenia)

CEEMAN is organizing an annual international case writing competition in partnership with Emerald Group Publishing Ltd. Besides funding the €1,500-worth CEEMAN/ Emerald prize for the author of the winning case, Emerald will publish the case in one of its journals and will also consider publishing other highly commended cases. As well as receiving a prize, the author of the winning case will be invited to the CEEMAN Annual Conference. The competition has no explicit relation to corporate sustainability issues.

http://www.ceeman.org

US Student Case Writing Competition (USA)

The US-based Society for Case Research is organizing in cooperation with *Business Week* an annual student Case Writing Competition. The competition is open to teams of up to five students attending a regionally accredited business or MBA program in the United States. Each team selected by its university will research and write a Case Incident (short case) based on a real-world business decision. The competition has no explicit relation to corporate sustainability issues. The annual call for cases is published via the Society for Case Research homepage:

http://www.bcj.org

John Molson MBA International Case Competition (Canada)

This competition is not a case writing competition but in fact an international event dealing with case studies in real time. The John Molson MBA International Case Competition is an annual event organized by a team of MBA students from the John Molson School of Business (Canada). The competition is open to teams of four students from business schools worldwide, and is recognized as the largest competition of its kind. Its main purpose is to bridge the gap between corporate and academic worlds, which ultimately enriches both students and executives alike. The prize money for the winning team is CDN$10,000. This competition has no explicit relation to sustainability or corporate sustainability issues.

http://mbacasecomp.com

6.3
Case Collections and Journals

Case Collections

CasePlace.org (USA)

CasePlace.org is a free online resource for up-to-date case studies, syllabi, and innovative teaching materials on business and sustainability—from corporate governance to sustainable development. It is designed for business school faculty—to facilitate new curriculum development and new connections among faculty with aligned interests. However, the site is free and open to students, executive educators, and anyone interested in learning more about social and environmental issues in business and in connecting with others who share these interests. It is a non-commercial website, seeking to make as many materials as possible available for free. The site is run by the Aspen Institute.

http://www.caseplace.org

Duke University: Center for the Advancement of Social Entrepreneurship Teaching Cases

This site lists a number of teaching cases that explore the social entrepreneurship process, including issues related to economic strategies, social enterprise, scale, and entrepreneurial philanthropy. The site lists 30 teaching cases on social entrepreneurship which can be an important trigger for the development of a broader understanding of value creation processes.

http://www.fuqua.duke.edu/centers/case/knowledge/casestudies/index.html

ICFAI Center for Management Research (India)

The Institute of Chartered Financial Analysts of India (ICFAI)'s Center for Management Research holds Asia's largest online collection of management case studies. ICFAI case studies are usually written from an industry or company perspective, rather than from the perspective of an individual decision-maker. In addition to training, these case studies are useful if you require information on industries, or on companies and their strategies. Though an increasing number of ICFAI cases deal with corporate responsibility topics, the majority of cases do not have explicit links to corporate sustainability issues.

http://icmr.icfai.org

The European Case Clearing House (ECCH) (see Chapter 6.1)

ECCH is an independent, non-profit, membership-based organization dedicated to promoting the case method of learning. The ECCH case collection of management case studies and journal article reprints is the largest in the world. It is a unique and accessible resource for business school and university teachers worldwide. It has no explicit link to corporate sustainability topics but most oikos winning cases are also published within the ECCH case collection.

http://www.ecch.com

Other sources

A number of leading universities manage their own case collections, including IMD Lausanne (Switzerland), INSEAD Fontainebleau (France), Harvard Business School (USA), and Ivey School of Business (Canada).

Selected Research Journals on Case Studies

The Management Case Study Journal (University of South Australia)

Founded in 2001, the journal is produced twice yearly online and contains cases that have application in graduate management education in the Asia Pacific context (Editor in 2007: Dr Barry Elsey). It welcomes contributions that provide opportunity for critique and debate. Teaching notes are most welcome and encouraged to supply such notes but as an optional extra. The journal is double-blind reviewed. It has no explicit link to corporate sustainability topics.

http://www.ojs.unisa.edu.au/journals/index.php/MCSJ

Case Research Journal

A leading North American case research journal, published quarterly by the North American Case Research Association. According to the publishers: approximately eight cases per issue; acceptance rate 15–20%; double-blind peer-reviewed. It has no explicit link to corporate sustainability topics.

http://www.nacra.net/crj

International Journal of Case Method Research and Application

Founded in 2007, this new, refereed *International Journal of Case Method Research and Application* (*IJCRA*) is available online. The journal is being published by WACRA: the World Association for Case Method Research and Application.

http://www.wacra.org/index.htm

6.4
About the oikos
Case Writing Competition
Concept and Award Committee

With the annual oikos Case Writing Competition oikos aims to promote the development of new, high-quality case studies in the field of sustainability, management, and strategy. Cases may take on topics and situations of real-world organizations in the following areas:

- Sustainability technologies and innovation
- Corporate sustainability and strategy
- Sustainability rhetorics and greenwashing
- Voluntary agreements and institutional change
- Organizational change and sustainability learning
- Corporate sustainability and corporate culture
- Sustainability as a business concept
- Sustainability networks and market development

The competition welcomes entries from all continents. The case studies should be suitable for use in management education and development, and should be related to managerial issues faced by organizations and individuals. Applicants may be teachers, research assistants or students of business administration (or related areas) at a registered university. Case entries may have more than one author, but each applicant may submit one case only. The case studies and associated material should concentrate on sustainability management and/or strategies, be presented in English, be based on real cases, be focused on a recent situation or development, and be released by management of the subject organization/company for use by other business schools. oikos accepts electronic submitted cases only. Each case must be accompanied by a completed case submission form (download PDF version at http://www.oikos-foundation.unisg.ch/case.htm) and a comprehensive teaching note.

Copyright ownership will remain with the author(s) and/or employer(s). Digests of the winning cases are published on the European Case Clearing House homepage (http://www.ecch.com). Inspection copies (without teaching note) will be published on the oikos Foundations homepage (http://www.oikos-foundation.unisg.ch). Statutory authors retain full copyright to all originally created works.

All submissions are subject to a **double-blind review** process. The Award Committee pays particular attention to the **concept and content**: the integration of the different sustainability dimensions, the topic relevance, and its ability to create a learning experience.

Each case submission must be accompanied by a comprehensive teaching note of ten pages maximum. Apart from the innovativeness, the Award Committee pays particular attention to the style of writing, the quality of presentation and the clarity of data.

The top three cases are awarded with a prize money. The annual first prize is **5,000 swiss francs** (second: CHF 2,000 and third: CHF 1,000). The author of the winning case is invited to present the case at a leading conference; from 2005 to 2007 the winning cases were presented at the European Academy of Management Conference. Details of the winning cases are also published on the oikos Foundation homepage (http://www.oikos-foundation.unisg.ch) and the European Case Clearinghouse homepage (http://www.ecch.com). Each case contributor receives a written short feedback on the submitted case.

Since the inception of the competition in 2003, oikos has been working with leading international faculty members in the field of sustainability and strategy within the case competition project. For 2008 the following faculty will comprise the Award Committee:

- Prof. Pratima Bansal, Ivey School of Business, Canada
- Prof. Frank M. Belz, Technical University of Munich, Germany
- Prof. Magali Delmas, University of California, USA
- Prof. Thomas Dyllick, University of St Gallen, Switzerland
- Prof. Minna Halme, Helsinki School of Economics, Finland
- Prof. Kai Hockerts, Copenhagen Business School, Denmark
- Prof. Andrew J. Hoffman, University of Michigan, USA
- Prof. P.D. Jose, Indian Institute of Management, Bangalore, India
- Prof. Steven J. Kobrin, The Wharton School, USA
- Prof. Bala Krishnamoorthy, NMIMS University, Mumbai, India (New Member 2008)
- Prof. Michael Lenox, Fuqua School of Business, Duke University, USA
- Prof. Mette Morsing, Copenhagen Business School, Denmark

- Prof. Stefano Pogutz, Bocconi University, Milano, Italy

- Prof. Forest Reinhardt, Harvard Business School, USA

- Prof. Juan Enric Ricart, IESE Barcelona, Spain (New Member 2008)

- Prof. Carlos Romero-Uscanga, EGADE Monterrey, Mexico

- Prof. Claude P. Siegenthaler, Hosei University Tokyo, Japan (New Member 2008)

- Prof. David Vogel, Haas School of Business, Berkeley, USA

- Prof. Michael Yaziji, IMD Lausanne, Switzerland

- Prof. Friedrich M. Zimmermann, Karl Franzens University Graz, Austria

Biographies of the Award Committee Members

Prof. Dr Tima Bansal, Richard Ivey School of Business, The University of Western Ontario, Canada

Tima Bansal is the Shurniak Professor in International Business at the Richard Ivey School of Business. Her research interests are primarily in sustainable development and in international business. She has investigated the motivations, processes, and outcomes of corporate greening using institutional theory, the resource-based view, and strategic issues management lenses. She has published several books and her research has also been published in academic journals such as *The Academy of Management Journal*, *The Strategic Management Journal*, and *The Journal of Management Studies*, in practitioner journals including *The Academy of Management Executive* and *Long Range Planning*, and in the popular press such as Canada's *Globe and Mail* and the UK's *The Independent*. She teaches strategic management and international business at the PhD, EMBA, MBA, and undergraduate levels, as well as executive programs. Tima received her doctorate from the University of Oxford.

Prof. Dr Frank Martin Belz, TUM Business School, Munich, Germany

Dr Frank-Martin Belz is full professor for Brewery and Food Industry Management at the TUM Business School, Technical University of Munich. His research focuses on sustainability innovations and sustainability marketing in consumer goods markets. He published a number of articles and books in these areas. Dr Frank-Martin Belz is also member of the editorial board of the journal *Business Strategy and the Environment* and a reviewer for a number of other scientific journals. He has been managing director of the oikos Foundation for four years (1999–2002) and was the president of the oikos Foundation from 2002 to 2004.

Prof. Magali Delmas, University of California at Santa Barbara, USA

Magali Delmas is an Associate Professor at the Donald Bren School of Environmental Science and Management at the University of California Santa Barbara. Her research examines the interaction between business strategy and public policy. More specifically she analyzes how various forms of regulation impact organizational change and how firms can influence regulation. Previous to embarking on an academic career she worked at the European Commission at the Directorate for Industry. She received her MA in Political Science from the University of Paris Sorbonne, and her PhD in Business Policy and Strategy from HEC Graduate School of Management Paris.

Prof. Dr Thomas Dyllick, Professor of Environmental Management, University of St Gallen, Switzerland

Thomas Dyllick is Professor of Environmental Management at the University of St Gallen, Managing Director of the Institute for Economy and the Environment and Vice President of the University. He serves on the Advisory Board of *Gaia, Ecological Perspectives in Science, Humanities, and Economics* and is a member of the Editorial Boards of *Greener Management International, Umweltmanagementforum* (*Environmental Management Forum*; *UWF*) and *Zeitschrift für Umweltpolitik und Umweltrecht* (*Journal of Environmental Law and Policy*; *ZfU*). His research interests are in the areas of sustainability and competitiveness, corporate sustainability strategies, and sustainability management systems.

Prof. Minna Halme, Helsinki School of Economics, Finland

Dr Halme is an associate professor at Helsinki School of Economics (HSE) and currently enjoys a five-year senior research fellowship of the Academy of Finland. Her current research focuses on business models for sustainable services and she is heading a project on material efficiency services to industry. She has worked with a number of European and national research projects on sustainable household services, sustainable organization cultures, actor networks and sustainable business strategies. She teaches masters', doctoral, and executive courses on corporate environmental management and social responsibility. She is also a visiting professor at the Seoul School of Integrated Sciences and Technologies, South Korea. Dr Halme is a member of the Editorial Board of the journal *Business Strategy and the Environment* and reviews for a number of other scientific journals. She is member of the Administrative Board of WWF Finland 2005, of the Action Planning Committee of the Greening of Industry Network, and belongs to the Community of European Management Schools (CEMS) Faculty Group of Environmental Challenges for Business.

Prof. Kai Hockerts, Copenhagen Business School, Denmark

Dr Hockerts is an Associate Professor at Copenhagen Business School where he is affiliated with the Center for Corporate Values and Responsibility. He holds a PhD in Management from the University St Gallen (Switzerland) and a Diploma in Business Administration from the University of Bayreuth (Germany). Before joining Copenhagen Business School (CBS), Kai was Adjunct Professor and Senior Research Programme Manager at INSEAD, Fontainebleau (France). Kai's business experience includes two years as a management consultant for Life Cycle Assessments and Eco-Design at Ecobilan S.A., Paris. He also worked at the New Economics Foundation, London, Dow Chemical Europe, Zürich-Horgen, and the Hamburger Umweltinstitut.

As part of his research work Kai has presented papers at numerous conferences and academic workshops including the Academy of Management Conference and the

Greening of Industry Network Conference. He is a co-organizer of the International Social Entrepreneurship Research Conference (ISERC) series, which in 2007 he brought to CBS.

Prof. Andrew J. Hoffman, PhD, Holcim (US) Professor of Sustainable Enterprise, Co-Director of the Erb Institute, University of Michigan, USA

Andrew (Andy) Hoffman is the Holcim (US) Professor of Sustainable Enterprise at the University of Michigan—a position that holds joint appointments at the Stephen M. Ross School of Business and the School of Natural Resources and Environment. Within this role, Andy also serves as Associate Director of the Frederick A. and Barbara M. Erb Institute for Global Sustainable Enterprise. Andy has published five books and over 50 articles/book chapters on environmental and social issues as they relate to business. Most recently, he published the report *Getting Ahead of the Curve: Corporate Strategies that Address Climate Change* with the Pew Center on Global Climate Change (October 2006). He was awarded the 2003 Faculty Pioneer/Rising Star award from the World Resources Institute and the Aspen Institute. His book, *From Heresy to Dogma*, was awarded the 2001 Rachel Carson Prize from the Society for Social Studies of Science. He holds a PhD from the Massachusetts Institute of Technology, awarded jointly by the Sloan School of Management and the Department of Civil and Environmental Engineering. Prior to academics, Andy worked for the US Environmental Protection Agency (Region 1), Metcalf & Eddy Environmental Consultants, T&T Construction & Design, and the Amoco Corporation. Andy serves on advisory boards of the Oakwood Healthcare System, University of Michigan Museum of Art, Earth Portal, Center for Environmental Innovation, and Canopy Partnership, as well as the Editorial Board of *Organization and Environment*.

P.D. Jose, Indian Institute of Management Bangalore, India

P.D. Jose is a Professor in the Corporate Strategy and Policy Area at the Indian Institute of Management Bangalore (IIMB). He is a Fellow of the Indian Institute of Management, Ahmedabad. He has a Postgraduate Diploma in Forestry Management from the Indian Institute of Forest Management, Bhopal and a Bachelor's in Science from the Institute of Science, Bombay University. Prior to joining IIMB, he was a member of the faculty at the Administrative Staff College of India, Hyderabad. He was also a Fulbright Fellow at the Massachusetts Institute of Technology, Boston and Kenan Flagler Business School, North Carolina, during 1999–2000. He has been associated as a consultant with several government agencies, state governments, and international organizations. Professor Jose has several publications in both international and national journals. He has presented papers and chaired special-interest sessions on environment and business in several international conferences as well as guest-edited a special issue of the journal *Business Strategy and the Environment*. He is a member of the International Planning Group of the Greening of Industries Network, which is a worldwide network of industries, international organizations, and universities.

Prof. Stephen J. Kobrin, Director, the Joseph H. Lauder Institute of Management and International Studies, Wharton School, University of Pennsylvania

Stephen J. Kobrin is the William H. Wurster Professor of Multinational Management at the Wharton School. He received his PhD in 1975 from the University of Michigan and holds an MBA from the University of Pennsylvania. His main research areas focus on international political economy, globalization, global strategy, and the impact of the information revolution. He teaches multinational management and international political economy in the Management Department of the Wharton School at the University of Pennsylvania. He has published, for example, in *The Journal of International Affairs* and the *Oxford Handbook of International Business*. He is a member of the Consulting Editors Board of *The Journal of International Business Studies*. Stephen J. Kobrin is a Fellow of the Academy of International Business and the World Economic Forum.

Prof. Michael Lenox, Fuqua School of Business, Duke University, USA

Michael Lenox is Associate Professor of Business at the Fuqua School of Business and has a secondary appointment as Associate Professor of Environmental Policy at the Nicholas School of Environment. Professor Lenox is the Area Coordinator for the Strategy Area and coordinates and teaches the core MBA strategy course. He pursues two distinct yet related research streams. The first is in the domain of technology strategy and policy. He is broadly interested in the role of innovation for economic growth and firm competitive success. The second stream is at the interface of business strategy and public policy. This works draws on emerging scholarship on the institutional, or non-market, strategies of firms and explores the prospects for industry self-regulation especially of environmental impacts. He has published in academic journals such as the *Strategic Management Journal*, *Academy of Management Journal*, *Management Science*, *Journal of Industrial Ecology*, and *Organization Science*.

Prof. Mette Morsing, Copenhagen Business School, Denmark

Mette Morsing, PhD, is Professor of CSR at Copenhagen Business School (CBS) and director of CBS Center for Corporate Responsibility. She specializes in the study of organizational sociology on issues of management, identity, corporate communications, and CSR. She has published a number of articles in journals such as *Human Relations*, *Corporate Reputation Review*, *Business Ethics*, and *Corporate Communication* and her latest books are *Corporate Social Responsibility*, with Prof. Andrew Kakabadse at Palgrave Macmillan, and *Corporate Communications: Convention, Complexity and Critique*, with Profs. Lars Thøger Christensen and George Cheney at Sage Publications. Morsing is a Vice Chair of the European Academy of Business in Society, and she is member of a number of European boards and committees on issues of CSR.

Prof. Stefano Pogutz, Bocconi University, Milano, Italy

Dr Stefano Pogutz is Assistant Professor of Management and Coordinator of the Specialized Master Program on Economics and Environmental Management at Bocconi University, Milan, Italy. He is a Senior Researcher at SPACE, the Research Center on Risk, Occupational Health and Safety, Environmental and Crisis Management, Bocconi University. His current research interests include sustainable development, environmental management, innovation management and cleaner technologies, and corporate social responsibility. Prof. Pogutz participated in a number of research projects at national and international level collaborating, among others, with the Italian Ministry of University and Research, the Italian Ministry of Labor and Social Policies, and the Eabis (European Academy of Business in Society). Since 1996 he has been a member of the Faculty Group on Environmental Challenges for Business Management in Europe,

Community of European Management Schools, and a frequent lecturer within the CEMS Master in International Management (CEMS-MIM). In 2006 his latest book, *Developing Corporate Social Responsibility: A European Perspective* (with Francesco Perrini and Antonio Tencati), was published by Edward Elgar Publishing, Cheltenham.

Prof. Dr Forest Reinhardt, Harvard Business School, Boston, USA

Forest L. Reinhardt is the John D. Black Professor of Business Administration at Harvard Business School. He heads HBS's Business, Government, and the International Economy Unit, a group of 15 faculty from various academic disciplines who study and teach about the economic, political, social, and legal environment of business. Reinhardt currently serves as the faculty chair of Harvard Business School's European Research Initiative. He is interested in the relationships between market and non-market strategy, the relations between government regulation and corporate strategy, the behavior of private and public organizations that manage natural resources, and the economics of externalities and public goods. He is the author of *Down to Earth: Applying Business Principles to Environmental Management*, published in 2000 by Harvard Business School Press. Like that book, most of his articles and papers analyze problems of environmental and natural resource management. He has written numerous classroom cases on these and related topics, used at Harvard and many other schools in MBA curricula and in executive programs. Reinhardt received his PhD in Business Economics from Harvard University in 1990. He also holds an MBA from Harvard Business School, where he was a Baker Scholar, and an A.B., cum laude, from Harvard College.

Prof. Carlos Romero-Uscanga, EGADE Monterrey, Mexico

Carlos Romero-Uscanga received his PhD degree in Management from ITESM Monterrey and a master's degree from ITAM Mexico City. He is an Associate Professor for Strategy and Environmental Management at EGADE Monterrey where he is also the Dean of Graduate Programs. He has been a Visiting Professor in EMI (Bolivia), the University of San Diego, the University of Texas at Austin, and the University of North Carolina. His research interests include environmental strategy, decision-making processes, globalization, social enterprise, and environmental management.

Carlos Romero-Uscanga is a Member of the Board of CEMS (Community of European Busines Schools). In addition to his membership of the oikos Case Writing Competition Award Committee he is also a case reviewer for the Social Enterprise Knowledge Network at Harvard Business School.

Prof. David Vogel, Haas School of Business, Berkeley, USA

David Vogel is the Solomon P. Lee Distinguished Professor of Business Ethics at the Haas School of Business, and Professor of Political Science at the University of California at Berkeley and the Editor of the *California Management Review*. He received his PhD from the Department of Politics at Princeton University and has taught at Berkeley since 1973. Vogel's research focuses on business–government relations, government regulation, and corporate social responsibility. Vogel's books include *Lobbying the Corporation: Citizen Challenges to Business Authority* (Basic Books, 1978); *Trading Up: Consumer and Environmental Regulation in a Global Economy* (Harvard, 1995) and *The Market for Virtue: The Potential and Limits of Corporate Social Responsibility* (Brookings, 2005). Vogel has also published more than 50 scholarly articles and essays. He has held the Jean Monnet Chair and the BP Chair in Transatlantic Relations at European University Institute and been a visiting professor at INSEAD, Sciences Po, Bren School of Environmental Management, and Hebrew University.

Prof. Michael Yaziji, IMD Lausanne, Switzerland

Michael Yaziji is Professor of Strategy and Organizations at IMD. With a PhD in management from INSEAD, Michael's educational background also includes a PhD in analytic philosophy from the University of California. His areas of special interest are strategy formulation and implementation, non-market strategy, stakeholder management, and change management. His current research focus is on relationships between corporations and non-governmental organizations (NGOs), e.g. Greenpeace, Friends of the Earth, PETA, and WWF. He studies both campaigns by NGOs against corporations as well as collaborative partnerships between corporations and NGOs. His recent publications on the topic include "Turning Gadflies into Allies" in *The Harvard Business Review* (2004) and "Toward a Theory of Social Risk: Antecedents of Normative Delegitimation" in *International Studies of Management and Organization* (2005).

Michael's articles have been translated into many languages and he is also a contributor to the *Financial Times*, *INSEAD Quarterly*, and *The European Management Journal*. His current book, *NGOs and Corporations*, published by Cambridge University and edited by Ed Freeman, will be on the bookshelves in the coming months.

Prof. Friedrich M. Zimmermann, Karl Franzens University Graz, Austria

In the 1970s and early 1980s, after his studies at the Universities of Graz and Munich, Dr Zimmermann focused on research in the field of tourism development planning and prediction. After qualifying himself as a university lecturer in 1987, he went to the USA as a guest lecturer and for research purposes and concentrated on "integrative and sustainable regional research and development." After temporarily holding a chair at the University of Munich, he was appointed to a full university professor for geography and head of the Institute for Geography and Regional Research at the University of Graz in 1997. Apart from his responsibilities as vice rector (since 2000), he is also a member of the Scientific Advisory Committee of Joanneum Research. In addition, he is the alternate president of both the board of directors of the Technikum Joanneum GmbH (Styrian University Colleges) and the Austrian-Canadian Liaison Group.

New Members of the Jury, 2008

Prof. Bala Krishnamoorthy, Professor and Head of Department, Business Policy and Environmental Management, NMIMS University, Mumbai

Dr Krishnamoorthy holds a doctorate (PhD) in Management from JBIMS, University of Mumbai and is a Postgraduate Diploma Holder in Planning from the School of Planning, CEPT, Ahmedabad. She has 19 years' experience through training and research activities. She underwent a Fellowship program at USETI, Washington, DC on Environmental Management and has published a volume on Environmental Management. Recently she received an International Felicitation in the area of Environmental Education and the WEE–IIEE–IAEWP Environmental Award. Her areas of interest areas include corporate environmental management, ethics, environmental management systems, ISO 14001, interpersonal relations, communication, leadership and manager-ial effectiveness, training for NGOs, and training for cooperative banks.

Prof. Dr Joan Enric Ricart (IESE Barcelona), Spain

Joan E. Ricart is the Carl Schrøder Professor of strategic management and Chairman of the general management department at IESE. He is also Associate Director of Faculty and Research. Recently, he was appointed President-Elect of the Strategic Management Society, an international organization composed of academics, business practitioners, and consultants dedicated to expanding knowledge and exchanging ideas on the strategic management process. He also served as president of the European Academy of Management (EURAM). He is director of the scientific committee of the European Institute for Advanced Studies in Management (EIASM) as well as member of the Harvard Business School–IESE Committee. Prof. Ricart holds a PhD in Managerial Economics from the Kellogg Graduate School of Management, a PhD in Industrial Engineering from the Polytechnic University of Catalonia, and a PhD in Business and Economics from the Autonomous University of Barcelona. His main areas of interest include strategic management, organizational design and sustainable development.

Prof. Dr Claude Patrick Siegenthaler, Hosei University, Tokyo

Since 2004 Claude Patrick Siegenthaler has held a tenure position as associate professor for environmental accounting at Hosei University Tokyo. He graduated as environmental economist from St Gallen University in 1993 and completed his PhD in 2005. He has been a visiting researcher with AIST in Tsukuba, RISTEX and ICU in Tokyo, INSEAD in Fontainebleau, and with ETH Zurich. His current research concentrates on Business Education for Sustainable Development.

Besides his academic work, he has founded and served on the board of several for-profit and non-profit organizations in the sustainability field. Claude Siegenthaler received, *inter alia*, the Switzerland Technology Award 2000, the Environmental Award from the Vontobel Foundation, and the TOYP Award from the JC Global Network Osaka.

6.5
About oikos

oikos is the International Student Organization for Sustainable Economics and Management, a leading reference point for the promotion of sustainability change agents. We aim to empower action competence for sustainable development among tomorrow's decision-makers. To target this objective, we strive to:

- Increase awareness for sustainability opportunities and challenges focusing on students of Management and Economics;

- Foster their ability not only to analyze long-term economic, environmental and social trends, but also implement sustainability-driven innovation;

- Create institutional support for these learning processes through the integration of sustainability issues in research and teaching at the world's faculties for Management and Economics.

oikos was founded as a local student group at the University of St Gallen, Switzerland in 1987. Ever since, oikos St Gallen has organized workshops, conferences, simulation games, and educational events to integrate sustainability issues into teaching and research of economics and management. In addition, institutional innovation is part of the oikos concept. In 1990, the oikos Foundation was created. In 1997, oikos decided to internationalize its activities and to strengthen sustainability awareness—not only among students in Switzerland, but also within faculties of Economics and Management throughout the world. oikos International was born.

Today, oikos is a global network of local chapters all working towards the same mission. With 20 chapters in 15 countries, the oikos network has the potential to reach 50,000 students worldwide. All chapters are neutral, non-political platforms for open-minded sustainability discussion. Local chapters aim at enriching students' curricula at their respective universities with sustainability knowledge. The international oikos projects focus on teaching (e.g. oikos Winter School, oikos Model WTO, oikos Case Writing Competition), research (oikos PhD Summer Academy, oikos PhD Fellowship

Program), and networking (oikos Spring and Autumn Meetings, oikos Award for Student Entrepreneurship in Higher Education).

The international oikos activities are funded by a circle of sponsoring companies and the oikos Foundation. Members of our circle of sponsors are actively engaged in the sustainable development dialog. Organizations that have supported oikos in the past and present include ABB, BP (Switzerland), Corymbo Foundation, Deutsche Telekom, Ernst Schweizer AG, Helvetia, Fondation Looser, Foundation for the Third Millennium, the Dow Chemical Company, Gasser, KPMG, Knecht & Müller AG, oikos Foundation, Novo Nordisk, Rhomberg, UBS, the Shell Foundation, Toyota, and Sustainable Asset Management (SAM), among others.

The headquarters of oikos is in St Gallen, Switzerland. Please refer to our website or the addresses below. More information about international oikos activities and the oikos Foundation can be found at: http://www.oikosinternational.org and http://www.oikos-foundation.unisg.ch.

Contact

oikos International
students for sustainable
economics and management

oikos International
President 2007: Nina Hug
hug@oikosinternational.org

Tigerbergstraße 2
9000 St Gallen
Switzerland

Tel. +41 (0)71 224 26 98
Fax +41 (0)71 224 26 98

oikos Foundation
for economy and ecology

oikos Foundation
Managing Director: Dr Jost Hamschmidt
hamschmidt@oikosinternational.org

Tigerbergstraße 2
9000 St Gallen
Switzerland

Tel. +41 (0)71 224 2595
Fax. +41 (0)71 224 2722

6.6
Literature

Abel, D. (1997) "What Makes a Good Case?" *ECCHO: The Newsletter of European Case Clearing House* 17: 4-7.

Barnes, L.B., C.R. Christensen, and A.J. Hansen (eds.) (1994) *Teaching and the Case Method* (Boston: Harvard Business School Press, 3rd edn).

Boehrer, J., and M. Linsky (1990) "Teaching with Cases: Learning to Question." In M.D. Svinicki (ed.), *The Changing Face of College Teaching* (New Directions for Teaching and Learning, no. 42; San Francisco: Jossey-Bass).

Bolton, M.A., J.A. Erskine, M.R. Leenders, and L.A. Mauffette-Leenders (1981) *Teaching with Cases* (London, Canada: Research and Publications Division, School of Business Administration, The University of Western Ontario).

Clawson, J.G., and S.C. Frey (1986) "Mapping Case Pedagogy." *Organizational Behavior Teaching Review* 11: 1-8.

Friedman, T.L. (2001) *The Lexus and the Olive Tree: Understanding Globalization* (New York: Anchor Books).

Ghoshal, S. (2005) "Bad Management Theories Are Destroying Good Management Practices." *Academy of Management Learning and Education* 4(1): 75-91.

Gilmore, T.N., and E. Schall (1996) "Staying Alive to Learning: Integrating Enactments with Case Teaching to Develop Leaders." *Journal of Policy Analysis and Management* 15(3): 444-456.

Heath, J. (2006) *Teaching and Writing Case Studies, A Practical Guide* (Wharley End: ECCH, 3rd edn).

Herreid, C.F. (1998) "What Makes a Good Case? Some Basic Rules of Good Storytelling Help Teachers Generate Student Excitement in the Classroom." *Journal of College Science Teaching*, December 1997/January 1998: 163-165; available online at http://ublib.buffalo.edu/libraries/projects/cases/teaching/good-case.html.

Hoffman, A. (2004) "Reconsidering the Role of the Practical Theorist: On (Re)connecting Theory to Practice in Organization Theory." *Strategic Organization* 2: 213-222.

Lane, Jill L. (2007) *Case Writing Guide*; available online at http://www.schreyerinstitute.psu.edu/pdf/CaseWritingGuide.pdf.

Leenders, M., and J.A. Erskine (1989) *Case Research: The Case Writing Process* (Ontario: School of Business Administration, University of Western Ontario).

Leenders, M., J. Erskine and L. Mauffette-Leenders (2001) *Writing Cases* (Richard Ivey School of Business, University of Western Ontario, 4th edn).

McKeachie, W.J. (1994) *Teaching Tips: Strategies, Research, and Theory for College and University Teachers* (Lexington, MA: DC Heath).

McNair, M.P., and A.C. Hersum (1954) *The Case Method at the Harvard Business School* (New York: McGraw-Hill).

Mintzberg, H. (2005): *Managers, Not MBAs: A Hard Look at the Soft Practice of Managing and Management Development* (San Francisco: Berrett-Koehler).

Pfeffer, J., and C. Fong (2002) "The End of Business Schools? Less Success than Meets the Eye."*Academy of Management Learning and Education* 1(1): 78-96.

Reinhardt, F.L. (1998) "Environmental Product Differentiation: Implications for Corporate Strategy." *California Management Review* 40(4): 43-73.

Tapscott, D., and D. Ticoll (2003) *The Naked Corporation: How the Age of Transparency Will Revolutionize Business* (New York: The Free Press).

Wassermann, S. (1994) *Introduction to Case Method Teaching: A Guide to the Galaxy* (New York: Teachers College, Columbia University).

Wüstenhagen, R., *et al.* (2007) "The Social Acceptance of Renewable Energy Innovation." *Energy Policy*, Special Issue, 35(5) (May 2007).

Yaziji, M. (2004) "Turning Gadflies into Allies." *Harvard Business Review* 82(2): 110-115.

Zell, D. (2005) "Pressure for Relevancy at Top-Tier Business Schools." *Journal of Management Inquiry* 14(3): 271-274.